Keep Your PC Cookin'

The Simple Care and Feeding of PCs

Keep Your PC Cookin'

The Simple Care and Feeding of PCs

Keith Aleshire

BANTAM BOOKS

NEW YORK • TORONTO • LONDON • SYDNEY • AUCKLAND

Keep Your PC Cookin': The Simple Care and Feeding of PCs
A Bantam Book/February 1993

ISBN 0-553-37178-9

Published simultaneously in the United States and Canada

Bantam Books are published by Bantam Books, a division of Bantam Doubleday Dell Publishing Group, Inc. Its trademark, consisting of the words "Bantam Books" and the portrayal of a rooster, is Registered in U.S. Patent and Trademark Office and in other countries. Marca Registrada, Bantam Books, 666 Fifth Avenue, New York, New York 10103

PRINTED IN THE UNITED STATES OF AMERICA

0 9 8 7 6 5 4 3 2 1

Dedication

To God, who helped me look away from the monitor and also see His glory . . .

. . . and to my wife, Pauline, who helps me balance my personal and professional needs while tolerating my late-night computer tinkering.

Acknowledgements

A special thanks to Michael Roney and the other staff at Bantam Books for embracing this book idea. They have made me what I am today...published.

Contents

II MAIN COURSE

Preface

Keep Your PC Cookin' was written to help you maintain, improve, and repair your computer. This book considers all DOS -based PCs, from the original IBM PC of 1981 to today's screaming 80486 models. Whether you own a "mature" computer or a blazing-fast 80486, *Keep Your PC Cookin'* gives you practical advice and hands-on instruction.

The IBM PC has been wildly successful since its introduction in 1981. Today, more than 50 million IBM or IBM-compatible computers are in use. Each of those 50 million PCs was purchased with some care and thought, just as yours was. You want your PC to stay viable—even powerful—in a world of "bigger, better, and faster."But how fast is fast?

- Do your software programs load quickly?

- Does the cursor move when you want it to, where you want it to, as fast as you want it to?

- Are you frustrated by waiting each time you save information to your computer?

- Do you have to wait for your computer to display what you need to see?

- Do you twiddle your thumbs while your computer is tied up printing?

- Are calculations and re-calculations in your spreadsheets finished fast, or do you have to get two cups of coffee while they work?

- Do you often find yourself watching the disk drive lights?

Computer performance is all these things. Primarily, though, performance is getting the most work done in as little time as possible.

You probably bought this book for one or several of the following reasons:

- **To preserve your investment in your computer.** If your computer has broken down or is on its last legs, this book can help.

- **To save money.** Repairing and upgrading your computer can save you money now until you are ready for a new one. If you have a new computer, maintaining it properly can save you costly repair bills later.

- **To take advantage of new software and hardware.** Some simple additions to your computer can allow you to use wonderful baubles like *DOS 5.0, Microsoft Windows,* and *OS/2.*

- **To further expand your knowledge of computers.** Adding to your computer and maintaining it provides you with more insight into how a PC works.

- **To determine whether or not to buy a new computer.** Sometimes, you may be better off buying a new computer. This book can point you toward your own conclusion.

Every computer owner has three options: stay with your current PC, improve it, or buy a different one altogether. *Keep Your PC Cookin'* helps you decide which avenue to take and how to get there.

Not all the techniques in this book may apply to your situation. The PC standard has evolved beyond what IBM originally envisioned. For example, you may not be interested in the expense of turning your PC into a multimedia PC (MPC), or you may not have the need for a math coprocessor to speed up your spreadsheet, if you own one. Despite these few exceptions, the bulk of this book should be helpful.

The Pareto Principle

This book follows the Pareto principle. You probably know it better as the "80/20" rule. The Pareto principle, named after nineteenth-century Italian economist Vilfredo Pareto, states that 80 percent of the value of a group of items is generally concentrated in only 20 percent of the items. For example, 80 percent of your paycheck goes to 20 percent of your bills. Or 80 percent of all television viewing is spent watching 20 percent of all programs. If you keep the 80/20 rule in mind, you will find it appearing in many places.

Over the years, I have noticed a trend for many general-purpose computer books to overwhelm the reader with hundreds of pages. It is intimidating to pick up and read, cover to cover, a two-inch-thick book that boasts 1300 pages. Unfortunately, according to Pareto, you probably are interested in only 20 percent of the book. Separating the wheat from the chaff is difficult.

This book takes a different approach, avoiding unnecessary details. For example, I do not need to list each voltage and its polarity coming off the power supply to tell you how to install a new power supply. Likewise, I don't need to explain how a fusing roller in a laser printer works to tell you how to replace its ozone filter. Your main concern is to fix a problem when it occurs or to make that power supply or printer last longer.

Keep Your PC Cookin' provides hands-on advice that applies to 80 percent of the possible situations in 20 percent of the pages of a heftier book. This smaller book provides much of the same information found elsewhere, but in a fresh, innovative approach that doesn't get bogged down in technical lingo.

When I spoke to a gentleman about this book, he said, "Oh, it's one of those *idiot* computer books." Au contraire, sir. *Keep Your PC Cookin'* provides sophisticated advice for *both* computer novice and professional. No one should be kept from pursuing some of the gutsier upgrades, like replacing the computer's motherboard—the very foundation of your computer.

Read on and enjoy.

How This Book Is Organized

Keep Your PC Cookin' is divided into three sections:

- **Appetizers.** The first five chapters prepare your PC for a long life. From how to open up your computer to keeping your work environment clean, these chapters may provide more benefit than any single improvement you may make your computer. They are:

  Improvements: Why Bother?
  Environment: Clearing the Air

Cracking Open the Case
Expansion Cards: Getting Onboard Safely
Power: Keep Your Juices Flowing

- **Main Course.** The middle part provides the "meat" of the book. These six chapters cover core improvements and repairs you can perform, from speeding up your microprocessor to replacing your hard disk. They are:

Thanks for the Memories
CPUs: Boning Up on Brainpower
The Motherboard: No Guts, No Glory
Storage: It's a Hard Life
Backing Up Your Hard Work
Preventing Floppy Fatalities

- **Desserts.** The latter part of this book covers the extras, the peripherals that are connected to your computer, like monitor or printer. Multimedia and cables are also included. These are:

Clear Vision
Multimedia
Printer Panaceas
Input Devices: Of Mice and Manicures
Bad Connections
PC Bio

PC Bio: An Important Appendix

Most chapters in this book have you turn to Appendix A: "PC Bio." There, you record information about your computer that you discover in that chapter. For example, in Chapter 3, "Cracking Open the Case", you open up your computer — possibly for the first time — and discover its inner workings. You then place several items of information into the worksheet — the size of your power supply, number and type of disk drives, and more. This appendix therefore becomes a one-stop list of basic facts about your PC. It can be invaluable as you consider which items can or need to be improved or replaced.

XT- and AT-Type Computers

Instead of stumbling over the names and combinations of each computer, I have divided all computers into two families: XT-type and AT-type. Let me define each:

- **XT-type computer:** A computer that uses an 8088-family microprocessor for its brain. This includes the 8088, 8086, 80186, 80188, NEC V20, V30, or V40 processors. Also, an XT-type computer has an 8-bit bus (which I'll describe later) and requires you to configure it by using switches inside its case.

- **AT-type computer:** A computer that uses an 80286, 80386SX, 80386DX, 80486SX, 80486DX, or higher processor. These newer computers have a 16-bit bus and are often configured by a software setup program that is either built-in or provided on a separate diskette.

If I refer to a true-blue computer from IBM Corporation, I will call it either an IBM PC, IBM PC/XT, or IBM PS/2.

Of Bits and Bytes

I'd like to throw out some measurement terms that will be used later. These terms are used in referring to both memory and disk storage.

Storage Amount (for memory and disks)

Bit	Short for "binary digit," a bit is used to measure how much information computers can store and process
Byte	Typically, eight bits make up a byte, that is, a single character such as a letter, number or symbol
Kilobyte (K or KB)	1024 bytes
Megabyte (M or MB)	1024K or 1,048,576 bytes
Gigabyte (G or GB)	1024M

Storage speed (for memory and disks)

Millisecond (ms)	one-thousandth of a second
Nanosecond (ns)	one-billionth of a second or the time it takes light to travel 12 inches

PART I

Appetizers

1 Improvements: Why Bother?

Improving, maintaining, and repairing your computer doesn't require the skill of a brain surgeon, the patience of a saint, or the bankroll of a Perot. Rather, it requires some quiet diligence and common sense. *Keep Your PC Cookin'* serves as a road map to whichever end you seek.

The very nature of the personal computer (PC) makes it ideal for improvements. The first PC unveiled by IBM in 1981 was built mostly from off-the-shelf parts. It consisted of a motherboard — the main PC circuit board — and five slots for connecting additional hardware. Not all those slots were filled. Some were left open to support circuit boards from other companies to enhance the PC. This built-in expandability continues today. By buying various *expansion cards* for these *expansion slots* you can add more power and features to your PC (see Figure 1.1). The result: You can customize your PC for today's and tomorrow's needs without having to buy a new one every year.

Your PC's ability to accept "plug-and-play" expansion cards as well as software programs from many different companies is called an *open architecture*. This open architecture allows you to have freedom of choice when buying PC components. Compare this to the closed architecture of a television set. Rarely, if ever, will you tear apart your TV to enhance its abilities or fix it. Unlike a TV or microwave oven, your PC does not have a sticker that says: "No user-serviceable parts inside." I have opened my PC dozens of times to add a new video card, hard disk, CD-ROM drive, and more. In some ways, improving your PC is no more difficult than changing a tire.

3

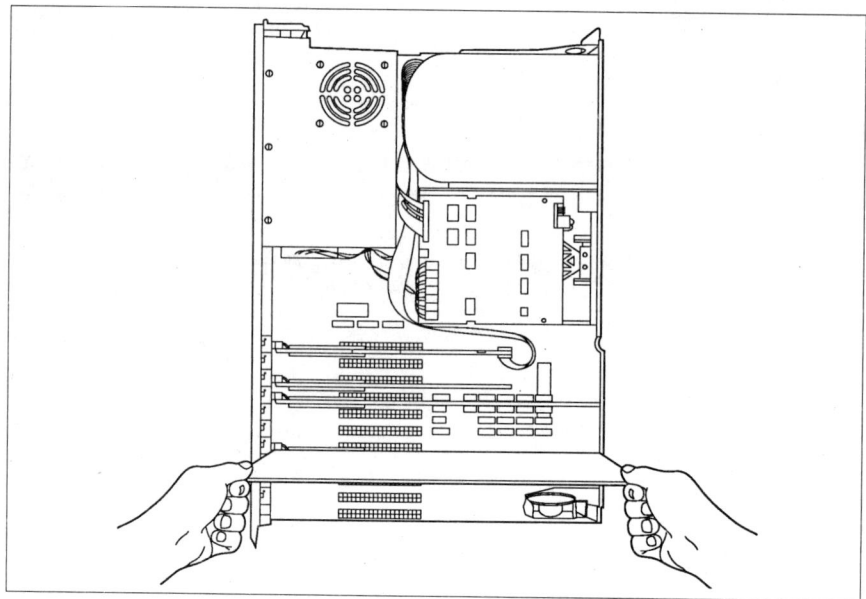

Figure 1.1 By inserting an expansion card into an expansion slot, you add new features and power to your PC.

To Tangle with Technology

The rise of the PC during the 1980s and beyond is a double-edged sword. We have enjoyed great leaps in power and ease of use. At the same time, we have seen PC prices plummet. The first IBM PC/XT cost about $5000. A decade later, you would be hard pressed to find a similar PC for more than $300.

If you currently own a PC, you probably paid more for it than it is worth today. Or a lot more power is available today for the same price you might have paid yesterday. That is the curse of acquiring new technology, and one you'll have to live with. You have no reason to kick yourself for buying a PC when you did. Four years ago, I paid more than $3000 for a 12-MHz 80286 computer with a 44-megabyte (MB) hard disk and a VGA monitor. Today, I could buy three of those for the same price...if I could find them. Like myself, you thoughtfully selected your PC at the time. To delay your purchase would have meant foregoing the benefits of your PC.

Indeed, PCs do become outdated. Since 1981, five new families of microprocessors have been introduced, each faster than its predecessor (see Figure 1.2). (The microprocessor is your PC's "brain.") For example, the 50-MHz 80486 processor is about 50 times faster than the

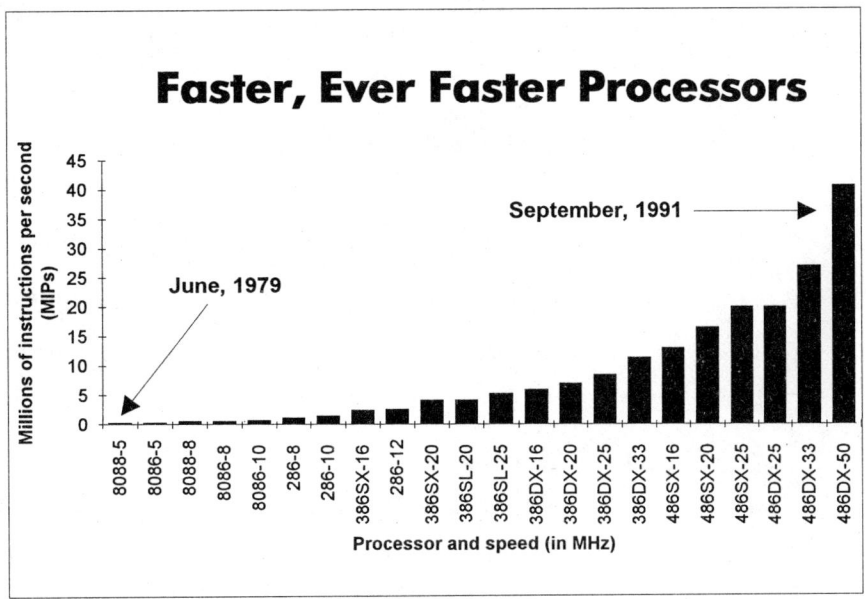

Figure 1.2 Prices for computers have fallen as power has multiplied.

one in the first IBM PC. This trend continues; a new microprocessor is introduced each year — its power doubles about every two years. Not only have the PC's brains been improved but also its brawn — faster hard disks, higher-capacity floppy disk drives, stunning color monitors, and more. In 1983, I purchased my first hard disk for a Radio Shack Model 4. With five megabytes of space for my programs and letters, I was in heaven. Today, I have a 212MB hard disk that is almost full. Oh, how things change!

In the face of such changes, you may develop "computer envy." You may want some of the features your friends or co-workers have that you don't, or you may have a strong need to upgrade your PC. Let's examine your reason for wanting to improve your PC.

Speed Bottlenecks

One obvious reason to improve your PC is to get your work done faster. There is nothing more agonizing than waiting for your PC to warm up and load your favorite game or business application. Those few seconds spent staring at your monitor may seem an eternity. Yet buying a newer PC may not solve the problem. Why not? Your PC's speed is a combination of factors — not just the speed of the processor. Remember this simple yet vital rule:

> **Aleshire's Axiom:** *The overall speed of your PC is limited by the speed of its slowest component.*

Five major potential bottlenecks can prevent your PC from performing to its utmost. They are, in order of importance:

1. Microprocessor (also called the central processing unit, or CPU)
2. Memory
3. Video
4. Disk storage
5. I/O (input/output) bus

These five bottlenecks inhibit your PC from having the maximum throughput, that is, performing the most work in the least amount of time. If you can improve each, you can truly have a "fast" PC without incurring the costs of a new one. The trick is to break through one or more of these bottlenecks that pinch off your PC's performance.

How do you relate this rule and the five bottlenecks to your PC? Your otherwise fast processor may have limited memory. If you bought more memory, your processor would have more elbow room to get the job done quicker. Likewise, a slow, disorganized hard disk could be improved with a simple software utility and therefore could more quickly feed the processor the stored information it wants.

Besides speed, you may simply want to improve the quality of your PC. For example, my brother was accustomed to the blotchy letters on his CGA (color graphics adapter) color monitor. A monochrome monitor, although not color, not only lets him view his construction drawings with better clarity but preserves his eyesight.

Running Newer Software

One strong reason to upgrade your PC is to run certain software and hardware you currently cannot run or can run only with difficulty. Newer versions of operating systems require minimum levels of PC hardware. For example, if you wish to use *Microsoft Windows*, it's best to have at least a 386SX PC, two megabytes (MB) of memory, a VGA (virtual graphics array) display, and a 40MB hard disk. If you want to use *DOS 5.0*, you need at least 2.8MB of free disk space and 512K of memory.

You may be interested in some high-resolution color games or graphics programs. To run a game like *F-117A Stealth Fighter* from MicroProse Inc., you need at least a VGA monitor — anything less and you cannot play. With such requirements, you may feel left out, unable to enjoy the marvelous software that is available. However, a simple addition or two to your PC may allow you to run some of these programs. Likewise, you may be unable to use a piece of hardware, such as one of the newer hard disk drives because your PC's internal circuitry cannot yet support it. A modest tweaking of your system will let you break that barrier.

Saving Money

A PC is no simple investment; it's dozens of times more expensive than a blender or other electrical appliance. It's also much more useful (unless you want a milkshake). Remember your options: Stay with your current PC and maintain it, upgrade it, or buy a different PC altogether.

By choice or by pocketbook, many of us will opt to keep our current computer. It's a known quantity and one that is paid for. Improving your PC is much less expensive than buying a new one. Even spending $1000 on a low-end 386SX PC can take a large bite out of any budget. Preserving what is already bought and paid for is a great motivation.

One advantage to upgrading your PC as opposed to buying a replacement is that you can pay as you go. It's not going to drain your checkbook or credit limit in one fell swoop. Maybe this month you can buy some extra memory and next month a software utility. Maybe with that tax refund you'll buy a new hard disk. And no matter how far you take your improvements, you'll always have a functioning PC. You don't have to wait for your financial ship to dock before buying a new PC nor ask that your credit card limit be extended. Best of all, you can make small changes now while you shop around for bargains for the truly big improvements you want to make.

Repairs: Who You Gonna Call?

You not only can save money by improving your PC but also by fixing it yourself when it breaks down. You don't have to be a computer technician or possess a Ph.D. Once, my PC's power supply died on me. I turned on the switch, the LED lights flickered and then went dim. Thirty minutes later, I had installed a new power supply. However, some repairs may require equipment you do not have and do not care to buy. How often will you need an AC power meter? In repairs requiring out-of-the-ordinary equipment, I often recommend you have someone else fix your PC.

Love Me Tender

For some, their current computer is quite adequate for their present needs. However, after several years, a PC could use some tender loving care to live out the rest of its natural life. Such care can be simple. When I lived with two cats several years ago, one would always perch in my lap while I was writing at the PC. Smokey's long, wispy hair would shed and find its way between the keys. Eventually, typing at the keyboard was akin to fondling fuzzy dice. A simple pulling of the keycaps and cleaning helped remove the outgrowth.

Other care may not be so obvious. Many of the internal workings of a PC are invisible. Suddenly and without warning, your PC may start making errors or even stop working. Often, these errors can be diagnosed and fixed long before they really mess things up. This preventive maintenance not only reduces or eliminates repair bills but also protects your work and your patience. Even if you aren't planning improvements anytime soon, use this book to maintain your PC for years of dedicated service. Then you can sell it knowing it was kept in tip-top shape.

Got a New PC?

If you have a relatively new computer (less than one year old), you are quite fortunate. You have a PC that is somewhat advanced. However, you can go still further. Like any computer owner, you may contemplate some improvements. This book suggests additions and tricks to help you get the most from your recent purchase. Also, you can learn how to protect your PC (and the work you do with it).

Simple preventive maintenance can also increase the resale value of your PC when it's time to move on to "greener processors." Since you are the first owner, you have an opportunity to ensure it is properly maintained. Then, when it's time to sell, you can clearly say to its new owner it has been well cared for.

Drawing the Line on Budget

Watch your budget. You could spend thousands of dollars to better your PC, but that may be overkill. Remember the 80/20 rule mentioned in the preface of this book? You can probably spend one-fifth the money to get about four-fifths of the improvement. To spend the remainder of your budget to squeeze the last remnant of speed from your computer is just diminishing returns.

When contemplating any improvement, consider the kind of work you do and your budget. For example, if you are using your PC simply to write letters and possibly the Great American Novel, you don't need to buy a hard disk controller with a whopping 128K built-in cache. The hard disk does not need to be improved for that kind of work. However, you may want to buy an antiglare screen to reduce the strain on your eyes. Likewise, if you are learning PC programming, you would want a faster microprocessor and more memory to speed the compiling of your programs. Without these improvements, you would be waiting long periods of time whenever you made a change and wanted to test it.

Try to anticipate your later needs. What else might you expect to be doing with your PC? At the same time, watch the PC industry. Do you think OS/2 might be the operating system of the future? Perhaps you should check whether you are in a position to run it, if required.

Leftovers

After upgrading your PC, you may have some technological leftovers. That 300-baud modem might be left after you installed a new fax/modem card. Or your monochrome video adapter might be replaced by a color video card. Hang onto these leftovers; you might need them later. If your replacement part has an inherent defect, it most often will die within two months of daily use. After that period, you may want to sell these leftovers to someone else or use them in another PC.

Have a Goal for Upgrading

You should have a strategy when upgrading your PC. It's not simply a matter of getting your machine to work faster and more reliably. Like traveling, you can elect to take a bus, your car, a plane, or the subway. You may even decide to walk. What's the difference? It all depends on how far you have to go, how much money you want to spend, and how quickly you want to get there.

First, consider what your PC keeps you from doing now. Is the screen too fuzzy to let you work for extended periods of time? Does the keyboard have a mushy feeling that multiplies your typing mistakes? Does the hard disk occasionally lose information? Can you not use shareware programs your brother-in-law passes on to you? This book should remind you of some limitations you may have forgotten.

Next, turn these present weaknesses into goals that can be measured later with each improvement. Without a goal that can be measured, you'll never know if you achieved it. Some possible goals might be:

- Work at my PC for two hours straight without eye fatigue.
- Use both 5.25- and 3.5-inch floppy diskettes.
- Hear each keystroke from my keyboard.
- Send and receive fax messages.
- Play color games.
- Double the size of my hard disk.
- Back up my hard disk every week.
- Print high-quality letters.
- Spend less time waiting for my program to run.
- Stop the flicker of my PC screen.

Write down these goals with as much detail as possible. Doing so has a twofold purpose: First, it helps you clearly identify what you want. Thoughts are fleeting, but written goals are less likely to be forgotten or lost in the shuffle of daily routines. Second, writing down your goals increases your personal commitment to them. And your degree of commitment is the single most important factor in achieving them.

Besides this book, seek help from computer magazines, which often have reviews of many products. My favorites include *PC Sources, PC Shopper, PC/Computing, PC Magazine, Computer Shopper,* and *PC World.* (see Figure 1.3) You can also get help from on-line services like the PRODIGY service's Computer Club and the many forums on

Figure 1.3 Computer magazines are a great place to find more information and low mail-order prices.

CompuServe and GEnie. Thousands of people from across the country use these services to share their experiences about improving their PCs. Locally, you can join a PC users group. Usually, such a group gets together once a month to discuss general questions and to learn in detail about some new product from either another member or a company official.

You can also get some rudimentary help from the salespeople at PC stores like Egghead Software, Software Etc., and the computer superstores that are popping up nationally. However, be wary; the staff may be no more knowledgeable than you are.

As you read this book, you'll see current "street" prices for each upgrade or repair. It's then up to you to determine if the benefits outweigh the costs. Again, consider your list of goals. When it's time to put the cash down for an improvement, first do some cost comparison. I'm a great proponent of mail-order buying, where the low overhead of these companies allows very competitive prices. Don't spend a lot of time paging through every magazine or even the 900 pages of *Computer Shopper*. Rather, jot down the prices of about five vendors. Statistically, the lowest price in that list is probably in the ballpark.

Next, can you afford the upgrade today? If yes, then order right away. If not, you have the following choices:

- Wait until you can afford it.

- Purchase another upgrade that is in your financial ballpark. For example, you may forego a new hard disk and instead get some extra memory, which costs less.

- Limit the features of your upgrade so it is affordable. For example, you can order a smaller hard disk but still gain its high speed.

Questions to Ponder

Below are some questions you should consider before reading on. They will help you realize how comfortable you are with your PC's level of technology and how imperative an upgrade is.

- How many levels of technology have you passed up since you bought your current PC?

   For example, today's hottest processor is the 80486. It was preceded by the 80386, 80286, 8086 and 8088. If you have an 8088 processor

Figure 1.4 Being selective in what you improve will make you and your computer happier.

(the one used in the first IBM PC in 1981), you are seriously in danger of being unable to run certain software and hardware.

- How often does your PC make you feel limited in what you can do?

Are you waiting too long for your hard disk to load your program or is the delay tolerable? Does your screen make your eyes tired? Do you frequently get messages from your programs that you don't have enough memory? Does your hard disk groan and grind or occasionally lose your work? Do you want to play the latest PC games but can't because you need a VGA monitor? Measure your PC's limits by the specific jobs you want to accomplish but can't. Put your wish list of features aside for the moment. They're the icing — we're talking about the cake.

- If you have to improve your PC, does it involve making several hardware and software purchases?

The cost of upgrading your PC can be deceptive if you have to rework almost your entire system. Not only do you have to install each part of the upgrade — and hope it works with the other components — but you also have to learn each component. Refurbishing your PC may make it an unstable friend.

- How often does your current PC conflict with those of friends, family, and colleagues?

For example, if you have a low-density, 5.25-inch disk drive, you may be unable to reliably share information with others who have 1.2MB drives. Or perhaps your monochrome (one-color) monitor doesn't let your friends show their work on your PC.

- Count the most appealing features of each upgrade recommended in this book. How many of them are truly important to you?

Count only those features you will actually use or need. Don't be distracted by bells and whistles, and don't be driven by the features a co-worker or neighbor has. For example, you could get an anti-glare screen for your PC but it may be useless if you work mostly at night. You could buy a larger hard disk but perhaps you could simply prune your drive of unneeded files. Be honest with yourself: How many features will really help you work smarter?

- How much work and time are you willing to devote to upgrading your PC?

Some of us have lots of free time, some don't. If it's a toss-up between money and time, you may prefer a little time and elbow grease to spending the money for a new PC or its repair. For example, replacing your PC's motherboard — the main circuit board — is time-consuming but very beneficial in giving it a boost.

• What are the real trade-offs when upgrading or repairing your PC?

You may be sinking money into old technology that could be set aside for a new PC later. Be selective about how far you want to go.

• What demands will your software or hardware upgrade make on your entire system?

Nothing is more aggravating than upgrading your PC only to discover that some other component is needed. For example, the puny 135-watt power supply found in an older PC may need to be replaced to handle a new hard disk or other additions.

• Would a whole new PC, not merely an upgrade, better satisfy your heart's desires?

You may love your current PC but have trouble recognizing when you've outgrown it. For example, you could invest in a memory card and larger hard disk so your older 80286 PC can run *Windows*, but perhaps you could instead save those monies for a newer 80386 PC that runs *Windows* in its optimum Enhanced mode. When the job at hand substantially outstrips your PC's abilities, an upgrade probably won't help. It's time to look elsewhere.

Software versus Hardware Enhancements

Improving your PC takes a twofold approach: software and hardware. You can purchase software programs on diskettes that either fix problems or provide more features. This is the least expensive route to improving your PC. You can purchase disk utility software, for example, that fixes some basic hard disk problems.

You can also buy hardware to replace existing components in your PC or add more power to it. For example, you can buy a new hard disk or a second floppy disk drive. Because PC hardware means purchasing a tangible, manufactured piece of equipment, you will be paying more than you would for software.

Enhancing your investment won't always be a pleasant task. In some cases, the cost may be high. It's the cost of installing new software and hardware, and then getting it to work with the rest of your PC. Yet if you were to purchase a new PC, you'd face some of the same challenges. Improving, maintaining, and repairing your PC may be your only recourse, or one you prefer to tackle yourself. As you work toward your goals, turn to this book in evaluating each improvement and then use it to avoid common pitfalls. Enjoy the challenge and take pride in each and every accomplishment.

2 Environment: Clearing the Air

The computer room of a large corporation is a special place. Mainframe computers can occupy an entire floor. Rows of high-speed disk drives hold thousands of megabytes of information.

Such a computer center is especially designed to protect and extend the life of its multi-million-dollar tenants. The air is filtered and cooled to a chilly 68 degrees Fahrenheit. Humidity is closely monitored. Cables are neatly tucked under raised floor panels. Halon gas extinguishers and smoke detectors are ready for the improbable electrical fire. An uninterruptible power supply and backup diesel generators with a two-day supply of fuel stand ready for power outages. Cigarette smoking isn't allowed, and food and beverages are taboo.

Your personal computer is no less important than a mainframe computer. To you, its information is as vital as any corporate ledger. You cannot furnish the protection a larger computer receives, but providing a better environment can extend its life as much as any act of preventative maintenance. In fact, setting up your computer work area correctly is probably the ultimate preventive maintenance.

Your computer does not always deteriorate visibly as do other office machines. A neglected typewriter, for instance, slowly accumulates dirt, grease, and dust that decreases the clarity of its typed letters. Eventually, its performance demands attention. Your PC, on the other hand, wears its badge of abuse silently. It keeps working until one day...nothing. At that point you may have to shell out hundreds, or even thousands, of dollars in order to put a functional PC back on your desk. Ironically, the preventative measures that will help you avoid this type of expensive situation are mostly free.

Dealing with PC Heat

Every time you turn on your PC, its electrical energy turns into heat. The components in your computer are heated and expand. When it is shut off, these components cool and contract. This thermal expansion and contraction place a stress on your computer. Keeping the temperature in your work area somewhat constant reduces this stress. If the temperature in your room varies greatly, your computer chips might work their way out of their sockets, causing computer errors. Also, wide temperature swings can crack the copper lines on your circuit boards, break your solder joints, or speed corrosion of your electrical contacts. Turning your computer on and off is like you repeatedly going from an air-conditioned room to the sweltering summer heat outside. The stress may eventually overwhelm your immune system and cause you to develop a cold or other illness.

According to the Arrhenius equation — used by electrical engineers — each 18-degree Fahrenheit rise in temperature reduces the life of an electronic component by 50 percent. Conversely, an 18-degree drop in temperature doubles the life of your computer. If you want to increase the life of your PC, keep the temperature cool and constant.

Your hard disk is also affected, since its internal platters may expand or contract with the temperature. For example, some hard disks use inexpensive stepper motors that are sensitive to temperature changes. In a few minutes, your hard disk may go from room temperature to over 100 degrees. Saving information at one temperature may make it difficult to find when it is retrieved at a different temperature.

When you first start your computer, do not use it immediately. Give it about 15 minutes to warm up. During that time, get ready for your work, grab a cup of coffee, or read the paper. This will help extend the reliability of data saved to your computer. IBM recommends these temperature ranges for the IBM AT computer, which most likely applies to your PC as well:

When your PC is off	50-110 degrees Fahrenheit
When your PC is on	60-90 degrees Fahrenheit

To reduce the extremes of temperature, keep your computer and its accessories, such as a printer, out of direct sunlight and away from vents and windows. You can also add better or extra cooling fans to the inside of your PC. (This is covered in detail in Chapter 5, "Power: Keep Your Juices Flowing.") If you move your computer from one temperature to another, such as from an outside car in the dead of winter to a cozy-warm office, treat it like a victim of jet lag. Give your PC several hours to one day before you use it. In some cases, the temperature change may cause water to condense inside the computer. If you turn it on, this condensation may cause a short circuit and destroy your computer.

Let Your PC Breathe

Your PC needs to "breathe" to release built-up heat. One way to reduce heat is to increase the amount of cooler air to your computer. Most PCs have a power supply with a built-in cooling fan. This fan is usually placed in the rear of your computer. You can hear the fan when your PC is on. It forces hot air from inside your computer to the outside. If the fan stops working, heated air could build up inside your computer and shorten its life. To provide ample air, you should place your PC so air circulation is not restricted or cut off. With proper ventilation, you can tell if the heat is being dissipated. Simply place your hand on the case; it should be mildly warm if not cool.

The body of your computer, the part with the disk drives, is called the system unit. The system unit should have a cover over each of the six to eight slots in the rear of the computer. Also, you should leave the system unit cover on and secure when using it. This way, the built-in fan forces fresh air to enter the system unit through the front openings and exit through the rear. There should be no other path for air to enter or leave.

Your monitor, or display, should also be free to breathe. Like your system unit, it also creates heat. Unlike your system unit, the monitor does not have a built-in fan. Therefore, it needs some extra breathing room. Avoid the temptation to use the top of your screen as a repository for paperwork. The open grillwork on the rear of the monitor is not for looks; it allows warm air to rise from the display. If blocked, the display interior may become too hot, shortening its life.

Both the system unit and monitor should have at least four inches of clearance around their exteriors to allow good airflow. The side of your system unit that has a fan should have at least six inches of room.

Leave It On or Off?

Is it better to leave a computer on or off when you're away for an extended period of time? Ah, yes, the eternal debate. Before answering this question, let's examine the mechanics of your computer. Foremost, your PC is a mixture of moving parts (hard disk platters, disk drive spindles, cooling fan, the power switch) and nonmoving parts (video card, memory chips). Keeping a part moving when it's not needed generates heat, friction, and general wear-and-tear. But moving parts suffer even more wear-and-tear when first started.

Nonmoving parts can be damaged from the sudden power surge when your PC is turned on. A phenomenon known as the "electron wind" can cause metal ions on your circuit boards to move and eventually cause a short circuit between two copper lines on the board. (See Figure 2.1.) The electron wind is generated by the burst of voltage when you turn your computer on. As computer components get smaller, with ever smaller gaps between these signal traces, there is a greater chance of the electron wind blowing your way and causing a problem.

There's also danger from heat. As mentioned earlier, the primary

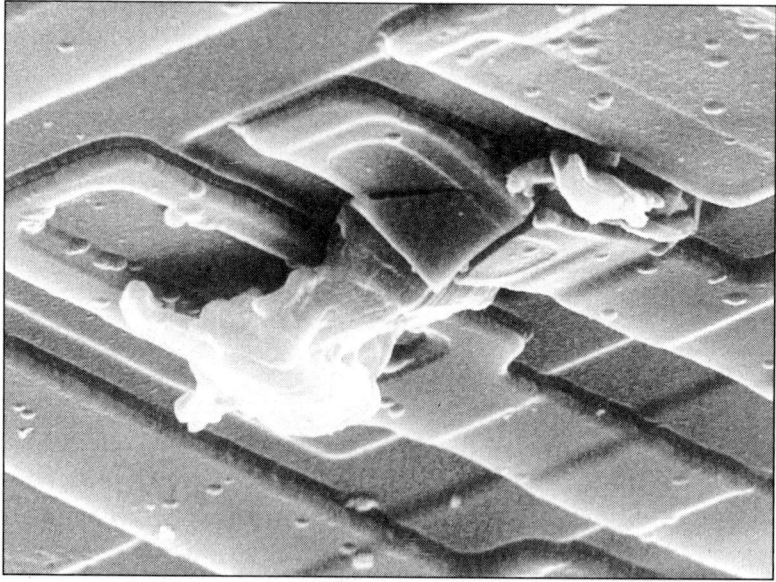

Figure 2.1 This electron microscope photograph shows copper particles that have caused a short circuit between two copper traces because of repeated turning on and off. (Courtesy of Sienna Technologies Inc.)

danger comes from the changes in temperature your PC endures when turned on or off. When you turn your computer on, it moves from room temperature to its operating temperature. When turned off, the built-up residual heat can put extra stress on the electronic components.

The power supply in your computer is the most susceptible to being turned on and off. The power demands of your hard-disk and floppy-disk drives are great when first turned on. During those first few seconds, the power supply must provide stable, extensive power to get those devices literally up to speed. (The hard disk platters spin at about 3600 revolutions per minute!) The power supply is severely strained by being turned on and off.

I recommend leaving your computer on during the day but not overnight. Generally, turn off your computer if you will be gone for more than a half-day. This not only saves precious energy but also money. Some people even recommend that you turn the computer on once a day and off once a day...and no more. The same applies to your computer printer. For your monitor, it's best to turn its brightness down when gone more than an hour. This prevents the image from being permanently burned into the monitor's internal phosphor surface. For less than $30, you can buy a software program called a screen saver or scr*een blanker*. Software screen savers display attractive dancing images on your screen to prevent such damage. *Microsoft Windows 3.1* includes some built-in screen savers.

In the long run, whether you leave it on or off when absent, your computer probably will be obsolete before it burns out.

Hazardous Foods

Your computer requires little care and feeding. Actually, it requires the absence of food or drink.

Coffee spilled on a table can easily be wiped up with a sponge. If your documents fall prey, they can be retyped or reprinted. If your keyboard gets soaked, you may have to disassemble it or get a new keyboard. (If your keyboard *does* get soaked, we provide advice on how to clean it in Chapter 14, "Input Devices: Of Mice and Manicures.") If any of your diskettes get soaked, the damage is multiplied. How much does it cost to replace a damaged diskette? Although a new diskette costs less than $1, your hundreds of hours of work cannot be so easily replaced. That 50-cent cup of coffee or other beverage may cost you or your company thousands of dollars.

You don't have to starve yourself at your computer. Rather, simply keep food and beverages to one side of or lower than your computer or keyboard. Liquids are the primary concerns. A spilled liquid quickly spreads across a surface and down. By keeping your container below the height of your computer, you reduce the likelihood of a spill reaching it. When I write at my computer, I often keep my coffee cup on the floor — but not where I may knock it over when getting to or from my desk.

If eating food, also keep it out of the way. Avoid crumbly foods like muffins or cookies. With such foods, gravity inevitably sucks the crumbs between your keys. It may be better to step away from your computer to eat your morsel or at least sit back. If you must have food and beverages nearby, you may want to get a plastic cover that protects your keyboard from spills but still lets you use it. One popular product is SafeSkin from Merritt Computer Products. This clear rubber product acts as a second skin for your keyboard. For the best fit, you must order one designed for the shape of your keyboard.

Where There's Smoke . . .

Smoke ashes and particles invariably find their way to your disk drives and diskettes. I recommend not allowing smoking within 20 feet of your computer.

Any foreign matter on your diskette may cause the read/write heads of your floppy-disk drive to be lifted from the diskette surface and pass over data to be read. A smoke particle is twice as large as the 1/1000-inch gap between this head and the diskette. Smoke contamination can also disturb the path of the flying disk drive head. It forces the head to rise over this obstruction and drop on the other side. The falling head overshoots its normal flying position and "crashes" onto the disk surface, removing the iron oxide coating and ruining not only the disk but the head as well.

If you got your computer at a fire sale (literally), then have it thoroughly checked out by a computer technician. Although the computer may have no external traces of damage, smoke particles can damage floppy diskette drives and other components.

Ashes to Ashes, Dust to Dust

Although you can keep food and drink from touching your PC, minute particles of dust inevitably cover and seep into it. This dust can corrode and discolor your computer and its internal components. Dust also can prevent it from keeping cool as it works.

A typical house accumulates about 40 pounds of dust each year. What's in dust? Usually soil particles, although 300 million tons of sea salt are placed in the air every year. In New Jersey, so much salt is blown inland that rime accumulates on power-line insulators, triggering blackouts. Some dust is even alive. Dust mites crawl in your bed and over rugs, digesting the millions of skin scales your body sheds each day. Yeast is also in the air, created by spores so tiny that 2800 can be placed on a one-inch length of thread. The smallest dust grains are actually moved around by the vibrations of air molecules and may not land for centuries.

Although they are tiny, dust particles can cause severe damage to your computer. Each computer chip, usually about the size of a baby's fingernail, is etched with thousands of microscopic lines. When a single particle lands on a chip, it's like a tree trunk falling across a road. For this reason, the chip manufacturing plants are at least 1000 times cleaner than a hospital operating room. Unfortunately, your computer work area cannot be so clean. With so much dust activity, you'll have to regularly clean your computer's exterior and occasionally its interior.

To extend the life of your computer, occasionally dust off the system unit, keyboard, monitor, and any other related equipment. How often? Here's one simple test: First, dust off your computer case and monitor. Then, count how many days before a noticeable layer of dust accumulates. Divide the number of days in half and dust that often.

When you dust, first turn off your computer. Then, take a soft, lint-free cloth and quickly wipe off your system unit and monitor. Use a toothbrush to sweep dust from the air intake vents on the fronts and rears of your system unit and monitor. Next, wipe the dust from between the keyboard keys. Avoid using solvents, cleaners, or any fluids. They may mar the finish of the case.

Likewise, dusting inside your computer can lengthen its life. Dust buildup leads to several problems. Dust acts like a winter coat on a hot summer day; it keeps the already hot electrical components from cooling off. Your computer not only goes from room temperature to

90 degrees but beyond with this dust overcoat. This excessive heat shortens its life.

Dust can also cause full or partial short circuits, which may cause your computer to behave erratically. Some components of dust may also accelerate corrosion of electrical contacts. Removing any type of debris or dust in your computer is in your best interests. In Chapter 3, "Cracking Open the Case," we discuss how to open your PC and clean its internal components. Basically, though, you use canned air to clear dust from inside your computer. You could blow the dust out yourself, but you are simply inhaling dust-infected air and exhaling it into the system. Compressed air in a can is much cleaner. You'll also need to remove the dust that accumulates near and on your computer's internal cooling fan.

Floppy disk drives are especially susceptible to dirt and dust, especially since they provide the biggest openings into your computer. The cool air being pulled into your computer often enters through the disk drive doors, bringing with it dust and dirt. In fact, if you place your hand in front of the disk drive opening, you should feel the air being drawn in. In later chapters, we'll discuss how to reduce the dirt that collects in floppy disk drives. Hard disks are not as susceptible to dust because the crucial head disk assembly, or HDA, is sealed shut.

Zap! Static Electricity

We're all familiar with static electricity; walking across a plush carpet builds up 20,000 to 30,000 volts of electrostatic energy, which is released by touching a metal doorknob. Only a few thousand volts are needed to lose information in your computer or the computer itself. Rarely does static kill a computer. Rather, it may cause your PC to "lock up," requiring you to restart it. One possible solution is to plug into a three-prong electrical outlet. The third prong connects your computer to the ground, there by draining off the built-up static electricity.

Static electricity is worst during the dry winter months or in extremely dry climates. Some precautions can reduce any static problems you may have. Antistatic mats for your desk or floor may be a worthwhile investment, especially if your computer is in a carpeted, low-humidity area. These mats drain off static electricity through a conductive grid. The pent-up energy is drained through a ground cord. A desk mat under your computer is best for areas too small for a floor mat. In some ways, it may be better antistatic insurance since rubber- or synthetic-soled shoes may render an antistatic floor mat ineffective. With a desk mat, you simply touch it once before switching on or returning to your computer.

If static problems continue, purchase an antistatic spray. An antistatic spray contains ionized water that counters the static energy. You can also make your own antistatic spray. Acquire a spray pump bottle and fill it with one-third fabric softener. Fill the rest with water and shake it up. Then just spray some on the rug every few days or until its effects wear off. In Chapter 4, "Expansion Cards: Getting Onboard Safely," I'll discuss how to prevent static from ruining circuit boards and other electronic components you are installing into your computer.

Magnetic Fields

Like static electricity, a strong magnetic field can also damage your computer. Magnetic fields are the most overlooked threat to computers. In particular, magnetism can damage your computer's hard disk and any floppy diskettes stored nearby.

Because data is stored magnetically, diskettes should not be stored near anything that generates a magnetic field. The major magnetic culprits are computer monitors, electric typewriters, radios, vacuum cleaners, stereo speakers, or any electrical device that has a motor or transformer. Even fluorescent desk lamps with transformers in the base emit a magnetic field strong enough to erase data. You should also avoid those magnetic paper clip dispensers and magnets used to hold paper to a file cabinet or to a copy stand.

Some telephones also can ruin your disks. A commonly overlooked source of magnetism is a phone that rings or chirps, rather than beeps. A powerful electromagnet causes the ringing. If such a phone is placed on or near a floppy diskette and rings, the magnetic field can scramble the information on those diskettes.

Some electrical devices are not hazardous. It is unlikely that X-ray machines and walk-through metal detectors used for airport security will damage diskettes. Doubtful. Airport metal detectors should be gentle enough for diskettes. A power of 25 gauss, a measurement unit of magnetism, can affect a 360K diskette. For higher-density diskettes, even more magnetism is required. Metal detectors in the United States use no more than one gauss.

To reduce the risk, reduce the potential magnetic hazards. Primarily, remove any magnets from the general area. If you use a bulk magnetic eraser to reuse older diskettes, use and store it away from your current ones. Place your computer printer away from your diskettes; its motor usually isn't shielded. Try to replace your phone with one that beeps but does not ring or chirp. After clearing most magnetic hazards, keep your data away from these and other magnetic hazards. How near is too near? Keep your diskettes at least six to 12 inches away from these devices. Some experts suggest two feet.

Humidity: Good or Bad?

Increasing the humidity of a room can reduce static electricity. In general, a humid environment, like a damp basement, poses no threat to your computer. However, some humidifiers cause more problems than they solve. Ultrasonic humidifiers use ultrasonics to provide a fine mist of water vapor into the air. Although the extra humidity reduces static electricity, it may put more contaminants into the air. You'll know if you have such a humidifier; a white deposit accumulates on or near it. This deposit is composed of minerals that can corrode your computer. For example, if this residue collects on your disk drive read/write heads, it can ruin the heads and scratch the disks. One way to have your humidifier and use it too is to use only distilled, or soft, water in it. Distilled water is free of minerals.

If you follow the advice in this chapter alone, you will greatly reduce the preventive maintenance and repairs needed by your computer. The work required to give your PC a proper working environment is minuscule compared to the dollars that could be extracted to repair it. As General George S. Patton Jr. said, "A pint of sweat will save a gallon of blood."

3 Cracking Open the Case

If you want to improve or repair your computer, you invariably will have to remove its cover. This chapter tells you how to work inside your PC.

Before we continue, you may need some background on the various parts of your computer. If you already know this stuff, you may skip to the next section.

What's In There?

Your computer is made up of many different physical parts called *hardware*. Your hardware runs *software*, computer programs you usually buy on a diskette that translate the instructions you send to your computer into a language it can understand.

The most crucial piece of software is the *disk operating system (DOS)*. The operating system gets your computer up and running and controls its activities. It is the foundation required by other software programs, like a word processor. These other software programs are called *applications*. Besides the operating system and application software, you also have *utilities*, which are small, usually inexpensive software programs that help you improve or repair your computer.

The hardware is composed of any part of your PC you can touch. The basic components are the *system unit*, *keyboard*, and *monitor*. You may also have other parts attached to your computer, perhaps a modem to connect your computer to others via phone lines, a mouse for selecting items with a click of a button, or a printer to put your work on paper.

When people talk about a computer, they usually are referring to the *system unit*. The system unit is the box that holds your computer's microprocessor, memory, disk drives, expansion slots, and video card. In other words, it holds the "guts" of your computer. It is the system unit that we need to open to improve your computer.

The system unit can be in either of two types of cases: *desktop* or *tower*. The desktop case is designed to fit on your desk with the monitor placed on top of it (see Figure 3.1). The desktop case comes in three sizes: regular, baby-AT, and slim-line. The baby-AT is a narrower version of the traditional desktop case. The slim-line case is a shorter version of the baby-AT.

The tower case was meant to sit upright next to your desk. It is often taller than it is wide. It too comes in three sizes: full tower, regular tower, and mini-tower. Desktop computers can be made into towers by turning them on their side and inserting them into a floor-mounted stand.

For desktop cases, the power on/off switch for your computer is often on the right side of your computer. It is usually an orange or red paddle switch. Some newer computers sport an on/off button on

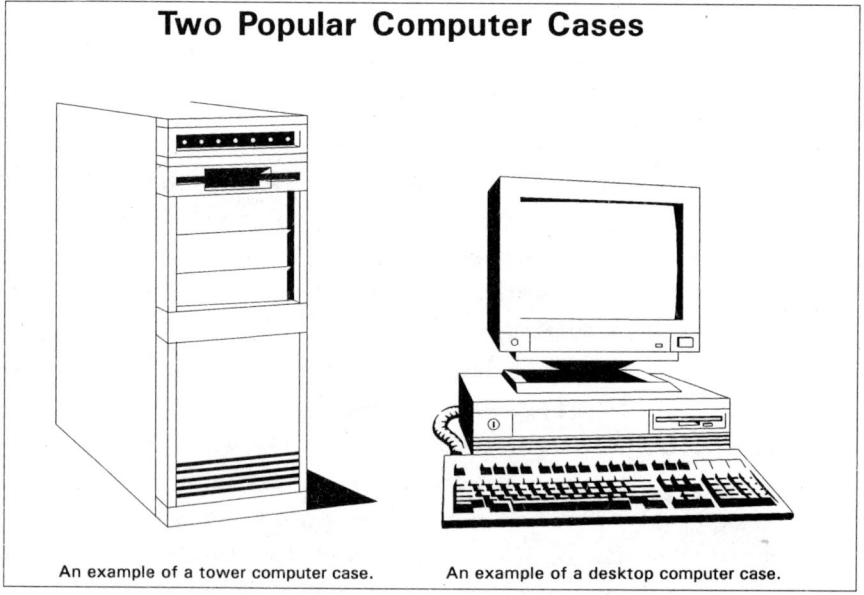

Two Popular Computer Cases

An example of a tower computer case.   An example of a desktop computer case.

Figure 3.1 The most popular case styles: tower and desktop.

the front. For tower cases, the power switch is often on the front. It too can be either a paddle switch or pushbutton.

Of course, PCs also come in portable configurations: laptops, notebooks, and palmtops. These generally feature on-off switches in the rear of the box, and can often be connected to "docking units" featuring desktop-style expansion ports, displays and keyboards. We're going to focus on conventional desktop PCs.

CPU and Memory: Brains and Brawn

The *microprocessor* (or just processor) is the "brains" of your computer. It is also called the central processing unit, or CPU. The microprocessor is a single computer chip inside the system unit that performs much of the work in your computer. There are other parts in your computer that assist the processor, but this computer chip is the most important factor of your computer's speed. Later, once we get your computer open, we'll discover which processor you have if you don't know already.

Your computer not only has a brain — it also has *memory*. As you work, the software program you are using and the information you give it are placed temporarily in your computer's memory. This is called *random access memory*, or RAM. When you turn off your computer, your work in this memory is lost. This is why you save your work to a file on a disk, which is permanent storage.

Memory and other parts of your computer are measured in *bytes*, a unit of information. Computer memory is measured in *kilobytes*, or just K. One kilobyte equals 1024 bytes. If your computer has 640K of memory, it can hold 655,360 bytes of software information at one time. Some software programs require a minimum amount of computer memory to work properly, such as 384K or 512K. You can usually find the memory requirements on the software packaging. Memory may also be measured in *megabytes*, or MB. A megabyte is equal to 1000K, or 1,024,000 bytes. Many computers have one, two, four, or eight megabytes of memory.

Disk Drives

The system unit has a decorative front panel called a *face plate* or *bezel*. Set in or behind the bezel, you usually have one or more *disk drives*. Disk drives are used to store and retrieve information to and from disks. Disk drives read information from a disk into memory, and they write information from memory to a disk.

There are two primary categories of disk drives: a *diskette drive* and a *hard disk drive*. The latter type can include 44 MB or 88MB removable cartridge systems, as well as high-density optical drives, which we discuss in the multimedia chapter. Diskette drives are probably the most noticeable when you look at the system unit; they have either a vertical or horizontal opening and levers or buttons on them. These are also called "floppy" disk drives because the computer diskettes you place in them are flexible. One feature of a diskette drive is that you can remove the diskette and store it elsewhere.

There are two sizes of diskette drives: 5.25- and 3.5-inch. These measurements are for the width of the diskettes they can hold. However, each size of diskette comes in any of three capacities: double-density (low-density), high-density, and extra-density, as shown in the following table. Like memory, disk drives are measured in kilobytes and megabytes.

Drive size	Low-density	High-density	Extra-density
3.5-inch	720K	1.44MB (1440K)	2.88MB (2880K)
5.25-inch	360K	1.2MB (1200K)	

Besides diskette drives, you may have a *hard disk*, which is also called a *fixed disk*. The hard disk is located inside your computer. It can hold many times more information than a single diskette and provides faster access to it. Because a hard disk can hold so much, it is more convenient to use than several floppy diskettes. The hard disk may be invisible from the outside or you may see its black plastic face with its LED light peering out at you. When your hard disk is being used, this LED is lit.

Your computer's disk drives each have a letter assigned to it so that your computer knows where to look to find instructions and information. On most computers, the diskette drive is called "drive A:" (A:). The hard disk is called "drive C:" (C:). If you have two diskette drives, the second one is called "drive B:" (B:).

The back of the system unit has several interesting features (see Figure 3.2). There are, of course, plugs for connecting your computer to the electrical outlet. There also is an opening for the power supply's

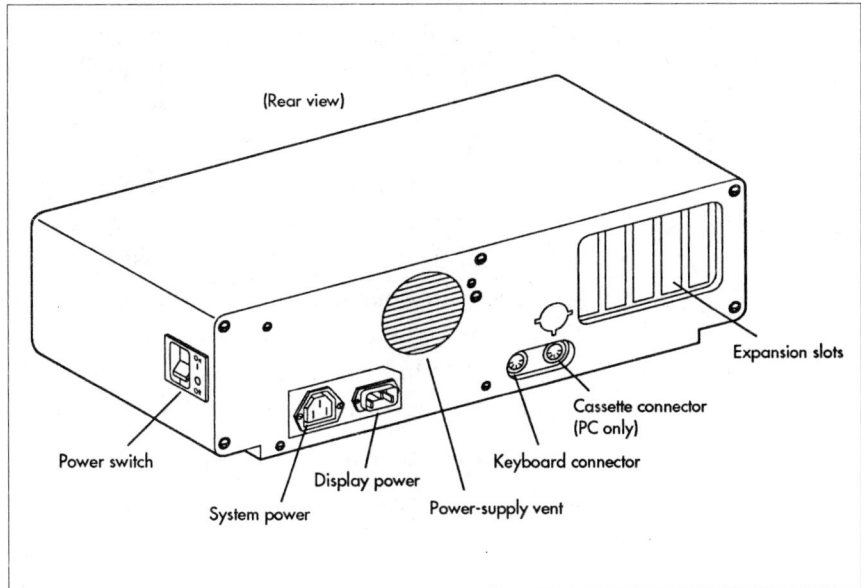

Figure 3.2 The rear of the system unit provides several important connections.

cooling fan to expel heated air. In a row, there are several narrow rectangular slots. These are called *expansion slots* or *ports*. Expansion slots allow you to add extra features to your computer, such as a color video card, a fax/modem, and more. Any item that fits in an expansion slot is called an *expansion card* or *add-on card*. Some expansion slots may already be filled; they may be used to connect your printer or monitor. The unused expansion slots have metal covers over them. If you are adding an expansion card, you must open the case to remove this metal cover.

Tools Needed

Now that we've explained the main parts of the computer, it's time to open it up. To open your PC, you'll need one basic tool: a medium-sized Phillips screwdriver

For all the procedures in this book, your toolkit should contain:

- Small Phillips screwdriver
- Small flat-blade screwdriver
- Medium flat-blade screwdriver

- Chip puller (to remove memory chips gently from your computer)
- Tweezers (to hold small parts in place)
- Needle-nose pliers (to straighten chips pins, remove jumpers, or crimp cables)
- Computer-grade compressed air (to blow away dust and dirt)
- Small makeup or camera lens brush (to gently remove dust and dirt)
- Toothbrush (to remove stubborn dust and dirt)
- Electronic-component cleaning solution (to clean electrical contacts)
- Foam cleaning swabs (to clean printheads and electrical contacts)
- Isopropyl alcohol (to clean parts)
- Silicone lubricant (to lubricate moving parts)

You can find most of these tools bundled in a "PC toolkit" that sells for about $30. I once received such a toolkit after subscribing to *PC World* magazine. Some "experts" recommend having soldering and unsoldering tools, logic probes, voltmeters, and other electronics testing equipment. The cost and expertise required for these tools is beyond the scope of this book. In 10 years of working with computers, I have never had to dabble with such equipment, and neither should you. Most repairs can be accomplished with these tools alone.

Opening the Case

Use the following procedure to open up your computer and get accustomed to seeing its "innards." Opening your computer is a completely natural occurrence and one I've performed often. It isn't brain surgery nor the domain of only technical "nerds." Instead, opening your computer is mandatory if you want to take advantage of your computer's ability to evolve and grow.

To remove your computer's case:

1. Park your hard disk heads, if required.

   On some older computers, you may have to manually park the hard disk's read/write heads. Most hard disks that use stepper motors must have their heads parked to safely move your computer. With such drives, a software utility often is included that moves the heads to an unused part of the hard disk. When in this position, the heads cannot damage data when the computer is bumped or moved. You usually run this utility by typing:

```
PARK  [Enter]
```

or

```
SHUTDOWN  [Enter]
```

If you have a computer manufactured by IBM, a program like SHUTDOWN.EXE or SHIPDISK.COM is available from the diagnostics or setup program.

2. Turn off your computer and unplug it from the electrical outlet.

3. Unplug any remaining cables from your computer.

    Various cables are connected to your computer, such as those to the keyboard, modem, monitor, and more. You may want to label each cable with some masking tape so you know to which port it should be reconnected. Grab each cable at the base and pull straight back, not at an angle. If you pull cables at an angle, you may damage or bend the pins of the connection.

4. Gently move your computer to an area where you will have ample room to disassemble it.

    Carry the computer in an embrace. In other words, don't hold the computer at arms length; you could damage your back. Bend at the knees to let your legs do as much of the lifting as possible.

5. With a Phillips screwdriver, remove the screws that hold the case to your system unit.

    Usually, five or six screws are found on the rear of your computer, on the outside perimeter at the corners and midpoints (see Figure 3.3). Any other screws are usually meant to hold internal components to the case. For example, four screws hold the power supply to the rear of your computer. Set aside these six screws so they won't be lost.

6. Firmly grasp the computer case from both sides and gently slide it back or forward (depending on the type of case you have).

On desktop computers, the case usually slides forward. The case usually includes the bezel, the attractive front of your computer. On floor-standing computers, like tower and mini-tower cases, the case is removed by sliding it backwards leaving the bezel behind. As you remove the case, be wary of any resistance that might be caused by

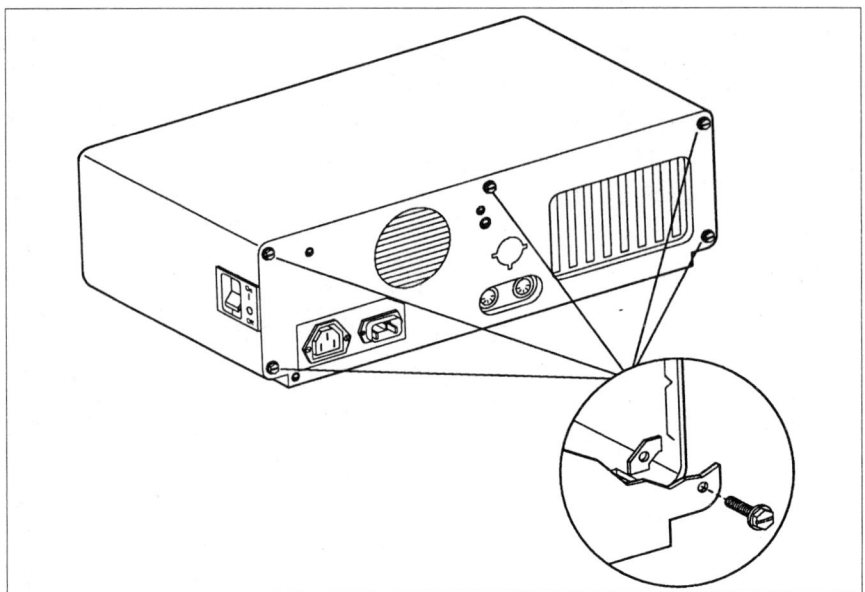

Figure 3.3 Six screws typically free your case for removal.

internal cables being snagged. Handle the case very gently during this procedure. If you feel any snags, try jiggling the cover, and peering inside the case to locate the source of the resistance. Set the case aside where it won't be scratched or marred. It's best to lay it flat on the floor so it doesn't tip over.

Danger: Static Kills

Before you touch anything inside your PC, you should be warned about static electricity. Some of the electronic parts in your computer can be damaged by extremely small amounts of electricity. Before touching anything, you must drain yourself of any built-up static electricity.

You can discharge static electricity by touching an unpainted grounded metal object, that is, a metal object that is in contact with the ground. For example, you can touch the metallic inside of your computer case lying nearby. You can also touch any electrical appliance that has a metal case, such as a lamp or stereo system. Touch this metal object briefly every few minutes.

You can minimize static electricity in several ways. Don't wear knit or wool sweaters, avoid fur or furry animals, don't walk on carpet, and don't touch rubber or plastic toys or balloons. Avoid any unnecessary moving around as you work. Avoid rubber-soled shoes and opt for leather. Ideally, removing your shoes and socks provides the best protection, but may be inconvenient or embarrassing.

You can get extra antistatic protection by using a *grounding wrist strap*. A ground strap is an elastic wristband with a built-in metal plate. You wear the wristband, which you attach by a wire to a grounded metal object, such as a power supply case. With a ground strap, you are continually being drained of static electricity.

If you ever remove an expansion card, described later and in the next chapter, grab it by its metal bracket. If you are handling memory chips, never touch the pins but instead pick them up by their bodies. If you must set an electronic component aside, place it on a special antistatic bag, which is usually pink or a shiny gray. Never place it on a table or carpet. You can buy antistatic bags and packaging at your local computer supply store. If you buy any electronic parts for your computer, keep their antistatic bags for future use.

Evaluating the Guts

Once the case is removed, I'd like you to notice some basics about your computer. First, the power supply is probably the largest part of your computer and most crucial (see Figure 3.4). It probably has a sticker on it that says, "CAUTION: Hazardous Area." This chrome steel, boxlike component provides power to all internal parts, like the disk drives and the motherboard — your computer's large, rectangular circuit board. Its fan also provides cooling for itself and your computer's heated electronics.

IMPORTANT: There should be a number on the power supply that states how many watts (W) it can support. Look for numbers like 135W, 150W, 200W, and so on. Place this number in the table in Appendix A: "PC Bio."

The power supply has multicolored wires attached to it. These wires, usually grouped in fours, provide power to the disk drives. Two sets of six colored wires also attach to the motherboard, your computer's main circuit board. These two power connectors are usually called P8 and P9, or P1 and P2.

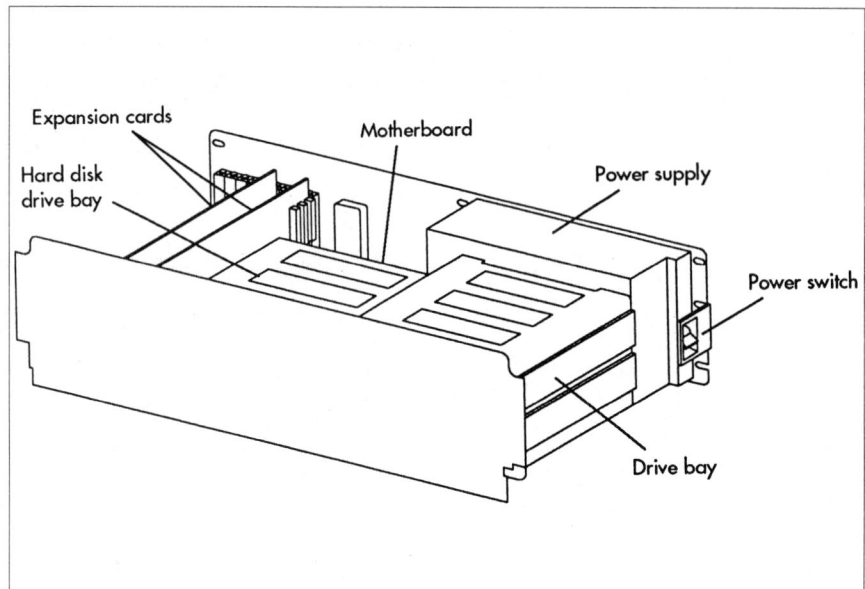

Figure 3.4 The various parts inside your computer.

Determining Drives

You'll also notice the disk drives. Floppy disk drives typically are held in place on a small metal bracket by four screws. Otherwise, they may be screwed to a bracket in the front by a screw on each side. The floppy disk drives are measured by the size of the disks they accept: either 3.5 or 5.25 inches. Your hard disk, if you have one, may be as large as a hardcover book or as small as a paperback; their sizes have greatly shrunk with advances in technology. The hard disk is usually encased in metal, although you may also see some of its electronic components on one side.

Your disk drives may be either of two sizes: *full-height* or *half-height*. Full-height drives are 3.25 inches high, 5.75 inches wide, and 8 inches deep. Older hard disks are often full-height. Diskette drives are usually half-height, that is, 1.625 inches high, either 5.75 or 4 inches wide, and 4 or 8 inches deep.

IMPORTANT: Measure your disk drives. Enter the size and height of each floppy diskette drive into the table in Appendix A: "PC Bio." If you have a hard disk, note whether it is full-height or half-height and place this information in the table. These measurements will be important in future chapters.

Next, notice the six to eight expansion slots in your computer. Some of these slots may already be filled by expansion cards. Others are vacant, waiting to be filled. The expansion cards in these slots may traverse the whole length of your computer case. Otherwise, these cards may be as small as six inches long. An expansion card that spans the length of your computer and fits into notches on the opposite side of the case is called a *full-length card*. Such a card is a little over 13 inches (35 cm) long. Older expansion cards, especially those that hold extra memory, often required this longer card to accommodate all the electronic components.

Expansion slots come in two sizes: *8-bit* and *16-bit*. An 8-bit slot has a single rectangular connector on the motherboard into which you plug expansion cards. This is called an *edge connector* because the edge of the expansion card is inserted into it. A 16-bit expansion slot uses two edge connectors (see Figure 3.5). An 8-bit connector is shown in Figure 3.6.

IMPORTANT: Count the total number of expansion slots and the number of expansion cards you have in your computer. Check whether they are 8-bit (one-connector) or 16-bit (two-connector) slots and cards. Enter these numbers into the table in Appendix A: "PC Bio."

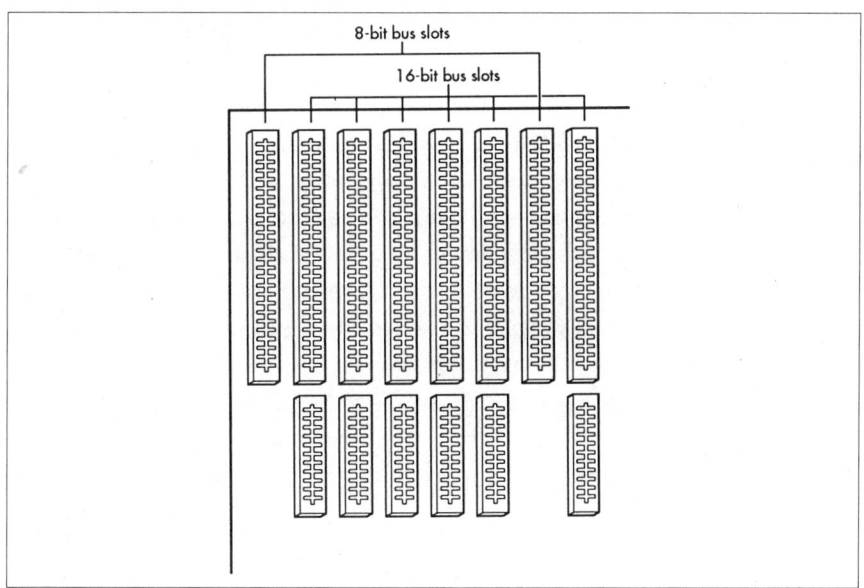

Figure 3.5 A 16-bit expansion slot has two edge connectors.

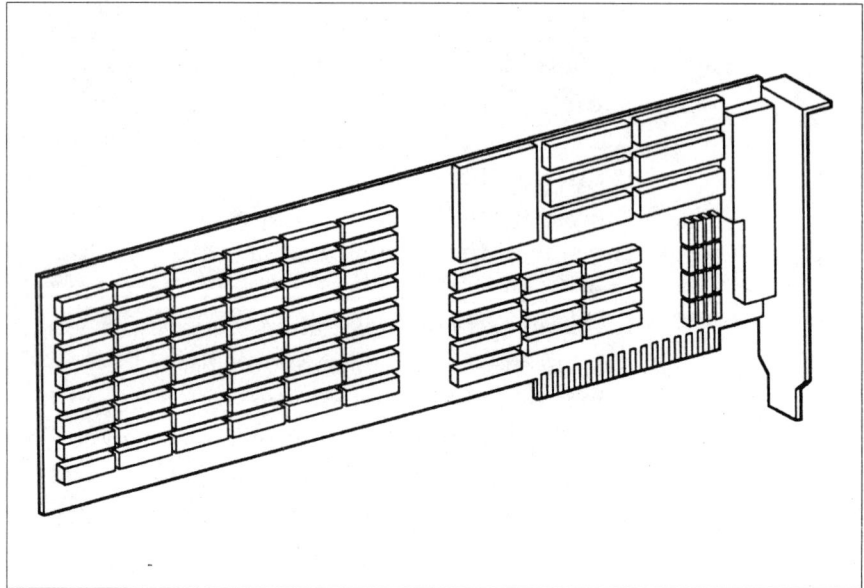

Figure 3.6 An 8-bit connector.

These expansion cards are inserted into connectors found on the *motherboard*. The motherboard is your computer's main circuit board. This flat, rectangular board occupies most of the bottom of your computer and its foundation. The motherboard is typically green or brownish with copper lines etched into it.

Finding the Brains

Your motherboard houses your microprocessor, your computer's "brain," as well as memory and other computer chips. The *microprocessor*, or just *processor*, is also called the *central processing unit (CPU)*. Which processor do you have? If you don't know, you can easily find out now that your computer is open. The processor is a single computer chip soldered to the motherboard. It is usually square (although it can be rectangular) and is often the largest computer chip inside your computer (see Figure 3.7). The microprocessor is usually located in the rear center of your case. There are numbers on this crucial computer chip that show the type of processor you own. Look for numbers like this:

- 8088
- 80286-*xx*
- 80386-*xx*

Figure 3.7 A picture of an Intel486 (80486) DX processor with its top removed. *(photo courtesy of Intel Corp.)*

- 80386DX-*xx*
- 80386SX-*xx*
- 80486SX-*xx*
- 80486-*xx*

where *xx* is the speed (in megahertz) of your microprocessor. The higher the number, the faster your computer. These numbers may be preceded by a letter or manufacturer's name.

IMPORTANT: Enter the type and speed of your microprocessor in the chart in Appendix A: "PC Bio."

The table on the next page lists the microprocessors found in PCs, their speed in megahertz (MHz), and the date they became available. You'll note that the table listings start way back in 1978 and continue to include the very latest 486 chips. You'll also notice the significant improvements in speed available in the newer CPUs. If the date on your processor is within two years of the listed date of availability, your computer is relatively new. Why? The dates listed are when these chips became available, not when they became affordable.

Processor	Speed (MHz)	Year Available
8086	5, 8, 10	June 1978
8088	5, 8	June 1979
80286	6, 8, 10, 12	February 1982
	16, 20	January 1989
	25	February 1990
80386DX	16	October 1985
	20	February 1987
	25	April 1988
	33	April 1989
	40	March 1991
80386SX	16	June 1988
	20	February 1989
	25	May 1991
80486DX	25	April 1989
	33	May 1990
	50	June 1991
80486SX	16	September 1991
	20	April 1991
	25	September 1991

IMPORTANT: Calculate the number of months between today's date and the microprocessor type and speed you have. Enter this number into the chart in Appendix A: "PC Bio."

Memory Chips

Besides the microprocessor, your motherboard also holds rows of memory chips. The memory chips are called *dynamic random access memory*, or *DRAM*, because they must be electrically refreshed by your computer or else the information is lost. These DRAM memory chips provide temporary workspace when you use a software program and load a file. This temporary workspace is called *random access memory (RAM)*.

Memory chips come in different sizes, depending on the computer

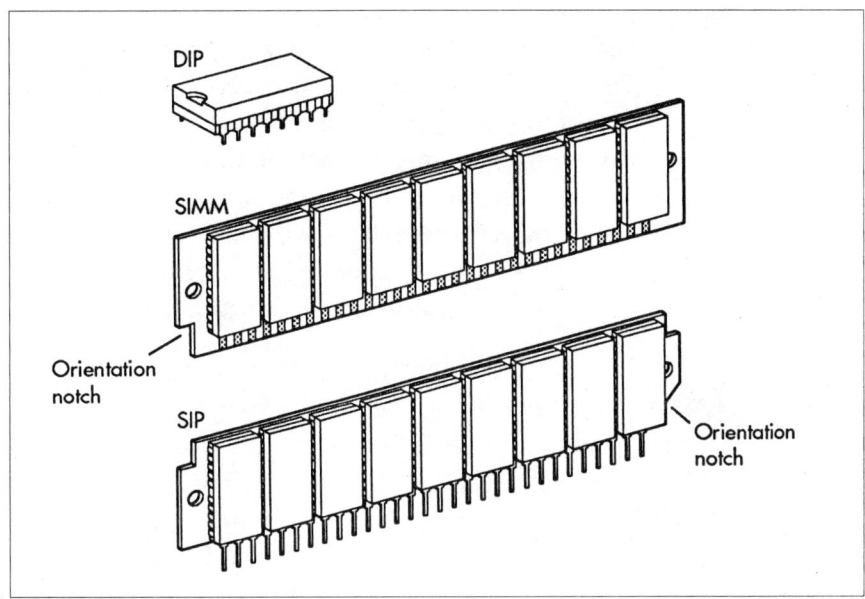

Figure 3.8 The differences among DIP, SIMM, and SIP memory chips.

you have (see Figure 3.8). Older computers use *dual in-line pin (DIP)* memory chips. A DIP memory chip is a rectangular chip that has 16 metal legs, eight on each side. To install such memory chips, you must plug each one into place, usually in groups of nine. Sometimes, DIP memory chips are permanently soldered to your motherboard.

A newer type of memory chip is the *single in-line memory module (SIMM)*. These modules combine several memory chips on a small circuit board. This board is then plugged into a socket on the motherboard. One advantage of this design is that you have fewer chips to install, reducing the chance of damage. In one move, you can install the equivalent of nine DIP chips. Also, using SIMMs eliminates chip creep, where memory chips work their way out of place because of the constant heating and cooling occurring inside your computer.

Another type of memory chip, although rarer, is the *single in-line package (SIP)*. The SIP uses DIP-like memory but is similar to the SIMM chip. This design contains several memory chips in one package. However, it looks like a comb because it has thin leads that are inserted into your motherboard. You find this type of memory in newer 80286 computers.

All memory chips must be installed into *memory banks*. A memory bank is a collection of memory chips that make up a block of memory. This memory is read by your processor in one pass. You may even see the words "Bank *x*" on your motherboard, where *x* is any number from 0 to 3. Examine your memory banks. An 8088, 8086, 80286, or 80386SX computer has four memory banks. An 80386DX, 80486SX, or 80486DX computer has two memory banks. Is any memory bank vacant? An empty memory bank may indicate an opportunity to speed up your computer by adding memory to it.

IMPORTANT: Enter how many memory banks your computer has in the table in Appendix A: "PC Bio." Look for words on the motherboard that say "Bank 0." How many banks are empty? Enter this number in the table, too. (In Chapter 6, "Thanks for the Memory," we'll discover what types of memory chips you have and which ones you need for the vacant memory banks.)

In older 8088, 8086, and 80286 computers, each memory bank contains nine chips. In newer 80286 and 80386SX computers, each memory bank holds either two 9-bit SIPs or two 9-bit SIMMs. The 80386DX, 80486SX, and 80486DX computers use 9-bit SIMMs or one 36-bit SIMM per memory bank.

On the memory chips — whether the DIP, SIP, or SIMM type — you will see an identifying number. The last two digits are especially important, since they indicate the speed of your memory. For example, one of my older computers has memory chips with the number "M5K4164ANP 51727F-15." The last two digits after this long number indicate the speed in nanoseconds. (A nanosecond equals one-billionth of a second and is abbreviated *ns*.) Since only two digits are used, this number may be the speed in tens of nanoseconds or simply nanoseconds. In this example, the memory chips are rated at 150 nanoseconds. Most memory chips range in speeds between 50 and 150 nanoseconds.

IMPORTANT: Enter the speed of your memory chips in the table in Appendix A: "PC Bio."

Besides the multicolored power cables, your computer also relies on *ribbon cables*. Ribbon cables are a bunch of independent wires, up to 50. In a way, these ribbon cables look like flattened packs of gray licorice. While the power cables provide power, ribbon cables allow electronic signals to pass between your computer's different internal parts. For example, you probably see a gray ribbon cable connected from one of your expansion cards to your floppy disk drive(s).

Cleaning Your PC

Before you replace the case, you may want to do some spring or fall cleaning inside your computer. Dust is your number one enemy. As the power supply's fan draws cooler air in through your computer, dust becomes an unwelcome visitor. It clings to your computer's electronic components, giving them undesirable insulation. It's best to dust the inside of your computer every six months. However, if you happen to go into your computer every so often, you might as well take advantage of the opportunity.

To clean your PC:

1. Use a toothbrush on the computer case to remove dust from its typically ribbed vents.

2. Brush the exhaust fan plate in the back of the computer to dislodge dirt.

3. Wipe the outside and rear of your system unit.

    Use a soft, lint-free cloth moist with water and a few drops of ammonia to clean the outside of the case. Next, clean the metal slot covers on the back of your computer. Do not use this cloth on the inside — water and electronics don't mix!

4. Loosen dust from inside your computer.

    Use a makeup or camera lens brush to loosen dirt and dust from components, like the computer chips attached to the motherboard. To reduce any static electricity, use short, slow strokes to remove the coat of dust. Use a toothbrush on the inside vents of the power supply. I once opened a veteran computer to find a beard of dust blocking the air intake vents. Scrape the dust growth off the vents.

5. Press down on the individual computer chips.

The heating and cooling occurring inside your computer can cause DIP chips — the ones with several legs inserted into the motherboard — to become loose. This "chip creep" can be prevented by pressing down on these chips to seat them. This not only counters the chip creep, but also removes any corrosion on the legs, providing a better connection. Before touching each chip, briefly touch a metal object to remove any static electricity. Always press down on the chip's black body, not the legs themselves.

6. Use compressed air to blow dust out and away.

A can of compressed air will help you clear dust from inside your computer. Make sure you get computer-grade air, not just air used for camera lenses. This canned air must be free of moisture and contaminants. A popular ingredient to look for is *chlorodifluoromethane*. Avoid canned air that uses Freon TF as a propellant; it generates static electricity as it leaves the nozzle, which could ruin electronic components.

Blow the dust away from your computer; you want to remove — not just move — the dust. You can also use a vacuum cleaner to gently remove dust that's collected in the cracks and crevasses of your PC. However, do not touch any of the electronic parts with the vacuum cleaner nozzles.

7. Loosen your disk drives and remove dust collected between them.

Dust also collects in your floppy disk drives. Loosen the screws that hold them in place and pull them slightly forward. You shouldn't have to remove any cables. If you have an older computer, you probably have a collection of dust and lint sitting on the drives. Blow this dust away with the compressed air. For stubborn dirt, use the makeup brush to loosen it. When done, reattach the drives.

Note: You can also clean your expansion cards. I discuss how to do this in Chapter 4, "Expansion Cards: Getting Onboard Safely." Since expansion cards are sensitive electronic components, I prefer to deal with these after you better understand how to work with them.

Closing the Case

When finished examining your computer, you'll need to replace its cover and use it again.

To close the case:

1. Put the outer case back on.

    As you slide the case on, avoid snagging any inside wires or cables. Tuck these in as you replace the case.

2. Install and tighten the five or six case screws.

    Use the first two screws to affix the bowed edges of the case, usually the lower left and right sides of the case. Attach the remaining screws to your computer.

    Do not overtighten the screws. Your computer is not a blender; it won't vibrate apart if the screws are not at the absolute tightest. There is a danger of possibly tightening the screws so much that their metal may chip, making it difficult or even impossible for you to remove the case later.

3. Once the case is on, return the computer to its normal location and attach all cables. Turn on your PC once more and enjoy.

Reattaching all the cables and cords can be a chore, especially since the cables are attached to the computer's backside where seeing is difficult. One simple trick is to place a mark on each cable so you know which end should be up when the cable is attached. Otherwise, you may try inserting the cable upside down, possibly damaging the connector. Use a permanent marker to put an identifying mark on each cable.

Now that you have been inside your computer at least once, you should be quite comfortable when opening it later. You may need to open your computer to clean it or to improve it. In the next several chapters, we will explore the various ways to better your computer. Your PC was meant to be improved, and a handful of screws no longer will prevent you from opening it up and getting the job done.

4

Expansion Cards: Getting On-Board Safely

The PC is flexible and has been since its creation in 1981. The original PC had five vacant slots inside its case. These slots were set aside so features could be added to your PC by inserting printed circuit boards from other manufacturers. (A *printed circuit board*, or *PCB*, is simply a flat piece of fiberglass, usually green, that is etched with copper wires and has several electronic components mounted on it.) These empty slots are called *expansion slots* or *expansion ports*. You may have between six and eight expansion slots in your PC. The circuit boards placed into them are called *expansion cards, expansion boards,* or *add-on cards.*

Although many improvements can be made to your PC, most require working with expansion cards. The features you get from these expansion cards are either required for your PC to operate or otherwise provide features above and beyond that of the typical PC. (See Figure 4.1). The expansion cards that are mandatory for your PC to operate are described below.

> *Note:* Some computers incorporate these mandatory features directly into the motherboard, your computer's main circuit board. One flaw of this design is that you cannot improve these features without tossing away the entire motherboard, which is costly and difficult to replace.

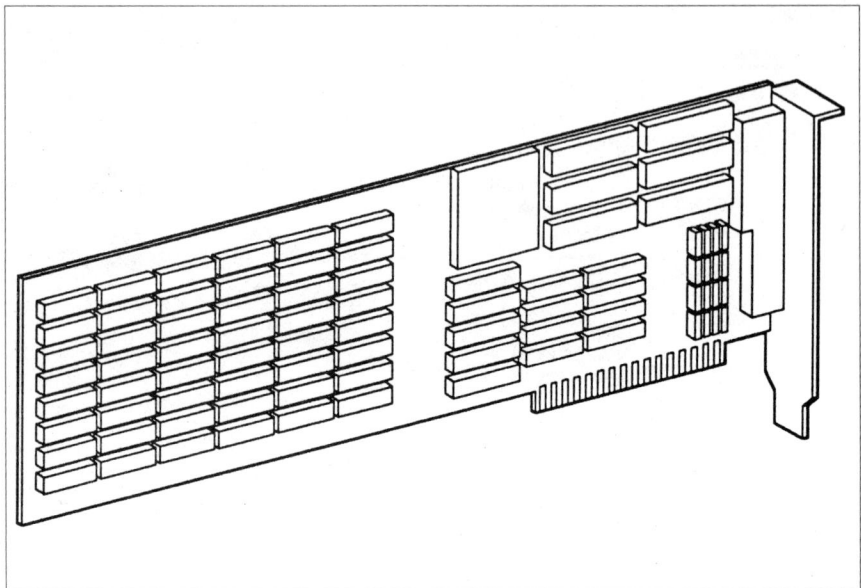

Figure 4.1 One example of an expansion card that enhances your computer.

- **Video card.** The video card lets you see your computer work. The *video card*, also called a *video* or *display adapter*, controls your computer screen so you can see it work. There are several different types of video cards, which we'll explain in Chapter 11 "Clear Vision." Basically, though, there are either monochrome (one-color) or color video cards. Some monochrome video cards also provide a connection for your printer.

- **Input/Output (I/O) cards**. Another crucial card is the *input/output (I/O) card*. The I/O card provides various connections to external hardware, like a computer printer. Some I/O cards provide only a parallel printer port and a serial port. Others take up two expansion slots to provide a parallel printer port, two serial ports, and a game port for a joystick. Such robust I/O cards are often called *multifunction I/O cards*. What do each of these ports do? The parallel printer port, or just parallel port, lets you connect a computer printer so you can print your computer work to paper. The two serial ports can be used to run a mouse (which lets you make a selection in a software program by pointing at it) as well as connect an external modem (which lets you communicate with other computers). The joystick port lets you use a joystick for use with computer games, and is especially useful for those that simulate flying.

- **Disk drive controller card.** The *disk drive controller card* is also important. Without a circuit board to run your disk drives, you cannot get information into or out of your computer. You cannot copy a file to a diskette to share with a friend or colleague, and you cannot load new software programs onto your computer. On newer computers, one expansion card may control up to two floppy diskette drives and two hard disk drives. Such expansion cards may also provide I/O ports for connection to other devices. For example, my disk drive controller takes up another expansion port by providing two serial ports, a parallel printer port, and a joystick port.

Nice-to-Have Cards

What other features can you get from expansion cards? Their uses are many, but you can have expansion cards that:

- Let you scan pictures and even text for use in desktop publishing or word processing programs.
- Add memory to your computer if your motherboard won't hold any more.
- Access an external tape drive or speed up an internal tape drive.
- Connect two joysticks to your computer for playing games with a friend.
- Access an external CD-ROM (compact disc read-only memory) drive, which may have an encyclopedia or other reference material on it.
- Add high-quality sound to games and other software programs.
- Turn your PC into a voice-mail and/or fax machine.
- Communicate with other computers or on-line services, such as the PRODIGY service, CompuServe, or GEnie.
- Speed up your computer by bypassing your processor — your computer's "brain" — and using its own instead.

Taking a Different Bus

Unfortunately, some expansion cards may not fit your computer because it may have a special circuit design. The *expansion bus* is a collection of wires that carry information between the different parts inside your computer. This expansion bus is what lets you add expansion cards to your PC.

The rectangular connectors you see on the motherboard into which you plug expansion cards are your gateways to the computer's bus. These are called *edge connectors* because the edge of the expansion card is inserted into them. Each connector contains two sets of pins, 31 on each side. Eight of the pins in each slot carry data. The other 54 are for supplying power to the expansion card and other functions.

The eight data pins on the edge connector are for the eight data lines on XT-type computers, which use either an 8088 or 8086 processor. XT-type computers have only one edge connector per expansion slot because these processors can only process 8 bits of information at a time. (A bit is a small unit of information.) A slot with a single edge connector is called an *8-bit slot* (see Figure 4.2).

When the AT, or 80286, computer was introduced by IBM, some of the connectors were enlarged with an additional 36-pin edge connector for a total of 98 pins. This second connector allowed expansion

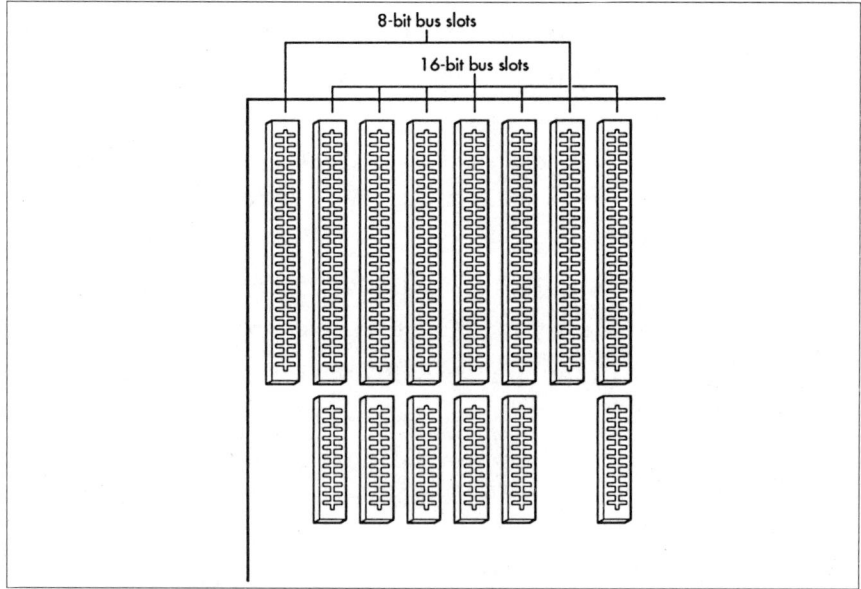

Figure 4.2 Sixteen-bit slots have two edge connectors; 8-bit slots have one.

cards to take advantage of the 16-bit speed of the 80286 processor found on such computers. A slot with these two edge connectors is called a *16-bit slot*. To accommodate both 8-bit and 16-bit expansion cards, the AT computer had a mixture of 8-bit and 16-bit slots. This tradition continues today.

When computers powered by the 80386 or 80486 processor became available, the expansion bus did not get larger. Although the new processors could move data in 32-bit chunks, speeding your computer's performance, no standard emerged. Such 80386 and 80486 computers still accept 8-bit and 16-bit expansion cards. You can easily tell if your expansion card is an 8-bit or 16-bit card. A 16-bit card has a gap between its two edges, or teeth. An 8-bit card has only one tooth to insert into the single edge connector on the motherboard.

Name That Bus

The 8-bit PC bus never received an official name and was simply called the *PC bus*. Today, it is called the *Industry Standard Architecture* or *ISA*. The ISA bus is the most common and popular bus available today.

In 1987, IBM introduced its line of Personal System/2 computers. The PS/2 computers didn't use the ISA bus. Instead, IBM created its controversial *MicroChannel Architecture* or *MCA*. Expansion cards for the older PC bus could not be used with PS/2 computers that have MCA. Likewise, you couldn't use an MCA expansion card in your PC. In other words, you couldn't salvage your color video card from your PC and put it into your PS/2 computer. For this reason, many people never considered the PS/2 computer, although IBM has since produced PS/2 computers that use the ISA bus. Although MCA was not very popular, it provided a 32-bit data path to move large amounts of data inside your computer much faster than with the ISA bus.

To counter IBM's renegade MCA bus, a consortium of PC makers decided to provide a 32-bit bus standard for their computers. A 32-bit expansion slot would allow an 80386 or 80486 computer to move data back and forth at top speed to a 32-bit expansion card. The new bus was called the *Extended Industry Standard Architecture*, or *EISA*. Unlike MCA, this new standard allows you to use your ISA expansion cards from your older computer with the new architecture.

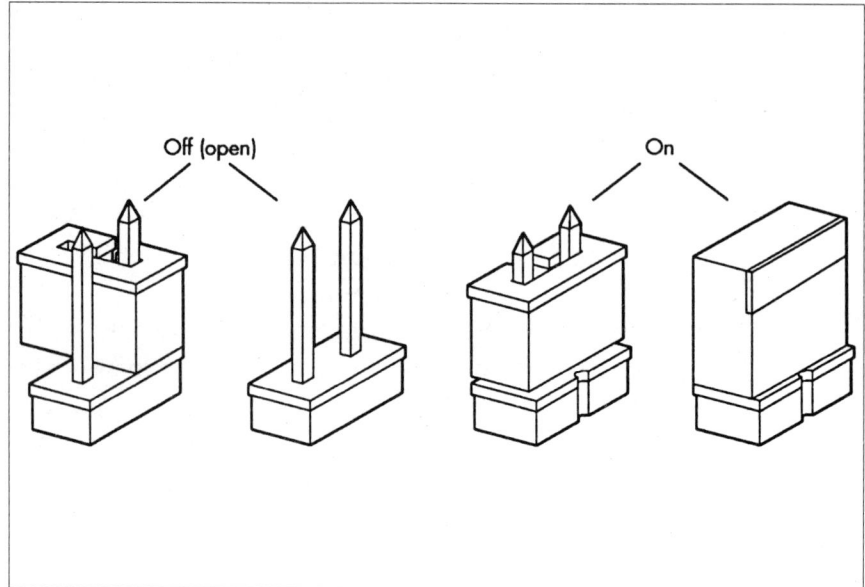

Off (open)   On

Figure 4.3 A jumper can be used to turn an expansion card option on or off.

Jumpers and DIP Switches

To configure your card, you often have to set *jumpers* or *DIP (dual-inline pin) switches.* For example, I installed a Diamond Stealth VRAM video card that required me to change the DIP switch to take full advantage of my NEC monitor.

A jumper, or *shunt,* is a common way to configure an expansion card (see Figure 4.3). It is simply a short piece of wire, encased in plastic, that lets you make an electrical connection between two pins on your card. A jumper is easy to remove and change, but you may want to use needle-nosed pliers to grab it. By simply sliding the jumper over two neighboring pins, you connect them, thereby changing the card's settings. On your expansion card, jumpers are usually designated by the letter "J" or "JP" followed by a number, like J3 or JP5.

You can also configure your expansion card with a DIP switch or one of it variants such as rocker or togg*le* (see Figure 4.4). A DIP switch is simply a small bank of switches. How small? The switches are spaced at 10 switches per inch, although many DIP switch banks have only four switches. They are easy to spot; they are usually blue or red. Each switch has two positions, on or off. On the switch's

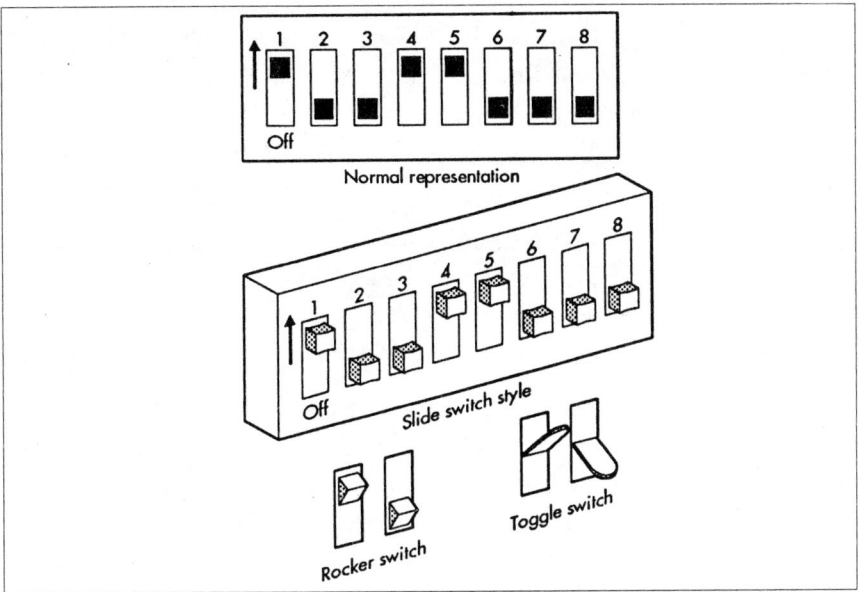

Figure 4.4 A DIP switch, in any of these three styles, modifies your expansion card.

plastic face, the word "ON" or "OPEN" may be printed. Don't confuse the two: "OPEN" means "off" (an open circuit). By setting each switch either on or off, you can tell your expansion card to behave a certain way. For example, a four-switch DIP switch lets an expansion card maker provide up to 24 combinations, although the features you can change on your card are usually fewer.

When Cards Don't Work

Fortunately, you often don't need to set DIP switches or jumpers. Most expansion cards have been preconfigured at the factory to work in most situations. Still, you may find yourself in a situation where a new expansion card doesn't work once installed. Why? The newly installed expansion card may be conflicting with others already installed.

How do you know there's a conflict? Both the new expansion card **and** the one with which it is conflicting do not work. For example, a just-installed modem may be preset for COM1 (the first serial communications port). However, you already have a COM1 port that is used for your mouse. You will find that neither the mouse nor the modem works. The solution is to change a jumper or DIP switch on the modem card to make it COM2, the second communications port. Once each has its own serial port, there is no conflict.

What causes such a hardware conflict? Four factors are involved with getting your expansion card to work:

- Direct memory access (DMA) channels
- Read-only memory (ROM) addresses
- Input/output (I/O) addresses
- Interrupt request (IRQ) lines

DMA channels are used to speed information to and from your computer's memory. Using your computer's processor to transfer this information can be slow. Using the DMA controller chips built into your computer, your expansion card can bypass the processor altogether. (Kind of like eliminating the middleman.) Your computer cannot support many expansion cards that use DMA channels; there are four channels on XT-type computers and eight on AT-type computers. However, the first three channels (0 through 2) are reserved for refreshing your computer's memory and controlling your disk drives.

DMA Channel	Purpose
0	Refreshes your computer's memory.
1	Used by your hard disk controller.
2	Used by your floppy disk controller.
3	Unused.
4–7	Available on AT-type and PS/2 computers but usually not used.

Some expansion cards have built-in read-only memory (ROM) chips that provide simple programs to control themselves. For example, an enhanced graphic adapter (EGA) video card or a disk drive controller may have such ROM chips. When your computer is started, these low-level programs are loaded by the expansion card into ROM *addresses.* If two expansion cards try to place their programs at the same address, neither will work.

I/O addresses and interrupts are the factors most likely to change on your expansion card. The I/O address is a place assigned in your computer's memory where it can "talk" to different parts of your computer. For example, there is an address for your keyboard. There are also addresses for your expansion cards. Some I/O addresses are set in stone. For example, a joystick controller (or game card) has a set address of 200-20F.

If you created a totally new expansion card, you would pick an address that is unassigned. However, there are a limited number of I/O addresses. Your PC, for example, is limited to three printer ports — LPT1, LPT2, and LPT3 — and two serial ports — COM1 and COM2. (With DOS 3.3 and later, you can also have COM3 and COM4; however, you must "split" the addresses for COM1 and COM2.) Likewise, you usually cannot have two video cards; the two will fight to the death for the video address space.

The *interrupt (IRQ)* is a method used by your expansion card to get your computer's attention when it needs it. When you type at your keyboard, for example, the keyboard controller chip inside your computer interrupts the processor so that each keystroke can be placed into the keyboard buffer, or storage area. If it were not for interrupts, your keystrokes would be lost until the processor was finished with its other work.

Like I/O addresses, the number of interrupts is limited. XT-type computers have five interrupts, 2 through 7. These interrupts are prioritized, with interrupt 2 being more urgent than interrupt 7. When an interrupt is used, your PC's processor stops dead in its tracks and handles the computer device with that interrupt. (See table on next page.)

Removing a Device Conflict

To remove any of these device conflicts, you need to change one or both of the conflicting expansion cards. However, some cards do not have jumpers or DIP switches. This means there is no possible way to remove the conflict. Instead, change the other card's settings. You can also remove conflicts by disabling parts of one expansion card. For example, I disabled a game, or joystick, port because I already had one. Likewise, you may need to disable a serial port or a parallel printer port.

If you have a somewhat older computer, such as a PC made in 1981 or 1982, you may need to buy a new BIOS (Basic Input/Output System) chip or chips to use some expansion cards. Likewise, some expansion cards may not work without a newer BIOS. (I discuss BIOS chips and how to determine if you should replace yours in Chapter 7, "CPUs: Boning Up on Brainpower.")

Interrupt	Device	Comments
0	Timer	
1	Keyboard	
2	Unused	Used in AT-type computers as a gateway to IRQ 8/15 or for EGA/VGA video cards.
3	COM2 (second serial port)	Used for a modem or mouse.
4	COM1 (first serial port)	Used for a modem or mouse.
5	Hard disk	XT-type computers only; otherwise available for AT-type computers to use.
6	FDC (floppy disk drive controller)	
7	LPT1 (first parallel printer port)	
8	Clock	Interrupts 8 through 15 are available only on AT-type computers and often not to expansion cards.
9	PC network	
10–12	Unused	
13	Math coprocessor	Used for speeding mathematical calculations, such as in spreadsheet or computer-aided design (CAD) programs
14	Hard disk	
15	Unused	

Installing and Replacing Cards

To add the special abilities of an expansion card, you must install it. You first need to open up your computer (explained in Chapter 3). Next, you may have to remove an existing expansion card and install its replacement. For example, you may be installing a color video card in lieu of your monochrome one. You may also be adding a new capability to your PC, perhaps adding a voice mail card to turn your PC into a sophisticated answering machine.

To remove an expansion card:

1. Turn off your computer and remove its case.

   For details on opening your computer, see the procedure in Chapter 3, "Cracking Open the Case."

2. Remove the screw that holds the expansion card in its slot (see Figure 4.5).

   Only one screw needs to be removed to free the metal bracket from the case. Set the screw aside where it won't be lost.

3. Remove the expansion card.

   Rock the expansion card back and forth along its length. In other words, do not twist the card from side to side but rather pull up alternately on each end. Be careful where you grab the card; there

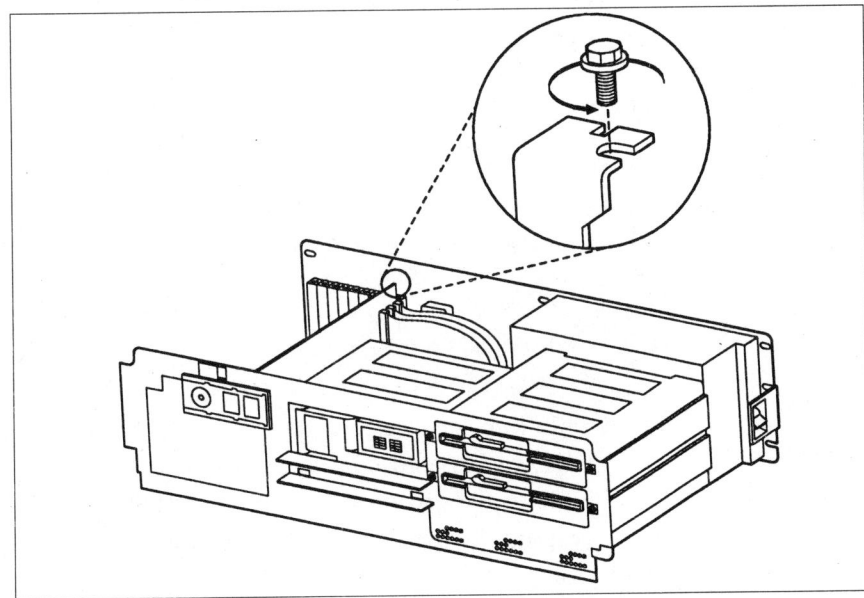

Figure 4.5 A single screw holds each expansion card in its slot.

may be delicate components that could be crushed. Carefully grab the card by its metal bracket and edges. DO NOT touch any of the components on the card since any static electricity you may have can damage the card. Also, do not touch the gold edge connectors. As you remove each expansion card, set it aside on a clean surface, preferably on antistatic packaging you have saved or an antistatic mat.

To install an expansion card:

1. Turn off your computer and remove its case.

   For details on opening your computer, see the procedure in Chapter 3, "Cracking Open the Case."

2. Select an empty expansion slot for your new card.

   Select a slot that matches the type of card you have. For example, you don't want to put a 16-bit card (one with dual edge connectors) into an 8-bit slot (one with a single edge connector). A 16-bit card was designed to take advantage of the larger 16-bit bus. If you have several empty slots from which to choose, you may want to place the new card in one as far away as possible from the others. This reduces any possible electromagnetic interference; that is, it reduces the possibility of stray radio signals from one card affecting another.

   > *Note:* You generally cannot use the eighth slot found in the IBM PC/XT. This is the expansion slot nearest the power supply. Cards in this slot do not work properly since it is electrically separate from the other slots.

3. Remove the screw that holds the metal plate that covers the empty expansion slot you've chosen.

   Only one screw needs to be removed to free the metal plate from the case. Set aside the screw where it won't be lost. Save the metal plate in case you remove the expansion card later. For example, you may want to sell your computer and keep some of the expansion cards for your next PC.

4. Remove the expansion card from its protective packaging.

Expansion cards are shipped in a special gray or silver antistatic bag. When you open this bag, carefully grab the card by its metal bracket and edges. DO NOT touch any of the components on the card since any static electricity you may have can damage the card. Also, do not touch the gold edge connectors.

5. Configure the expansion card.

   You may have to set jumpers or DIP switches to configure the card for your computer. See the instructions that came with the card.

6. Place the card in the edge connector.

   First, touch a metal object nearby, such as the inside of your computer's cover, to drain yourself of static electricity. Then, holding the card by its metal bracket and edges, place it in the expansion slot. Rock the expansion card back and forth along its length. In other words, do not twist the card from side to side but rather push down alternately on each end. There may be firm resistance as you press on the card; this is natural. Watch the motherboard to gauge how much force to apply. You should not have to push so hard that the motherboard bows downward, almost touching the bottom of the case.

7. Attach the screw to hold the expansion card.

   Tighten the screw to hold the expansion card in place. Do not overtighten this screw; you may need to remove the screw later.

8. When done, replace your computer's case and return your PC to working order.

9. In some cases, you may have to use your computer's Setup program to recognize the new expansion card.

   If you installed a memory expansion card, you would have to start your computer and use the Setup program to tell it the new total amount of memory. This Setup program is either built into your computer or provided on a diagnostics diskette that came with it. On some computers, you must set a jumper to tell it the new total amount of memory. Likewise, you would have to tell your Setup program if you installed a color video card in place of a monochrome one.

   If you have an XT-type computer or older AT-type, you do not have a built-in Setup. Rather, you may have to set jumpers on your motherboard to recognize changes. Consult your owner's manual.

10. Test the new expansion card.

To ensure your expansion card was well built, leave your computer on for 24 to 72 hours. You can also get a diagnostic program, such as QAPlus from Diagsoft, to run tests repetitively that stress the new card. This testing is called the *burn-in*. For example, many computer manufacturers claim to burn in your computer for 48 hours. Believe it or not, this stress is good for the expansion card. If it fails the burn-in period, you can always return it or have it repaired or replaced before the warranty period expires. If the expansion card passes your burn-in test, there is a greater chance that the card will last a very long time. How? The expansion card has no moving parts, so it will not wear out except because of bad manufacturing or poor-quality components. This is what the burn-in period tests.

Cleaning the Cards

Although we discussed cleaning the inside of your computer in Chapter 3, your expansion cards could also use special cleaning. Use this procedure every six months and more frequently if your computer is either in a harsher, dusty environment or is left on more than 40 hours a week. Also, removing the expansion card and reinstalling it provides a better connection to your motherboard, since the card may be loosened by the heating and cooling your computer undergoes.

To clean your expansion cards:

1. Remove the expansion card from its slot.

   Use the previous procedure to remove the expansion card. Watch out for static electricity!

2. Move the card away from your computer.

   If you are going to clean your expansion card of dust, it's best to move it away from the rest of the computer. If you must set the card down to clean it, place it on an antistatic bag or other antistatic packing material.

3. Loosen dust from the electronic components on the card.

    Hold the expansion card by its edges and/or the metal bracket. Do not touch its components. Use a makeup or camera lens brush to loosen dirt and dust from your computer's components before spraying. To reduce any static electricity, use short, slow strokes to remove the coat of dust. I also recommend you wear a grounding strap, as mentioned in Chapter 2, "Environment: Clearing the Air."

4. Use compressed air to blow dust out and away from the card.

    Use computer-grade air, not the canned air used for camera lenses. This air must be free of moisture and contaminants. Also, be sure the propellant used is not Freon TF; it generates static electricity as it leaves the nozzle, which could ruin the electronic components.

5. Clean the electrical contacts on the card.

    The copper pin edge connectors should be cleaned, since these provide the vital connection to your computer's bus. Use a cleaning swab. These swabs should be made of foam so they leave no lint behind; do not use the more common cotton swab. Dip the swab in an electronic-component cleaning solution and wipe each contact. Such a solution normally contains isopropyl alcohol, trichloroethylene, or Freon. Do not use a rubber eraser to clean these contacts. Not only can eraser crumbs be left behind, but the eraser may wear away the contact's copper coat.

6. After the contacts are dry, reinstall the expansion card.

    With expansion cards, you can enhance your computer and extend its useful life. In the next several chapters, we will examine many improvements to your computer that require expansion cards. With some tender care, you can ensure any added expansion cards will work successfully for years.

5 Power: Keep Your Juices Flowing

Your PC is placed under a lot of stress every time you flick on the power switch. This stress, in fact, makes your computer's power supply one of the most likely components to fail. You can take several measures to increase the life of your computer by making sure it has clean, adequate power.

The power supply (see Figure 5.1) has several duties. When you turn on your computer, it must charge the 110-volt alternating current (AC) from your electrical outlet into both 5- and 12-volt direct current (DC). It must bring the computer's hard disk from a dead stop to 60 revolutions each second. It has to run the floppy diskette drives on demand, operate tape drives, provide current to expansion cards like your modem, run your PC speaker and more.

Your PC contains sensitive electronic components that can be ruined by just a touch of static electricity. The electricity coming from your local utility to your outlet often fluctuates. Your power supply must keep this current stable; it must anticipate and adjust to these changes. The stability of the power supply is so crucial that it sends a Power Good signal to your computer. If this signal isn't present, the computer doesn't run.

Changing this higher voltage into a lower voltage generates heat and lots of it. And the greater the demand on your power supply, the more heat generated. One engineering principle is that the hotter a PC gets, the shorter its expected life becomes. This is one reason why the power supply has its own cooling fan. The fan also provides cool

Figure 5.1 The power supply provides the lifeblood to your computer by converting AC voltage to DC voltage. *(Photo courtesy of PC Power & Cooling Inc.)*

air to the rest of the computer, which generates heat as the electronic circuits are powered. The fan doesn't blow cool air into the computer. Rather, it blows hot air out the rear. The result of this decompression is that cooler air is pulled into the front of the computer through its vents and openings and then over the components of the motherboard.

> *Note:* If your fan ever stops working—and you should notice its silence—then turn off your computer *immediately*! Without this fan running, the built-up heat will destroy your PC.

Keep Your PC Well-Grounded

Your first concern should be your electrical outlet and how you use it. Your computer should be plugged into a three-prong, grounded wall outlet. The third prong provides good contact with the ground to drain off harmful electricity.

If you are also using one or more printers, displays, and other devices, you should be sure your electrical system can handle the workload. Some people use a master power switch or power strip to turn on several computer devices at one time. Although convenient, this one-switch system creates a large simultaneous demand for power. This strain can shorten your computer's life. Try to avoid using such a system, or at least turn on your printer separately.

Similarly, you may be turning on your monitor by plugging it into the AC outlet built into the back of your PC. Unfortunately, it was meant for the original monochrome (single-color) display. To use this outlet, the display's electrical cord must be of a special design. Some people use a special "cheater" cord to plug the monitor into the computer's AC outlet. If your power supply is not overtaxed (which we'll discover later), it should be able to handle the extra workload. For now, you may want to avoid the "cheater" cord and plug the monitor into its own outlet.

Leave It On!

A computer is not a blender. You can leave it on unattended if you are away for an extended period. Nothing will burn out. In fact, your computer may last longer if left turned on.

The power supply is most vulnerable when being turned on and off. During those first few seconds after being turned on, the power supply must provide extensive power to your entire computer. It must convert, stabilize, and apply various voltages to very sensitive mechanical and electronic components. Each time you turn on your computer, the power supply is endangered by the rush of electricity. Turning your computer on and off also causes thermal expansion and contraction; that is, your PC goes from room temperature to as high as 130 degrees Fahrenheit. When turned off, the built-up heat puts even more stress on the power supply and the rest of your computer.

The life of an electronic component is directly related to its operating temperature. For each 18-degree drop in operating temperature, your computer's life is doubled. As a general rule, turn your computer on and off once a day...and no more. Keeping your PC at a constant temperature is probably one of the best ways to lengthen its life. This same rule applies to your printer and monitor.

Note: In 1992, Apple Computer, IBM, and six other computer makers signed an agreement with the Environmental Protection Agency to produce energy-efficient computers. The voluntary EPA Energy Star Computers Program aims to save $1 billion a year in power costs, or enough electricity to supply the states of New Hampshire and Vermont. The companies have agreed to design systems that will automatically switch to a power consumption level of 30 watts or less when left unattended. Companies that meet the requirement can display the EPA Energy Star logo on their systems and in ads.

Low Power Problems

A wimpy power supply can dampen your efforts to expand your computer. Some computers have adequate power supplies for present needs. However, adding an internal modem or other expansion card, a larger hard disk, a CD-ROM drive, or a tape drive can strain the power supply. Eventually, it will simply stop working. Generally, you want to place the least demand on the biggest power supply possible. The less your power supply has to work, the longer it will last.

Some computers have an inadequate power supply out of the gate. For example, the original IBM PC had a 63.5-watt power supply. Adding a video card, a math coprocessor chip, and a full 640K of memory overwhelms it. The IBM PC/XT had a 130-watt power supply, and the original IBM PC/AT featured a 192-watt supply. (The AT's power supply was novel; it had a variable-speed, thermostatically controlled cooling fan. The hotter it got, the faster the fan spun to pull in cooler air.)

Most computers have a 150- or 200-watt power supply, certainly adequate for modest needs. Some computer manufacturers use the smaller power supplies to cut costs. In 1992, Zeos International, a mail-order computer maker, trimmed costs by incorporating 200-watt power supplies instead of 300-watt models. The company said the lower-wattage supplies should be adequate since computer components now require less power. Still, the lower wattage reduces the power supply's life since it must work at near-total capacity. If your power supply is overstressed, you can buy a heavy-duty replacement power supply and install it yourself (described later).

Calculating Your Workload

If your power supply is overworked, you may want to replace it before it fails. If it is operating near full capacity, your computer may act strangely. Odd behavior may include locking up, faulty reading and writing of data to your disk drives, or incorrect video displays and memory errors.

How do you know if your current power supply can handle its current workload? You must calculate the power drain required by your different components, such as disk drives, number of expansion cards, and more. Using the chart below, you can discover at what capacity your power supply is working. Some of the numbers for this chart, such as power supply rating, you can find in Appendix A: "PC Bio" if you have been entering the information there.

Unlike others, I'm not going to recommend you find or calculate the individual power consumption of each component. Instead, use this simple chart to "guesstimate" the power required for your computer. Although measuring the power required in amperes (amps) would be better, using watts makes the calculations much simpler.

Component	Qty	Watts per comp.	Subtotal wattage
Motherboard	1 x	30 watts	30 watts
Expansion cards*	___ x	5 watts	___ watts
Full-height hard disks*	___ x	40 watts	___ watts
Half-height hard disks*	___ x	25 watts	___ watts
Floppy diskette drives*	___ x	15 watts	___ watts
CD-ROM drive	___ x	30 watts	___ watts
Tape drive	___ x	40 watts	___ watts
TOTAL REQUIRED			___ watts
CURRENT POWER SUPPLY*			___ watts
% CAPACITY		Divide total watts required by the power supply	___ %

*You can get this information from Appendix A: "PC Bio."

IMPORTANT: Enter the capacity of your power supply in Appendix A: "PC Bio."

Ideally, your power supply should be operating at 50 percent capacity to reduce its heat and lengthen its life and that of your computer. For example, here is what my computer's situation was until I replaced its power supply:

Component	Qty	Watts per comp.	Subtotal wattage
Motherboard	1x	30 watts	30 watts
Expansion cards (internal modem, sound card, game card, disk drive controller card, scanner card, video card, tape drive controller)	7 x	5 watts	35 watts
Full-height hard disks	0 x	40 watts	0 watts
Half-height hard disks	1 x	25 watts	25 watts
Floppy diskette drives	2 x	15 watts	30 watts
CD-ROM drive	1 x	30 watts	30 watts
Tape drive	1 x	40 watts	40 watts
TOTAL REQUIRED			190 watts
CURRENT POWER SUPPLY			200 watts
% CAPACITY		Divide total watts by the power supply	95.0 %

As you can see, my power supply was operating at near-total capacity. That strain means excess heat and a shorter lifespan for not only the power supply but also my computer's other parts. When I installed a 300-watt power supply, the drain was only 63 percent (190 watts needed/300-watt power supply). Although 50 percent is ideal, this figure is much more reasonable, considering how decked out my computer is.

Replacing the Power Supply

If you do decide to replace the power supply, the operation can be quite easy, probably requiring less than one hour. The cost of a power supply may range from $50 to $250, depending on the type and features you want. Fortunately, power supplies come in only four sizes. When you order a power supply, you need to provide the following information:

- **The size of your computer.** You may have a desktop, baby-AT, slim-line desktop, tower, mid-tower, or mini-tower case. The size of the case often determines the size of its power supply. Also, XT-type power supplies differ from those used in AT-type computers. Some computer makers, such as Compaq, use proprietary power supplies. Fortunately, companies like PC Power & Cooling Inc. also provide these nonstandard supplies for Compaq Deskpro and original Portable computers.

- **Type and location of power switch.** You need to get a power supply with the identical on/off power switch you currently have. Most desktop computers have an on/off switch built into the power supply. To turn on the computer, you usually flick an orange or red paddle switch on the right side of the computer. Some computers have a remote switch on the front of the computer. This switch may also be a paddle switch; however, some computers use either a pushbutton or rocker switch.

IMPORTANT: Enter the type of power switch required for your computer in Appendix A: "PC Bio."

- **Wattage requirements**. Using the chart above, you can tell the salesperson what size power supply you have now and to what capacity it is operating.

- **Special requirements**. You should also consider any other special requirements. For example, will the power supply be used in a hostile environment, such as a dusty office? Is noise a factor? Some power supplies provide a silencing feature that slows the fan down if the cooling isn't needed. Do you have two hard disks the power supply must run? Is your supply of electricity stable? Some power supplies have built-in features to protect your computer from power fluctuations. If the power supply is for a very important computer, such as a network file server, you should tell the salesperson so.

A typical PC with one hard disk used in an average, air-conditioned office for non-critical purposes can get by on a 220-watt power supply. One company that specializes in replacement power supplies is PC Power & Cooling Inc. The Carlsbad, California, company has been in business since 1985 and offers a 30-day money-back guarantee on its products. Its ThermaSense(TM) power supplies have a thermostat that adjusts the speed of the cooling fan to your PC's needs. I installed a Turbo-Cool 300S power supply into my own computer. On a hot, muggy day (I have no air conditioning), I notice the fan trying harder to cool things down. On a cooler day, the fan is mildly humming along. The company also has economical but powerful power supplies for XT and AT computers.

If you simply want to silence an existing power supply, you can add The Silencer from Quiet Technology Inc. This device, a cylindrical probe about 2.5 inches long and three-eighths of an inch in diameter, mounts inside the typical power supply and connects to the fan's power leads. It reduces fan noise by varying the speed of the fan to maintain an internal temperature of 79 to 82 degrees Fahrenheit.

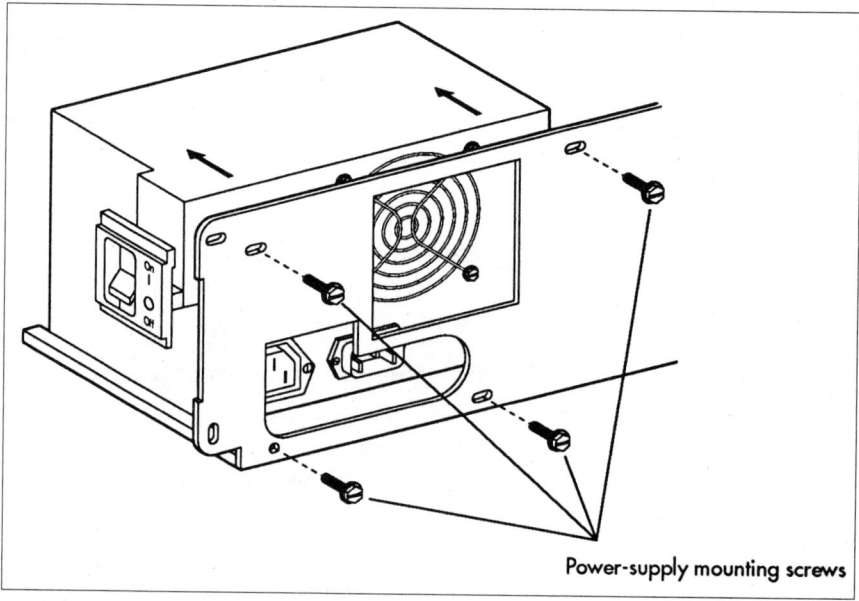

Power-supply mounting screws

Figure 5.2 Four screws hold your power supply to the system unit.

To replace the power supply:

If you need to replace your power supply, follow this procedure.

1. Turn off your computer and remove its case.

    For details on opening your computer, see the procedure in Chapter 3, "Cracking Open the Case."

2. Remove the four screws that hold the power supply to your system unit (see Figure 5.2). Set these screws aside where they won't be lost.

    Before removing the power supply, write down how it is situated in the case. For example, jot down which side of the power supply has the power cord connectors.

3. Gently remove the four-wire power connectors to your disk drives and any other devices.

    The power supply usually provides power to the following:

    *   Four to six 4-wire power connectors for accessories like hard disks, tape drives, and floppy disk drives.

    *   Two 6-wire power connectors that attach to your motherboard, which is the main circuit board forming the foundation of your computer.

    Wiggle or rock each connector back and forth until the connector is free. You don't need to remember how the cables are connected since their ends are specially molded to fit only one way.

4. Remove the pair of power cables connected to your motherboard (see Figure 5.3).

    Again, rock each connector back and forth until it is free. These two power cables are usually called P8 and P9, P1 and P2, or PS1 and PS2. When they are connected to the motherboard, note that the pairs of black wires are next to each other. Again, these cables only fit one way.

5. If you have a remote switch, free it from the front of your computer.

    If you have a remote on/off switch, one that is not built into the power supply but is attached to it by a long wire, you will have to remove that as well. The remote switch is usually found in tower cases.

    To remove the remote switch, you need to gently pry off the front

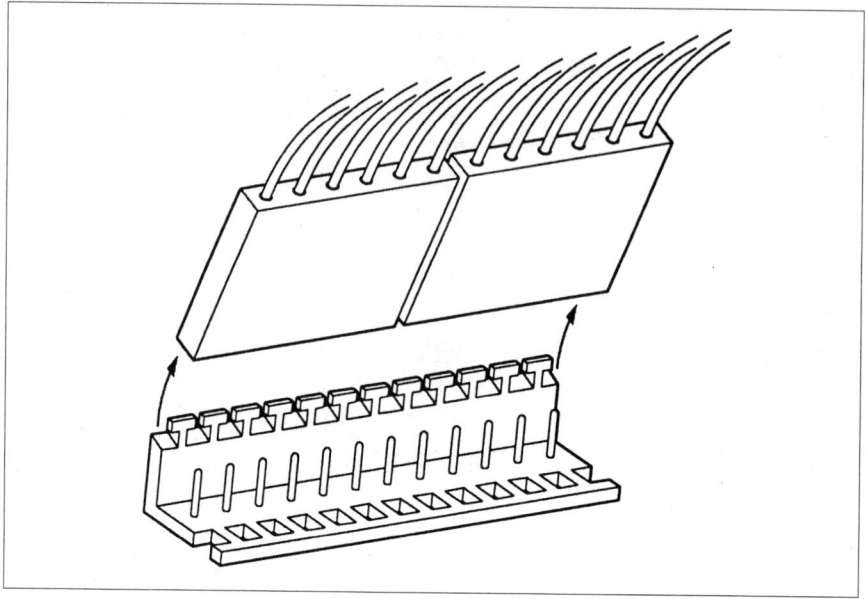

Figure 5.3 The two power cables to your motherboard (usually called P8 and P9) must be removed.

bezel, or face plate, of your computer so the screws holding the remote switch in place can be removed. Remove the two screws holding the remote switch and set them aside. You may also have to remove a plate that supports the switch. Set those two screws and bracket aside. With the remote switch loosened you can now remove the power supply.

6. Remove the power supply from the case (see Figure 5.4).

   If a remote switch is present, gently thread it and its cable back toward the rear of the computer so it can be removed. Then, gently remove the power supply from its position.

7. If the replacement power supply lacks an on/off switch or arrived with the wrong type of switch, you will have to salvage the old one.

   Remove any black electrical tape surrounding the old power supply switch's base. This exposes the four connectors to the switch. Note the color of each wire going to each part of the switch. Usually the colors are, starting in the upper-left corner and going clockwise: white, black, brown, and blue. These colors may vary from manufacturer to manufacturer. You may want to

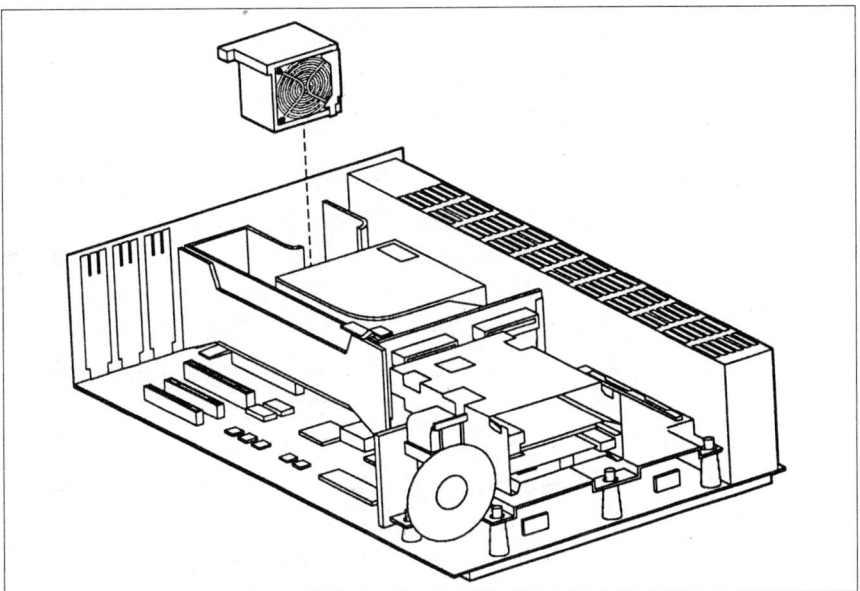

Figure 5.4 Once the power cables are removed, lift the old power supply from the case.

use a pair of needle-nosed pliers to grasp the base of each of the connectors as you remove them. Rock each connector back and forth until free. Remove the switch from the new power supply, if present. Then put the old switch onto the connectors of the new power supply. Be sure you put the wires on in the exact order as in the old power supply.

> *Note:* To save yourself trouble, be sure you order the right power supply switch. There are three types: pushbutton, rocker, and paddle.

8. Place the new power supply into the case in the same orientation as the old one. Do not reattach any screws yet.

9. If you have a remote power switch on the new power supply, thread it and its cable back into its location.

   Reinstall the supporting bracket and attach the switch to it. Next, reattach the front bezel, if you removed it.

10. Attach the new power supply to the case.

   Use the four screws you set aside to attach the power supply to the case.

11. Attach the power connectors to the motherboard and other parts.

   Attach P8 and P9 (or P1/PS1 and P2/PS2) to the motherboard. Once attached, check that the two pairs of black wires on each connector are next to each other. Next, attach the power cables to the disk drives and any other device that requires power. Note that the connectors are notched or specially shaped so they can't be incorrectly placed.

   Make sure the pins of each power supply connector are centered before you make each connection. Sometimes they may wobble or retreat as you put the connector on. Grabbing the base and a portion of the wires will hold these pins in place. You shouldn't have to use undue force.

12. With the case off, attach the electrical cord and briefly turn on the computer to test the power supply.

Caution: For your safety, do not touch any part of the case except the switch and keep others away from the computer. Working with electricity is perfectly safe *as long as you follow the rules of safety!*

   You do not need to attach any other cables; we simply want to test the power. Turn on the computer briefly to test if the power supply and its switch work. You will hear its cooling fan start and the computer begin its warm-up testing. As soon as you know the power works, turn off your PC.

13. Replace your computer's case and return it to working order.

   Since you have been working inside your PC, check that the gray ribbon cables are firmly attached and were not dislodged during your work. Also make sure that no alien objects, such as screws, have fallen inside the case. Use the procedure in Chapter 3, "Cracking Open the Case" to safely replace your computer case and return it to working order.

**Keep Your
PC Cool**

Not only does a power supply provide power — it also provides cooling. You can do a simple test to see if your PC is cool enough. First, measure the temperature in the room where your computer is used. Next, place a thermometer directly in the flow of air being expelled by the power supply's rear fan. The air coming out of the PC should be no more than 10 degrees Fahrenheit warmer than the room temperature. If it is too warm, you may want to consider one of three options:

1. Get a larger capacity power supply to reduce the heat generated.

2. Purchase a larger computer case so the heat can be dissipated more easily.

3. Install an extra cooling fan to pull additional cool air into the computer.

There is another, less expensive option: On XT-type computers, a little tape on the lower front of your computer can decrease its internal temperature and therefore extend its life. First, remove the front bezel of your PC, although that may mean removing the entire case. Next, take some electrical tape and seal the ventilation holes in the front of your computer. These 1/8- to 1/4-inch diameter holes or vertical slots may be in rows. If your computer lacks these holes, you need do nothing. By sealing these holes, more air is pulled in through the front of the computer and over the heat-generating components. The internal temperature may be cooled by 10 to 20 degrees Fahrenheit. This is no renegade procedure; IBM factory-sealed their computers this way on every XT and XT-286 it sold.

If your computer is not overworked but you would like more cooling, you can install a second cooling fan (see Figure 5.5). These auxiliary fans cost about $30, much less than the price of a new power supply. Most computers have space and screw holes for an extra fan in the front inside of the system unit. This fan blows more cool air on the expansion cards and over the motherboard, extending their lives. Some auxiliary fans have thermostats that adjust the fan's speed to the temperature. For example, PC Power & Cooling offers a fan with such a thermostatic control.

When you purchase a cooling fan, you need to tell the salesperson the size of the vent where the fan will be installed. You must open your computer and measure the distances between the four screw holes. If you have a full-length expansion card in your computer, you

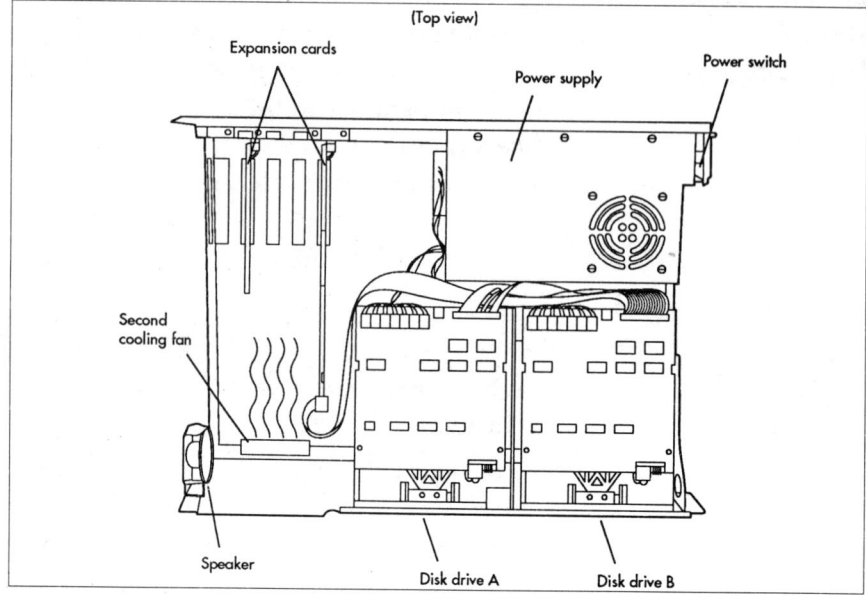

Figure 5.5 A second cooling fan can help pull fresh air into your computer.

cannot mount a second fan. The full-length card extends the full length of your computer case into notches on the front side of the case. This, unfortunately, is where the fan must be installed. If you don't have any full-length expansion cards, use the next procedure to install a cooling fan.

To install a cooling fan:

1. Turn off your computer and remove its case.

   For details on opening your computer, see the procedure in Chapter 3, "Cracking Open the Case."

2. Remove any plastic braces that are covering the front vent in the expansion slot area.

   These plastic braces hold the far edge of a full-length expansion card. If you don't have a full-length expansion card, you can remove the plastic braces and install the second fan. The braces are usually held in place by two notches.

3. Attach the fan to the power supply.

   The fan has a power connector coming from it. This connector must be attached to the power supply for the fan to operate. If the power supply doesn't have a spare power connector, the fan will have to share the power connector that runs to another device, such as a disk drive. In this case, the fan should include a "Y" connector to share the power with that device. Detach the power connector from the power supply to the device and then attach it to the single end of the Y connector that came with the fan. Take the forked ends of the Y connector and hook one end to the device and the other to your fan. Since these connectors are specially shaped, you cannot attach them incorrectly.

4. Determine the way the fan should blow.

    These cooling fans unfortunately don't show which way they are blowing the air. Plug your PC into the outlet. With one hand, hold the fan by its edges but do not touch its blades. Next, turn the computer on briefly. Determine from which side of the fan air is being blown. This side is the one that should be facing into the computer, blowing air *into* it. Turn off your computer.

! **CAUTION:** Hold only the fan's outer body. You do not want to cut yourself on the fan's spinning blades!

---

5. Install the fan.

    Place the side of the fan that blows air out facing into the computer cavity. The opposite side will be the side touching the inner face of the system unit. Take four screws and mount the fan to the system unit. If the fan didn't come with screws, you probably will need four 1.5 x 5/32-inch screws.

6. After the fan is attached, again turn on the computer to check the airflow. The outside air should be blown *into* your computer.

7. Replace the case and return your PC to working order.

Extra Power Protection

Your computer's power supply has plenty of built-in power protection. In fact, many supplies are designed to handle 115-volt electricity that can vary from 104 to 127 volts and power surges of up to 6000 volts. Despite this, there are four electrical enemies you may face:

1. Voltage spikes
2. Power surges
3. Brownouts or power sag
4. Blackouts

These four can cause loss of data and even destruction of your computer equipment. Do not think you are above power problems. According to the National Power Laboratory, a division of Best Power Technologies Inc., a typical office has 443 power errors annually, each of which could gravely affect computerized systems, causing data loss or crashes.

Voltage spikes — also called *transients* or *overvoltages* — are short-duration surges in the power line. They can be quite short, as brief as a billionth of a second. While voltage spikes generally are unnoticed by lights and other electrical equipment, your computer may be damaged by them.

Power surges are longer versions of voltage spikes, lasting several milliseconds. Power surges are invisible to the naked eye; you won't know when you're under attack. Some symptoms of these problems include your computer restarting itself or simply shutting down, although the monitor may still be on. If this happens, turn the power switch off, wait a few seconds, and then turn it back on to reset its internal circuit breaker.

An electrical *brownout*, or *power sag*, is when the line voltage falls below that required by the computer and other electrical devices. During a brownout, you will see lights dim, electrical motors slow down, and the display on your computer's monitor may shrink.

A *blackout* involves complete interruption of power for more than a fraction of a second. Power failures cost U.S. businesses $12 billion yearly. (Hopefully, you aren't in an elevator at the time — or in the middle of some unsaved computer work.)

Despite the built-in protection of the power supply, you may want more if your computer is used for very critical work or is in an area that has troublesome electricity. There are three ways to add extra power protection (see Figure 5.6):

1. Surge protectors
2. Line conditioners
3. Backup power supplies

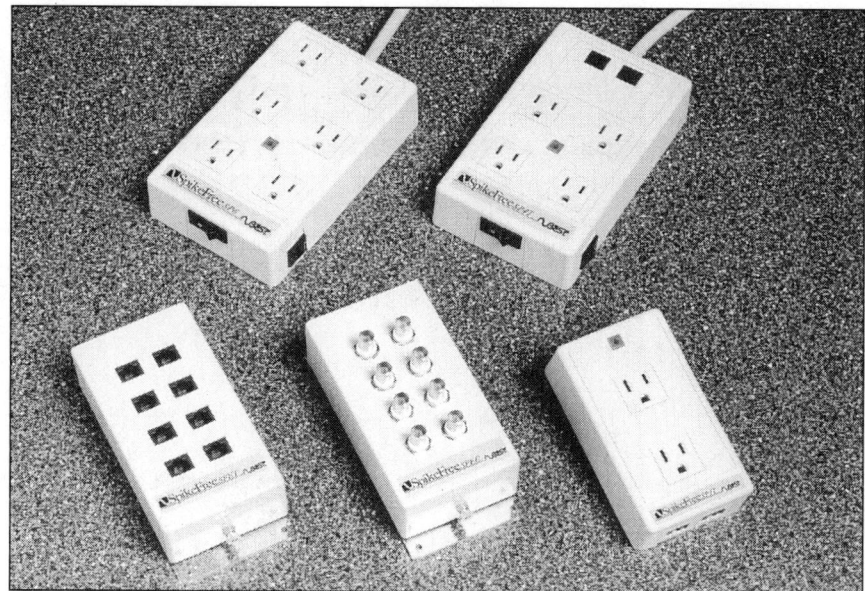

Figure 5.6 A surge protector (supressor) can smooth the power your PC receives, but it is a crude solution. *(Copyright 1992, Best Technology, Inc., Necedah, Wis. 54646.)*

Surge protectors provide the simplest and crudest power protection. You insert a surge protector between your computer and the electrical outlet. Costing between $20 and $200, these devices absorb the high-voltage spikes caused by nearby lightning strikes and power equipment. However, they only protect against power surges; they can't help when the power drops or dies completely. Surge protectors are often built into those power strips that allow you to plug several electrical devices into one outlet.

Surge protectors often use metal-oxide varistors (MOVs) to divert voltages above a certain level. Unfortunately, they won't stop a direct lightning strike. After a large surge or many small ones, the protector often stops working without notice. Look for three features in a surge protector: a status light that informs you when a large surge has occurred, support of the Underwriter Laboratories 1449 standard, and a circuit breaker that can be reset. Avoid a circuit breaker that uses fuses that must be replaced every time it is blown. Any surge protector that meets these qualifications is a good one.

Line conditioners provide stable power during brownouts. The voltage might dip below that needed to operate your computer. Line conditioners also weed out other electrical noise, such as radio-

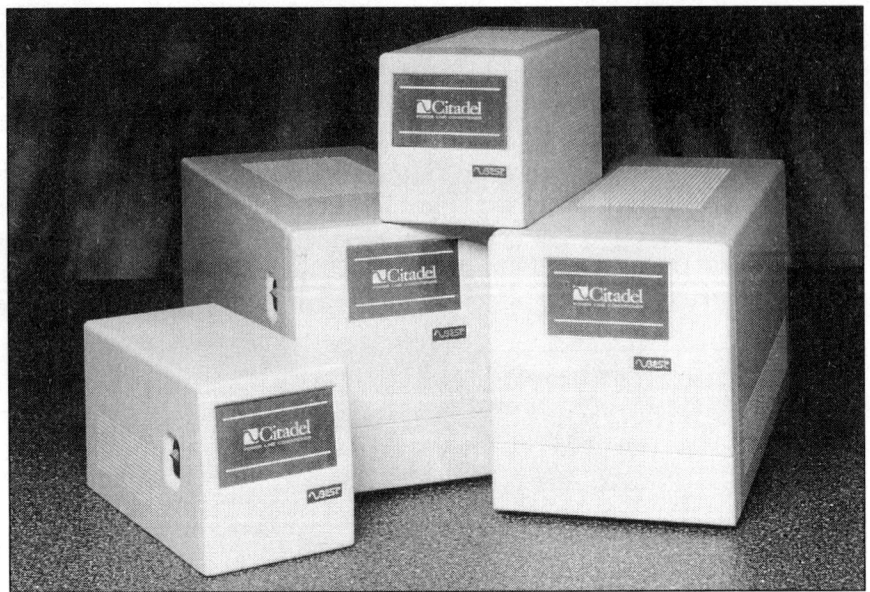

Figure 5.7 Like a water purifier, a line conditioner actively purifies the incoming power to your computer. *(Copyright 1992, Best Technology, Inc., Necedah, Wis. 54646)*

frequency interference (RFI) and electrical "noise" caused by motors and generators.

The line conditioner solves many problems. Like a water filter, it purifies the power. It also whitens the brownouts and suppresses high voltage and current. In other words, it acts as a buffer between the outlet and your computer. A line conditioner is like a sophisticated surge protector and more; you won't need both. Unlike a surge protector, which is passive, the line conditioner constantly monitors and adapts to changing power conditions. It contains capacitors, transformers, and other electronic components to perform its job. Some power supplies include built-in line conditioning. A line conditioner costs between $150 and $300.

Backup power supplies provide the best protection. If you are in an area prone to blackouts or you want the best protection from a temporary outage, a backup power supply is ideal. There are two types of backup power supplies: standby power supply (SPS) and uninterruptible power supply (UPS). The two are often confused.

A *standby power supply* (SPS) senses when the regular AC power is lost and switches over to a standby battery. This change usually

Figure 5.8 A backup power supply, such as an SPS or UPS, provides enough power so you can save your work after a complete power outage. *(Copyright 1992, Best Technology, Inc., Necedah, Wis. 54646)*

occurs in less than 50 milliseconds. The power inverter in the SPS turns the battery's power into 110-volt AC power for use by your computer. The power usually lasts for only 15 minutes, which gives you time to save your work and safely turn off the computer. A superior SPS includes a ferroresonant transformer, which stores a small amount of electricity for a smooth transition from AC to your SPS battery. An SPS, which costs between $200 and $2000, can benefit from a line conditioner.

An *uninterruptible power supply* (UPS) provides the best overall solution to your power needs. A UPS includes line conditioning and continuous power from a battery. In some ways, a UPS is very similar to an SPS, except that you always run from the battery. When a power outage occurs, the UPS does not make any changes in its operation, except that it cannot charge the battery during the outage. It continues to turn the stored battery power into 110-volt power. When the power is restored, the UPS battery is recharged.

Because a UPS relies on its battery, it is isolated from the AC outlet. In this way, it is the ultimate line conditioner and surge protector. A good UPS has a ferroresonant transformer for even better line conditioning and protection. When looking for a UPS, find one whose power inverter provides a sine wave or modified square wave. Avoid one that uses a simple square wave. Your computer's power supply may be too sensitive to accept this cruder power. However, square-wave output is fine for an SPS.

The cost of a UPS varies, depending on the amount and duration of the power it provides. You may want to get a UPS that can operate multiple PCs or one PC and your peripherals, like a printer and monitor. A UPS is more expensive than an SPS. Most UPS units cost between $500 and $4000.

Some companies label their SPS with a ferroresonant transformer as a "UPS." However, a true UPS is always running from the battery. How do you tell the difference? If the so-called UPS mentions a "switch time," then it is a SPS, not a UPS. Since a true UPS always uses its battery, it never switchs from the AC outlet to the battery. However, a ferroresonant transformer SPS can be a cheaper alternative to a true UPS.

When Lightning Strikes

Lightning is probably the PC owner's greatest electrical worry. To what extent can lightning affect your computer? In July 1992, Kevin L. Erwin Consulting Ecologists Inc. suffered $40,000 worth of damage to its microcomputers and network equipment after a nearby — not direct — lightning strike, despite using surge protectors. The lightning bolt bypassed power lines and, instead, went over the coaxial cable that links the business' network across two buildings. Besides losing equipment, the firm had two days of downtime and also had corrupted data files.

How should you handle a lightning storm? Even though lightning may not strike your building, it can affect nearby electrical facilities and damage your computer. During a severe storm, save your work and turn off your computer. Leave the computer plugged in. Believe it or not, this gives the lightning the fastest path to the ground. However, you may want to unplug the telephone line to your modem; electrical spikes and surges can find their way to your computer through this line. A simple way to add extra protection to your equipment in a lightning storm is to tie overhand knots in the power cord.

The knots make the lightning surge work against itself and burn out the power cord, not your computer.

With ample power and cooling, your computer will be able to live out a full life without getting "hot under the collar." An adequate power supply can provide ample energy for the power-hungry improvements you'll find in the rest of this book.

PART II

Main Course

6 Thanks for the Memory

Your PC seems most obsolete when it runs short on memory. The increasing sophistication of today's software challenges the memory ceiling imposed by DOS, and Microsoft Windows programs demand even more. On top of this, certain expansion cards require memory-hogging software in order to work, or you may want memory-resident programs nearby. All of these demands require memory.

A Memory Primer

Your PC has a "brain," the processor. However, the processor needs to have a memory in which to store information on which it is working. This is called the *random access memory*, or simply *RAM*. The amount of RAM is measured in *kilobytes (K)*. A kilobyte equals 1024 bytes (a byte holds a single character or nuMBer). A *megabyte (MB)* equals 1024K. For example, the first IBM PC had 16K of memory. Today's computers often have memory amounts of 512K, 640K, 1MB, 2MB, 4MB, 8MB, or more.

RAM is a type of short-term memory; when the power is turned off, the contents of this memory are lost forever. (This is why you must save your work to a floppy or hard disk before you turn off your computer.) In effect, this memory is used as a temporary workspace, just like the top of your desk. When you want to work on a project, you take your materials out of your desk drawer and put them on your desk within reach. With memory, you load a computer program and a file from your disk drive and put it into memory, where it is close at hand. Like your desk, the bigger this workspace, the less time you spend searching for something in its drawers. Therefore, adding memory can speed up your computer.

Unfortunately, the disk operating system, or DOS, places an upper limit on how much memory your PC can access at one time. In other words, you can have as big a "desk" as you want, as long as it isn't bigger than your office. In most cases, your PC can hold only 640K — or 655,360 bytes — of information at one time. This is an artificial limit created more than 10 years ago. Who would have thought today's software would require that much? With this limitation, memory-hungry programs may give you messages like "Program too big to fit into memory," or "Out of memory."

If your computer already has 640K of memory, don't think you have reached this memory ceiling and therefore cannot add any more. Over the years, several interesting innovations allow you to use memory above the "640K barrier." (Technically, this limit is 1MB, or 1024K.) I have 16MB (16,384K) of memory and would like some more. Besides bypassing this barrier, you may be able to squeeze some extra memory from your PC by changing its configuration.

Memory Defined

If the operating system limits you to 640K of memory, then how can you obtain and use more? The answer to this question lies in understanding the three types of memory available: conventional, extended, and expanded. (See Figure 6.1).

You are already familiar with *conventional memory*; it is the memory into which you load your programs and work. Conventional memory, also known as base or low memory, is any memory below 1MB, although only 640K of it is directly available for your work.

Extended memory (XMS) is memory above 1MB. This memory is usually not directly available to your PC, except through special programs I'll mention later. Also, this memory is only available in 80286 and higher computers.

Expanded memory (EMS) is, for the most part, converted extended memory. Introduced in 1985, expanded memory relies on a technical trick known as *paging* or *bank-switching*. Paging involves accessing large amounts of memory by swapping it — in 16K chunks — into

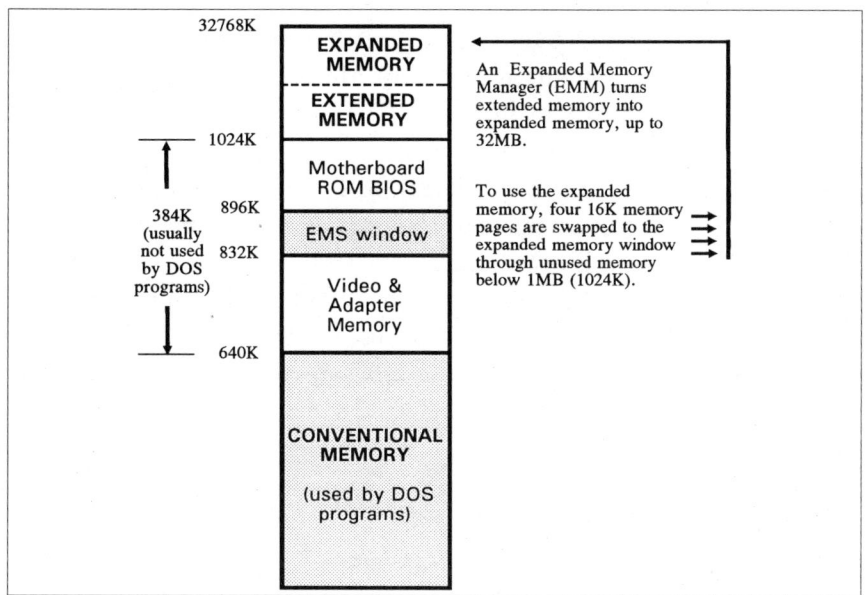

Figure 6.1 How your computer uses conventional, extended and expanded memory.

and out of a 64K memory window. This window to expanded memory is placed in the unused memory between 640K and 1MB. The computer is thus fooled into working beyond the first 1MB. In effect, you can give your programs up to 32MB more memory.

Usually a software utility called an *expanded memory manager (EMM)* manages this expanded memory. This utility must conform to version 4.0 of the Lotus/Intel/Microsoft Expanded Memory Specification (LIM EMS 4.0). Older standards exist, such as LIM EMS 3.0 and the Enhanced EMS (EEMS). Developed in 1987, the LIM EMS 4.0 specification lays the ground rules for how expanded memory is created and used. Any software program you own that supports this type of expanded memory can now have access to it. One popular spreadsheet program, *Lotus 1-2-3*, supports this type of memory.

The basic advantage of expanded memory is you will have more room for your work, such as more rows in your spreadsheet or more records in your database without seeing "memory full" or "out of memory" messages. Over 5000 programs support expanded memory. If they don't, they may if you use them within a windows environment such as Quarterdeck's *DESQview*, which does support expanded memory. A second benefit of expanded memory is that you can eliminate the conflicts between memory-resident — also called terminate-and-stay resident (TSR) — programs and your main program. For example, you can move a program like Borland's *Sidekick Plus* out of the 640K area altogether.

Through software and sometimes hardware, your computer can create expanded memory. In 8088, 8086, and 80286 machines, you can add EMS by installing an EMS memory expansion card and adding an EMS driver (a small program to control the expansion card). Fortunately, some 80286 computers have the built-in ability to turn some extended memory into expanded memory. For example, if your 80286 computer is based on a Chips & Technologies chip set — a core part of your motherboard's design — it already has the hardware needed to turn this extended memory into expanded memory.

With an 80286 computer, you can really put extra memory to work. *Move 'Em*, which is included with *386Max* from Qualitas Inc.; *QRAM*, which is included with *QEMM-386* from Quarterdeck Office Systems; and *Turbo EMS* from Merrill and Bryan Enterprises Inc. are good examples. They use this expanded memory to put memory-resident programs (like *Sidekick*, for example) and device drivers (for networks, RAM disks, and so on) into the area above 640K. By placing these programs and drivers above the 640K barrier, you have more memory for your regular software programs. Best of all, these programs cost less than $100.

You may not need to purchase a third-party program to get expanded memory. A few years ago, I overcame the sluggishness of Aldus' *PageMaker* by replacing my 1MB of memory with 4MB RAM. Using a software utility provided by my computer's manufacturer, I turned 3MB into expanded memory. This type of expanded memory is called *LIM-ulation* because a software utility makes your motherboard's memory emulate the operation of expanded-memory cards.

In 80386 and higher computers, the ability to use expanded memory is built in, but an EMM is needed to turn extended memory into expanded memory. An EMM is included with DOS 5.0 (EMM386.EXE) and built into Microsoft Windows. Older versions of DOS have a driver called EMM386.SYS. *QEMM-386* from Quarterdeck and *386Max* from Qualitas are two other utilities that can create expanded memory as well as helping you squeeze more memory from your computer.

A Tour of Your Memory Needs

Adding memory usually is not an end in itself. Any extra memory you add must be used to load various software utilities which in turn speed up your computer. Adding conventional memory to get your computer up to 640K (technically, 1MB) is your first priority. This memory is the foundation upon which your computer operates.

To discover your own personal memory needs, you need to find out the following:

- Your version of DOS
- The amount of memory in your PC
- The amount of free memory in your PC
- The memory required by your programs

As mentioned earlier, the first 640K of memory — conventional memory — is used by the operating system, DOS. Your software program (a word processor), your work (a letter), and part of the operating system coexist in this first 640K of memory.

The amount of memory required by DOS varies with each version. Today's *MS-DOS* requires about three times as much memory as six years ago. The table and graph below show how much memory each version takes, not counting startup files such as AUTOEXEC.BAT.

DOS Version	Memory used (in K)	Main features
1.0	10	Original IBM PC operating system; supported 160K floppy drives.
1.1	12	Supported 320K floppy drives and added the time a file was last saved to the directory listing.
2.0	24	Supported 10MB hard disk formatted 180K and 360K floppy disks, and added hierarchical file structure (directories and such).
2.1	24	Supported half-height floppy drives.
3.0	38	Supported 20MB hard drive, 2K cluster and high-density 5.25-inch floppy drives (1.2MB).
		Continued

DOS Version	Memory used (in K)	Main features
Continued		
3.1	38	Supported local area networks (LANs).
3.2	44	Supported 3.5-inch (720K) floppy drive and added XCOPY command.
3.3	54	Supported high-density 3.5-inch (1.44MB) floppy drive and many 32MB hard disk partitions.
4.0	64	Supported expanded memory and drive partitions as large as 2GB (1024MB); added a DOS shell and disk caching software.
4.01	67	Bugs in version 4.0 fixed.
5.0	61	Provided advanced memory management, a DOS macro capability and on-line help, and support for 2.88MB floppy drives.

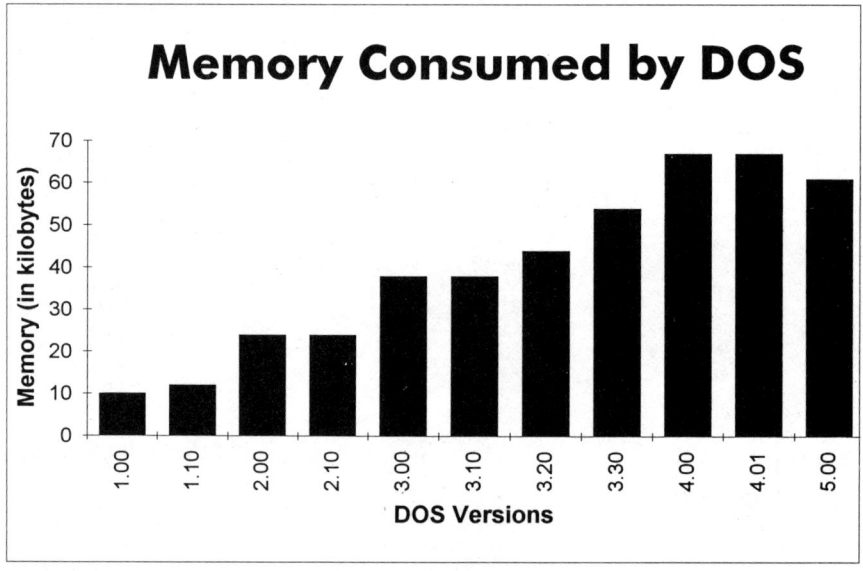

Figure 6.2 Typically, the memory required by the operating system has increased over the years.

**To deter-
mine your
version of
DOS:**

Before you add memory to your computer, if you ever need it, you
must determine what version of DOS you have.

1. Turn on your computer.
2. From the DOS prompt (C:\ or A:\), type:

```
VER [Enter]
```

The maker and version number of your operating system then
appears:

```
MS-DOS Version 5.00
```

IMPORTANT: Enter this version nuMBer and the manufacturer in Appendix A: "PC
Bio."

**To find out
how much
memory
you have:**

1. Turn on your computer.

    Your PC, when turned on, performs some diagnostic tests. One
    of the tests checks its memory.

2. As it warms up, watch the total amount of memory checked.

    Your computer will count through the memory at least once.
    Watch for the final, highest number. This number is normally
    measured in K (kilobytes). Some common values may be 512K,
    640K, 2048K, 4096K, 8192K, and so on.

3. If the number is greater than 1024K, divide the amount by 1024K
    and round up to the nearest whole number. This is the number
    of megabytes of memory you have.

    For example, my computer counts up to 16256K. Therefore,
    16256K ÷ 1024K = 15.875 = 16MB. (It seems 128K of memory is not
    counted as my computer warms up.)

IMPORTANT: Record both these numbers in Appendix A: "PC Bio."

The total amount of memory you own is different than how much
you have free and available. Why? Part of the operating system must

occupy part of your conventional, or low, memory. Also, you may have your PC load some small DOS utilities or memory-resident programs — like a pop-up calculator or the software that runs your mouse. All of these eat away at your total conventional memory. After DOS and these other programs are loaded, the remaining memory is called *free memory*. This remaining memory is what's available to load your main program, like a word processor, and any files to go with it, such as a letter.

To find free memory:

To find out how much memory is left, you can use either of two DOS commands: CHKDSK or MEM. (MEM is a command found only in DOS version 4.0 and higher.)

Using CHKDSK:

This command, often called "Check Disk," provides a limited report about how much disk space, as well as memory, you have used. Unfortunately, this DOS command does not report on memory above 640K.

1. Turn on your computer.
2. From the DOS prompt (C:\ or A:\), type:

```
CHKDSK[Enter]
```

Your computer will then display various information about your disk drive space and memory. It may look like this:

```
105906176  bytes total disk space
  4468736  bytes in 11 hidden files
   174080  bytes in 66 directories
 98244608  bytes in 2199 user files
  2969600  bytes available on disk
     2048  bytes in each allocation unit
    51712  total allocation units on disk
     1450  available allocation units on disk
   655360  total bytes memory
   585680  bytes free
```

The last line is the most important — how many bytes you have free. Divide this number by 1024 — there are 1024 bytes in a kilobyte — to calculate how many K of memory you have free. In the example above, 585680 ÷ 1024 = 572K.

IMPORTANT: Record this amount of free memory in Appendix A: "PC Bio." Enter the nuMBer in the space provided ahead of the words "before changes."

Using MEM:

The MEM command is available only with DOS 4.0 and higher. Unlike CHKDSK, the MEM command provides in-depth information about your computer's memory, including memory above 1MB.

1. Turn on your computer.
2. From the DOS prompt (C:\ or A:\), type:

```
MEM [Enter]
```

This command displays how much memory you have available. The information displayed may seem cryptic, however, like:

```
   655360   bytes total conventional memory
   655360   bytes available to MS-DOS
   603328   largest executable program size
   655360   bytes total EMS memory
   262144   bytes free EMS memory
 15990784   bytes total contiguous extended memory
        0   bytes available contiguous extended
             memory
  9191424   bytes available XMS memory
   MS-DOS   resident in High Memory Area
```

The first section reports on conventional memory. You can get the same information from using CHKDSK. The first line shows total conventional memory available. The third line ("largest executable program size") shows the amount of free memory.

The second section shows statistics on EMS (expanded memory). This section appears only if you have loaded an expanded memory driver that conforms to LIM EMS 4.0.

The third section shows your extended memory. Don't be alarmed if you have 0 bytes of available contiguous extended memory. This memory is often converted into XMS memory by the HIMEM.SYS driver — a small software program loaded in CONFIG.SYS startup file. Some of this XMS memory is then diverted to your expanded memory manager EMM386.EXE, which creates expanded memory, or other programs, such as Microsoft Windows.

Last, MEM indicates whether DOS is resident in the High Memory Area. If not, you may not have the line

```
DOS=HIGH
```

in your CONFIG.SYS startup file, described later.

IMPORTANT: If using the MEM command, record the numbers from each section in Appendix A: "PC Bio." Enter the largest executable program size, the total EMS memory and free EMS memory, available contiguous extended memory and available XMS memory, and whether or not MS-DOS is resident in the High Memory Area. Divide these numbers by 1024 to get the amount of memory in kilobytes (K). Enter these numbers in the spaces provided ahead of the words "before changes."

For Memory Misers

In the previous section, you discovered how much free memory you have. How much of your 640K (655,360 bytes) is left to run your software? Divide your free memory (in K) by 640K. In the example above using the MEM command, 603328 bytes are available. Dividing by 1024, this equals about 589K. Next, divide this free memory by 640K, the amount available to DOS. In our example, 589K ÷ 640K = 92%. In other words, about 8 percent of our total memory is eaten up by the operating system and other software before you can load your main program.

IMPORTANT: Calculate your percentage of free memory in Appendix A: "PC Bio."

Of course, if you often get "Out of memory" error messages, then some extra memory could be helpful. But what if you could eke out more from your current memory avoid having to buy any more? If your free memory is about 85 percent or less, you probably could use a memory tune-up. You can modify your two startup files — AUTOEXEC.BAT and CONFIG.SYS — to maximize your existing memory.

If you have an 80286 computer and use DOS 4.0 or greater, you can use the DOS memory manager HIMEM.SYS to get an additional 64K of memory. If you own an 80386 (DX or SX) or higher computer, you can also use EMM386.EXE to free up more memory. This DOS utility lets you "create" extra memory. If you have at least 1MB of memory, you can turn the 384K area above 640K into usable memory. How? This 384K region is reserved for various computer hardware, such as your video card. Fortunately, some of this reserved memory is unused, leaving pockets of memory. From this memory no-man's land, EMM386.EXE can reclaim more memory for your programs.

When you reclaim these pockets of memory, they are turned into *upper memory blocks*, or *UMBs*. With UMBs, you can shovel more parts of DOS out of conventional memory and into this upper memory area. Likewise, you can move device drivers — small software programs required to run some hardware devices, like a mouse — as well as terminate-and-stay-resident (TSR) programs, like a print spooler or a pop-up calculator. With these various programs loaded into the UMBs, you can have the most memory for your primary programs.

To create the most memory:

If you have an AT-type computer, DOS 4.0, and at least 640K of memory, this procedure can give you more memory. Since your computer needs are unique, some parts may not work. However, this procedure has some built-in safety precautions to prevent possible problems.

1. Turn on your PC.
2. Make a bootable diskette.

   Every computer owner should have a "boot disk." This floppy disk is a kind of emergency disk if your computer suddenly does not start from its hard disk. It may go through the motions of warming up, but somehow it simply doesn't bring you to a DOS prompt (C:\).

For example, if you make a deadly change to the startup file CONFIG.SYS, your computer won't start. It won't be broken, but it won't let you work on it. Having a boot disk lets you bypass the CONFIG.SYS file and start your computer from your floppy disk drive. You can then get to your CONFIG.SYS and correct your error.

To make a bootable diskette, place a blank diskette in drive A:, your first and possibly only floppy disk drive. (Boot diskettes usually do not work from drive B:.) From the DOS prompt, type:

```
FORMAT A: /S [Enter]
```

This command formats the diskette. The /S switch at the end adds system information to the diskette so it can start your computer when needed.

3. Copy any crucial files to your new boot disk.

You may want to copy some important DOS files to your boot disk. Here are some I recommend:

ATTRIB.EXE	Changes a file's attributes, such as hiding it from view, preventing it from being deleted, and so on.
BACKUP.EXE	A crude but effective backup program.
CHKDSK.EXE	Provides disk and memory information.
EDLIN.EXE	Allows you to edit a text file, such as CONFIG.SYS or FDISK.EXE changes the size of your hard disk before formatting it.
FORMAT.COM	Formats a disk drive.
EDIT.COM (DOS 5.0 only)	Allows you to edit a text file, such as CONFIG.SYS or AUTOEXEC.BAT.
MIRROR.COM	Records information about one or more disks for easier

	recovery (DOS 5.0 only).
QBASIC.EXE (DOS 5.0 only)	Needed for EDIT.COM to work.
QBASIC.HLP (DOS 5.0 only)	Needed for EDIT.COM to work.
RESTORE.EXE	Works with BACKUP.EXE to restore a backed-up file or directory.
SYS.COM	Makes a formatted disk bootable by adding the system information to it.
UNDELETE.EXE	Restores a file that you accidentally deleted (DOS 5.0 only).
UNFORMAT.COM	Restores a disk erased by the FORMAT command (DOS 5.0 only).

To copy these files to the boot disk, type:

```
COPY C:\DOS\filename A: [Enter]
```

where *filename* is the name of the files above.

4. Reboot your computer to ensure the boot disk works.

   Leave the boot disk in drive A:. Restart your computer by either pressing the three keys Ctrl-Alt-Del at the same time or by shutting your PC off and turning it on again. The computer should read the boot disk and bring you to a plain DOS prompt of "A:>." If this works, remove the boot disk and restart your PC. If not, try formatting the disk again.

5. Verify the name of your DOS directory.

   For your safety, verify the name of the directory where your DOS files are located. Some people name their DOS directory "DOS5," "DOS50," or simply "DOS."

   From your PC's root, or top, directory, type:

```
DIR *. [Enter]
```

This command lists the directories off your root directory. Re-meMBer the name of your DOS directory. If different than C:\DOS, use your directory name in lieu of C:\DOS.

6. Make a backup copy of your CONFIG.SYS file.

To protect yourself, first make a backup copy of your CONFIG.SYS file. From the DOS prompt (C:\ or A:\), type:

```
COPY C:\CONFIG.SYS C:\CONFIG.BAC [Enter]
```

7. Edit your CONFIG.SYS file.

Now that you have a working boot disk, you can tweak your files to have the most memory. If you have DOS 5.0, type:

```
EDIT C:\CONFIG.SYS [Enter]
```

The DOS 5.0 editor loads your primary startup file CONFIG.SYS. If you don't have DOS 5.0, use the DOS EDLIN command or your own word processor. The CONFIG.SYS file loads device drivers and configures your computer for its work each time you start it. Here is an example of my CONFIG.SYS file:

```
DEVICE=C:\DOS\HIMEM.SYS
DEVICE=C:\DOS\EMM386.EXE  FRAME=E000  NOEMS
DOS=HIGH,UMB
BUFFERS=3
FILES=40
DEVICEHIGH=C:\DOS\SMARTDRV.SYS 2048 1024
DEVICEHIGH=C:\DOS\RAMDRIVE.SYS 2048 /E
STACKS=0,0
LASTDRIVE=D
FCBS=1
```

Your CONFIG.SYS file should be similar to the first five lines, but probably not exactly. Let me explain each:

• DEVICE=C:\DOS\HIMEM.SYS

HIMEM.SYS is an extended memory manager that opens up a world of memory opportunities. This file turns extended memory into XMS (eXtended Memory Specification) memory. Once turned into XMS memory, it can be manipulated for various uses.

One feature of HIMEM.SYS is that it creates the *High Memory Area*, or *HMA*. The High Memory Area is the 64K area between 1024K and 1088K. With HIMEM.SYS loaded, the HMA becomes an extension of your PC's conventional memory. In other words, you get an extra 64K of memory. You must type the full path to the HIMEM.SYS file. If your DOS directory is not called C:\DOS, replace it with the path to your DOS directory.

- `DEVICE=C:\DOS\EMM386.EXE FRAME=E000 NOEMS`

EMM386.EXE is the expanded memory manager, or EMM. Use this line only if you have at least an 80386 computer; it should not be used for 80286 computers. If your DOS directory is not called C:\DOS, replace it with the path to your DOS directory.

EMM386.EXE relies on HIMEM.SYS and therefore should be the second line. EMM386 creates expanded memory, which can be used by select programs, like *Lotus 1-2-3*. Even if you don't have programs that can use expanded memory, you will want this EMM loaded. Why? This program turns pockets of memory in the 384K region into Upper Memory Blocks, or UMBs. These precious UMBs can be used to store the device drivers, parts of the operating system, and memory-resident programs, leaving more room in the conventional memory.

If you have no programs that require expanded memory, use the NOEMS switch. This switch sacrifices possible expanded memory for more UMBs. If you need expanded memory, replace NOEMS with RAM, creating a default amount of expanded memory.

The switch FRAME=E000 creates an additional 64K of upper memory. This memory segment isn't used on most PCs. Adding it loads EMM386.EXE and moves the EMS page frame from memory position D000 (its default position) to E000. If your computer has a conflict with this switch, it will display the message:

```
WARNING: Option ROM or RAM detected within
page frame.
```

If you get this message, remove this switch and everything should be fine. Alternative switches to try include:

- `I=E000-EFFF`

- `I=E000-F7FF`

If something in the E000 segment prevents you from using it, you might consider a third-party replacement for EMM386.EXE, such as *QEMM-386* or *386Max*. These utilities are adept at finding unused areas above 640K to convert to Upper Memory Blocks. You'll get more upper memory and you'll be able to keep your 64K page frame, too.

I've seen other switches recommended that create more upper memory from that reserved for certain types of video cards.

Switch	When to use it
I=B000-B7FF	If you own an EGA card connected to a color monitor.
I=B800-BFFF	If you own an EGA card connected to a monochrome monitor.
I=A000-AFFF	If you own a Hercules or compatible monochrome video card.
I=A000-B7FF I=BC00-BFFF	If you own a CGA video card.
I=A000-AFFF I=B100-BFFF	If you own a monochrome video card.

Sometimes, using these switches is more trouble than it's worth, especially since some of these changes often conflict with *Microsoft Windows* or other programs. If you don't use *Windows*, the first switch is very helpful. Your line in CONFIG.SYS should then read:

```
DEVICE=EMM386.EXE  NOEMS  FRAME=E000  I=B000-B7FF
```

- `DOS=HIGH,UMB`

Once the High Memory Area (HMA) and Upper Memory Blocks (UMBs) are created, you can put a majority of the operating system into these areas. DOS has three main programs: IO.SYS, MSDOS.SYS, and COMMAND.COM. As you use your PC, COMMAND.COM may be reloaded several times. In a way,

COMMAND.COM is like a memory-resident (TSR) program. When considered this way, COMMAND.COM can be placed in this upper memory region. The result: more conventional memory for your real work. If you have an 80286 computer, this line should simply read:

```
DOS=HIGH
```

• `BUFFERS=3`

Buffers are used to speed up your hard disk. With the BUFFERS command, a portion of memory is set aside by DOS to store information read from your disk. Accessing information already in memory is much faster — up to 100 times faster — than reading information from the hard disk.

If you set the nuMBer of buffers high enough, such as 99, DOS frequently finds the information it needs in the buffered memory, saving itself the work of accessing your disk drive. In this example, the nuMBer of buffers is reduced to three. Why? Later, the disk caching software SMARTDRV.SYS is loaded, which is a better way to speed up your hard disk than the cruder BUFFERS command.

If you do not use disk caching software, which is described fully in Chapter 9, "Storage: It's a Hard Life," then increase the nuMBer of buffers to between 30 and 99. RemeMBer: When you increase the nuMBer of buffers, you are trading memory that could be used by your program for a faster hard disk. You will have to decide which setting is best based on your hands-on use. However, selecting a nuMBer of 44 or less allows the buffered memory to occupy DOS's upper memory, preserving the conventional memory.

• `FILES=40`

When DOS starts, memory is reserved to track the nuMBer of computer files you are using. Loading your word processor, for example, may require opening up five files. The more files you expect to open, the larger this nuMBer should be. You can have up to 255 files open at one time. A value of 20 is adequate for most people. Some programs, such as *Microsoft Windows*, require a higher number of files — like 40. Check your software programs to see how many files they require open. If you exclude this line, the default number of files is eight.

You can reduce the number of files from 40 in increments of 10 to determine how many you need. You will get an error message, "Out of files," if you lower the number too much and then try to run a program that requires more. Simply increase the number and try running the program again. Like the BUFFERS command, the larger number you specify, the less memory is available for your programs and work.

- `DEVICEHIGH=C:\DOS\SMARTDRV.SYS 2048 1024`

Once you have upper memory (created by HIMEM.SYS and EMM386.EXE), you can load device drivers and memory-resident programs into it. Using the phrase DEVICEHIGH= tells DOS that you want to load a device driver (a small software program) into upper memory. In this case, you want to load the disk caching software SMARTDrive, which comes with DOS 5.0, into upper memory. If your DOS directory is not called C:\DOS, you can replace it with the path to your DOS directory where the file SMARTDRV.SYS is located.

Disk caching software speeds up your PC by reading a part of your hard disk into your computer's faster memory. Then, when your application needs to retrieve data, it can get it directly from RAM rather than by going out to the disk. In a way, the disk caching software tries to anticipate what files you want next from your hard disk. If wrong, it makes the corrections. (For more information about disk caching, refer to Chapter 9, "Storage: It's a Hard Life.")

To use SMARTDrive, you must have at least 512K of extended memory or 256K of expanded memory.

The numbers after SMARTDRV.SYS indicate how big the disk cache should be. The first number is the size of the disk cache, in kilobytes, when you are using a DOS program. The second number is how big the disk cache should be when you are using Microsoft Windows. Below is the recommended size for these two numbers based on the total amount of memory you currently have in your PC:

Total memory	Recommended disk cache when not using *Windows* (in K)	Recommended disk cache when using *Windows* (in K)
2MB	1024	512
3MB	2048	1024
4MB	2048	1024
5MB–6MB	2048	2048
7MB	2048	2048
8MB	2048	2048
9MB	2048	2048
10+ MB	2048	2048

To use expanded memory for your disk cache — the preferred option for 8088/8086 computers that have an expanded memory card — add the switch /A at the end of the line, like this:

```
DEVICEHIGH=C:\DOS\SMARTDRV.SYS 2048 1024 /A
```

Note: With *Windows* version 3.1, *SMARTDrive* was changed from a device driver (SMARTDRV.SYS) to an executable program (SMARTDRV.EXE). Instead of being loaded from CONFIG.SYS, *SMARTDrive* is loaded from the AUTOEXEC.BAT startup file. I discuss this later.

```
• DEVICEHIGH=C:\DOS\RAMDRIVE.SYS 2048 /E
```

The file RAMDRIVE.SYS is a software utility that temporarily creates a disk drive in your computer's memory. This *RAM drive*, or *virtual disk* as it is sometimes called, can be created from conventional, extended, or expanded memory.

RAM drives are much faster than hard disk drives because your computer can read information much faster from memory than from a hard disk. A RAM drive is best used for storing temporary files required by *Windows*, DOS, or other programs. A variable called TEMP, described later, can point these programs to use the faster RAM drive.

Again, using DEVICEHIGH= loads the *RAMDrive* program into the upper memory created by HIMEM.SYS and EMM386.EXE. The nuMBer following the filename is the size of the RAM drive in kilobytes. In the example above, the size is 2MB (2048K). The last switch, /E, tells DOS to create the RAM disk from extended memory. To create the RAM drive in expanded memory, the preferred option for 8088/8086 computers that have an expanded memory card, use /A. Once a RAM drive is created, it automatically is assigned the next available drive letter, perhaps drive E:. The RAM drive then behaves like a disk drive, except that it is temporary. If you turn off your PC or lose power, the information on this RAM drive is lost.

If your DOS directory is not called C:\DOS, replace it with your path to your DOS directory where the file RAMDRIVE.SYS is located. Below is the recommended size for your RAM disk based on the total amount of memory you have and what *Windows* mode you are using:

Total Memory	Recommended Ram drive in *Windows'* Standard mode (in K)	Recommended Ram drive in *Windows'* 386 Enhanced mode (in K)
2MB	0	0
3MB	512	0
4MB	1024	0
5MB-6MB	2048	1024
7MB	2560	1536
8MB	3072	2048
9MB	4096	3072
10+ MB	4096	4096

• STACKS=0,0

The STACKS command sets aside memory for running your hardware devices, like CD-ROM drives, sound cards, and so on. You can conserve some memory by setting stacks to zero. However, if your computer locks up while you are running *Microsoft Windows* in 386 Enhanced mode or you receive a message

"Internal stack failure," change this setting to STACKS=9,256, the default installed by *Windows*.

> *Note:* STACKS=0,0 is the default for PC and PC/XT computers. AT-type (80286 and higher) computers have a default of 9,128.

- LASTDRIVE=D

The LASTDRIVE command tells DOS the maximum nuMBer of drives it can access. Without this line, the default nuMBer of drives is through drive E:. However, each letter uses about 100 bytes more than the preceding letter. Therefore, if your CONFIG.SYS file does not have this command and you have fewer drives than E (5), then add this command. Replace D with the highest-lettered drive you have. Some computers are configured with LASTDRIVE=Z, wasting over 1K of memory. That's not much waste, but it adds up.

> *Note:* If you decide to use a RAM drive, the last drive must include the letter for it. For example, if you have drives C: and D: but then create a RAM drive using RAMDRIVE.SYS, the last drive must be E:, not D:, to reflect the RAM drive.

- FCBS=1

File control blocks, or FCBS, are used in older software programs. By setting this to one, you minimize the memory reserved for these FCBs. If a program complains that it can't open a file that uses an FCB, increase this setting. If you don't have an FCBS setting, the operating system loads a default value of 4.

8. Remove any other memory-hogging lines from CONFIG.SYS.

Some lines in CONFIG.SYS may load unnecessary or extravagant software that eat away at your memory and reduce the critical working room required by your applications. Here are some I believe are wasteful:

Command	Why It's Wasteful
BREAK=ON	Slows down your computer by checking more often for your pressing the Ctrl-C or Ctrl-Break key.
DEVICE(HIGH)= C:\DOS\ANSI.SYS	Only required by a handful of software programs to provide color.
DEVICE(HIGH)=C:\ DOS\COUNTRY.SYS	Only needed for non-English computer users.
DEVICE(HIGH)=C:\ DOS\DISPLAY.SYS	Only needed for non-English computer users.
DEVICE(HIGH)=C:\ DOS\EGA.SYS	Only needed for EGA monitors for use with the DOSSHELL.
DEVICE(HIGH)=C:\ DOS\KEYBOARD.SYS	Only needed for non-English computer users.
DEVICE(HIGH)=C:\ DOS\PRINTER.SYS	Only needed for IBM Quietwriters and Proprinters to print non-English characters.
DEVICE(HIGH)=C:\ MOUSE\MOUSE.SYS	Only needed if you have DOS programs that use a mouse. Otherwise, *Microsoft Windows* can recognize your mouse without this mouse software being loaded.

9. Save your changes to CONFIG.SYS.

   If using the DOS Edit utility, press Alt-F (the Alt and F keys at the same time) to open the File menu. Press "X" to exit. Select "Yes" to save the file on leaving.

10. Restart your computer.

    Whenever you make changes to the CONFIG.SYS startup file, you must restart your computer to make the changes effective. You can press the three keys Ctrl-Alt-Del at the same time to do a "warm boot." Otherwise, you can press your computer's reset button (if you have one) or turn it off and then on again.

11. Make changes, if necessary.

    If your PC becomes frozen, also called "locking up," some of the changes made may be wrong or inappropriate. If so, place the boot disk into drive A: (the first disk drive) and reboot your computer. If you didn't make a boot disk, you can use the original DOS disks that came with your computer. These are often "bootable."

Once you get your computer started, you have two choices:

• Edit the CONFIG.SYS file further.

• Restore the backup of your CONFIG.SYS file made earlier (CONFIG.BAC).

To edit your CONFIG.SYS file, type:

```
C:\DOS\EDIT C:\CONFIG.SYS [Enter]
```

Note: Replace C:\ with whatever drive your computer starts from, if necessary.

Next, edit your CONFIG.SYS further or check for any typing mistakes. Save the file. Remove the diskette from drive A: and restart your computer.

To restore your original CONFIG.SYS, type:

```
COPY C:\CONFIG.BAC C:\CONFIG.SYS [Enter]
```

Next, restart your computer to make the changes effective.

12. Make a backup copy of your AUTOEXEC.BAT file.

   You can also conserve memory by altering your AUTOEXEC.BAT file, the other startup file for your computer. To protect yourself, first make a backup copy of your AUTOEXEC.BAT file. From the DOS prompt (C:\ or A:\), type:

```
COPY AUTOEXEC.BAT AUTOEXEC.BAC [Enter]
```

13. Edit your AUTOEXEC.BAT file.

   From the DOS prompt, type:

```
EDIT C:\AUTOEXEC.BAT [Enter]
```

The DOS 5.0 editor loads your other startup file, AUTOEXEC.BAT. If you don't have DOS 5.0, use the DOS EDLIN command or your own word processor. This file further configures your computer and can include DOS commands you want carried out every time you start it. For example, you can have AUTOEXEC.BAT automatically load your menuing program. Here is an example of my AUTOEXEC.BAT file:

```
@ECHO OFF
PROMPT $P$G
PATH C:\;C:\DOS;C:\BAT;C:\UTILS;C:\WINDOWS;
  C:\PCTOOLS;
SET PCTOOLS=C:\PCTOOLS\DATA
C:\WINDOWS\SMARTDRV.EXE 2048 1024
MD D:\TEMP
SET TEMP=D:\TEMP
loadhigh C:\DOS\DOSKEY.COM
CLS
```

Your AUTOEXEC.BAT file should be similar for the first three lines, but probably not exactly. Let me explain each:

• `@ECHO OFF`

The ECHO OFF command prevents the lines in the AUTO-EXEC.BAT file from being displayed as your computer starts. This simply prevents the screen from being cluttered with information as each line in AUTOEXEC.BAT is run. The @ syMBol, available in DOS 3.3 and later, prevents the ECHO OFF line itself from being displayed.

• `PROMPT $P$G`

The PROMPT command lets you change how the DOS command prompt looks. Without this command, your prompt looks like this when you start your computer:

```
C>
```

These are just a few of the commands you can use to add zest to your prompt:

Code	Purpose
$P	Current drive and directory
$G	> syMBol
$L	< syMBol
$Q	= syMBol
$T	Current time
$D	Current date
$_	Moves cursor to next line

Simply add these codes in the order you want them to appear. I prefer to see only my current path — drive and directory — and the greater than syMBol. To do this, I type:

```
PROMPT $P$G
```

• `PATH C:\;C:\DOS;C:\BAT;C:\UTILS;C:\WINDOWS;
  C:\PCTOOLS;`

The PATH command tells DOS where to search for your most popular program files. This way, you can type the program's startup command without having to go to the directory in which it is located. DOS looks to your PATH statement and finds the program file. Each path is separated by a semicolon (;). When creating your path, always include drive letters with the directory names. I recommend you always have a path to your DOS directory as well as to your root directory (C:\).

One caveat: Limit the size of your path; the longer the path, the longer it takes DOS to find the program you want to run. You are limited to 127 characters for the path line. Also, each path requires some of your precious memory. One way to limit your path is to create a directory for several batch files. A batch file (.BAT) is a text file you create to run several DOS commands or programs in one step. By having a path to a directory of batch files — mine is C:\BAT — you can have access to several programs without having to include each directory in your path. For example, I use the database program *Q&A* from Symantec. Instead of having the directory C:\QA in my path, I created a batch file, using the DOS 5.0 *Edit* program, called QA.BAT. This short file contains these simple but useful commands:

```
@ECHO OFF
C:
CD \QA
QA
```

I use @ECHO OFF to not display the lines of the batch file. The batch file switches to drive C: and then to the QA directory. Finally, it runs the program QA.COM. By using batch files, you can reduce the length of your path considerably. Another way to reduce your path is to place several of your DOS utilities, like PC Tools and Norton Utilities, into one directory called C:\UTILS. Then, provide a single path to this directory.

• `SET PCTOOLS=C:\PCTOOLS\DATA`

Some programs create *environment variables* using the SET command. You normally don't have to create these yourself. The installation program, in this case *PC Tools*, automatically adds this line to the AUTOEXEC.BAT file for you.

• `C:\WINDOWS\SMARTDRV.EXE 2048 1024`

If you have Windows 3.1, you should use SMARTDRV.EXE in the AUTOEXEC.BAT file instead of the older SMARTDRV.SYS, which is loaded in the CONFIG.SYS file. As mentioned earlier, the two numbers represent the size of the disk cache when running DOS programs and Windows, respectively. Consult the previous table for which sizes you should use based on how much total memory your computer has.

• `MD D:\TEMP`

If using a RAM drive for a program like Windows, you need to create a directory where it can place the temporary files it creates. By using the RAM drive, the program can access these temporary files much faster. A directory is needed instead of the root directory (D:\) because there is a limit to the number of files you can place in the root directory. This temporary directory can also be used by the DOS 5.0 Shell's task swapping. With task swapping, you can quickly switch between two or more programs.

• `SET TEMP=F:\TEMP`

Once the temporary directory is created, you need an environment variable to point to it. Both *Windows* and DOS 5.0 look to a variable called TEMP for directions where to place their temporary files.

• `LOADHIGH C:\DOS\DOSKEY.COM`

The above command loads the DOSKEY program into upper memory. (DOSKEY is a DOS 5.0 program that lets you create DOS macros — recorded keystrokes — and recall and edit previous commands, saving you from typing repetitive keystrokes.) The LOADHIGH command is the AUTOEXEC.BAT version of the DEVICEHIGH command used in CONFIG.SYS. Like DEVICE-HIGH, LOADHIGH places certain software into upper memory. When LOADHIGH is used, DOS 5.0 tries to put the program after it into upper memory. If there is no room, the program is loaded into conventional memory. You can use LOADHIGH to load any memory-resident — also called terminate-and-stay-resident (TSR) — program. For example, you could place the software that brings your mouse to life (usually MOUSE.COM) or a pop-up calculator into upper memory. You cannot use LOADHIGH with typical software programs, like your word processor.

> *Note:* You do not need to load MOUSE.COM in the AUTO-EXEC.BAT file if you only use *Microsoft Windows. Windows* can recognize your mouse without this software utility. By not loading this utility, you can save about 20K of memory.

• `CLS`

The CLS (clear screen) command clears the screen of any text and leaves you a blank slate from which you can issue commands to your computer. This is simply an aesthetic touch.

14. Save your changes to AUTOEXEC.BAT.

    If using the DOS Edit utility, press Alt-F to open the File menu and press "X" to exit. Select "Yes" to save the file on leaving.

15. Restart your PC.

Whenever you make changes to the AUTOEXEC.BAT startup file, you must restart your PC to make the changes effective. You can press the three keys Ctrl-Alt-Del at the same time to do a "warm boot." Otherwise, you can press your computer's reset button (if you have one) or turn it off and then on again.

16. Make changes, if necessary.

Unlike CONFIG.SYS, a wrongly changed AUTOEXEC.BAT file normally doesn't cause your computer to freeze, or lock up. If you want to restore the original AUTOEXEC.BAT, type:

```
COPY C:\AUTOEXEC.BAC C:\AUTOEXEC.SYS [Enter]
```

Next, restart your computer to make the changes effective.

17. Measure how much memory you now have.

After these major changes, check how much memory you now have. If you have DOS 4.0 or greater, type:

```
MEM [Enter]
```

If not, use the CHKDSK command. From the DOS prompt, type:

```
CHKDSK [Enter]
```

IMPORTANT: In either case, record the amount of free memory in Appendix A: "PC Bio." If you used the MEM command, also provide information on the various EMS and XMS memories. When entering this information, use the spaces provided before the words "after changes."

Compare the amount of memory you now have to the earlier amount. Do you find that you still need more? Try running any demanding software programs that you couldn't run before or couldn't run without them being slow. Do they run efficiently now, or are they still slow? Do you still get "Program too large to fit in memory" or "Out of memory" messages? Then perhaps you do need to add some extra memory. This can be accomplished by adding memory chips to your PC's motherboard. This fairly easy procedure is described in the Adding Memory section below.

Built-In Limits

The amount of memory you can add to your computer is limited by the type of processor it has. The number of memory locations your processor can address is equal to 2^n power, where n represents the nuMBer of address lines. The 8086 and 8088 processors support a maximum of 20 address lines, so they are limited to addressing 1,048,576 bytes, or 1MB of RAM. The 80286 and 80386SX have 24 address lines, the 80386DX and 80486DX/SX have 32. Below is a chart showing the maximum memory with which your computer can work. Unfortunately, it may not be designed to hold this maximum. For example, my 80386 computer can hold a maximum of only 32MB of memory, about 4064MB short of its potential!

Processor	Maximum Memory
8088	1MB (1024K)
8086	1MB (1024K)
80286	16MB
80386SX	16MB
80386DX	4096MB (4GB)
80486SX	4096MB (4GB)
80486DX	4096MB (4GB)

As mentioned earlier, DOS limits your computer software to the first megabyte. However, the upper 384K of that 1024K is reserved for other uses by your computer. The first 128K of this 384K is used as memory for your video display. The next 128K is reserved for special control programs for your expansion cards. The last 128K is reserved for special control programs for your computer. If you have an XT-type computer, you are limited to one megabyte, although you can still add expanded memory.

Uses of Memory

After this first megabyte, you can add extended memory. Extended memory can be used in many ways. As shown earlier, having extended memory and DOS 5.0 allows you to load memory-resident programs into upper memory, freeing up more conventional memory for your main software programs. If you have Microsoft Windows, then the 640K limitation imposed by DOS is broken; all the extended memory is available to *Windows* programs, such as *Microsoft Excel* or *Ami Pro*.

With some programs, such as *Windows* and *DESQview*, you can use extended memory to load several programs at one time and move among them. This is called *task switching*. If you have a computer that uses an 80386 or higher processor, you can even have your programs performing work in the background — printing or downloading a file from an electronic bulletin board system (BBS) — while you are working in another program in the foreground. This is called *multitasking*.

Expanded memory can be useful — but only if your software supports this type. If you have a favorite software program that supports expanded memory — and over 5000 do — then having expanded memory would be a boon.

Both extended and expanded memory can be used for a disk cache, thereby speeding up access to your hard disk. If you work with databases or other space-demanding programs, the improvement can be phenomenal. The disk caching utility *SMARTDrive* comes free with DOS 4.0 and higher and also with *Microsoft Windows*. Most disk caches let you use either expanded or extended memory, although caches in extended memory are slightly faster. Although Microsoft's *SMARTDrive* is not quite as slick as other disk cache utilities, it has one advantage: It automatically frees memory when *Windows* needs more memory.

If you own an XT-type computer — one that uses the 8088 or 8086 processor — you are limited to the traditional 640K limit imposed by DOS. However, you can add a memory expansion card and use the extra memory for your programs that support the LIM EMS 4.0 specification. This type of expanded memory lets you add up to 32MB of expanded memory. Most important, you can use the expanded memory for a disk cache to speed up your hard disk.

Adding Memory

Adding memory can be an inexpensive solution. The cost of memory at the time of this writing was about $30 per megabyte. A small dose can be a big boost to your computer's performance. How do you add memory? There are three options, listed in order of convenience and cost:

1. Add memory to vacancies on your motherboard.
2. Obtain higher-capacity memory for the motherboard.
3. Purchase a memory expansion card.

Motherboard Memory

Your motherboard may have room for more memory. While most 80286 and higher computers can take additional memory chips directly on the motherboard, most PCs and PC/XTs will need a memory expansion card to gain the benefits of extra memory.

Memory chips come in different shapes and sizes. Yet, all memory chips in which you are interested are called DRAM, or dynamic random access memory. DRAM chips are the most common type of computer memory. These memory chips need to be energized hundreds of times per second to hold information. If you shut off the power, the information is lost.

There are three types of DRAM chips: *DIP, SIMM* and *SIP* (see Figure 6.3). Your computer may use one or possibly a mixture of these, as we discovered in Chapter 3, "Cracking Open the Case." The maker of your computer's motherboard determines what type of DRAM chips are used; you will have to rely on your owner's manual to determine this. If you are unsure, I will help you discover what you have.

Early computers used DIP (dual in-line pin) memory chips. A DIP memory chip is a rectangular chip that has 16 metal legs, eight on each side. To install such memory chips, you must plug each one into place. DIP chips are installed in multiples of nine. For example, you

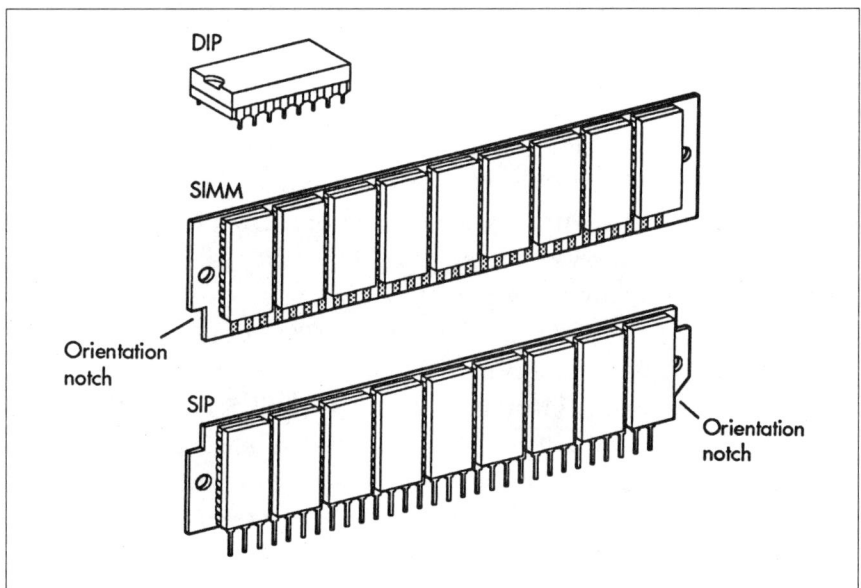

Figure 6.3 Your memory chips may be either the DIP, SIMM or SIP variety.

must install 36 separate 256-kilobit (K) chips to acquire 1MB of memory. Sometimes, the DIP memory chips are permanently soldered to your motherboard.

To install several memory chips in one step, some manufacturers use *memory packages*, where several memory chips are stored on small circuit boards. There are two types of memory packages: *SIMMs (single in-line memory module)* and *SIPs (single in-line pin)*.

The typical SIMM has nine memory chips on the circuit board with edge connectors. The nine chips mean the SIMM is a 9-bit SIMM. (Only PCs made by IBM use the 36-bit SIMM.) These connectors are then plugged into a socket on the motherboard. One advantage of this design is that you have fewer chips to install, reducing the chance of damage. In one move, you can install the equivalent of nine DIP chips. Also, using SIMMs eliminates chip creep, where memory chips work their way out of place because of the constant heating and cooling occurring in your computer.

The SIP memory package is similar to the SIMM in that it contains several memory chips in one unit. However, the SIP uses DIP-like memory and has thin metal leads that plug into your motherboard. In some ways, a SIP looks like a coMB with metal teeth. You find this type of memory on newer 80286 (AT) computers.

Memory Banks and SIMMs

Whichever type of memory chips you have, they are installed into *memory banks*. A memory bank is a collection of memory chips that make up a block of memory. Each bank of memory is read by your processor in one pass. A memory bank must be completely filled with memory chips for it to work.

Early 8088, 8086, and 80286 PCs have four memory banks that are each nine chips wide. These memory banks may be labeled 0 through 3 or A through D. The first eight chips are for holding data. The ninth is a parity chip meant to ensure the numMBers of the other eight are correct. Each chip is measured in *bits* and eight chips make up a byte. For example, imagine you had the first two banks full of 256-kilobit chips. How much memory is that? Well, 18 chips (9 chips x 2 banks) of 256-kilo*bit* memory equals 512 kilo*bytes*.

More modern 80286 computers can usually take four banks of 256-kilobit (K) chips to make 1024K (1MB). Newer 80286 computers can handle up to 4MB on the motherboard using 1-megabit chips. With 80386SX-based computers, four memory banks are used, requiring 18 chips or sometimes two 9-bit SIMMs each. 80386DX, 80486SX, and 80486DX computers have two memory banks, each using four 9-bit SIMMs or one 36-bit SIMM.

Below are three tables of some common combinations of chips. The quantity of chips precedes their sizes. The table immediately following is for computers that use only DIPs, typically PCs with either 8088 or 8086 processors. It also applies to some 80286 computers:

Total Memory	Bank 0	Bank 1	Bank 2	Bank 3
512K	9x256K	9x256K		
576K	9x256K	9x256K	9x64K	
640K	9x256K	9x256K	9x64K	9x64K
1MB	9x256K	9x256K	9x256K	9x256K

The next table is typical of more modern 80286 and 80386SX computers that use only SIMMs or SIPs. Note that the memory capacity is much greater.

Total Memory	Bank 0	Bank 1	Bank 2	Bank 3
1MB	2x256K	2x256K		
2MB	2x256K	2x256K	2x256K	2x256K
	2x1MB			
3MB	2x256K	2x1MB		
4MB	2x1MB	2x1MB		
5MB	2x256K	2x256K	2x1MB	2x1MB
6MB	2x1MB	2x1MB	2x1MB	
8MB	2x1MB	2x1MB	2x1MB	2x1MB
9MB	2x256K	2x256K	2x4MB	
10MB	2x1MB	2x4MB		
12MB	2x1MB	2x1MB	2x4MB	
16MB	2x4MB	2x4MB		

This table shows the possible memory variations for 80386DX and 80486 computers that use only SIMMs:

Total Memory	Bank 0	Bank 1
1MB	4x256K	
2MB	4x256K	4x256K
4MB	4x1MB	
5MB	4x1MB	4x256K
8MB	4x1MB	4x1MB
16MB	4x4MB	
17MB	4x4MB	4x256K
20MB	4x4MB	4x1MB
32MB	4x4MB	4x4MB

Unfortunately, the memory capacities of motherboards vary by manufacturer.

Memory Chip Speeds

The size of memory chips is only one concern. The other is speed. Memory chips are rated by their reaction time, which is measured in *nanoseconds*, or billionths of a second. How fast is a nanosecond? One nanosecond, abbreviated ns, is the time it takes light to travel 12 inches.

The smaller the speed rating, the faster the chip. For example, a 60-ns chip is faster than a 100-ns chip. Generally, faster chips cost more. It won't hurt to install chips that are faster than required for your motherboard or memory card; buying faster memory chips can be a boon if you intend to transplant them to a faster computer in the future. Unfortunately, the faster memory won't speed up your computer; your computer's design permits working at a certain speed and no faster.

The speed of a memory chip is printed on its surface. On the memory chips — whether the DIP, SIP, or SIMM type — you will see an identifying number. The last two digits after the dash (–) are especially important, since they indicate the speed of your memory. For example, one of my older computers has memory chips with the number "M5K4164ANP 51727F-15." The last two digits after this long number indicates the speed in either nanoseconds or tens of nanoseconds. In this example, the memory chips are 150 nanoseconds fast. Today's faster memory is around 60 ns.

Most motherboards use tricks to allow the use of slower memory. One technique is called *interleaving*, which splits memory into two banks. Your computer then alternates between the two banks for the fastest possible speeds. *Wait states* are also used so slower memory can be employed. A wait state simply means your computer must wait before accessing its memory. The wait states are usually measured in processor, or CPU, cycles. These cycles that your computer must wait are like missed beats. For example, if you take slower memory from an old PC and put it into a newer computer, the newer computer may operate at 1 or 2 wait states, rather than 0 or 1, respectively. The more wait states, the slower your computer.

Installing Extra Memory on the Motherboard

Installing extra memory onto your motherboard is the least expensive way to add memory to your computer. In Chapter 3, "Cracking Open the Case," I had you notice the speed of your memory and whether you had any room for more. If you do have a vacant memory bank, there is a fairly easy way in which you can install extra memory and use it to significantly speed up your PC. The following steps show you how to do it.

To install DIP memory chips in a vacant memory bank:

1. Turn off your computer and remove its case.

   For details on opening your computer, see the procedure in Chapter 3, "Cracking Open the Case."

2. Locate the banks of memory chips and the vacant memory bank.

3. Jot down the numbers on the DIP memory chips present in the full memory bank and order additional memory for the vacant bank or banks.

   The chips in the other memory banks are probably the type of memory chips you need to order. The current DIP chips probably have these numbers included in the chip's part number printed on its top:

DIP Type	Size
4164	64K x 1 bit
4264	64K x 2 bits
4464	64K x 4 bits
41128	128K x 1 bit
42128	128K x 2 bits
44128	128K x 4 bits
4256	256K x 1 bit
41256	256K x 1 bit
42256	256K x 2 bits
44256	256K x 4 bits
41100	1024Kx1 bit
41000	1024K x 1 bit

The vacant memory bank requires nine DIP chips, eight to make one byte and the ninth to verify the accuracy of the other eight. Therefore, your computer probably requires one of the 1-bit chips

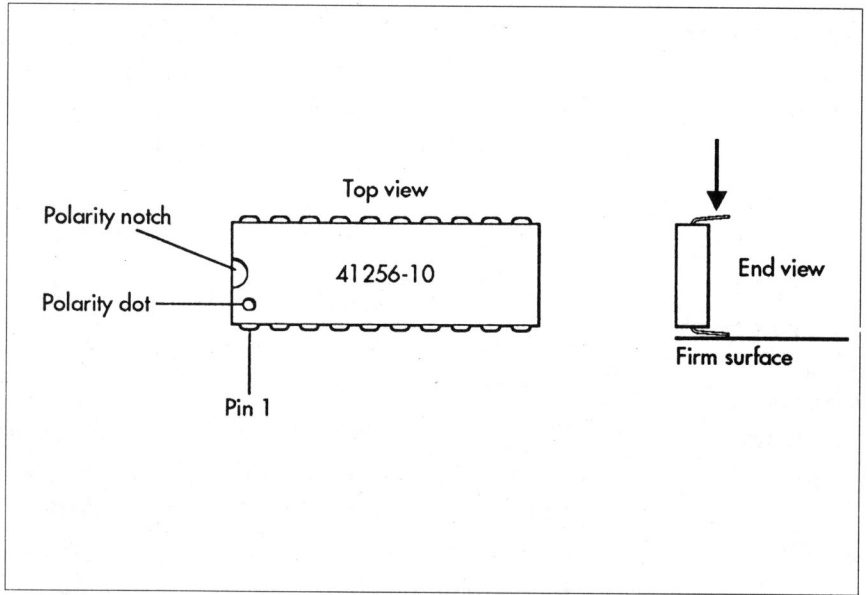

Figure 6.4 With DIP memory, you must bend the legs to right angles on a firm surface before installing them. Also, install the DIP chips with the correct polarity.

listed above. In most cases, you would want to add chips that match the current ones. For accuracy, consult your owner's manual about the type of chips to add. If you don't have an owner's manual, consult the previous table of possible memory configurations for DIP chips. Remember, if you add extra memory to your computer, its speed must be equal to or less than that of the memory already installed.

4. Prepare the DIP memory chips for installation (see Figure 6.4).

Memory chips are very sensitive to static electricity. Keep them in their antistatic container until they are needed. Otherwise, place them on an antistatic bag that came with an expansion card or some other electronic component.

Before installing each DIP chip, touch a piece of metal briefly, such as your computer's metal case, to drain yourself of built-up static. For DIP type of memory chips, you often have to slightly bend the pins, or legs, so they will match the sockets. Grasp each chip between your thumb and forefinger. Place the chip with all of the pins on one side against a firm surface, such as a table. Apply enough pressure to bend all the pins on one side so they are perpendicular to the chip body. Turn the chip over and repeat this procedure for the legs on the other side.

5. Install the DIP memory into the sockets.

Each DIP memory chip must be installed pointing in a certain direction. Each chip has a polarity marking on one end. This marking may be a polarity notch, a circular indentation or both. The chip socket may have a corresponding notch. Otherwise, the motherboard may have a printed legend that indicates the orientation of the chip.

The most difficult part of installing DIP memory chips is getting all 18 leads of each chip to fit their assigned holes. Set the chip on the socket into which you wish to install it. The leads should fit directly into the holes of the socket, and the chip should drop slightly into the holes. Before you do anything else, check the alignment of the chip.

Press each chip firmly into its socket. Apply firm pressure but don't bend the circuit board too much. To be sure the chip is properly seated, press each of its ends down one more time individually. After each chip is installed, use a flashlight to inspect it. Make sure that none of the leads of the chip has folded underneath the chip and that none of the leads has slipped outside the socket. If a lead is folded under or bent outside the socket, remove the chip and straighten the lead by squeezing it between the jaws of a pair of pliers. Then carefully reinstall and reinspect the chip.

Sometimes, a single leg may accidentally miss its socket. If the memory chip is installed backwards or a single leg is out of place, your computer will not work properly.

6. Tell your PC about the extra memory.

If you own an 8088, 8086, or older 80286, you need to physically configure your PC to recognize the extra memory. Usually a jumper or switch has to be changed on the motherboard to make the change effective. (A jumper is a small cap that connects two pins together.) Consult your owner's manual about these changes.

How do you know how much memory you've added? You already know how much memory you started with, based on what your computer reported during its warming up. Using the tables above, you are adding that many kilobytes of memory for each memory bank you fill with that type of memory. For example, imagine you have 512K of memory in your PC. You check and discover that two of the four memory banks are empty. I decide to add 128K of memory (2 banks x 64K) to create a total of 640K. Since each memory bank requires nine DIP chips, that means they are one-bit chips. From the chart, you see that you need eighteen 4164 chips. What speed do you get? Get a speed that matches the speed of the other chips already installed. For example, a chip with the phrase "-12" imprinted on it means 120-nanosecond-fast memory.

If you have an 80286 computer and don't have jumpers to change, don't worry. More modern 80286 computers like yours can be told of the new memory through a setup program, rather than by moving a jumper. This setup program may be either on a diagnostics diskette or built into your computer's motherboard. Usually you can get to this setup program as your computer warms up; it is part of your computer's BIOS, or Basic Input/Output System. The BIOS provides a setup program to record the new amount of memory to a CMOS (complementary metallic oxide semiconductor). The CMOS is a special type of memory chip that requires little power to store information. Even when your computer is turned off, its memory contents are saved by a trickle of power from an AA or small nickel-cadmium battery. You can later tell this setup program how much memory you have.

7. Once all the chips are installed, attach your keyboard and monitor to your PC and plug it into the electrical outlet.

   For now, leave your computer case off so you can fix any wrongly installed chips.

8. Turn on your computer.

   If you have a newer 80286, you need to tell your setup program that you have additional memory. Usually on warming up, the 80286 computer will recognize that something has changed and will display an error message. From there, you can access the setup program and make the changes. If you must use a setup program from a diskette, insert the setup diskette into your computer before turning it on.

   If your PC gives a message such as "Parity error" or does not recognize the new memory, either you have a defective memory chip or you have installed it improperly. Remove the cover and inspect your work. If your PC relies on jumpers to configure the memory, be sure they were set correctly.

9. Attach your computer's case and return to normal operation.

To install SIMM/SIP memory chips

SIMM and SIP memory chips are very similar. Several memory chips are bundled into one package. Unlike DIP memory, SIMM/SIP memory lets you install all nine chips in one motion rather than one at a time.

1. Turn off your computer and remove its case.

   For details on opening your computer, see the procedure in Chapter 3, "Cracking Open the Case."

2. Locate the banks of memory chips and the vacant memory bank.

   There are usually two memory banks that hold four SIMMs or SIPs apiece.

3. Jot down the numbers on the SIMM/SIP memory chips present in the full memory bank and order additional memory for the vacant bank.

The chips in the other memory bank are probably the type you need to order. The current SIMM/SIP chips probably have these numbers within the chip's part number printed on its top:

SIMM/SIP Type	Size
1256	256K x 1 bit
14256	256K x 4 bits
11000	1024K x 1 bit
14400	1024K x 4 bits
41000	4096K x 1 bit
44000	4096K x 4 bits

For example, one of my computers has eight megabytes of memory, four 1MB SIMMs in each bank. The first bank has SIMMs made of three chips each. Two of the chips are the 14400 kind (1024K x 4 bits), which together make up eight bits. The third chip, the ninth bit, is an 11000 chip (1024K x 1 bit) that checks the accuracy of the other two. The second memory bank uses SIMMs composed of the typical nine chips, one for each bit. These are the 11000 type of chips, 1024K x 1 bit. It doesn't matter what type chips are used for the SIMM/SIP, although a three-chip SIMM/SIP requires less room. In my computer, the three-chip SIMMs are shorter, allowing me to install an expansion card over them.

If you have a vacant memory bank, you probably want to add chips that match the current ones. For accuracy, consult your owner's manual about the type of chips to add. If you don't have an owner's manual, consult the previous table of possible memory configurations for SIMM/SIP chips. RemeMBer, if you add extra memory to your computer, its speed must be equal to or less than that of the memory already installed.

4. Prepare the SIMM/SIP memory chips for installation.

Memory chips are very sensitive to static electricity. Keep them in their antistatic bag until they are needed. Otherwise, you can place them on an antistatic bag that came with an expansion card or other component. Before installing each SIMM/SIP chip, touch a piece of metal briefly, like your computer's metal case, to drain yourself of built-up static.

5.   Install the SIMM/SIP memory into the sockets (see Figure 6.5).

Each SIMM/SIP must be installed pointing in a certain direction. Each chip has a polarity notch on one end of the circuit board. A SIMM has a notch cut into one side; a SIP has a diagonal notch. These notches physically prevent the memory module from being installed wrongly. If the module is reluctant to enter its socket, try turning it around.

Place each SIMM at about a 45-degree angle, lining up the copper-colored connectors on the memory module with the socket on the motherboard. The chips on the module should face away from the angle of the socket. Since four modules must be installed into the bank, you must insert the modules in a certain order so each subsequent module has room to be inserted at this angle.

Firmly insert the SIMM into the socket. Next, pivot it backwards to an upright position until it touches the plastic latches on both sides of the socket. Carefully press the SIMM against these latches

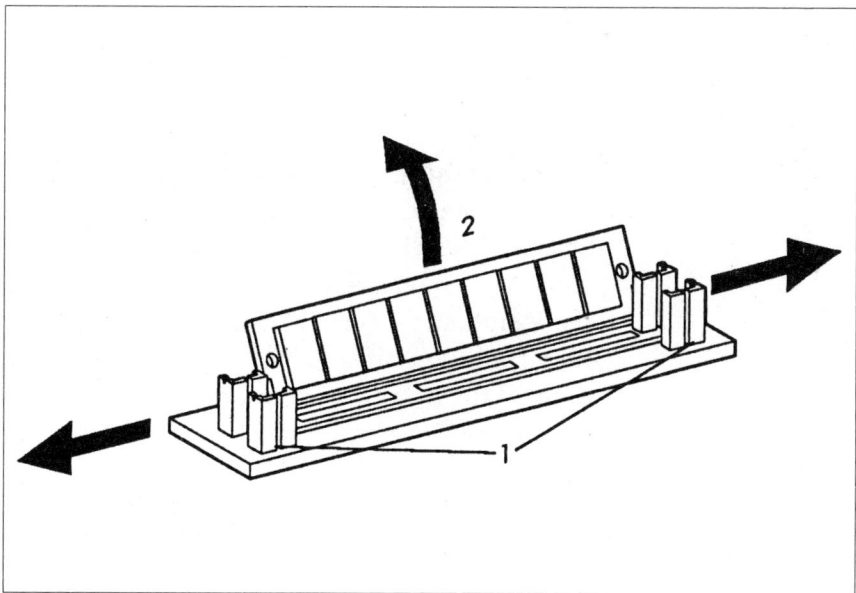

Figure 6.5 Insert the SIMM at a 45-degree angle and snap it into place.

until they snap around the edges of the SIMM and clamp it firmly into place. The circuit board serving as the bacKone of the SIMM should be perpendicular to the circuit board holding the socket.

A plastic finger from the socket latch should poke slightly through the alignment hole at the edge of the SIMM (if there are holes in the SIMM), or the side latches of the socket should wrap around the board of the SIMM. For each SIP, insert the module straight into its socket. You should feel it slide into the grasp of the socket's contact fingers.

6. Inspect your work.

    Use a flashlight to inspect the installation. Make sure each module is not bowing out but is directly in line with its socket. For SIMMs, you should see only the top rim of each contact finger at the top of the socket. If you see more, if one end of the SIMM is deeper in the socket than the other, or if the latches don't properly engage, remove the SIMM and reinstall it.

7. Once all the chips are installed, attach the keyboard and monitor to your PC and plug it into the electrical outlet.

    For now, leave your computer case off so you can fix any incorrectly installed chips.

8. Turn on your PC.

    You need to tell your setup program that you have additional memory. This setup program may be either on a diagnostics diskette or built into your computer's motherboard. Usually you can get to this setup program as your computer warms up. This program is part of your computer's BIOS, or Basic Input/Output System. The BIOS provides a setup program to record the new amount of memory to a CMOS (complementary metallic oxide semiconductor). The CMOS is a special type of memory chip that requires little power to store information. Even when your computer is turned off, its memory contents are saved by a trickle of power from an AA or small nickel-cadmium battery.

    Usually on warming up, your PC will recognize that something has changed and will display an error message. From there, you can access your computer's setup program and make the changes. Sometimes, your PC will already guess how much memory you have and just have you approve the changes to the setup program. If you must use a setup program from a diskette, insert the setup diskette into your computer before turning it on.

How do you know how much memory you've added? You know how much memory you started with, based on what your computer reported during its warm-up and/or the CHKDSK command. Using the previous chart, you are adding that many kilobytes of memory for each memory bank you fill with that type of memory. For example, if you have a memory bank filled with four 1MB SIMMs, you can add four 1MB SIMMs to the empty bank, making a total of 8MB. In your computer's setup program, you would indicate 640K of base memory and the remainder for extended memory.

If your computer gives a message such as "Parity error" or does not recognize the new memory, either you have a defective memory module or you have installed it improperly. Remove the cover and inspect your work.

You may find that the SIMMs are not seated properly in their sockets. While inspecting them, make sure the PC is unplugged, and guard against static electricity.

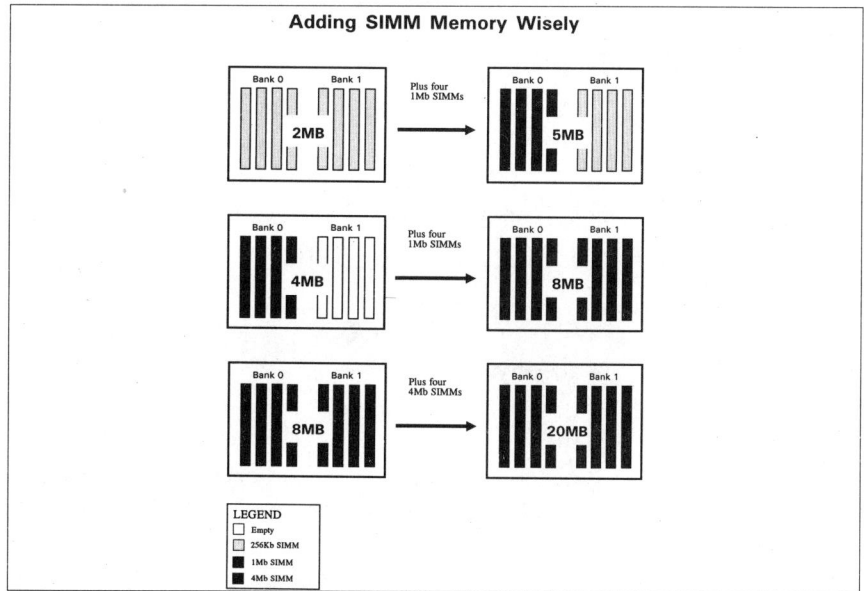

Figure 6.6 By using higher capacity SIMM memory, you can increase your total memory with little waste, as shown in this chart.

Replacing Memory on the Motherboard

Besides adding memory to vacant memory banks, you can also increase the amount of memory by replacing low-capacity memory with high-capacity memory. In most cases, the waste is minimal, since most of the existing memory chips can be used (see Figure 6.6).

For example, I had a computer whose two memory banks were filled with eight 1MB SIMMs. All the memory banks were filled, yet I wanted more memory. The solution was to remove all or part of the current SIMMs and replace them with higher capacity SIMMs. In my situation, I removed four of the 1MB SIMMs from the first memory bank and replaced them with four 4MB SIMMs. The result: 20MB of memory instead of 8MB. I then took the four 1MB SIMMs I removed and placed them in my wife's computer. To discover which low-capacity memory can be replaced, consult your owner's manual. Otherwise, the charts below may help.

Below is a chart showing combinations of DIP memory for 8088, 8086, and some 80286 computers:

Total Memory	Bank 0	Bank 1	Bank 2	Bank 3
512K	9x256K	9x256K		
576K	9x256K	9x256K	9x64K	
640K	9x256K	9x256K	9x64K	9x64K
1MB	9x256K	9x256K	9x256K	9x256K

This table is typical of more modern 80286 and 80386SX computers that use only SIMMs or SIPs:

Total Memory	Bank 0	Bank 1	Bank 2	Bank 3
1MB	2x256K	2x256K		
2MB	2x256K 2x1MB	2x256K	2x256K	2x256K
3MB	2x256K	2x1MB		
4MB	2x1MB	2x1MB		
5MB	2x256K	2x256K	2x1MB	2x1MB

Continued

Total Memory	Bank 0	Bank 1	Bank 2	Bank 3
Continued				
6MB	2x1MB	2x1MB	2x1MB	
8MB	2x1MB	2x1MB	2x1MB	2x1MB
9MB	2x256K	2x256K	2x4MB	
10MB	2x1MB	2x4MB		
12MB	2x1MB	2x1MB	2x4MB	
16MB	2x4MB	2x4MB		

This table shows the possible memory variations for 80386DX and 80486 computers that use only SIMMs:

Total Memory	Bank 0	Bank 1
1MB	4x256K	
2MB	4x256K	4x256K
4MB	4x1MB	
5MB	4x1MB	4x256K
8MB	4x1MB	4x1MB
16MB	4x4MB	
17MB	4x4MB	4x256K
20MB	4x4MB	4x1MB
32MB	4x4MB	4x4MB

For example, you could go from 2MB of 256K SIMMs to 5MB by buying four 1MB SIMMs and putting away the four extra 256K SIMMs. Or, you could go from 2MB of 256K SIMMs to 9MB by buying two 4MB SIMMs and pocketing the four extra 256K SIMMs.

The table on the following page shows the possible memory variations for 80386DX and 80486 computers that use only SIMMs.

In this situation, you could go from 2MB to 5MB by buying four 1MB SIMMs and putting away the four extra 256K SIMMs. Likewise, you could go from 17MB to 32MB by buying four 4MB SIMMs and putting away the four 256K SIMMs. How you decide to configure your memory is, of course, dependent upon your own needs and budget.

Total RAM	Bank 0	Bank 1
1MB	4x256K	
2MB	4x256K	4x256K
4MB	4x1MB	
5MB	4x1MB	4x256K
8MB	4x1MB	4x1MB
16MB	4x4MB	
17MB	4x4MB	4x256K
20MB	4x4MB	4x1MB
32MB	4x4MB	4x4MB

Removing Memory

To replace lower capacity memory with higher capacity memory, you have to be very careful. First, be sure to briefly touch a piece of metal, such as your computer's case, to drain yourself of harmful static electricity. After removing memory chips, place them on or in an antistatic bag for safety.

If you are removing DIP memory, you must be very careful to avoid bending the legs. The best method for removing DIP memory is to put a flat object under both ends of the chip and lift upwards. I recommend using two flathead screwdrivers or two of those metal plates that cover the expansion ports. If you pry up only one end, the legs will be bent or broken.

Before removing SIMM or SIP memory, be sure the latches, if present, are undone on both ends. Then tilt the chip down and out. Try to grab the memory chips by the edges of the circuit board, rather than touching the chips themselves.

Using a Memory Expansion Card

If you own an 8088, 8086, or an older 80286 computer, adding a memory expansion card may be the only way to get additional memory. The memory is often expanded memory, since older computers such as the 8088 or 8086 can only address 1MB. With expanded memory, your PC can run any of thousands of programs that support expanded memory. Also, a memory expansion card often includes utilities that can use the expanded memory to speed up your computer.

The memory expansion card, just like any other expansion card, is placed in an expansion slot inside your PC. With a special software utility, your computer can then access the memory chips on this card. One disadvantage of the memory expansion card is that it is plugged into the expansion slot and not into the motherboard itself. What's the difference? The PC's data bus talks to expansion cards at a sluggish 8 MHz. Any installed card is limited to this slower bus speed, no matter how fast the computer. The extra memory available on the card cannot be quickly accessed by your computer. This drawback may be minor, however. If your PC is an 8088, 8086, or a slower (sub-12 MHz) 80286, then the slow bus speed is not such a detriment.

A memory expansion card can be purchased for between $50 and $300. The cost of memory is usually extra, since many of these cards come with either no memory or a skimpy 512K. The total capacity of these cards ranges between 2MB and 32MB. The typical total capacity is 8MB. If you don't need much memory — maybe 2MB to cache your hard disk and maybe put some memory-resident programs above the 640K barrier — then save some money by purchasing the 2MB version. If you have programs that support expanded memory, such as Lotus 1-2-3, you may want a board with a higher total capacity.

To add memory beyond a certain point, some boards require a *piggyback card*, which is also called a *daughterboard*. These cards plug into the side of a main memory board and provide sockets for more memory. Avoid piggybacks if you can; the add-on card requires another of your valuable expansion slots. Also, a piggyback can be as expensive as the main memory card.

The memory expansion card should meet the Lotus/Intel/Microsoft 4.0 expanded memory specification, or LIM 4.0 EMS for short. An 8088 or 8086 computer requires an 8-bit memory expansion card. Some companies, however, sell expansion cards that double as both 8- or 16-bit cards. Such a dual-purpose card can be reused later with an 80286 computer. However, you wouldn't want to use such a card with an 80386 or faster computer — the 8-MHz bus speed would slow the memory to a crawl. I recommend you buy an inexpensive 8-bit only model, unless you know for certain you will be upgrading to an 80286 computer that cannot accommodate more than 640K memory on its motherboard.

Figure 6.7 The line of Intel AboveBoard memory expansion cards offers additional memory, up to 8MB on one card. *(Photo courtesy of Intel Corp.)*

Older PCs that are limited to 512K of memory require an expansion card just to reach the base 640K of memory. No problem; many memory expansion cards let you use some of the expanded memory to "backfill" your conventional memory to 640K. The remaining memory is used as expanded memory. In some cases, you may want to disable as much memory on your motherboard as possible so you can keep all your memory eggs in the expanded card basket. By primarily using the memory expansion card, you reduce having to bounce between the memory on your motherboard and the memory on the card.

Some expansion cards, such as the Intel AboveBoard Plus I/O, provide extra features besides memory, including serial and parallel ports and a real-time clock. With the clock, you won't have to enter the date and time each time your PC starts. The serial port can be used for an external modem or a mouse.

When looking for an expansion memory card, also consider the following:

• The maximum amount of memory the card can hold
• Optional I/O ports, such as a serial or parallel port

• Bundled software to take advantage of the expanded memory, such as disk caching or print spooler utilities

When you receive your card, you must configure and install it. Many memory cards feature switchless installation. You install the card and configure it via a setup program. The program asks you how you want to use the memory and then stores your answers into an electrically erasable, programmable read-only memory (EEPROM) chip. This program should also modify your CONFIG.SYS startup file to load the EMS device driver.

If you own an 80286 computer whose motherboard uses the Chips & Technologies NEAT chip set, you won't need a memory expansion card. With this type of motherboard design, the memory on the motherboard can emulate expanded memory at any speed. This is called *LIM-ulation*. Check your owner's manual for how to invoke this feature; usually a software utility, or driver, called a *LIMulator* must be loaded to convert the extra memory into expanded memory.

Being out of memory doesn't mean you're out of luck. Extra memory can be the perfect tonic for your upgrade blues.

7

CPUs: Boning Up on Brainpower

Your PC is an assembly of many expensive parts, including a case, power supply, hard and floppy disk drives, parallel and serial ports, video card, and so forth. At the heart of all computers is the *motherboard*, the typically horizontal circuit board that contains the guts of the PC. The motherboard includes such crucial components as the microprocessor, memory, and more.

A simple addition or two to your computer's microprocessor, can make it last longer. The speed of this electronic "brain" is the biggest stumbling block to your computer operating at peak efficiency. More than any other factor, these improvements can speed up or improve your computer:

- Replacing your computer's processor
- Replacing your computer's crystal
- Installing an accelerator card
- Adding a math, or numeric, coprocessor
- Installing a newer or different BIOS (Basic Input/Output System)

Processor Primer

The *microprocessor*, *processor* or *central processing unit (CPU)*, is the "brains" of your PC. The processor is a single computer chip inside your computer that performs much of the work. Other parts of the PC assist the processor, but this computer chip is the engine providing speed.

Figure 7.1 A photograph of an Intel i486 (80486) processor. *(Courtesy of Intel Corp.)*

Most likely, your PC's processor was designed by Intel Corp.; however, companies like Advanced Micro Devices (AMD) also make microprocessors. Although all PC microprocessors are members of the Intel 80x86 family, they come in different strengths: 8088, 8086, 80286, 80386, 80386SX, 80486SX, 80486DX, and so on. For example, the Intel 8088 used by IBM in the original IBM PC and PC/XT computers is about one-third as fast as the 80286. Each processor, usually a square computer chip measuring about one inch on each side, contains thousands of small transistors. These small transistors are the building blocks of computer technology. For example, the 80486DX processor contains about 1,200,000 transistors (see Figure 7.1).

The speed of your processor is based on two factors: the speed of its clock oscillator and the number of bits it can process at one time.

Beating the Clock

A processor's power is determined by the speed at which its clock oscillator runs. This clock synchronizes every part of the processor; it provides the "heartbeat" to your PC. Every action your PC performs uses at least one clock cycle and often several. For example, an 80386 CPU has an average instruction-execution time of 4.4 cycles.

The speed of this clock is measured in millions of cycles per second, or megahertz (MHz). If one PC has a faster clock oscillator than another, it gets the same amount of work done in less time. In other words, the higher the clock speed, the faster your PC runs.

Surprisingly, your processor doesn't contain this clock oscillator. It is a separate component in your computer, often called the *clock crystal*. Rather, your processor is rated to run at a certain minimum clock speed. An 80286 processor rated at 12 MHz is guaranteed to work with a clock oscillator running at 12 million cycles per second. The original IBM PC and XT with their 8088 processors were designed to run at 4.77 MHz. The first IBM PS/2 Models 25 and 30 used the 8-MHz 8086 chip. Today's computers operate at higher clock speeds — 40 MHz and even higher.

The Data Bus

Besides its clock speed, a processor is measured by the amount of information it can move at one time. This information is measured in *bits*, short for "binary digit." A bit is used to measure how much information computers can store and process. Typically, eight bits make up a byte, that is, a single character (a letter, number, or symbol). The movement of these bytes inside your computer is similar to highway traffic. If a highway has only one lane in each direction, only one car can pass at any one time. To handle more traffic, you can add another lane and thereby double the number of cars that can pass at one time. These highways are called *data buses*.

Both the 8088 and the 8086 are 16-bit processors. In other words, they process information two characters at a time. However, this measurement is only for *inside* the processor. There may be a different number of "lanes" for talking to the other circuitry in your PC. These external lanes are called the *external data bus*.

While both the 8088 and the 8086 chips are designed internally as 16-bit chips, the 8088 communicates to the rest of the computer using only eight bits. Thus, the 8088 is a 16-bit internal, 8-bit external chip. When IBM introduced its first PC in 1981, it chose the 8088 processor over the full 16-bit 8086. Why? IBM could make the PC affordable by using this less-expensive processor and 8-bit electronic components for the rest of the PC. In other words, the 8088 is just a lower-cost version of the 8086. This design allowed the first PC, with 16K of memory and no disk drives, to be sold for $1355, about $300 less than a similarly configured Apple II system. Below is a table of processors, speeds, and data bus.

Processor	Speeds (in MHz)	Internal-External Data Bus (in bits)
8088	5, 8	16, 8
8086	5, 8, 10	16, 16
80286	8, 10, 12, 16, 20, 25	16, 16
80386DX	16, 20, 25, 33, 40	32, 32
80386SX	16, 20, 25	32, 16
80486DX	25, 33, 50	32, 32
80486SX	16, 20, 25	32, 32

80286: The Coming of the AT

Intel introduced the 80286 in 1984, after the 8088 and 8086. IBM used the 80286 chip in its IBM PC/AT (Advanced Technology). Its primary advantage over older processors was its ability to operate in two different modes. The first, called the "real mode," allows the 80286 processor to work just like an 8088 or 8086 processor, enabling computers built around it to use software designed for the original IBM PC and PC/XT.

The second mode of the 80286 is called the "protected mode." An 80286 (or AT) computer operating in protected mode has capabilities not found in the 8088/8086 chips. For example, the 80286 computer can use 16 megabytes of primary memory, whereas the 8088/8086 computer can use only one megabyte (1024K) of memory. Thus, the 80286 computer can run much larger programs. Also, the 80286 was designed to allow several programs to run simultaneously. This is called *multitasking*. A computer user could now use one PC to perform several tasks at the same time.

Unfortunately, most of the benefits of protected-mode operation found in the 80286 cannot be used, since the current operating system used in most PCs does not provide access to these features. In 1987, Microsoft Corp. and IBM announced a new operating system called OS/2 that was designed to tap the power of the 80286's protected mode. Unfortunately, those multitasking features did not work quite as well as originally planned. Programs designed for DOS would "crash" when the 80286 computer switched to protected mode.

Because of its problems with multitasking, the 80286 was treated simply as a fast 8088/8086 computer. Although the 80286 is a 16-bit processor like the 8086, it can run at faster clock speeds. And the 80286 is very fast indeed. Running software at the same clock speed, an 80286-powered computer is at least three times as fast as an 8086.

The 80286's clock speed rose steadily over the years. The Intel version of the 80286 processor topped out at 12 MHz, but other chip makers who built 80286 processors under reluctant license from Intel built faster versions, up to 25 MHz. The first IBM PC/ATs were designed to run at 6 MHz. Many AT-compatible computers today run at speeds of 12 to 20 MHz.

80386: A "Perfect" 80286

With the introduction of the 80386 processor, Intel corrected the 80286's problems with switching to protected mode. Unlike the 80286, the 80386 processor is a true 32-bit processor, processing four bytes at a time. Effectively, this change alone makes the 80386 at least twice as powerful as the 80286.

Besides doubling the amount of information that can be processed, a third operating mode was added to the 80386. Like the 80286, the 80386 has a real mode and a protected mode. Also, it includes what is called the "virtual real mode." In virtual real mode, an 80386 computer can run as if it were multiple 8086 PCs, each running independently of the others and at the same time. Also, the 80386 chip can directly access up to four gigabytes (4096MB) of memory, 256 times what the 80286 can use. With multitasking that works, you can carve that memory into separate "virtual 8086s," each of which appears to the software to be an 8086 computer with one megabyte of memory all to itself.

The 80386 bottom line: More calculations can be done, as if you had several PCs operating in your 80386 computer. Also, the 80386 processor is ideal for any application that involves graphics, such as CAD (computer-aided design) or serious desktop publishing. The

80386 is much better at task switching than the 80286. However, an 80386-based computer using DOS cannot access the virtual real mode; it provides no additional functions compared to the original IBM PC, other than a significant increase in speed. The 80386 has the ability to run at speeds up to 40 MHz.

The newest version of OS/2, 2.0, is designed to take advantage of the 80386's improved multitasking, and it makes use of those improvements, including the ability to run multiple DOS programs at the same time. However, nonmultitasking DOS software runs little faster on an 80386 than on an 80286 at the same clock speed.

Poor Man's 80386

There's also a version of the 80386 with only a 16-bit external data bus — the 80386SX. Consider the 80386SX a "poor man's 386." It allows you to use the memory management/multitasking features of the 80386 without paying the full price for an 80386 computer. Intel and computer manufacturers often refer to the full-size 80386 as the 80386DX, to contrast it with the SX. The 80386SX is limited to speeds of 16, 20, 25, and 33 MHz.

The relationship between the 80386SX and the 80386 is similar to that of the 8088 and 8086, respectively. The 80386SX has all the features of the 80386, except that it talks to the rest of the computer in 16-bit chunks instead of 32 bits. Computers built around the 80386SX can use less-expensive 16-bit components while still providing the 80386's more powerful features. Because of the halved external data bus, the 80386SX is slower than a regular 80386 running at the same clock speed.

Gaining More Speed

As these computer processors become faster, the *random access memory (RAM)* — where programs and data are temporarily stored — has difficulty time shoveling data to them in time. Several technological tricks are used to prevent this bottleneck.

To speed up the number-crunching power of computers, math coprocessors are often added. These additional computer chips speed up mathematical calculations. Most computers have a math coprocessor socket for either the Weitek or Intel (or Intel-compatible) math coprocessors. However, your software must support the extra power. Usually, spreadsheets (like Lotus 1-2-3), drafting, and programming tools support a math coprocessor. (Math coprocessors are discussed later in this chapter.)

Another technique to speed up 80386 and faster computers is memory caching. Memory caching is used to have more data in memory poised to be fed to the computer's processor. On high-end 80386 and 80486 computers, small amounts of super, high-speed memory are used to keep pace with the processor. (Don't confuse memory caching with disk caching, which speeds up the hard disk. The concept is similar, however.) Such memory caches are a way to deliver memory speed while keeping costs down. Typical cache sizes range from 64K to 256K. Cache memory, at 25 nanoseconds or less, is expensive and usually reserved for high-end computers.

Caching provides a significant increase in speed. An 80386 computer that has caching is about 40–50 percent faster than without it. Some computer manufacturers have combined the affordability of 80386SX computers with caching to provide a delicate balance of power and low price.

For Power Users: The 80486

The 80486 processor (or i486) from Intel is a top-of-the-line, enhanced version of the 80386. The 80486 processor does not require math coprocessors or memory caching. These extra capabilities are already built-in.

The 80486 combines three formerly separate chips into one: an 80386DX processor, a math coprocessor, and an 8K on-board memory cache. Although the 8K cache is smaller than those found on some 80386 computers, it is more effective because it is built into the 80486 processor. However, an external cache sometimes is added to an 80486 computer for more speed.

Theoretically, the 80486 was designed to be completely compatible with the 80386, but in practice there are a few minor differences. The 80486 runs significantly faster than an 80386 — about 40 percent faster at identical clock speeds. And software programmers can squeeze an extra 10 percent to 15 percent performance by using a compiler that capitalizes on the 80486's design. As a result, the 25-MHz 80486 runs as fast as or faster than a 33-MHz 80386. The 80486-based computers are irresistible to power users, for whom the added speed means faster engineering, science, desktop publishing, or spreadsheet recalculations.

Like the 80386, the 80486 also comes in a "castrated" SX style. Unlike the 80386SX, the 80486SX does not have a smaller external data bus of 16-bits. Instead, the SX means that the math coprocessor is disabled. If you do not have math-intensive work, the 80486SX is an enticing choice.

Avoid Radical Upgrades

You can certainly upgrade your IBM PC/XT to an 80486 processor. But sometimes the result is an expensive and lopsided system. The lightning speed of the processor would be slowed by the limping hard disk, and some expansion cards may not won't work with the new processor. Remember Aleshire's Axiom:

> *The overall speed of your computer is limited by the speed of its slowest component.*

As a general rule, avoid radical upgrades since they upset the balance among the various components in your PC. A more modest upgrade, such as moving from an 80286 to an 80386SX processor, provides the most upgrade bang for your buck.

Replacing Your Processor

Adding a faster processor to your computer is the single most important upgrade you can undertake. The processor not only speeds up your PC but also determines which programs it can run. An increasing number of applications and operating systems, such as *AutoCAD 386*, *DESQview 386*, and *OS/2* 2.0, require an 80386 or 80486 processor.

Unfortunately, adding a faster processor is not a plug-and-play operation. In fact, 8088, 80286 and 80386 processors each require a different socket; you cannot simply pop out your current processor and replace it with a newer model. Rarely do such "brain transplants" work.

Even replacing, for example, an 8-MHz 80286 processor with a 12-MHz 80286 processor will not speed up your computer. Why not? The processor is not the only component that determines your computer's speed. The separate clock oscillator mentioned earlier paces the processor. In other words, the speed imprinted on the processor specifies its minimum operating speed, but the clock determines how fast it actually runs.

Replacing Your XT-Type Processor

In some cases, you can increase the speed of your computer despite the restrictions of the clock crystal. In PC and PC/XT computers, the Intel 8088 processor can be replaced by the faster 10-MHz NEC V20. If you own an 8086-based compatible, such as the original Compaq Deskpro, use a NEC V30. IBM PS/2 Models 25 and 30 cannot use the NEC processors.

Once the NEC processor is installed, don't expect your PC that operates at 4.77 MHz to double in speed. Because the NEC processor uses the old clock oscillator in your PC, it runs at the same speed. However, the NEC processor is designed to get more work done in fewer clock cycles. The new processor particularly shines in programs that rely heavily on math operations, as in spreadsheets. The improvement won't be drastic, possibly between 10 and 20 percent. Yet for $20, adding a NEC processor is an inexpensive way to boost performance. Unfortunately, these replacement processors are becoming rare and many electronics distributors offer them but require a minimum order of at least $25 to $250.

To install a new XT processor:

1. Turn off your computer and remove its case.

   For details on opening your computer, see the procedure in Chapter 3, "Cracking Open the Case."

2. Locate your processor.

   Look for numbers such as "8088" or "8086" imprinted on the top of the processor.

3. Remove the processor.

   To best remove the processor, use a chip puller. A chip puller resembles a U-shaped pair of tweezers, often made of aluminum. On the ends, the chip puller has curved hooks with which to grab onto the end of computer chips. Chip pullers usually cost about $1. If you don't have a chip puller, use a small flathead screwdriver with a three-inch blade. Then carefully bend the last quarter-inch of the blade 90 degrees to form a right angle.

4. Install the new processor.

    First, briefly touch a nearby piece of metal, such as your computer's cover, to drain yourself of built-up static electricity. Next, remove the new processor from its antistatic packaging. Gently place the processor in the empty socket and push down evenly to install it.

5. Replace your computer's case and return your PC to working order.

A Faster Clock

You can increase the heartbeat of your PC by replacing its clock oscillator with one that beats a little faster. However, your PC may have a mild heart attack at the accelerated pace.

The clock oscillator is a silver-colored electronic part about the size of one or two after-dinner mints, depending on your computer. A small sliver of quartz is contained in this tin container. It is located on your motherboard. A one-mint oscillator is probably a 4-pin DIP oscillator crystal. A two-mint oscillator is probably an 8-bit DIP oscillator.

This speed-determining oscillator may be either soldered to your motherboard or socketed, that is, plugged in and therefore removable. In 8088 and 8086 computers — PC and PC/XT computers — the oscillator is most likely soldered to the motherboard, making its removal difficult. However, early 6-MHz IBM ATs and newer computers have socketed clock oscillators you can easily pry out.

By operating at a higher clock speed, your processor may be able to keep pace. Why? Processors are not built to work at exactly 8 MHz, 12-MHz, and so on. They are made in batches and tested to see which clock speed they can reasonably handle. For example, a 12-MHz 80286 processor may be able to handle a clock speed of 16 MHz.

You can find a replacement oscillator in electronics stores. A clock oscillator needs to run at twice the processor speed. To upgrade a 6-MHz 80286 PC to 8 MHz, for example, you need a 16-MHz crystal. I recommend not installing a replacement oscillator that is more than 20 percent above the current speed, although you could go as much as one-third above the current rate.

If you own a genuine IBM PC/AT with a BIOS (Basic Input/Output System) dated after 11/15/85, you cannot easily speed up your crystal. IBM revised its startup diagnostics to prevent the PC from operating if a faster-than-normal crystal is detected. (The BIOS, described later, is a program that is embedded in an electronic chip on your motherboard.) Makers of speed-up devices circumvent this annoyance by maintaining the original clock speed until after the PC warmed up. Then the speed is increased to a preset maximum. Some varispeed devices use a rear-panel dial to set the maximum clock speed. Through trial and error, you find the best speed to safely operate your PC.

To find the date of your BIOS:

With a BIOS, the date is as important as the version number is for your software programs. This date is encoded into the BIOS chip itself. Instead of opening up your computer or buying a special utility program, you can find out the date with a simple DOS program. Run the DEBUG program located in your DOS directory. From the DOS directory, type:

```
DEBUG [Enter]
```

A hyphen (-) prompt appears on the left side of the screen. Then type:

```
D F000:FFF0 [Enter]
```

A row of numbers appears. The BIOS date should appear in the right-hand column. Write down the date. To exit DEBUG, type:

```
Q [Enter]
```

If the date of your PC/AT BIOS is earlier than November 15, 1985, replace the original oscillator with a faster one.

Not Crystal Clear

Usually, other parts of your PC, like your video card, rely on this crystal's frequency for smooth operation. An upgrade may cause your computer to act erratically. A better upgrade path would be to replace your processor with a newer one, either through the addition of an accelerator card (discussed later in this chapter) or a new motherboard (discussed in Chapter 8). If a higher speed crystal is installed, you may experience difficulties, like these:

- Lowered reaction time to games and other time-sensitive programs.

- Inaccurate times in communications software.

- Refusal to start when warming up.

- Erratic behavior, sometimes "locking up."

- Electronic "snow" on your monitor, or the monitor scrolls or starts up in 40-character-wide mode rather than 80.

- Failed diagnostic tests of your monitor, although it works fine otherwise.

- Memory errors, indicating your memory chips are not fast enough for your accelerated crystal.

For these reasons, I recommend you back up your hard disk before installing a faster crystal. See Chapter 10, "Backed Up Against the Wall."

A faster crystal may require other additions. Many people recommend buying a heat sink to siphon off the heat generated by the faster processor. The heat sink is a piece of metal that attaches to your processor to remove excess heat. Some heat sinks include a small fan that cools the processor.

When the clock speed is faster than 8 MHz, older memory chips may need to be replaced with ones rated at 120 nanoseconds or faster. On older PCs, the memory chips in memory bank 0 are soldered in place, requiring a soldering iron to remove them. Leave such electronic surgery to a service technician. If both the crystal and memory chips in bank 0 are soldered in place, you may want to replace the motherboard rather than pay for these services. The expense is just too great.

To replace your crystal:

1. Turn off your computer and remove its case.

   For details on opening your computer, see the procedure in Chapter 3, "Cracking Open the Case."

2. Locate the crystal of your PC.

The crystal is a silver-colored part. The speed imprinted on its top should be about double the rated speed of your processor. For example, my 40-MHz 80386 computer has a crystal rated at 80 MHz. You may have to remove some expansion cards or one or more disk drives to find the crystal.

3. Remove the original crystal.

   If the crystal has a binding strap on it, cut and remove it. Then pry the crystal from its socket, preferably using a chip puller. If your crystal is soldered to the motherboard, you may want to avoid the frustration of de-soldering it and consider another way to speed up your computer.

4. Install the new crystal.

   Gently place the crystal in the socket and push down evenly to install it.

5. Replace your computer's case and return your computer to working order.

6. Turn on and test your accelerated PC.

Once the crystal is installed, perform these extensive tests:

- Save and load files from the faster PC. If the tests fail, you may need to reformat your hard disk or use a slower crystal.

- Format a diskette in each floppy diskette drive you have.

- Print several documents and carefully examine them. Look for missing line feeds, garbled text, or other strange behavior.

- If you have a math coprocessor (described later), use a spreadsheet or BASIC program and try to divide by zero.

If any problems occur, you are pushing a component of your accelerated PC beyond its designed limits. The solution is to replace the component or use a slower crystal.

Of course, there are other ways in which you can add speed to your PC. One of the most popular solutions is adding an accelerator expansion card, which we discuss in the next section.

Pedal to the Metal

Accelerator expansion cards, or *accelerator boards*, are not as popular as they once were but still can add ample zip to your PC. An accelerator card is a single expansion card installed into one of your computer's expansion slots. The accelerator card contains the essential elements of a PC: processor and memory. Usually, your original processor is removed from its socket on the motherboard and a cable is attached in its place. There are a number of accelerator expansion cards that will enhance your XT- and AT-type computer. Some bring an old PC up to the speed of an 80286 or 80386 computer. Others perform more modest speed increases.

The falling prices of high-powered computers and other upgrade options make accelerator cards less attractive. An accelerator card only improves your processor's speed. Your other PC components — printer and serial ports, video display, and hard disk — remain unchanged. Ironically, an accelerator card often costs the same as an entirely new motherboard. The advantage of an accelerator card is its easy installation compared to the more daunting task of replacing one's entire motherboard. For the cost-conscious consumer, an accelerator card can extend the life of a PC another two or three years for a modest price and effort.

Despite the ease of installation, an accelerator card has one Achilles' heel: bus speed. Most PCs have the typical ISA — Industry Standard Architecture — expansion bus. An accelerator card placed in an ISA expansion slot is slowed from the start; the ISA bus operates at a sluggish 8 MHz, slowing communications between the accelerator card and the rest of your computer. For this reason, many accelerator cards connect to your processor's socket.

In an ISA bus computer, you have to remove your old processor, attach a delicate cable in its place, and forfeit one of your expansion slots. The sacrifices are minimal compared to the doubled or tripled speed. Few ISA accelerator cards are available for the 8088- or 8086-based PC. One popular model was the InBoard 386/PC from Intel Corp. The InBoard 386/PC gave old PC and PC/XT computers the power of an 80386. Unfortunately, Intel discontinued manufacturing the InBoard 386 in early 1992.

If your expansion bus is an EISA (Extended Industry Standard Architecture) or an MCA (MicroChannel Architecture), an accelerator card becomes a more attractive choice. The card works at top speed in the expansion slots of such computers. Why? The buses of these two types of computers operate at breakneck speed. Also, you don't need to remove your old processor. Overall, an accelerator card for a MicroChannel or EISA PC is the easiest and most effective upgrade. If you have an older MicroChannel PC (usually a PS/2), don't hesitate to add an accelerator card. The bus in these computers was designed to embrace accelerator cards. The newer processor can take over your PC as if it was the original processor.

Besides the processor itself, most accelerator cards include extras. Some accelerator cards include their own memory, up to 640K, or a smaller amount of cache memory to speed up communications between the accelerator card and the rest of your computer. Software is also included. The Intel InBoard products, for example, speed up the video display and include software that quickens the hard disk to match the newfound speed. These powerful extras can keep your computer off the scrap heap a little longer.

One warning: Before buying an accelerator card, beware of compatibility problems. Make a call to both companies, computer and accelerator card, to find out about compatibility roadblocks. Also, don't expect miraculous improvements from an accelerator card. Your computer still has the low-speed data bus it always had, and its hard disk and companion controller still operate at their original speeds. For this reason, many companies, like Intel, include some form of disk-caching software that will speed up your disk drives in the accelerated system.

Some accelerator cards run in synchronization with the motherboard clock circuits and others do not. The ones that run in synch with the motherboard are more efficient. However, the asynchronous accelerator cards have the advantage of being compatible with more brands of computers. The synchronous cards only work with PCs that have an 8088 processor running at 4.77 MHz. You cannot install them in any other computer, including "turbo" XT compatibles, unless they can be run at the slower speed.

One popular accelerator card is the SOTA 386si, which is an 8-bit card for use with 8088- and 8086-based PCs and PC/XTs. An asynchronous card, the SOTA 386si is fast, increasing the speed of an 8088-based PC eightfold. It has a 16-MHz 80386SX processor and 16K of cache memory. It also supports version 4.0 of the Lotus/Intel/Microsoft Expanded Memory Specification (LIM EMS 4.0). The SOTA 386si has an optional memory piggyback card, or daughterboard.

This piggyback card attaches to the accelerator card, adding up to 4MB of memory to your computer.

To install an accelerator card:

1. Turn off your computer and remove its case.

   For details on opening your computer, see the procedure in Chapter 3, "Cracking Open the Case."

2. Remove the main processor from the motherboard.

   Sometimes, the accelerator card requires you to install the processor on the accelerator card. Others have you put it away for a rainy day.

3. Plug the accelerator card into an open slot.

   For convenience, select an expansion slot as close to the processor as possible. Remove the expansion slot cover and install the accelerator card.

4. Connect the cable from the accelerator card to the processor socket.

5. Replace your computer's case and return your PC to working order.

6. Turn on your PC.

7. Install any software drivers, if needed.

   For the Kingston Technology SX/Now! product, for example, you must add the line

   ```
   KTCCACHE -E
   ```

   to your AUTOEXEC.BAT startup file. Fortunately, this utility only turns on the card's high-speed cache and does not require any memory.

8. Restart your computer and test your PC.

Look Ma, No Slots!

Accelerator cards for 80286-based computers may not require an expansion slot at all. A variation of the accelerator card allows you to plug a small circuit board into your 80286 socket to transform it into an 80386SX PC (see Figure 7.2). You simply remove your 80286

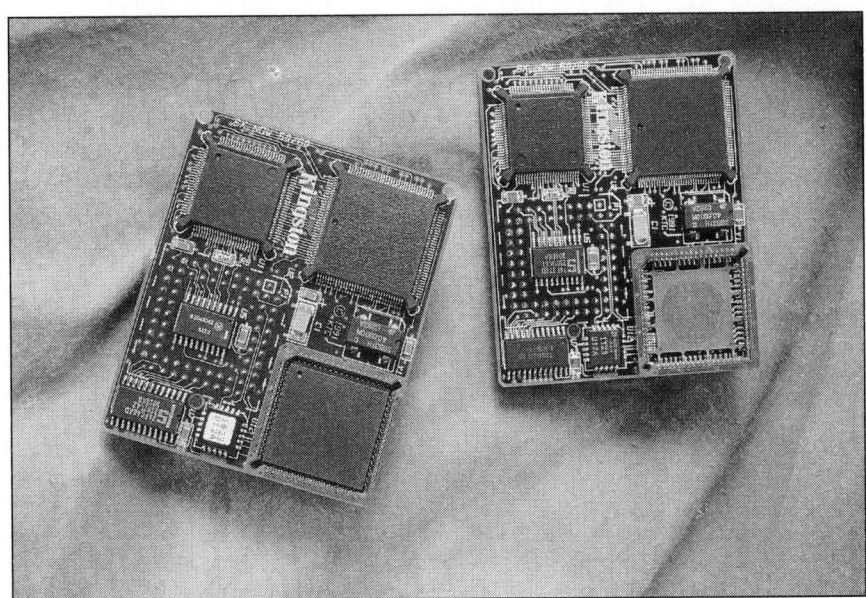

Figure 7.2 Some accelerator cards, such as Kingston Technology's SX/Now!, plug directly into your 80286's processor socket. *(Photo courtesy of Kingston Technology Corp.)*

processor and plug in the circuit board. No expansion slot is required for the upgrade.

Kingston Technology, Cumulus Corp., and SOTA make such cards. Because each motherboard design is different, these cards work with only certain brands of computers. Cumulus Corp. offers its 386SX card for many 80286 computers, including the Compaq Deskpro 286 and Tandy 3000. Kingston Technology's SX/Now provides 20-MHz and 25-MHz 80386SX power to Compaq and IBM PS/2 computers. SOTA offers its Express/386 accelerator for AT computers in 16-, 20-, and 25-MHz versions. These accelerator cards sell for between $300 and $600.

Upgradable PCs

A recent trend in extending the life of a PC is the replaceable processor/memory module. This new technology may make accelerator cards obsolete. In early 1992, Intel introduced speed-doubler, or clock-doubler, technology for 80486 computers. Chips based on this technology come in two versions: DX2 and OverDrive processors. They

Figure 7.3 The DX2 processor provides clock-doubled speed for new computers. *(Photo courtesy of Intel Corp.)*

run at one speed inside the processor and at half that speed when addressing the PC's memory and other components. The technology works on Intel 80486DX and 80486SX processors running at 16, 20, 25, and 33 MHz. There are no OverDrive or DX2 options for 80386 computers.

The DX2 is a type of processor that comes on new PCs (see Figure 7.3). For example, you can buy a new PC with a 80486DX2/50 processor. This processor thinks at 50 MHz inside the processor but talks to the rest of the computer at 25 MHz. An 80486DX2/66 processor is also available, operating at 66 MHz inside the processor and 33 MHz to the rest of the PC.

The OverDrive chip is a processor that replaces the 80486SX processor already in your computer (see Figure 7.4). These chips fit in the vacant 169-pin "performance upgrade socket" that your motherboard already has. (This is also called the 80487SX math coprocessor or OverDrive socket.) Such OverDrive sockets are available to 16- , 20-, and 25-MHz 80486SX computers. Once you plug in the new OverDrive processor, the original processor does no processing.

You can also replace the processor in 25- and 33-MHz 80486DX computers with a 168-pin OverDrive chip. You simply remove the

Figure 7.4 The OverDrive chip from Intel can double the clock speed of your computer; simply plug in the new processor. *(Photo courtesy of Intel Corp.)*

existing processor from its 168-pin socket and replace it. The dizzying speeds of these new replaceable processors may require heat sinks and/or extra cooling fans to dissipate the built-up heat. The unwanted heat can slow down the processor, shorten its life, and cause erratic behavior.

Math Coprocessors

The next best thing to replacing the computer's brains is to give it a calculator. A *math*, or *numeric, coprocessor* will do just that. A math coprocessor is a computer chip that aids the heart of your computer by relieving it of certain mathematical (also called floating point) operations. Not all math operations will use the math coprocessor. Common operations such as addition, subtraction, multiplication and division are done by the processor. For sophisticated math operations — cosines, sines, tangents, square roots — a math coprocessor can speed the number-crunching up to 100 times, boosting overall performance by 200 to 1000 percent.

Unfortunately, not all software programs can benefit from a math coprocessor. They must be written to take advantage of this mathematical speed. Traditionally, spreadsheet, scientific, graphics, and computer-aided design (CAD) software receive a boost from a coprocessor. For example, CAD software requires many calculations to track every dot on your screen. Modeling and simulation software also require tremendous mathematical power. Usually, programs such as word processors do not, although Microsoft Word *for Windows* does support a coprocessor. About one in 10 software programs supports a math coprocessor. If your work involves software that accesses a math coprocessor and you do indeed use sophisticated mathematical functions, a math coprocessor can be a great addition — no pun intended. Often costing less than $150, a math coprocessor becomes a very focused upgrade.

How is a math coprocessor added to your computer? Most computers have a socket — an empty hole — for a math coprocessor, usually next to the main processor. Computers that have an 80486DX processor do not require a math coprocessor; it's already built into the chip. Because of space limitations, some computers don't have a coprocessor socket. Below are the names of the coprocessors needed to assist your main processor:

Processor	Coprocessor
8086	8087
8088	8087
80286	80287
80386SX	80387SX
80386SL	80387SX
80386SLC	80387SX
80386DX	80387DX or Weitek 3167
80486SX	80487SX or Weitek 4167
80486DX	Built-in, no Intel coprocessor needed, or optional Weitek 4167

As you can see, computers based on the 8088 and 8086 microprocessors require an 8087 coprocessor. Systems based on the 80286 require the 80287, and so on.

The type of coprocessor is not the only information you need to order one. You also need to know the speed required by your computer's design. Like your processor, this speed is measured in megahertz (MHz). For example, the 8087 coprocessor comes in three speeds: 5 MHz, 8 MHz, and 10 MHz. Each is designed to match the speed of the computer.

As a rule, a coprocessor's speed must match the speed of the main processor. If you have a 12-MHz 80286, you should order a 12-MHz 80287 coprocessor. In general, if a coprocessor operates at a higher speed than the main processor, it will work without difficulty or error. There is one exception: The 8087 processor must run at the same speed as the main processor. For example, an IBM PC/XT with a 4.77-MHz 8088 processor requires a 5-MHz 8087. Computers that use 80286, 80386, and 80486SX processors do not require a math coprocessor to run at the same speed as the main processor. The design of the motherboard determines at what speed the coprocessor will run. Most computers have the math coprocessor run at the same speed as the main processor. However, do not get a math coprocessor that is slower than your main processor; the coprocessor will fail.

Determining the speed of math coprocessors can be confusing. The 5-MHz 8087 used by typical PCs and PC/XTs usually is labeled by Intel Corp. as the 8087. The 8-MHz 8087 used in the PS/2 Model 30 and Compaq DeskPro is identified as the 8087-2. The 10-MHz version is called the 8087-1. With other coprocessors, finding the speed is easy. Like the system used with processors, the suffix gives the maximum speed rating of the chip. Thus, the 80287-6 runs at up to 6 MHz. An 80387-25 is rated to operate at 25 MHz.

Computers based on the 80286 processor and some early 80386 PCs use the 80287 coprocessor. While the 8087 and 80287 coprocessor look identical — they both fit into a 40-pin socket — the two are not compatible. The 80287 is asynchronous, not necessarily operating at the same speed as the main processor. In most 80286 PCs, the 80287 coprocessor operates more slowly than the main processor, typically at two-thirds of the processor's speed. For example, an 8- MHz IBM PC/AT runs the 80287 coprocessor at 5.33 MHz. Newer 80386-based PCs use 80387 coprocessors, although early 80386 computers had sockets to accept either an 80287 or 80387. Why? The 80387 processor didn't become available until more than a year after the 80386 processor was introduced, leaving the 80287 the only available chip for upgrading early 80386 PCs.

Figure 7.5 The Intel line of math coprocessors gives your computer a mathematical helping hand by relieving it of burdensome calculations. *(Photo courtesy of Intel Corp.)*

There are four major manufacturers of math coprocessors. Intel Corp., manufacturer of most microprocessors, is the leader. Others include Advanced Micro Devices (AMD), Cyrix, and Weitek Corp.

When a Weitek?

An alternative to an Intel or Intel-compatible coprocessor is the Weitek math coprocessor (see Figure 7.6). The Weitek Abacus 3167 (or just Weitek 3167) is for the 80386 PC; the Weitek Abacus 4167 (or Weitek 4167) is for the 80486 PC.

Weitek math coprocessors are designed for high-end computer needs, such as three-dimensional graphics, computer-aided design and machining (CAD/CAM), simulations, and structural analysis. Weitek coprocessors deliver 1.5 to 3 times the performance of an 80387. Although more expensive than an Intel math coprocessor — $350 to $750 for a sliver of silicon — a Weitek coprocessor can be one of the most cost-effective improvements for your workhorse PC. Some animation work, for example, may require an entire eight-hour day to process, even with a conventional math coprocessor. With a Weitek coprocessor, that time may be reduced by several hours.

Figure 7.6 A Weitek math coprocessor is for the most demanding mathematical needs, such as AutoDesk 3D Studio modeling software. *(Photo courtesy of Weitek Corp.)*

Not all computers can handle a Weitek coprocessor. The chip requires a special 112-pin coprocessor socket called the *Extended Math Coprocessor (EMC)* socket. This socket has three rows of holes on each of the four sides. In many computers, this math coprocessor socket accommodates both Intel and Weitek coprocessors. The inner two rows of pins are used by the Intel or compatible coprocessor and the third outer row accommodates the Weitek processor. Other computers, such as the Tandy 4000, support only the Weitek coprocessor. If installing a Weitek coprocessor, be very careful to place the chip in this outer perimeter. Otherwise, you may damage your computer. Please note that even an 80486DX computer, which has its own built-in math coprocessor, can benefit from a Weitek. Some computers have two sockets to use both simultaneously.

Besides having the proper socket, the Weitek coprocessor requires specially written programs to take advantage of its power; it won't work with software written for Intel coprocessors. The Weitek coprocessor works when your computer is operating in *protected mode*, while DOS programs work in *real mode*. To use the Weitek coprocessor, such 32-bit software must use a DOS extender to access memory above the 1MB threshold. In other words, most high-end scientific and CAD programs support the Weitek coprocessor. Before purchasing a Weitek coprocessor, be sure your software will make use of it.

Once a math coprocessor is chosen, installing it is easy. You simply buy the chip, plug it in, and flip a switch or run a setup program to recognize it.

To install a math coprocessor:

1. Turn off your computer and remove its case.

   For details on opening your computer, see the procedure in Chapter 3, "Cracking Open the Case."

2. Locate the coprocessor socket.

   The coprocessor socket is often next to your computer's processor. This socket is usually square, consisting of three rows of pin holes. For 8088/8086 and 80286 computers, the coprocessor socket is rectangular. Don't confuse empty ROM (read-only memory) sockets for the coprocessor socket. The ROM sockets usually come in pairs and are no more than one inch apart. Also, the coprocessor socket generally has more pins: 40 versus 28 for each ROM. Computers that accommodate both an 80287 and 80387 coprocessor have a rectangular socket for the 80287 processor, as well as a square socket of 68 or more connections for the 80387 processor.

3. Remove any expansion cards that prevent you from reaching the coprocessor socket.

   You can avoid bloodied knuckles by removing expansion cards that are in your way. In some cases, you may have to remove your disk drives or power supply to reach the coprocessor socket.

4. Remove the coprocessor from its protective packaging.

   Before touching the coprocessor, touch a piece of metal briefly, such as your computer's metal case, to drain yourself of built-up static electricity.

5. Prepare the coprocessor for installation.

Math coprocessors that are in DIP (dual in-line pin) cases have metal legs that must be bent to fit in the socket. These are usually 8087 and 80287 coprocessors. Math coprocessors for 80386 and 80486 computers do not require such preparation. Slightly bend these legs so they will match the sockets. Grasp the coprocessor between your thumb and forefinger. Place the chip with all of the pins on one side against a firm surface, like a table. Apply enough pressure to bend all the pins on one side so they are perpendicular to the chip body. Turn the chip over and repeat this procedure for the legs on the other side.

6. Place the coprocessor on the socket (see Figure 7.7).

    Align pin 1 on the coprocessor with pin 1 on the socket. To align the pins, be sure the notch on the coprocessor faces the same direction as the notches on other chips in your computer. There should also be a matching notch or other symbol on the coprocessor socket. Other coprocessors indicate pin 1 with a recessed dot directly above or adjacent to the pin. On square math coprocessors, one of the three corners is truncated, indicating pin 1. You may also find a printed or embossed dot above this corner

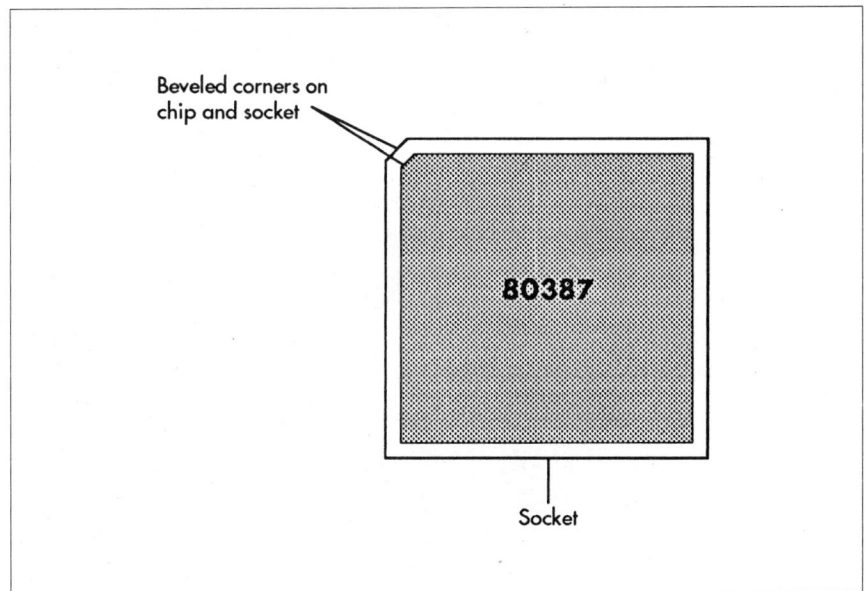

Figure 7.7 The math coprocessor must be placed in the socket so that the beveled corners match.

of the chip. The socket for such chips should show a similar marking on the pin 1 corner. Either the outside edge of the socket is truncated or one corner of the inner edge is angled at 45 degrees.

On some early IBM PC/AT computers, the coprocessor socket was installed backwards, with the notch facing toward the back. Install the coprocessor with its own notch facing forward toward the front of the computer's case.

Many computers accommodate both Weitek and Intel co-processors. Instead of two rows of connections all the way around, the socket has three rows for 112 pins. When fitting an 80387 coprocessor into such a socket, place it into the inner two rows of pins, ignoring the outer row. Once installed, the socket should look the same from all sides; you shouldn't see two rows of pins on any one side. If so, you installed the chip too far over by one row. If you are installing a Weitek coprocessor, all three rows of pins should be covered.

7. Carefully press the coprocessor into its socket. Do not bend any pins.

   Inspect the installation with a flashlight. With DIP-type coprocessors, look for any legs that might have bent under the pressure. If so, remove the coprocessor and straighten the bent legs with the jaws of a pair of pliers.

8. Reinstall any expansion cards you removed.

9. Turn on your computer.

   If the math coprocessor is installed with its notch or beveled edge facing in the wrong direction, your computer will fail on warming up and the chip may be destroyed.

10. Use your setup software or diskette to tell your PC to use the coprocessor.

    Usually, your computer will notice the presence of a math coprocessor and ask you to run a setup program to acknowledge its existence. You often have to run the setup program that is built into your computer or use a setup or reference diskette that came with your computer. Just tell the setup program that you now have a math, or numeric, coprocessor. On XT-type computers, a

DIP (dual in-line pin) switch must be set to indicate a math coprocessor is present.

11. Test your math coprocessor.

Once done, run a software program you know will take advantage of the coprocessor.

12. Replace your computer's case and return your PC to working order.

Upgrading Your BIOS

Your computer is just a conglomeration of electronic and mechanical parts — a hard disk controller here, a memory chip there, and a cooling fan back there. Like the Oz Tin Man, your computer needs a brain.

The Basic Input/Output System, or BIOS, provides the crude brains that gets your computer's components working together (see Figure 7.8). Without it, your computer is simply an overpriced, 40-pound paperweight. You can even add your own brain transplant. A simple $30 to $90 BIOS replacement can give your PC faster performance and more features.

Figure 7.8 Although not well known, the BIOS is what makes your computer IBM-compatible. *(Photo courtesy of American Megatrends Inc.)*

Software on a Chip

The BIOS is a collection of small computer programs embedded into an EPROM (erasable programmable read-only memory) chip or chips, depending on the design of your computer. That collection of programs is the first thing "loaded" when you start your PC even ahead of the operating system. Simply put, the BIOS has three main functions:

1. Tests your computer's components when it is turned on. This is called the Power-On Self-Test, or POST. The POST tests your computer's memory, its motherboard, video adapter, disk controller, keyboard, and other crucial components.

2. Finds the operating system and loads, or "boots" it. This is called the *bootstrap loader routine*. If an operating system is found, it is loaded and given control of your computer.

3. Once an operating system is loaded, the BIOS works with the processor to provide software programs easy access to your computer's specific features. For example, it tells your computer how to work with the video card and hard disk when a software program requires it.

With these responsibilities, the BIOS is like a computerized traffic cop, ensuring your computer's safety when it starts and providing smooth flow for the demands software and DOS place on it.

Any program that works with your computer, usually works through the BIOS. As mentioned earlier, the BIOS is a collection of programs, also called routines. To use a BIOS routine, such as reading a file off your computer, a software program must issue the right *interrupt,* a special instruction to the processor. The interrupt causes the processor to stop in its tracks and start the requested routine. It does this by looking in a table of interrupt vectors to find out where in memory the specific BIOS routine is located. Once the routine is located, it's run.

On AT-type computers, the BIOS has another function; it lets you change your computer's configuration without having to open your computer and set various DIP switches and jumpers. Usually during your computer's warm-up, you can start this built-in setup program to tell your computer about added memory, disk drives, a different video adapter, or a change in date and time.

The BIOS doesn't actually hold this information. Rather, it provides a setup program to write this information to a CMOS (complementary metallic oxide semiconductor). The CMOS is a special type of memory chip that requires little power to store information. Even when your computer is turned off, its memory contents are saved by a trickle of power from a AA or small nickel-cadmium battery. By using a CMOS and the BIOS setup program to access it, you can configure your computer from your keyboard rather than wrestling with a screwdriver. On an XT-type computer, you still must open your computer and set DIP switches and jumpers.

True Compatibility

The BIOS also is the heart of what makes your IBM-compatible computer "compatible." It provides standard rules for using the various electronics inside your computer. The first BIOS debuted on the IBM PC in 1981. If your computer is to be compatible with the PC standard, your BIOS must duplicate the operation of that first BIOS. Of course, manufacturers of "clone" computers cannot copy the IBM BIOS. Like any software program, the BIOS is protected by copyright law. Rather, companies use a BIOS that mimics the operation of the IBM BIOS without copying IBM's code.

Instead of creating their own BIOS, many computer makers buy a BIOS from specialists like American Megatrends Inc. (AMI), Award Software, Microid Research, or Phoenix Technologies Ltd. These companies then usually use an ultraviolet light to "flash" the BIOS code onto programmable chips for use in their computers. Providing BIOS code is a hefty business. Phoenix Technologies, for example, receives about $20 to $30 million each year by selling BIOS chips. With an IBM-compatible BIOS, companies like Gateway 2000, Dell Computers, and Zeos International have been able to offer IBM-compatible computers for years.

Although companies try to mimic the first BIOS, the slippery, evolving PC standard requires the BIOS to adapt to changes in technology. For example, a different BIOS is needed for various computer designs. Each computer motherboard relies on a chip set, which is the motherboard's core. The chip set provides a computer with characteristics that hopefully sets it apart from "the other guy's." Popular chip sets include VLSI, Suntac, Opti, and Chips & Technologies. However, the number of chip sets doubles every year, requiring a BIOS tailored for each.

The BIOS not only provides IBM compatibility but also the ability to recognize some accessories you might add to your computer. The first IBM PC had its BIOS set in stone. Extra programming code couldn't be added to the small domino-sized chips. This limitation posed a problem, since the first PC BIOS didn't expect such things as hard disks or requiring more than 64K of memory. The PC-2, the PC-1's replacement, featured a new BIOS that was flexible, an innovation that continues today.

Let me show you how the new BIOSes are flexible. Imagine you just installed a new VGA video card into one of your computer's expansion slots. As your computer warms up, the BIOS performs its self-test (POST) and accesses the basic BIOS programs. Then, the BIOS seeks any extra BIOS code needed to run that VGA card. The chips containing those extra pieces of BIOS code are not found on your motherboard. Instead, they are on the video card. Once found, these *BIOS extensions*, as they are called, are loaded.

Of course, the process is not perfect. Sometimes, the default address where a card looks for a BIOS routine is already used by another card, making the new card unusable. The DIP switches and jumpers on expansion cards let you reassign the address so the new card works. If you own a PS/2 or any computer that uses the Micro-Channel Architecture (MCA), you don't need to worry about any such hardware conflicts. When the PS/2 was introduced in 1987, IBM revised its BIOS to support MCA. One advantage was that jumpers or DIP switches no longer had to be set. All configuring of expansion cards was done by software.

Another drawback of BIOS extensions is not only possible hardware conflicts but simply the valuable memory they occupy. A portion of your computer's memory between 640K and 1024K is reserved for BIOS extensions. If you have an 80386 or 80486 computer and DOS 5.0, you can reclaim the unused portions of this memory for your other software. However, BIOS extensions may leave little room for this reclaimed memory.

There are good reasons for expansion cards to use BIOS extensions. One reason is speed; the basic BIOS routines can be slow. For example, all IBM BIOS routines place characters one at a time onto your computer display. It is much faster to bypass the BIOS and blast this text onto the screen. Also, your use of hardware may be restricted by the BIOS. For example, an expansion card may let you format a floppy disk for use by a different computer system, such as an Apple Macintosh. However, the basic BIOS routines restrict you to reading, writing, and formatting disks with the standard IBM disk formats. BIOS extensions let the expansion card overcome these hurdles. Today, many hardware manufacturers enhance or bypass the BIOS by writing their own programs to control their products.

When to Upgrade

Adding a new BIOS can allow you to use new accessories for your PC. With a new BIOS you can use programs and hardware you otherwise couldn't use or could use only with difficulty and frustration. Yet upgrading your BIOS is no panacea. It may not solve some inherent incompatibilities or limitations of your PC. Some people have misconceptions about the BIOS. For example, an XT-type computer doesn't always require a new BIOS when a high-density diskette drive is added. The necessary BIOS code is often found on the floppy disk controller that is connected to the new drive. Likewise, you can't add a feature like shadow RAM if your motherboard design doesn't support it. (Shadow RAM is a feature that copies some of the BIOS programs into your PC's faster memory rather than the slower ROM. or read-only memory.)

So when would you want to update your BIOS? Since the BIOS is the "glue" between hardware and software, it can play an important part in error-free or increased performance of your PC. Following are 15 reasons to update your BIOS.

1. **To support DOS 5.0.** With DOS 5.0, you can load device drivers into the High Memory Area (HMA), giving you more memory for your other work. However, some peripherals (hard disks, video cards, and so on) may not work properly when their drivers are "loaded high." A new BIOS can overcome these problems. It is often recommended that BIOS chips prior to 1989 be replaced to support these features.

2. **To remove conflicts with *Microsoft Windows* and *OS/2* software.** According to industry sources, this is the single most popular reason why people buy a new BIOS. The demands *Windows* and *OS/2* place on your computer hardware causes incompatibilities and "glitches." The problems are often erratic, varying from one PC to another, but common complaints are the inability

to use Windows' 386 Enhanced mode or frequent "locking up" of one's computer.

3. **To support high-density or new disk drives.** If you want to use the new 2.88-megabyte disk drives with your AT-type computer, you'll need an updated BIOS. Likewise, an AT may need a newer BIOS to support 1.44MB drives. (Some PC makers did not equip early AT clones with the newer BIOS chips to support the high-density drive.) You can check your BIOS setup program or owner's manual to see if your computer supports these higher-density drives.

Once the proper BIOS upgrade is installed, adding a new disk drive is as simple as selecting the correct drive from the setup program. For XT-type computers, adding a 3.5-inch or high-density (1.2MB) 5.25-inch disk drive often does not require a new BIOS. The floppy disk controller for such a drive usually provides the needed BIOS code. However, a new BIOS often allows you to use the existing controller.

4. **To support more and newer types of hard disks.** The BIOS contains a table of possible hard disk drives, including the heads, sectors, and cylinders of each. This is called the *drive table*. The BIOS uses this table to recognize the hard disk. If your hard disk isn't in the table, you're out of luck.

In 1984, IBM's PC/AT BIOS recognized only 15 types of hard disks. This drive table is limited in size. The first 24 entries often match those in the IBM BIOS. The remaining entries vary from one BIOS manufacturer to another. To support larger and newer hard drives, such as the popular IDE (integrated drive electronics) models, the BIOS may need to be updated.

How do you tell you need a new BIOS? An IDE drive may be added using your current BIOS if the BIOS supports a newer feature that lets you "define" your drive. That is, it lets you enter the characteristics of your drive. With AMI BIOS, drive type 47 is reserved for this user-defined drive. With a Phoenix BIOS, you can define drive types 48 and 49. However, if you are adding a gargantuan one-gigabyte or larger drive (1024MB), there may not be enough room for the digits required. If you cannot define your drive and the new hard disk you want to add is not listed in the drive table, it's time for a new BIOS. Recent BIOS chips can automatically sense the characteristics of IDE drives so you don't even have to crack open a manual. For example, pressing the question mark key (?) interrogates the drive.

5. **To prevent data loss and improve drive performance.** Some older BIOS chips (pre-April 1990) may have timing problems with IDE drives. This could cause some data loss. By supporting newer drives, the BIOS can use the proper timing for your hard disk. This gives you the fastest speed, but may not be noticeable.

6. **To provide compatibility with a Novell network.** Novell NetWare software looks for a specific hard disk in the BIOS drive table. If the drive type isn't listed, the computer will not work with the network. A new BIOS can provide an updated list of the drives available. The BIOS vendor may have to hard-code the drive parameters into the chip.

7. **To support enhanced keyboards (101/102-key).** Sometimes, you may want to use an enhanced keyboard with 101 or 102 keys. Occasionally, the BIOS plays a role in its compatibility.

8. **To speed up your keyboard.** Many BIOSes let you change the typematic (repeat) rate of your keyboard as well as the delay before a keystroke is repeated.

9. **To provide better power-on diagnostics testing.** Today's BIOSes provide faster and more thorough testing of your computer as it warms up. During the Power-On Self-Test (POST), various components are checked. These include your PC's central processing unit (CPU), system timer, the video display adapter and its built-in memory, the computer's main memory, the keyboard, and all disk drives. If something is wrong, you often will hear a series of beeps and see a brief message, which helps you diagnose the problem. However, most PCs beep once or twice to signal the end of this start-up test. Some BIOSes even have extras such as testing of your hard disk's surface and low-level formatting.

10. **To support VGA (virtual graphics array) monitors.** Sometimes, your BIOS may have to be updated to support VGA. Some video cards require a BIOS after a certain date.

11. **To provide more than two serial (COM) and parallel (LPT) ports.** Sometimes, a BIOS supports extra serial ports (up to four) and parallel ports (up to three). These extra serial and parallel ports can be used for mice, modems, or printers. For example, if you need to redirect printing from LPT1 (your first parallel printer port) to COM3 (your third serial port), you would need to get an updated BIOS.

    In most cases, your computer can accept extra serial devices without buying a new BIOS. For example, many modems can be configured for COM3 or COM4. The communications software often supports those extra ports by writing programming code directly for the modem, bypassing the BIOS. Check your software before buying a new BIOS.

12. **To provide password security.** Among the new bells and whistles of some BIOS models is a feature to provide password security to your computer. You enter the password each time you start or reboot your computer. If you don't know the password, you can't get in.

13. **To keep the right date and time by supporting daylight savings time.**

14. **To change drives to boot from.** Some BIOSes let you specify which drive the computer should check first for the operating system. Usually, a computer first checks the floppy disk drives (A: then B:, if present) and then drive C:. By changing the boot-up sequence to drive C: then drive A:, you can quickly start your computer and save wear-and-tear on your disk drives. Some BIOS products even let you swap the order of floppy disk drives, so that drive A: becomes B: and vice versa. This can be handy in rebooting your computer from a different-sized diskette in drive B: or easing the installation of software that seeks drive A: but requires the size and format of drive B:. (In this last case, you can use the DOS ASSIGN command to swap drives temporarily.)

15. **To support up to four floppy disk drives.** Some newer BIOS manufacturers support up to four disk drives. Why would you need four disk drives? You could have a newer 2.88MB drive, a 1.44MB drive, a 1.2MB drive, and a 360K drive. One advantage

of having a 360K drive is that you can confidently read a 360K 5.25-inch disk formatted on a low-density drive. (Often, information saved to a 360K disk formatted in a low-density drive cannot be read or altered by a high-density 1.2MB drive.) You can have four floppy disk drives without a new BIOS, but then drivers would need to be loaded.

Checking the Age of Your BIOS

Before you rush out to buy a new BIOS, you may want to find out the age of your current one. With a BIOS, the date is as important as the version number is for your software programs. The date is encoded into the BIOS chip itself. Instead of opening up your computer or buying a special utility program, you can find out the date with a simple DOS program. Run the DEBUG program located in your DOS directory.

To find the age of your BIOS:

1. From the DOS prompt (C:\) directory, type:

```
DEBUG [Enter]
```

A hyphen (-) prompt appears on the left side of the screen.

2. Next, type:

```
D F000:FFF0 [Enter]
```

A row of numbers appears. The BIOS date should appear in the right-hand column. Write down the date.

3. Exit DEBUG.
To exit DEBUG, type:

```
Q [Enter]
```

You can also create a BASIC program to display the BIOS date. Simply enter these four lines:

```
10  DEF SEG = &HF000
20  FOR x = &HFFF5 TO &HFFFF
30  PRINT CHR$(PEEK(x));
40  NEXT
```

Replacing the BIOS

Like a computer manufacturer, you too can buy a BIOS chip. A handful of mail-order companies specialize in replacement BIOS chips. You need to provide certain information about your computer, including

- **Size of the BIOS chips.** To determine this look for a number printed directly on the chip. It may or may not be covered by a label. For example, the number may be "27C128."

- **The chip set, or design, used on your motherboard.** You can discover the chip set by looking for a large square chip about the same size as the processor. Record the numbers off the chips. Some manufacturers include VLSI, Suntac, Opti, and Chips & Technologies. If no chip set is found, your computer may use discrete logic. To determine what BIOS you can use, ask your BIOS salesperson.

If you currently use an AMI BIOS, simply record the reference number displayed as your computer warms up.

When you order a BIOS upgrade, it usually means installing two chips. However, newer computers may require only one. The street price of a BIOS chip varies with the type of computer and manufacturer. Some BIOS makers provide more features than others. Below are approximate street prices:

Model	Street price
PC & PC/XT	$60–$80
80286	$80–$90
80386SX & 80386DX	$70–$130
80486SX & 80486DX	$80–$130

Sometimes the keyboard controller BIOS chip (chips #8042, #8242, or #8742) has to be replaced as well, since it is a partner to the BIOS. This controller costs $20 to $40. Note that true IBM PC/AT models 5162, 5170, and 5170/339 have it soldered to the motherboard.

To replace your BIOS:

Replacing the BIOS is relatively easy. Installation usually requires removing the current BIOS and inserting the replacement chip(s) in the same slots and then running the BIOS setup program.

1. Before replacing, gather information about your computer.

    You should first go into your BIOS setup program (called CMOS) and print the screens or jot down the facts about your current computer, including the amount of memory, video display, and — most important — the various parameters for your hard disk, like the number of heads, sectors, and cylinders. You will need to reenter this information after the new BIOS is installed. To enter your BIOS setup program, you often have to press the Delete key or F1 as your computer warms up. If you have an older PC, your BIOS may not have a setup program. Instead, collect the information about your PC, and about your hard disk.

2. Remove the cover from your computer's system unit.

3. Locate the BIOS chip(s).

    The BIOS chip is usually a 28-pin DIP type chip. In other words, it is a rectangular chip that has 14 metal legs on each side. These legs are inserted into a socket on your motherboard. XT-type computers use a single BIOS chip while most AT-type computers use either one or two. These BIOS chip(s) could be anywhere. Older computers place them in the center. Newer 80386 and 80486 computers place the BIOS near the processor. For example, my single BIOS chip is a 28-pin DIP chip located on the front of the motherboard near the math coprocessor socket. The keyboard BIOS chip is near the connector where the keyboard is plugged in.

4. Remove any expansion cards that prevent you from reaching the BIOS.

    Set the expansion cards aside on some antistatic packaging.

5. Remove the old BIOS chip(s).

    Note where the BIOS chip(s) are located and how they are positioned. A small notch or other marking indicates the end of the chip where pin one is located. If your computer uses two BIOS chips, one may be marked either HI or ODD, or simply H or O. The other will be marked LO, L, E, or EVEN.

    A small screwdriver can be used to gently pry the BIOS chip from each end, although two extra metal expansion slot covers or a specialized chip puller are ideal for removing the chips. Do not put your prying tools under the socket itself — you could damage it or the motherboard. To avoid bending or breaking the BIOS chip's metal legs, alternate prying up each side until the chip is free and then lift the chip straight up.

6. Remove the new BIOS chip(s) from its protective packaging.

   Before touching each BIOS chip, touch a piece of metal briefly, such as your computer's metal case, to drain yourself of built-up static.

7. Install the new BIOS chip(s).

   Carefully plug in the new BIOS chip(s). Be sure you replace the HI or ODD chip and the LO or EVEN chip in its correct socket. Make sure the chips are facing the right direction. If you plug in the BIOS incorrectly, it will be destroyed. You'll know when that happens — a small flash of light is emitted. If any metal legs get bent, carefully remove the chip and use long-nose pliers to straighten them. If you are installing a BIOS chip for an XT-type computer, a small circuit board is often installed to convert the 28-pin BIOS chip to the 24-pin socket. Also, such early PCs have four ROM chips that contain the BASIC programming language for cassette players (cassette BASIC). These must be removed.

8. Reinstall any expansion cards you removed.

9. Replace your computer's case and return your PC to working order.

10. Turn on your computer.

   For AT-type computers, the BIOS will probably report an incorrect configuration and force you to enter its setup program to make the changes. You may have to enter the date, time, the type of drives, and type of monitor you are using. After saving the correct information, your computer should restart itself and behave normally with the new BIOS. For XT-type computers, nothing has to be done.

   Newer BIOS techniques allow the BIOS to be updated with Intel Corp.'s flash memory. This means you can upgrade your BIOS without having to open your computer. Flash memory is similar to the

EPROMs used to store the BIOS, except that it can be erased and reprogrammed with software. In other words, you can upgrade your BIOS from a floppy diskette. Upgrading your computer's processor or one of its supporting cast may not be for everyone, but it may be necessary to partake in the rich features of today's newest hardware and software. Instead of coping with laggardlike speed or older software, a new component or two can keep the lid from shutting prematurely on your PC's coffin.

8
The Motherboard: No Guts, No Glory

The motherboard is your computer's main circuit board. It contains your computer's processor, memory, and several other crucial components. In other words, the motherboard forms the foundation for your entire computer (see Figure 8.1).

The decision to replace the motherboard is a difficult one, with both pros and cons. The biggest drawbacks are the time and technical savvy required. Unlike other improvements, a motherboard replacement requires you to remove all expansion cards, disconnect all cables, extract all disk drives, and remove the power supply.

Basically, if you are comfortable installing an internal hard disk in your computer, you can handle installing a new motherboard. If not, you may want to add an accelerator card or extra memory (covered in Chapters 6 and 7). These improvements may be a better boon to your computer than facing the unknown. However, such improvements bear their own problems; you may have to load memory-hogging device drivers — small software programs — to run the accelerator card or face incompatibility with another piece of hardware. When you replace the motherboard, you don't have to worry about matching anything to your computer because you're essentially replacing the whole thing.

The benefits of adding a new motherboard may outweigh any concerns. For example, there may be two reasons for you to replace your motherboard:

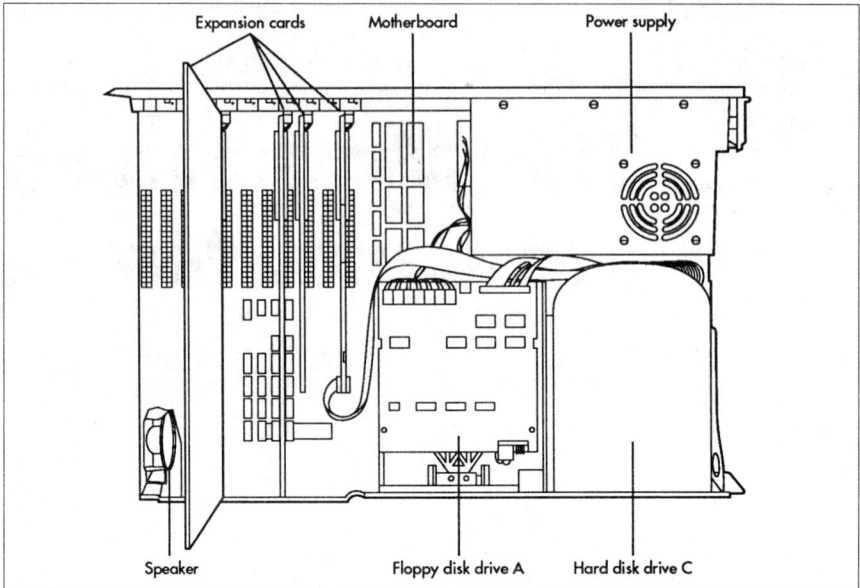

Figure 8.1 The motherboard forms the foundation of your computer by holding expansion cards, memory chips, and your computer's "brain" — the processor.

1.   Your current motherboard is dead or dying.

2.   You want to increase the speed and enhance the features of your computer.

   If you find yourself in the first category, you may have no other options. Replacing your motherboard essentially gives you a new computer in the old box. You not only get a new processor but also faster memory and new features (such as password protection). If you find yourself in the second group, you must be willing to invest the time to reap the fruits of such new speed and features. For example, if you want to run Microsoft Windows in its deluxe 386 Enhanced mode, you need an 80386-based computer. Replacing your 80286-based motherboard with an 80386 model is about the only remaining option.

   Installing a new motherboard is very economical, costing as little as $75 (memory extra) and rarely more than $500. Otherwise, your computer case, disk drives, power supply, video card, monitor, and other components usually can be used with it. In one installation, a new motherboard can give you access to software you couldn't run before, greater speed, and more memory.

Replacing the motherboard is also preferable to endless patching of an outdated computer. The computer may become such a hodge-podge assembly of components that scuttling the motherboard may be a better fate than continuing with such a Frankenstein-like creation. As you continue to upgrade your computer, you may encounter hidden incompatibilities and problems.

Although replacing your motherboard will greatly improve your computer's speed, there still are some bottlenecks. Certainly, the new or faster microprocessor and any extra memory will provide faster performance. For example, you may add the horsepower required to run Windows, but your CGA monitor won't work with it. Likewise, some older computers may not accept a standard-sized motherboard, thus requiring a new case.

An outdated power supply rated at 135 or 150 watts should be replaced with at least 200 watts to provide ample, "clean" power to the new motherboard. If you're considering a fast 80486 motherboard, consider a power supply with extra cooling abilities: the extra cooling can extend the life of this processor. A new power supply with a fan that spins only as fast as needed to dissipate the heat will let your PC operate quietly.

The biggest bottleneck to a new motherboard is the hard disk. The original hard disk may slow the new processor to a crawl. Of course, you could always purchase a new hard disk (discussed in Chapter 9 "Storage: It's a Hard Life"). One inexpensive remedy is to use a disk-caching utility. This software program will place a part of your hard disk into your computer's memory where it can be accessed up to 100 times faster. As you use your computer, the disk cache constantly changes what it is holding in memory, always trying to second-guess what you want next . Popular disk-caching programs include Super PC-Kwik from Multisoft Corp. and SMARTDrive, which comes free with Microsoft Windows and DOS 5.0.

If you are replacing an 80286-based motherboard with an 80836 or 80486 motherboard, you have a lesser chance of facing such bottle-necks since the speed improvement is not that outlandish. In this situation, you're undertaking more of an incremental upgrade, rather than a wholesale, dramatic refurbishing of an older or outmoded PC. Therefore, the case and power supply, and possibly even the hard disk, will work perfectly well with either the 80386 or 80486 motherboard.

The Guts of the Mother-board

There are three types of motherboards: *standard*, *active*, and *passive*. The standard motherboard contains all the electronic circuitry required for your computer, including the processor and memory. The standard motherboard is the most common type sold.

The passive backplane motherboard contains all the expansion slots the computer might need to accept expansion cards, like a video card. The passive backplane motherboard has no place for a processor or memory. Instead, the processor is placed on an expansion card and plugged in. The advantage is that your computer can later be easily upgraded. The active backplane motherboard is similar to the passive backplane motherboard, except that there are sockets for memory chips on it. Some variations of it allow you to put the chip set and even read-only memory (ROM) on it. An active backplane motherboard can be troublesome because its processor requires its own version of some components.

Most of the computer chips are soldered to the motherboard and require little attention. Here are the important parts on a motherboard:

- **Processor.** The processor is your computer's "brain." It is the number one determining factor for how fast your computer is. The processor may be an 8088, 8086, 80286, 80386, 80486, or some variation. The processor also works at a certain speed, which is measured in megahertz (MHz). With a new motherboard, you primarily are trying to get the next-higher processor or one that is faster. For example, you can purchase a 20-MHz 80286 motherboard for about $75 to replace a 10-MHz 80286. Or, you can purchase an 80386SX motherboard to replace an 80286 motherboard. The new processor not only provides more speed but can let you run programs you couldn't run before. For example, some software programs require an 80386 or higher processor. If you have an 80286 motherboard in your computer, you may want to replace it with an 80386 version.

- **Random access memory (RAM).** Your computer relies on several computer chips for its working memory. When you use your computer, the current program and your work are stored in RAM. Some motherboards hold only so much memory. For example, some computers hold only 640 kilobytes, or K, of memory, the amount of memory available to your typical software program. Replacing your motherboard with a newer model may allow you to have more memory, up to 32MB (more than 32,768K!). This memory can be used to run programs you couldn't run before (like *Microsoft Windows*), speed up your computer with a disk cache or RAM disk, or free up more of your first 640K of memory by loading parts of the operating system into memory above that.

- **Read-only memory (ROM).** Your computer's motherboard has a handful of ROM chips on it. The most important ones contain the BIOS (Basic Input/Output System). The BIOS is a small program that is put inside one or two ROM chips. The BIOS is a crucial part in your computer; it is the "boss" that ties all your computer's parts together. It recognizes and remembers new disk drives and memory and it handles demands from your software programs to use various parts of your computer. The BIOS also helps set the date and time in your computer's clock. A replacement motherboard usually comes with the ROM BIOS chip already installed. The new BIOS chip may give you access to functions you didn't have with your older motherboard, such as password protection to keep others off your computer.

- **Expansion slots.** Expansion cards — like a video card — plug into slots on the motherboard called expansion slots. Between six and eight slots, depending on the type of PC you own, are found in the upper-left quadrant of the motherboard. These expansion slots come in two sizes: 8-bit and 16-bit. XT-type computers have only 8-bit slots, limiting you to certain types of expansion cards. AT-type computers have 16-bit expansion slots. Having 16-bit slots lets your expansion cards work faster with the rest of the motherboard.

It Won't Fit

If you replace your entire motherboard, the most important concern is size. The new motherboard must match the layout and size of your computer's case.

Basically, motherboards come in two sizes: XT (8.5 by 13.5 inches or smaller) and AT (12 by 13.5 inches or smaller). Because of their smaller size, XT motherboards are also called "baby AT" motherboards. If you own a genuine PC/XT or PC/AT, finding a motherboard is easy, since these computers use these standard sizes. Most other PCs also use the standard XT- and AT-sized motherboards. What matters is that the new motherboard isn't bigger than the space you have inside your case. Generally, these boards come drilled with enough holes that you can find a match for the posts and standoffs that hold your current motherboard (see Figure 8.2). The location of the keyboard connector is also a concern, although you can use a drill to create a new opening in the back of your case if the new keyboard connector doesn't match the position of the connector on the old motherboard. Oddly enough, the original IBM PCs use a different size motherboard. They require either a special replacement motherboard or a new case, which costs under $100.

IMPORTANT: Use a tape measure to find which size motherboard will work in your PC. Check your motherboard size in Appendix A: "PC Bio."

XT motherboards typically are for 8088- and 8086-based computers. AT motherboards are for 80286-, 80386-, and 80486-based computers. While most XT-sized motherboards are designed to fit in place

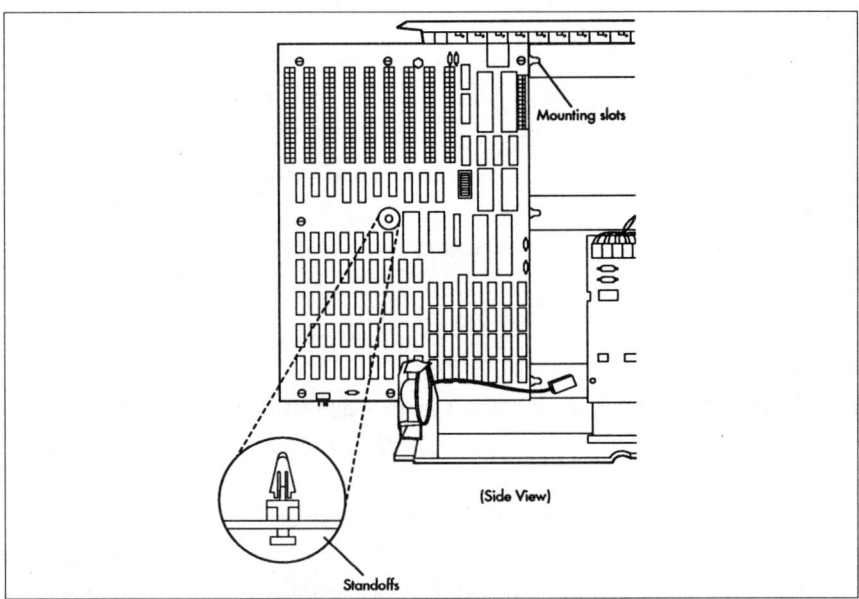

Figure 8.2 Plastic standoffs suspend the motherboard above the metal case.

of an AT-sized board, the reverse is rarely possible because of constraints in case size. In other words, order an AT-sized motherboard only if your old PC has one. In other cases, you'll want an XT-sized board.

Even smaller motherboards are available. This smaller size may make the motherboard more difficult to install because it requires different screw placement than standard-sized boards. Other computers, such as those from Compaq, Epson, NEC, Hewlett-Packard, ALR, and AST, use odd-sized motherboards. With these odd-sized computers, you have three options:

1. You may still be able to use a standard-sized motherboard in these computers but you may have to drill or saw part of the case to make it fit. If so, ensure all metal shavings are removed before installing the new motherboard. If not, these particles could quickly short-circuit and destroy the motherboard.

2. Like the IBM PC, replace the case and power supply to accommodate the new motherboard. Other components — the disk drives, input/output card, video card — can be salvaged for the new motherboard and case.

3. Try to find a motherboard that fits in your uniquely designed computer.

Don't worry about the spacing between expansion slots. All computers except IBM's original 1981 PC use an 0.8-inch spacing for their expansion slots. This same dimension is almost universal in replacement motherboards.

Watch Out There are a few roadblocks to replacing your motherboard, especially if you are adding an AT-type motherboard to your XT-type computer. If you are moving your computer from an 8088- or 8086-based motherboard to an 80286- or 80386-based motherboard, you will need to modify your keyboard or order a new one. The new motherboards use a different keyboard signal. Many keyboards, however, have a switch that converts them from XT to AT operation.

The expansion card that runs the hard disk in an XT-type computer is different than those used with an AT-type motherboard. In an XT-type computer, the hard drive controller contains information about the drive. With AT-type motherboards, this hard drive information is contained on the motherboard itself in the BIOS chip. To use the XT-type controller with your new motherboard, you must tell the BIOS that you have no hard drive at all. This way, the motherboard won't interfere with the drive controller. A second solution is to re-place your controller with an AT-style (16-bit data transfer) control-ler. This should double the speed of your hard disk since the 16-bit controller can "push" information between the hard disk and the motherboard at twice the speed of the XT's 8-bit controller.

Many replacement motherboards have built-in input/output (I/O) ports. These I/O ports may include parallel, serial, and game ports. The parallel ports are used for connecting to printers, the serial ports are often used for attaching mice and modems, and the game ports are for using joysticks. The built-in I/O ports pose two pitfalls: im-proper fit and hardware conflicts. These built-in I/O ports may not match the holes in your case. Although you can fix this problem with an electric drill or hacksaw, you'd be better off with a motherboard that uses the conventional I/O ports that are installed into the expan-sion slots.

Another possible downfall is hardware conflicts. If you already have these I/O ports on an expansion card you are bringing from the original computer, you must be careful the two sets of ports are not fighting each other. For example, you should disable one set of the parallel ports to avoid having two LPT1s (the name for the first parallel port). If both the motherboard and the expansion card are fighting for the same parallel port, neither will work. Most ports can be either switched off or reassigned. For example, the second or third parallel port can be changed to LPT2 and LPT3, respectively.

XT-type computers have a real-time clock on an I/O expansion card, and the AT-type motherboard has the clock built in. If you transfer such a board from an XT, try to switch off its clock to prevent conflicts. Also, remove any software driver — a small computer pro-gram — that runs the clock from your CONFIG.SYS and/or AUTOEXEC.BAT files. With a clock built into the new motherboard, you no longer will need the software driver.

One last pitfall is an inadequate power supply. Some older XT-type computers have small 135- or 150-watt power supplies. To support the new motherboard, get one with at least 200-watts. A new motherboard requires that extra power to give you the increased capability you need.

Choosing a Motherboard

When you chose a new motherboard, the first consideration is the processor. This choice boils down to two factors: your budget and your software.

For the budget minded, a 20-MHz 80286 motherboard can be purchased for under $75, almost doubling the speed of most other 80286 computers. High-end motherboards can cost you several hundred dollars. My recommendation is to buy as much horsepower as you can now so the motherboard replacement will satisfy your needs for as long as possible.

The type of software you run or may run is also a crucial factor. For example, if you want to run Windows software, you should opt for a motherboard with an 80386SX, 80386DX, or 80486 processor on it. The choice will be how much you can afford. For standard word processing and spreadsheet applications, an 80286 or 80386SX processor is ample. If you require strong graphics, desktop publishing, or computer design work, then aim for a fast 80386 or 80486 processor. Remember that a faster processor is no panacea. A new motherboard will not speed up your aging hard disk. Putting a jet engine on a horse carriage just makes the wheels fall off.

Below are listed some basic differences among different processors, starting with the low-end 80286 to the advanced 80486DX.

80386SX over 80286

With the 80386SX processor, you can use *Windows, DESQview,* or other multitasking software to run several programs at the same time. The 80386SX also accommodates advanced memory management features found in DOS 5.0, QEMM-386, 386Max, Memory Commander, DR DOS 6.0, and others, to move memory-resident programs out of the first 640K of memory used by your main program. However, these utilities include 80286 versions (like QEMM's QRAM) that provide the same benefits. The 80386SX also understands 32-bit instructions that are used by the next generation of operating systems, including OS/2 2.0 and Windows NT.

80386DX over 80386SX

The 80386DX has a full 32-bit bus that doubles the speed of data moving inside your computer. This especially improves the performance of software that moves a lot of data, such as graphics or database programs. The 80386DX also supports higher clock speeds, measured in megahertz (MHz). This higher clock speed — up to 40-MHz — quickens your computer work.

80486SX over 80386DX

The 80486SX has a more efficient design for better performance at the same or slower clock speed, which benefits all software. The 80486SX also has an 8K built-in memory cache for faster performance. Future multiuser, multitasking software may use the 80486SX instruction set to provide extra features. The 80486SX can later be upgraded with an OverDrive processor, which doubles the speed of the computer.

80486DX over 80486SX

The 80486DX has a built-in math coprocessor that speeds number-intensive software, such as animation, statistical, spreadsheet, and computer-aided design software. The 80486DX also comes in faster clock speeds, up to 66 MHz. Like the 80486SX, a new processor can be added that doubles the speed of the computer.

Don't Forget the Extras

Besides getting a new processor, you can also get extra memory on your motherboard. If you are using Microsoft *Windows*, get at least 8MB. If not, get at least 4MB RAM. The extra memory can be used for a disk cache or with a memory manager program like *386Max* from Qualitas or *QEMM* from Quarterdeck. These programs free up more of your conventional memory for your main programs by loading the operating system, device drivers, and other crucial software out of the way.

The capacity and speed of this memory is another important concern. Try to get a motherboard that supports up to 32MB or 64MB using an array of eight or 16 SIMM sockets. Also, motherboards are designed to take memory chips of particular speeds, rated in nanoseconds (ns), or billionths of a second. Most 80386DX and 80486 motherboards use chips rated between 60 and 80 ns, with faster clock speeds requiring faster memory. It's possible for a motherboard to use slower memory chips, but your computer may be slowed by the extra wait (or "do-nothing") states needed to accommodate this slow memory. Therefore, trying to save money by purchasing the slower chips may not help you at all. Stick to the recommended chip speeds.

Buying a Mother-board

Once you have decided what processor to get on the motherboard, you have to choose from several brands, with more added daily. A few manufacturers have been around for years, such as AMI, Hauppauge, Mylex, and Micronics. When ordering, be sure you can get a refund if the new motherboard doesn't fit properly into the case. You also reduce your risk with a one-year parts-and-labor warranty. A 15 percent restocking fee is common for nondefective returns, but you can find many places that sell motherboards with no-questions-asked, money-back guarantees and no restocking fee.

You want to buy from a manufacturer that provides good before- and after-sales support. See how well the salesperson steers you to the best motherboard for your needs.

- Do they give good answers to your performance questions?

- Can they tell you what size motherboard you need without you dismantling your computer?

- Do they know the details about maximum memory and the existence of a memory cache?

If the salesperson doesn't answer all your questions, move on to the company's technical support staff. Their answers will indicate how well you may receive competent technical support later. If you like what you hear, ask if the company can mail you a list of specifications on the motherboards in which you are interested. You can pick up a lot from the details of these "spec sheets." Although unlikely, it also would be advantageous to see a few pages from their installation instructions. Unfortunately, most motherboard manuals are skimpy.

An important part of a motherboard is the ROM BIOS, mentioned earlier. It pays to stick with a well-known BIOS brand because the BIOS largely determines compatibility of your PC-compatible. Well-known BIOS companies include American Megatrends Inc. (AMI), Award, Quadtel, Microid Research, and Phoenix. Because the BIOS is more or less a software program, ask the salesperson about its features. Can you access the built-in setup program with a hotkey? Does the hard disk table support custom drive entries in case your drive isn't listed? Does it provide password protection, support for more than two diskette drives, and more? Also important, find out the date of the BIOS. If it is more than a year old, ask for a newer one. The newer the BIOS, the better your odds for complete compatibility with today's software and hardware. I once ordered a motherboard with a two-year-old BIOS chip on it. Although it worked, it did not provide some of the nice bells and whistles I have on a newer version.

Here are some tips for shopping for a new motherboard:

- **Physical appearance.** Examine the copper traces (connections) with a magnifying glass. Do they have ragged edges? Look at where these traces bend. A high-quality motherboard has traces with no sharp angles and preferably smooth, rounded corners.

- **Ground planes.** Hold the motherboard up to the light. If you can't see through, the motherboard may have several layers. The more layers, the more sophisticated the board. A multilayered board has several layers of traces — both top and bottom — sandwiched in between the outer layers. A good motherboard has a ground plane in one of the inner layers to reduce electromagnetic interference from the layers of high-speed circuitry. This ground plane improves the performance of your motherboard.

- **Memory sockets.** Select a motherboard that allows at least 4MB of dynamic random access memory, or DRAM. This memory is your computer's working memory. If you intend to use *Microsoft Windows*, try to get a motherboard that supports up to 32MB. There are three types of memory sockets: DIP, SIP, SIMM. Your motherboard may be able to accept more than one, possibly allowing you to use memory chips from your current motherboard. Don't count on this, though; often, the memory from your original motherboard is too slow for your new one. The manual that comes with your new motherboard recommends what speed memory, measured in nanoseconds (ns), you'll need. The most popular socket today is the SIMM type. These single in-line memory modules allow you to install several memory chips in one movement. Conversely, some newer 80286 motherboards support both SIP (single in-line pin) and DIP (dual in-line package) memory.

- **Static Memory.** An 80386SX and higher computer gets some of its speed from a small block of high-speed memory chips. These chips are called *static random access memory*, or *SRAM*, and are collectively called a *memory cache*. This memory cache is used to have more data poised to be fed to the computer's processor. Typical cache sizes range from 64K to 256K. An 80486 processor has an 8K cache already built in, but can also benefit from such a cache. Caching provides a significant increase in speed. An 80386 computer that has caching is about 40 to 50 percent faster than without it. Some computer manufacturers have combined the affordability of 80386SX computers with caching to provide a delicate balance of power and low price.

- **Chip set design.** The chip set is the heart of your motherboard. What kinds of chips are used? Are there lots of little components or just a few very large chips? The best boards usually use VLSI (very large-scale integration) circuits, requiring fewer parts. Such boards are superior because the fewer parts, the fewer chances for any one of them to fail.

- **Optional chips.** Usually, motherboards come with no DRAM memory chips (0K). However, an 80386 or faster motherboard that supports static RAM often includes some or all of the SRAM chips. Some motherboards may be offered without the processor, which is also called the CPU, or central processing unit. Be careful; the CPU on a high-speed 80386 or a 80486 motherboard costs at least $100. Include the cost of any chips you must add when comparing prices of various motherboards.

Installing a Motherboard

Once you have your motherboard, extra memory chips, and CPU (if one wasn't included in the motherboard), replace your motherboard.

To install your new motherboard:

1. Back up your hard drive.

   Before replacing your motherboard, you should have an up-to-date backup of your hard disk. Before doing any critical work like replacing your motherboard, you should protect your investment. Refer to Chapter 10, "Backing Up Your Hard Work" for tips on selecting and using backup software.

2. Before replacing your motherboard, record information about your PC.

   You should first go into your computer's BIOS setup program (also called CMOS), and print the screens or jot down the facts about your current computer, including the amount of memory and, more importantly, the various parameters for your hard disk — cylinders, heads, sectors, and so on. You will need to reenter this information after the new motherboard is installed. To enter your setup program, you often have to press the Delete key or F1 as your computer warms up. Refer to your computer's manual.

3. Park the heads on your hard disk, if required.

   On some older computers, you may have to park the hard disk's read/write heads. Most hard disks that use stepper motors must have their heads parked to safely move your computer. With such hard disks, a software utility often is included that moves the heads to an unused part of the hard disk. When in this position, the heads cannot damage data when the computer is bumped or moved. You usually run this utility by typing:

   ```
   PARK [Enter]
   ```

   or

   ```
   SHUTDOWN [Enter]
   ```

   If you have a computer from IBM, a program like SHUT-DOWN.EXE or SHIPDISK.COM is available from the diagnostics or setup program.

4. Create a large work area.

   Use a large table or work bench. Clear about three to four times the amount of space that your computer system unit covers. You'll need this much room to comfortably replace the motherboard.

5. Attach a grounding wrist strap, if you have one.

   Replacing a motherboard invites danger because of the static electricity you may accidentally create. Besides frequently touching a metal object to drain yourself of static electricity, you can get extra protection. For example, you could work on a special antistatic mat or use a grounding strap. A grounding strap is an elastic wristband with a built-in metal plate. You wear the wristband, which you then attach by a wire to a grounded metal object, such as a power supply case. With a grounding strap, you are continually being drained of static electricity. More information on these products is in Chapter 3, "Cracking Open the Case."

6. Unplug your computer from its electrical outlet. Remove all cables and then its case.

    Place your computer on the work area and remove its case. Usually, six screws must be removed from the back. Set the case aside.

7. Remove each expansion card from your computer and set aside.

    Your computer may have from six to eight expansion slots. Some of these expansion slots may be filled with expansion cards, such as a video card or an internal modem. Before removing your motherboard, each of these expansion cards must be removed.

    First, place a piece of tape on each expansion card, noting its numbered position in the slots. For example, if you have an expansion card in the second slot, place a piece of tape with the number "2" on it. The location of an expansion card is not usually important, but for some XT-type computers, the eighth slot is a special type of slot. To be safe, it's best to put the cards back into their original locations.

    Use a Phillips screwdriver or hex-nut driver to remove the screw holding each expansion card in place. Then firmly grab the card and remove it by lifting straight up. You may have to slightly rock the card along its length to remove it from its slot. As you remove each expansion card, set it aside on a clean surface, preferably on antistatic packaging you have saved or an antistatic mat.

    Some expansion cards, such as the disk drive controller, may have ribbon cables that attach to the hard disk and floppy diskette drives. Use tape to mark which cable is attached to which connector on the card. Clearly marking these connections is very important for putting your computer back together.

8. Remove the disk drives (see Figure 8.3).

    You must next remove the floppy, hard disk, tape, and/or CD-ROM drives. Each drive has two cables connected to it. One provides power to the drive, and the other transmits data read from the disk to the disk drive controller. Use a piece of tape to mark which connector is attached to which drive. Also, note the order of the drives in the case. Is the 5.25-inch disk drive on top of the 3.5-inch drive? Is the tape drive in the third or fourth drive bay opening in your computer?

    Once marked, disconnect the cables from the drives. You may also see a small ground wire, which has to be disconnected. Next, remove the screws holding each drive. Usually two to eight retaining screws hold each drive in place. Remove the screws for one drive at a time, to avoid letting the drives fall. Remove each drive and set aside. Most drives are removed by sliding them forward and out, although hard drives may have to be removed from the inside of the case.

9. Remove the power supply.

The power supply is probably the largest part of your computer. It probably has a sticker on it that says, "CAUTION: Hazardous Area." This chrome steel, boxlike component must be removed for you to extract the old motherboard.

Before removing the power supply, you must remove any power cables connected to the motherboard. You probably have removed the cables that attach to the disk drives. Next, remove the two sets of six colored wires that attach to the motherboard. These two power connectors are usually called P8 and P9, or P1 and P2 (see Figure 8.4). Note their position and how they are installed. Usually, the black leads on each connector face each other.

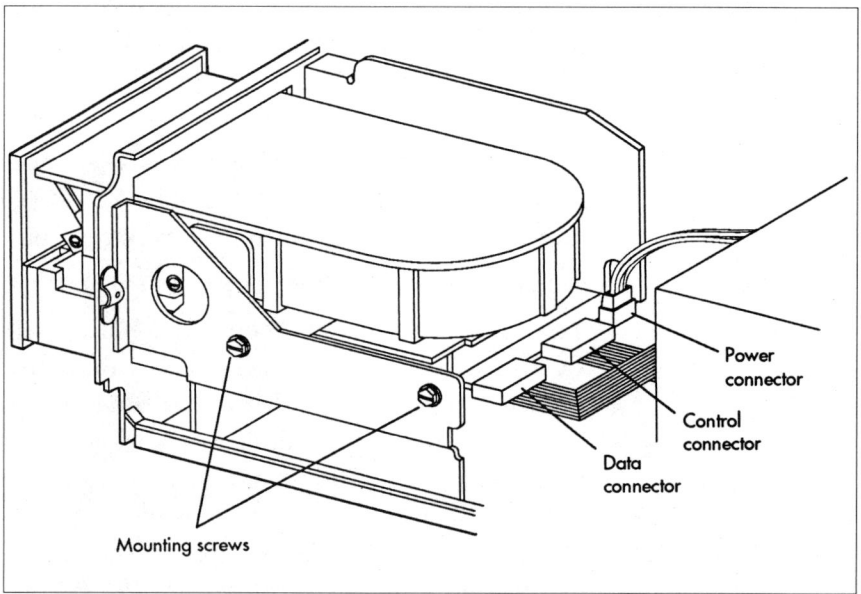

Figure 8.3 Before removing each drive, remove the data and power cables.

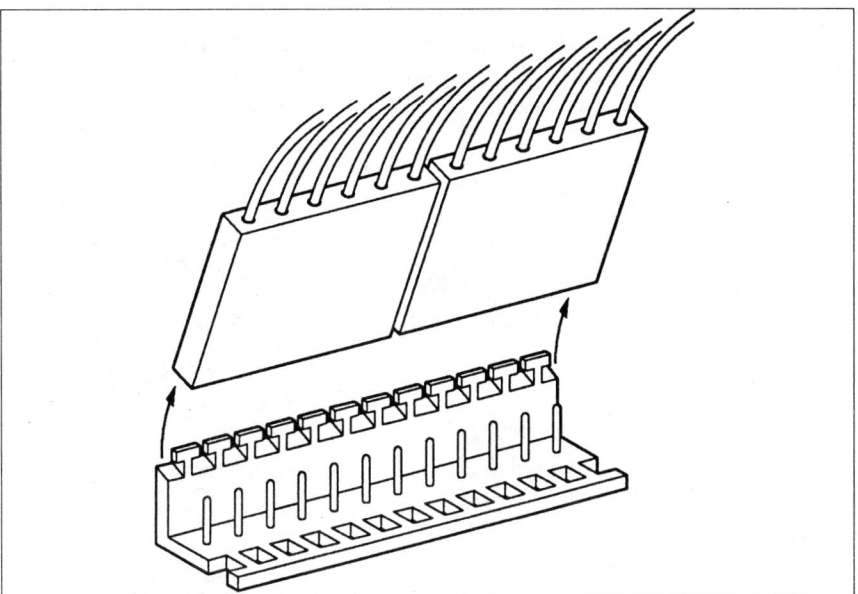

Figure 8.4 The two power cables to the motherboard (usually called P8 and P9) must be removed.

Always grasp the connectors themselves; never pull the wires.

Next, remove the screws that hold the power supply to your computer's case. Once loose, slide the power supply forward and remove. In some computers, an interlocking tab may help hold the power supply in place. Sliding the power supply forward will free it of this tab.

10. Remove any other connectors.

There may be some electrical connectors attached to the motherboard. These may include wires for the speaker, keyboard lock, turbo speed, hard disk light, and reset button. Remove these.

11. Remove the motherboard.

Once the expansion cards, drives, and power supply are removed, you can remove the motherboard. The motherboard is held in place by two kinds of fasteners: retaining screws and standoffs– white plastic pop-in fasteners. First, use a screwdriver to remove the retaining screws and any insulating washers that are used with them. Next, use long-nosed pliers to squeeze the tips of the standoffs to free the motherboard. You may also have to slide the motherboard around to free it of the standoffs. Lift the motherboard up and out of the case and set it aside on a clean or anti-static surface.

12. Use a soft brush and a can of compressed air to clean the inside of your computer case.

Removing dust and other contaminants can prepare your new motherboard for a long life. Especially clean the front vents of your computer, since this is where air is pulled into the computer. Dust often builds up on this grillwork. Remove dust that's accumulated on the power supply vents as well. Use canned air and the brush to remove dust from your floppy disk drives and expansion cards. When using the brush, use gentle, slow strokes to avoid static electricity.

13. Remove the new motherboard from its protective antistatic bag.

If not using a grounding wrist strap, briefly touch a piece of metal before opening the bag. Grab the motherboard by its edges and place it on a clean part of your work surface or on the anti-static packaging itself.

14. If needed, install memory onto the motherboard.

If you are installing the DIP type of memory, bend the legs on both sides so they form 90-degree angles to the body of each chip. Be sure each chip is installed in the right direction. Each chip has a polarity marking on one end. This marking may be a polarity notch, a circular indentation, or both. The chip socket may have a corresponding notch. Otherwise, the motherboard may have a printed legend that indicates the orientation of the chip.

The most difficult part of installing DIP memory chips is getting all 18 metal legs of each chip to fit their assigned holes. Set the chip on the socket in which you want to install it. The leads should fit directly into the holes of the socket, and the chip should drop slightly into the holes. Before you do anything else, check the alignment of the chip.

Press each chip firmly into its socket. Apply firm pressure but don't bend the circuit board too much. To be sure the chip is properly seated, press each of its ends down one more time individually. After each chip is installed, use a flashlight to inspect it. Make sure that none of the leads of the chip has folded underneath the chip and that none of the leads has slipped outside the socket. If a lead is folded under or bent outside the socket, remove the chip and straighten the lead by squeezing it between the jaws of a pair of pliers. Then carefully reinstall and reinspect the chip. Sometimes, a single leg may accidentally miss its socket. If the memory chip is installed backwards or a single leg is out of place, your computer will not work properly.

If installing SIMM- or SIP-type memory, again each must be installed pointing in a certain direction. Each chip has a polarity notch on one end of the circuit board. A SIMM has a notch cut into one side; a SIPP has a diagonal notch. These notches physically prevent the memory module from being installed incorrectly. If the module is reluctant to enter its socket, try turning it around.

Place each SIMM at about a 45-degree angle, lining up the copper-colored connectors on the memory module with the socket on the motherboard. The chips on the module should face away from the angle of the socket. Since four modules must be installed into the bank, you must insert them in a certain order so each subsequent module has room to be inserted at this angle.

Firmly insert the SIMM into the socket. Next, pivot it backwards to an upright position until it touches the plastic latches on both sides of the socket. Carefully press the SIMM against these latches until they snap around the edges of the SIMM and clamp it firmly into place. The circuit board serving as the backbone of the SIMM should be perpendicular to the circuit board holding the socket.

A plastic finger from the socket latch should poke slightly through the alignment hole at the edge of the SIMM (if there are holes in the SIMM), or the side latches of the socket should wrap around the board of the SIMM. For each SIP, insert the module straight into its socket. You should feel it slide into the grasp of the socket's contact fingers.

15. If needed, install the processor and/or math coprocessor.

The processor and optional math coprocessors usually are square chips with many leads emerging from the bottom. These chips usually have a corner mark that indicates where pin 1 is located. Pin 1 is used to mark the direction in which the chip should be installed. Match that up with the corner mark on the socket. Plugging in the processor incorrectly can destroy it.

16. Position the new motherboard (see Figure 8.5).

If your computer uses plastic standoffs, put them into the case's slots first. When you install the motherboard, push the stems through the motherboard's mounting holes. If the new motherboard also uses screws, be sure you use insulating washers to separate the metal screw from the motherboard. Do not yet fully tighten the screws. You may have to shift the motherboard slightly for proper alignment.

If the holes in your new motherboard don't match the mounting holes of the case, you will have to create your own. With the motherboard lying flat in your case, poke a pencil through the mounting holes in the motherboard and mark their positions on the bottom of the case. After you remove the board, drill holes matching these positions and install your own mounting system — screws and spacers to hold the motherboard in place.

17. Test the placement of the expansion slots and tighten the motherboard screws.

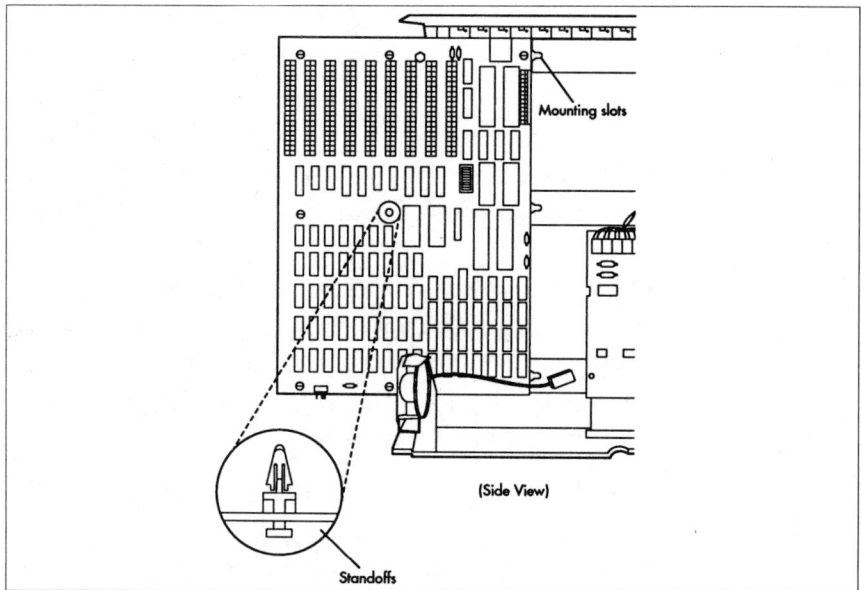

Figure 8.5 Pinching a standoff with pliers will push it through a motherboard mounting hole.

Take one of the expansion cards you set aside and install it into the motherboard. Be sure it lines up properly with the rear mounting holes and the screw hole in the top of the slot. Once the expansion card is screwed in, tighten the screws that hold the motherboard in place.

18. Reinstall the power supply.

Install the power supply and attach it to the case with its original screws. Plug the two 6-lead power cables — labeled P8 and P9, or P1 and P2 — into the motherboard. When plugged into the motherboard, these connectors should have their black leads next to each other.

19. Reinstall the expansion cards into the motherboard's slots.

Install each expansion card into the same slot from which you removed it. In some cases, the order is important.

20. Attach the other cables to the motherboard.

Reattach the cables for the speaker, keyboard lock, turbo speed, hard disk light, and reset button. Refer to the manual that came with your new motherboard for their exact positions.

21. Attach the monitor and keyboard to your computer and plug the monitor and computer into an electrical outlet.

22. Turn on your PC.

Before closing up your computer, test your new motherboard. Your PC should immediately come to life — the power supply fan should start spinning and text should appear on your monitor after it warms up. You should see the computer counting its new memory. Don't worry if it says there are no drives present or they are not working. If it does not start or beeps at you, switch off your PC and double-check your work.

23. Turn off and reassemble your PC.

Once your new motherboard has passed this simple test, install the remaining parts of your computer, such as the disk drives. Do not yet attach the computer's cover.

24. Again, test and set up your PC.

Turn on your computer again. You should be given an error message and told to run the computer's setup program. Go into the setup program (usually by pressing the function key F1). This gives you the opportunity to set up parameters like the type of disk drives you have, the amount of memory, the type of display, today's date, and so on. Often, the setup program correctly guesses the answers to most of these questions.

25. Attach your computer's case and return your PC to its normal work area.

Place the old motherboard into the antistatic bag that came with the new one and store away. After installing a new motherboard, I leave my computer on continuously for two weeks. This tests the quality of the motherboard; if it survives two weeks of continuous operation, it probably will last years.

Although replacing the motherboard can be challenging, it is — one hopes — a one-time operation that greatly increases the speed and compatibility of your computer. In one move, you can extend the life of your PC by a few years if not more.

9 Storage: It's a Hard Life

Mass storage is simply that: large. You can store and retrieve large amounts of information using any of several mass storage devices. These include

- Hard disk drives
- Removable storage devices
- Portable storage devices
- Tape drives

Note: You'll find CD-ROM (compact-disc read-only memory) drives in Chapter 13, "Multimedia."

The Hard Way

The most popular mass storage device today is the hard disk, which is also called a *hard drive, Winchester drive,* or *fixed disk drive.* Most computers have a hard disk, although yours might have just one or two floppy diskette drives. A hard disk is similar to a floppy diskette with four exceptions:

1. A hard disk usually is not removed from the computer as a floppy diskette is. All your information and programs are stored in one convenient place.

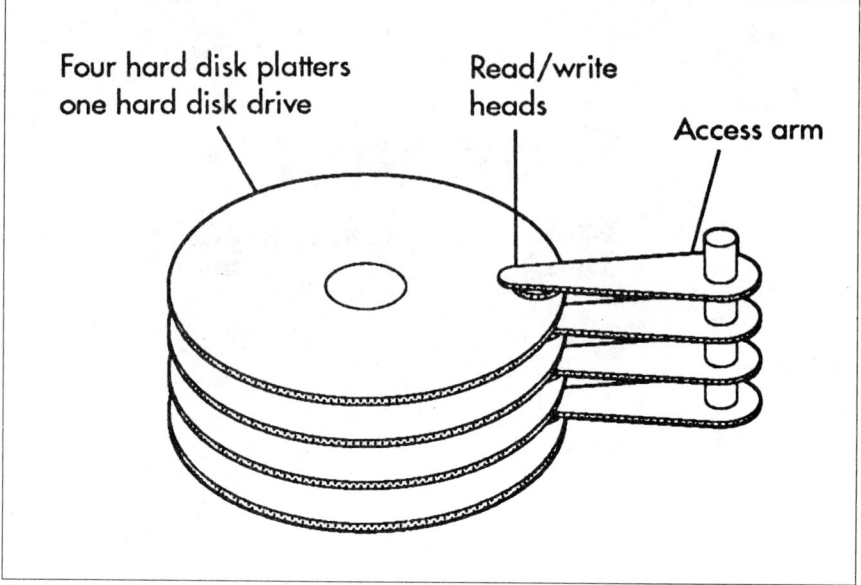

Figure 9.1 A hard disk contains several disk platters and several read/write heads.

2. A hard disk is several times faster than a floppy diskette.

3. A hard disk can store much more information than a floppy diskette (usually about 150 times more!).

4. A hard disk can store and retrieve your information more than 10 times faster than it can from a floppy diskette drive.

Overall, a hard disk is simply a high-performance disk drive. It gets its great speed and capacity because it is permanently mounted inside your computer and sealed. This allows it to be built to very fine mechanical tolerances. In other words, bumping your computer while its hard disk is working could damage it.

Cylinders, Tracks, and Stuff

The hard disk is made of several round platters stacked on top of each other (see Figure 9.1). These platters spin at great speeds — 3600 revolutions per minute or faster. The platters are made of iron oxide, which can easily be magnetized and demagnetized. Read/write heads, just like those on a cassette player, record and play back in-

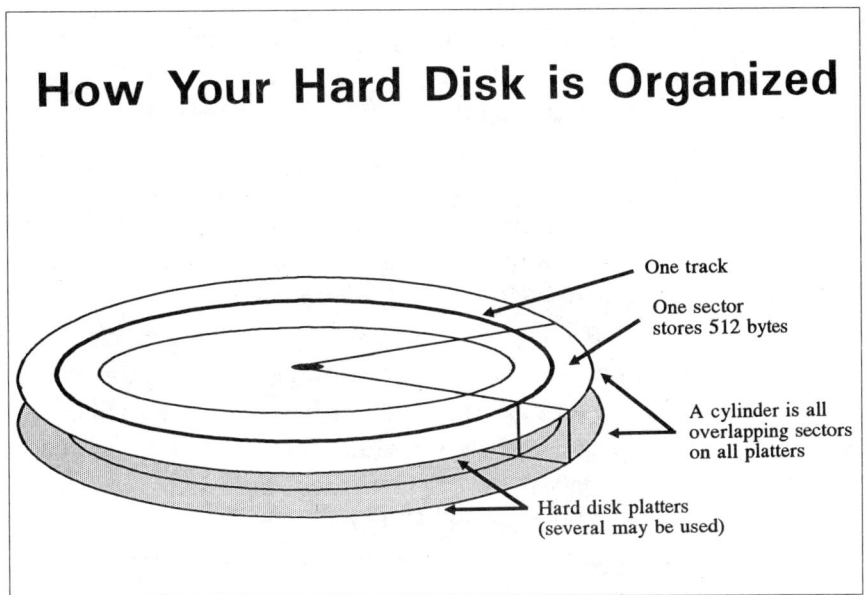

How Your Hard Disk is Organized

One track

One sector
stores 512 bytes

A cylinder is all
overlapping sectors
on all platters

Hard disk platters
(several may be used)

Figure 9.2 A hard disk is broken down into circular tracks, pizza-sliced sectors, and overlapping cylinders.

formation to and from these platters. Unlike a cassette player, a read/write head never touches the platter's surface; it is suspended a few thousandths of an inch above it. With the platters spinning 60 times each second, these heads literally fly over the surface.

Because hard disks have several platters, they have several read/write heads. One read/write head is placed on top and another on the bottom of each platter, since information can be recorded on both sides. For example, a hard disk with five platters will have 10 heads. Because these heads and platters are so sensitive to contamination and vibration, they are sealed into what is called a head-disk assembly, or HDA. The air within this chamber is then microfiltered.

In a way, a hard disk is similar to a phonograph record. Yet instead of reading information from it in a long, continuous spiral, the hard disk reads data from any of several hundred concentric rings. Each ring is called a *track* (see Figure 9.2). Some hard disks have more than 1000 tracks. Tracks are numbered starting from the outside of the disk, beginning with track 0. The next track is 1, and so on. The innermost track on a floppy disk is track 39 (for a 40-track disk) or 79 (for an 80-track disk). With a hard disk, the tracks that lie one above another are called *cylinders*. In other words, all track 0s on the several platters make up a cylinder. Cylinders are also numbered. Cylinder 0 is all track 0s from each side of every platter.

Your computer often doesn't require an entire track to save your information, so it divides each track into smaller portions. Like a pizza, the tracks are cut into slices called *sectors*. Floppy disks are divided into eight, nine or 15 sectors. Hard disks are divided up into 17 or more sectors. Each sector holds a certain amount of information, usually 512 bytes. The address of each sector is recorded to the hard disk when you use the DOS (disk operating system) FORMAT command. When your computer records information to its hard disk, it remembers the location based on the cylinder, track, disk side (or head), and sector where the recording was made.

Once a disk is formatted, the smallest chunk of data is this small 512-byte sector. DOS could keep track of each and every sector — whether it's in use by your files or available for use. But the work involved in keeping track of this information is too much. Instead, DOS deals with multisector units called *clusters*. Clusters vary in size depending on the size of your disk. A 30MB hard disk has a cluster size of 2048 bytes, or four sectors. A 1.2MB floppy disk is formatted with a cluster size of one sector — 512 bytes.

By the way, hard disks are not perfect. Some sectors may have physical flaws in them. When a hard disk leaves the factory, these "bad sectors" are marked so no information is saved to them. Usually, no more than 2 percent of your hard disk contains bad sectors. Bad sectors are a "natural" disk-making phenomenon, so don't worry about them. DOS keeps track of which sectors it cannot use because of these physical flaws.

Getting Up to Speed

A hard disk is classified by four factors:

1. Physical size, either full-height or half-height
2. Capacity, measured in megabytes (MB)
3. Speed, measured in milliseconds (ms)
4. Interface, the method used to "talk" to the rest of your computer

First, what does a hard disk look like? Your hard disk, if you have one, may be as large as a hardcover book or as small as a paperback; their sizes have greatly shrunk with advances in technology. The hard disk is usually encased in metal although you may also see some of its electronic components on one side. The drive may be either of two sizes: *full-height* or *half-height*. Full-height drives are 3.25 inches high, 5.75 inches wide, and 8 inches deep. Older hard disks are often full-height. Half-height disks measure 1.625 inches high and either 5.75 or 4 inches wide, and 4 or 8 inches deep. Smaller drives are available, as small as 1.3 inches wide, but these are popular only in laptop computers.

The capacity of a hard disk is measured in *megabytes*, or *MB*. One megabyte equals roughly one million bytes. A byte is equivalent to a single character or digit, such as the letter A or the number 1. (Technically, a megabyte equals 1,048,576 bytes, but who's counting?) The size of the hard disk in the original IBM PC/XT was 10MB. Today's typical computers have hard disks with capacities beyond 100MB. There are even hard disks that hold gigabytes (GB) of information. (One gigabyte equals 1024MB.)

Your hard disk is quite fast. Most information can be retrieved in one-tenth of a second. Most of this time is spent physically moving the read/write head to the position where the information is stored. The time spent to locate this data is called the drive's *seek time* or *access time*. Since the data may be located either on the inner or the outer parts of a platter, this time is usually based on the average seek time. This access time is measured in thousandths of a second, or milliseconds (ms). When you look at an advertisement for a hard disk, its speed is usually listed in milliseconds, such as 28 ms. A typical hard disk may have an access time of 40 ms. A fast hard disk may have an access time of 15 ms.

Face-to-Interface

Both floppy disk drives and hard disks require an expansion card called a *disk drive controller*. This controller card plugs into an expansion slot on the motherboard and is connected to the drives with ribbon cables (see Figure 9.3). The cable to a hard disk is usually a 34-pin cable. Most disk controllers can handle up to two floppy disk drives and two hard disk drives.

The hard disk and its controller must support the same *drive interface*. Basically, the interface is a software and hardware method of passing information between your hard disk and the rest of your

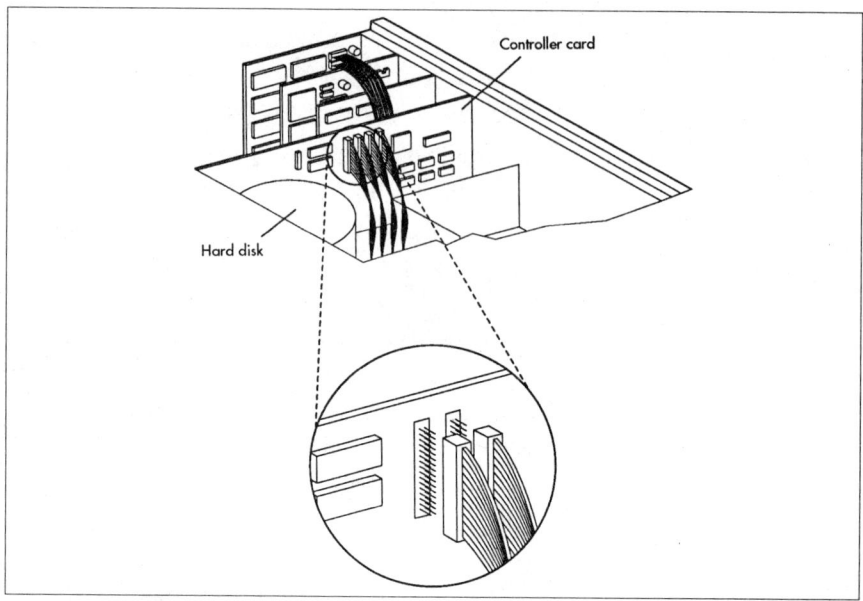

Figure 9.3 The hard disk is connected to your computer by one or more cables to the controller card.

computer. The interface used often determines the maximum amount of data that can be "shoveled" to your computer. The amount of data that can be moved is called the *data transfer rate*, measured in kilobytes per second. This figure is often more important than the speed of the hard disk. A hard disk may be able to find your stored information in 15 ms but, once found, how fast can it be delivered to your computer?

One way to increase the data transfer rate is to squeeze more information onto the hard disk's tracks. The denser the information on the disk, the less the heads have to move. The magnetic recording scheme, also called the *data encoding*, used in a hard disk allows you to do just this. The first of two popular encoding schemes is *Modified Frequency Modulation*, or *MFM*. Using MFM, each bit of data is represented by one magnetic spot on the disk. (This magnetic spot is also called a *flux*.) With MFM, a hard disk can be sliced into 17 sectors to provide a data transfer speed of up to 625K per second.

A newer recording scheme called *Run Length Limited*, or *RLL*, puts even more information on a hard disk, allowing more than 26 sectors on the disk. With RLL, the speed of the hard disk and electronics allow two to seven bits to be recorded in one flux. This is called 2,7

RLL. There are other variations of RLL that double the capacity of MFM hard disks. This higher density allows a data transfer rate of up to 937K per second.

Besides the recording method, the interface also involves the physical connection between the hard disk and the rest of the computer. There are primarily four physical interfaces:

1. **ST506/412.** Pioneered by hard disk manufacturer Seagate Technology, this interface was used in early hard disks, usually 40MB and smaller. Data can be moved between the hard disk and the rest of the computer at 625K per second. With the ST506 interface, either the MFM or RLL recording schemes are used. Some ST506 hard disks support both, but the disk controller only supports one or the other. In other words, some MFM-type hard disks can work with an ST506 RLL controller and increase its capacity 50 percent and its speed to 937K per second. Still, this data transfer rate is no match for the speed of many 80386 and 80486 computers. The ST412 interface is an improvement to the ST506 standard. All new ST506 drives/controllers incorporate these enhancements. Therefore, the terms ST412, ST506/412, and ST506 all refer to the same standard. If your computer was purchased before 1990, it's hard disk probably uses the ST506 interface.

2. **ESDI.** The Enhanced System Device Interface, or ESDI, once was the Cadillac of interfaces but now finds its popularity waning. It was developed to eliminate some problems with the ST506 interface. For example, an ESDI hard disk has a data transfer rate of up to 3MB per second, more than double that of the ST506. Also, an ESDI hard disk can be larger than 1024 cylinders and more than 17 sectors per track. The speed of an ESDI controller must match or exceed that of the ESDI drive it controls.

3. **SCSI.** The Small Computer Systems Interface, or SCSI, is another high-end interface. It allows you to connect up to seven devices and not just hard disks. For example, one SCSI controller lets you connect up to seven hard disks, tape drives, CD-ROM drives, or printers. In other words, you can add up to seven SCSI devices to your computer while using only one expansion slot for the one SCSI controller. Unfortunately, not all SCSI controllers work with every SCSI device. The SCSI-1 interface provides data transfer speeds up to 5MB per second. The SCSI-2 interface provides rates

of up to 10MB and possibly more. The SCSI-3 interface proposes enhanced features and the ability to handle more than eight devices. SCSI controllers often have difficulties working with disk utilities and parts of the *Windows* software. These difficulties are slowly being solved.

4. **IDE.** The Integrated Drive Electronics, or IDE, interface appeared a few years ago as an inexpensive, effective hard disk interface that competes with the ESDI and SCSI interfaces. A more accurate name for IDE is the ANSI (American National Standards Institute) AT Attachment standard. Unlike other interfaces, the IDE interface puts the controlling electronics not on the controller card but on the drive. An IDE drive still needs an expansion card to connect to your computer, but this card is quite "dumb," since the real brain is built into the drive. (Most IDE cards cost under $25.) IDE drives offer data transfer rates up to 4MB per second. The IDE interface supports drives that use either the MFM or RLL recording scheme.

Unfortunately, you cannot examine your hard disk and tell if it supports one interface or another; all the cables and connections are identical. To discover what interface your drive uses, check your computer's manual or invoice.

How DOS Organizes Your Disk

To find a specific file in a vast sea of many megabytes, the hard disk needs an efficient index system. It needs to know the head, cylinder, and sector where that information is located. Your hard disk also needs to know which parts of the disk are free for saving new files and which parts are occupied by existing files. The way this information is organized on the disk is called the logical format of the disk. DOS organizes your hard (and floppy) disks into five main areas:

1. Boot record
2. File Allocation Table (FAT)
3. Root directory
4. Data area
5. Master Boot Record (MBR) or partition record

The boot record, FAT, and root directory form the *system area*. When you use the DOS FORMAT command on a hard disk, you are not physically formatting; that was done at the factory. You actually are doing a *logical format*. (On a floppy disk, FORMAT does the physical **and** logical formatting.)

The *boot record* always occupies the second sector of the first track of the first disk side — sector 2, track 0, side 0. (The first sector is reserved for the Partition Table.) The boot record allows the hard disk to start your computer by reading a very short program, called the *boot code* or *bootstrap loader routine*. This program then loads the rest of the operating system. Besides the boot code, the boot record also contains information about your hard disk, including the number of bytes per sector, the total number of sectors on the disk, the number of sectors per track, and the number of heads.

The *File Allocation Table*, or *FAT*, is a table that tracks the status of all sectors. It tracks which files occupy which sectors as well as which sectors are available for new or expanded files. When a file needs to be enlarged — you've added some paragraphs to a letter, for example — the File Allocation Table finds the closest sector that is free to store the part of your file that outgrew its previous location. If the FAT becomes damaged, some or all of the data may be lost. The FAT is so critical to keeping track of your files that DOS stores two identical copies of it. If one goes bad, the other acts as a backup.

For speed, the FAT really tracks clusters, which are groups of sectors. Since clusters are created by DOS, their size may vary, from one to eight sectors, to keep the FAT from being too cumbersome. If even a fraction of a cluster is occupied by one of your files, the FAT forbids other files from being saved to the rest of that cluster. This wasted space is called slack. The bigger the cluster, the more slack you have. Clusters reflect a trade-off between speed and space. If your clusters were smaller, you could have less waste. However, smaller clusters create a larger FAT, requiring more reading and writing to this table as you save and delete files from the hard disk. The more reading and writing, the slower your PC.

The *root*, or *main*, *directory* is the last part of the system area. The root directory (C:\) is the top directory under which you create subdirectories, such as C:\DOS or C:\WINDOWS, to store your files. In a way, the root directory is like an entire file cabinet. Subdirectories underneath the root directory are similar to the cabinet's drawers. To finish the analogy, each drawer contains files, such as MOM.LET.

Besides the system area, you also have a *data area*. The data area is the rest of your disk. Following the root directory, the data area is used to store your work.

Last, the *Master Boot Record* or *partition record* is used to divide one physical hard disk into several disks. It also allows different operating systems, such as DOS and OS/2, to share one hard disk. The hard disk is broken up into subsets called *partitions*. The partition record specifies the disk location and length of each operating system's partition.

Speeding Up Your Hard Disk

Besides a hard disk "dying," most hard disk users have these two complaints:

1. Hard disks are too slow.
2. Hard disks are almost always full, requiring constant pruning before new files or software can be added.

There are several ways to speed up your hard disk. Some require an investment in extra hardware, and others require you to buy an inexpensive software utility or use the free utilities that came with DOS. Below are some ways to speed up your computer:

*   Increase BUFFERS in your CONFIG.SYS startup file.
*   Use the DOS FASTOPEN utility.
*   Use a RAM, or virtual, disk.
*   Shorten your DOS path.
*   Use a disk caching software utility.
*   Defragment your files.
*   Create smaller partitions.
*   Change the interleave factor of your hard disk.
*   Order a new hard disk controller.

Optimizing Buffers

Some ways to reduce the demands on your hard disk are quite simple, using commands and utilities that come free with DOS. The first step is to optimize the number of buffers in your CONFIG.SYS startup file. A line in your CONFIG.SYS file reads (or should read):

```
BUFFERS=xx
```

where *xx* is the number of buffers. Buffers are used to improve disk performance. With the BUFFERS command, a portion of memory is set aside by DOS to store information read from your hard disk. Clearly, accessing information already in memory is much faster — up to 100 times faster — than reading information from the hard disk.

The higher the number of buffers, the faster your hard disk. If you set the number of buffers high enough, such as 99, DOS frequently finds the information it needs in the buffered memory, saving itself the work of accessing your disk drive. DOS 4.x and 5.0 allocate the number of buffers in your system according to how much memory you have installed. If you have a large hard disk, even Microsoft Corp. recommends more buffers than the defaults. With 640K or more of RAM, DOS defaults to 15 buffers (a buffer contains 512 bytes plus 16 for overhead). For hard disks up to 40MB, Microsoft recommends a setting of 20 buffers; up to 80MB, 30 buffers; up to 120MB, 40 buffers; and for 120MB and larger disks, 50 buffers.

If you are using disk caching software, described later, you can reduce buffers to three since disk caching is superior to the cruder BUFFERS command. If you simply eliminate the BUFFERS statement from your CONFIG.SYS file, you will have the default value of 15. If you do not use disk caching software, increase the number of buffers to between 30 and 99. Remember: When you increase the number of buffers, you are trading memory that could be used by your software for a faster hard disk. You will have to decide which setting is best based on your hands-on use. Also, you must restart your computer each time you change the number of buffers. If you have DOS 5.0 and are using Upper Memory Blocks (UMBs), selecting a number of 44 or less allows the buffered memory to occupy this upper memory, preserving your first 640K of memory. For information on UMBs and changing your CONFIG.SYS file, refer to Chapter 6, "Thanks for the Memory."

Using FASTOPEN

DOS isn't the smartest operating system in the world. In fact, it is quite forgetful. For example, DOS searches for a file every time you request it — even if you just used that file. You can speed up DOS by using its FASTOPEN command, which has been available in all versions of DOS since 3.0. FASTOPEN tells DOS to remember where it found files so that it can find them again quickly, without stepping through a tedious search. It works best with database and compiler software.

To use FASTOPEN every time, you can add it to your AUTO-EXEC.BAT startup file. Otherwise, you can simply type FASTOPEN at the DOS prompt whenever you want to use it. The command, given either from the DOS prompt or in your AUTOEXEC.BAT file, would be

```
FASTOPEN c:=xx d:=xx
```

where *c:* and *d:* are the drives you want to use FASTOPEN on and *xx* is the number of files to track. One rule of thumb is to give FASTOPEN one file for every megabyte on your hard disk. For example, if your drive C: is a 40MB hard disk, you would want a setting of 40. If you have expanded memory that supports version 4.0 of the Lotus/Intel/Microsoft Expanded Memory Specification (LIM EMS 4.0), you can have FASTOPEN use this memory instead of your precious conventional memory. To use this, add a /X at the end of the command, like this:

```
FASTOPEN D:=40 /X
```

If you have an 80386 or 80486 computer and are using DOS 5.0, you can load FASTOPEN into upper memory. To load FASTOPEN into upper memory, type:

```
LOADHIGH FASTOPEN c:=xx d:=xx
```

! **WARNING:** FASTOPEN requires some memory — at least 3K. This memory may best be used by increasing the number of buffers. Also, since FASTOPEN is a terminate-and-stay-resident (TSR) program, it may conflict with some of your other software. For example, you shouldn't use FASTOPEN when running a defragmentation program, described later. You may lose information.

Modifying Paths

DOS organizes your hard disk into what is called *tree-structured directories*. The top directory, usually C:\, is called the *root directory*. Directories and subdirectories are then placed underneath the root directory. Tree-structured directories are a great way to organize your hard disk. You can have a directory called C:\DOS for just your DOS programs, and you can have a directory called C:\LETTERS \JANUARY for your January correspondence.

The PATH statement is used in your AUTOEXEC.BAT startup file to tell DOS where to search for your most frequently used program files. This way, you can type the program's startup command without having to go to the directory in which it is located. DOS then looks to your PATH statement and finds the program file from among the directories listed. When you install new programs, these programs normally add their directory to your path. A typical path looks like this:

```
PATH C:\DOS;C:\WINDOWS;C:\BAT;C:\WP;C:\
```

Although very useful, the PATH statement can get unruly, slowing your hard disk and causing it to work too hard. To find the starting cluster of a file (which is where DOS must always start reading a file), DOS needs to read through each layer of subdirectories along the way. This research requires the disk's read/write heads to move a lot when a file is buried under several layers of subdirectories. In other words, the longer the path, the longer it takes DOS to find the program you want to run. Besides slowing down your computer, each directory listed in the path requires precious memory. Fortunately, DOS limits you to a total of 127 characters for the path line. Still, you should limit the path statement to the bare essentials.

If you want to take advantage of all the speed your hard disk has to offer, trim the number of directories DOS must search through. The fewer alternative paths you specify, the less time it will take DOS to zero in on the program you want. Also, organize the list of directories in the PATH statement in descending order of use. In other words, put the most frequently used directories first. This also increases the speed of DOS finding your program. In the example above, I place my \DOS and \WINDOWS directories near the top. You should also create directories right off the root directory and not any deeper. In other words, put your program — say *WordPerfect* — in the directory C:\WP5 and not C:\PROGRAMS\WP5. The closer you are to the root directory, the faster DOS will find your files.

When changing or creating your path, always include drive letters with the directory names. I recommend you always have a path to your DOS directory as well as to your root directory (C:\). Also, note that each path is separated by a semicolon (;).

One way to limit your path statement is to create a directory for several batch files. A batch file (.BAT) is a text file you create to run several DOS commands or programs in one step. By having a path to a directory of batch files — mine is C:\BAT — you can have access to several programs without having to include each directory in your path. For example, I use the database program *Q&A* from Symantec. Instead of having the directory C:\QA in my path, I created a batch file, using the DOS 5.0 *Edit* program, called QA.BAT. This file contains these commands:

```
@ECHO OFF
C:
CD \QA
QA
```

I use @ECHO OFF to not display the lines of the batch file. The batch file switches to drive C: and then to the QA directory. Finally, it runs the program QA. By using batch files, you can reduce the length of your path considerably. Another way to reduce your path is to place several DOS utilities, such as PC Tools and Norton Utilities into one directory called C:\UTILS. Then, provide a single path to this directory.

Creating a Virtual Disk

A *RAM (random-access memory) drive*, also called a *virtual disk*, is another way to speed up your computer. DOS includes a utility called VDISK.SYS or RAMDRIVE.SYS, depending on your DOS version and manufacturer. This utility temporarily creates a disk drive in your computer's memory. This RAM drive can be created from conventional, extended, or expanded memory.

RAM drives are much faster than hard disks because your computer can read information much faster from this type of memory than from a hard disk. A RAM drive is best used for storing temporary files required by *Windows*, DOS, or other programs. A variable called TEMP can point these programs to use the RAM drive. Otherwise, you can create a RAM drive and copy your program and/or work files to it. Then, use your program and work files from the RAM drive instead of the hard disk. It will be much faster. When done, copy the files from the RAM drive back onto your hard disk. One warning: You need ample memory to copy your program and files to a RAM drive, often one megabyte or more. Also, if you suffer a power surge or outage while using a RAM drive, your work is lost. A disk in memory is gone when you turn off the power.

The RAM disk utility is loaded from your CONFIG.SYS startup file. The line that loads it typically looks like this:

```
DEVICE=C:\DOS\RAMDRIVE.SYS 2048 /E
```

The number following the RAM drive's filename is the size of the RAM drive in kilobytes. In the example above, the size is 2MB (2048K). The last switch, /E, tells DOS to create the RAM disk from extended memory. To create the RAM drive in expanded memory, the preferred option for 8088/8086 computers, use /A. Once a RAM drive is created, it is automatically assigned the next available drive letter, such as drive D or E. The RAM drive then behaves like a disk drive.

If you are using DOS 5.0 and have upper memory blocks (UMBs), you can place the RAMDRIVE.SYS into upper memory so it won't take memory away from your other programs. Use the DEVICEHIGH command:

```
DEVICEHIGH=C:\DOS\RAMDRIVE.SYS 2048 /E
```

If using a RAM drive for a program like Win*dows* or DOS, you need to create a directory called \TEMP into which it can place the temporary files these programs create. A directory is needed instead of the root directory because there is a limit to the number of files you can place in a root directory. For example, my AUTOEXEC.BAT file has the following lines in it to create a \TEMP directory on my RAM drive (drive F:) and tell *Windows* TEMP variable to use it:

```
MD \TEMP
SET TEMP=F:\TEMP
```

Following is the recommended size for your RAM disk based on the total amount of memory you have and the *Windows* mode you are using:

Total Memory	Recommended RAM drive in *Windows'* Standard mode (in K)	Recommended RAM drive in *Windows'* 386 Enhanced mode (in K)
2MB	0	0
3MB	512	0
4MB	1024	0
5–6MB	2048	1024
7MB	2560	1536
8MB	3072	2048
9MB	4096	3072
10+MB	4096	4096

For more information on RAM drives, consult your Windows or DOS manuals.

Caching Out   A *disk cache* is the most effective way to improve your hard disk's performance and extend its life. A disk cache is a software program you run to dynamically duplicate parts of your hard disk to your computer's memory. Once in memory, the contents can be read at top speed. DOS versions 4.x and higher and *Microsoft Windows* include a disk caching utility; however, more advanced disk caching utilities are available.

Unlike the BUFFERS feature mentioned earlier, the disk cache attempts to anticipate your requests for information on your hard disk, typically by retaining the information you've most recently accessed. (The assumption is that this information is what you will most likely need next.) A disk cache is generally more versatile than a RAM disk because it is dynamic; the contents of the cache change as you read other programs and work on files.

All disk caching programs copy frequently read sectors of your hard disk into your computer's much-faster memory. All offer track buffering — reading ahead on the disk so the next block of data is already loaded. The "smarter" caches add redundancy checking, skipping over unchanged sectors when saving data. Some disk caching programs also buffer, or delay, writing to your hard disk. In other words, it will save information in its memory to your hard disk when your computer is not so busy doing other work, usually waiting no more than one second. This is also called "delayed writing." This waiting period adds significant speed but may cause information to be lost if your computer were suddenly turned off. Because of the small delay, often less than one second, this concern is minor.

A disk cache only helps with certain kinds of computer work. If your work generally is loaded into memory and doesn't access the hard disk much (as with spreadsheets and word processors, for example), disk caching won't improve performance. In fact, performance may suffer if the caching program uses expanded memory that could be better used by the spreadsheet. Conversely, disk caching definitely helps software that uses your hard disk often. For example, almost any disk-caching utility will make dBase IV or other database software programs run about three times faster.

Disk caching utilities let you adjust the size of the cache (bigger is usually better), and most let you use either expanded or extended memory, although part of the disk caching software must use some of your lower 640K of memory. Caches in extended memory are slightly faster than ones in expanded memory. Most disk caches are easy to install but provide extra options to "fine tune" the cache for maximum performance. The manual should clarify how to tune your disk caching.

For non-Windows programs, a 1MB (1024K) cache is best. If memory is precious, use a 256K cache. You'll lose only 10 percent in performance over a 1MB cache. For Windows users, a disk cache of up to 2MB (2048K) is recommended, as shown below:

Total Memory	Recommended disk cache when not using Windows (in K)	Recommended disk cache when using Windows (in K)
2MB	1024	512
3MB	2048	1024
4MB	2048	1024
5–6MB	2048	2048
7MB	2048	2048
8MB	2048	2048
9MB	2048	2048
10+MB	2048	2048

You may have free disk caching software already on your computer. SMARTDrive is one disk caching utility included with Microsoft Windows 3.0 and DOS 5.0. Typically, SMARTDrive is not quite as slick as other caches, but it does have two unique advantages: It automatically frees memory when Windows needs more, and it is small enough to fit into any upper memory you may have available. Other disk caching software programs are often too large. To use SMARTDrive, you must have at least 512K of extended memory or 256K of expanded memory. SMARTDrive typically is found as the file SMARTDRV.SYS. To load it, you must add the following line to your CONFIG.SYS startup file:

```
DEVICEHIGH=C:\DOS\SMARTDRV.SYS xxxx yyyy
```

where *xxxx* and *yyyy* are the size of the cache (in K) when running DOS programs and running Windows, respectively. Use the chart above to select the best sizes based on your total memory. If your DOS directory is not called C:\DOS or you are using SMART-DRV.SYS from your Windows directory, you can insert the correct path. To use expanded memory for your disk cache — the preferred option for 8088/8086 computers that have an expanded memory card — add a /A at the end of the line, such as:

```
DEVICEHIGH=C:\DOS\SMARTDRV.SYS 2048 1024 /A
```

A newer version of SMARTDrive included with Windows 3.1 has better performance and is easy to use. Unlike other versions of SMARTDrive, this one can be run from the DOS prompt or AUTOEXEC.BAT startup file instead of the CONFIG.SYS startup file. In fact, the name has changed from SMARTDRV.SYS to SMART-DRV.EXE. By simply typing SMARTDRV, the program senses if it should be loaded into any available upper memory and which drives to cache. Also, this new version allows delayed writing to your disk, increasing its speed. If you have SMARTDRV.EXE, you should add the following line to your AUTOEXEC.BAT file:

```
C:\WINDOWS\SMARTDRV.EXE 2048 1024
```

As mentioned earlier, the two numbers represent the size of the disk cache when you are running DOS programs and Windows, respectively.

If you don't have SMARTDrive or prefer a superior disk cache, you can buy an off-the-shelf program for about $100. Commercial disk-caching programs include PC-Kwik Corp.'s Super PC-Kwik Disk Accelerator, PC-Cache included with Central Point Software's PC Tools, or Norton Cache included with Symantec's Norton Utilities. One popular shareware (try-before-you-buy) program is HyperDisk. Besides the cost of a disk caching program, you may have to spend an extra $50 to $100 for more memory if your computer doesn't have at least 2MB.

Gathering Fragmented Files

Every time you use your hard disk, it gets a little slower. Why? As your disk is used over time, its files are distributed in various places on the disk. This "fragmentation" is caused either by a new file filling in the empty holes left after you deleted older files or by an existing file having outgrown its number of sectors after you added extra information to it. Although your files may be split into pieces, the File Allocation Table (FAT) safely tracks which sectors each file occupies.

Unfortunately, finding and loading these fragmented files takes longer, since the hard disk heads must keep moving around the disk platters to retrieve or store different pieces of each file. The more fragmented your disk, the slower it becomes. The remedy is to use a *disk defragmentation* software utility, which is also called a *disk optimizer, disk compactor,* or *hard disk compression* program.

A disk defragmenter gathers the scattered sectors that make up each file and rewrites them in continuous, contiguous order on the disk. With the file in one piece, your hard disk can nimbly read it. The best defragmentation programs also close up the spaces left by deleted files and let you place often-read files (such as .EXE or .COM) and subdirectories (such as C:\DOS) at the front of the disk for faster access. They should also let you pick either a "quick" defragmentation or a "full" defragmentation. The benefit of optimizing your hard disk is great. Some benchmark tests have operated twice as fast after a disk is optimized.

Disk optimizers are typically included in hard disk utility packages like Central Point Software's PC Tools and Symantec Corp.'s Norton Utilities. For example, I use the Norton Utilities' SpeedDisk about once a week. (See Figure 9.4). When my drive becomes 10 percent fragmented, I take the time for a full optimization. If less, I might do

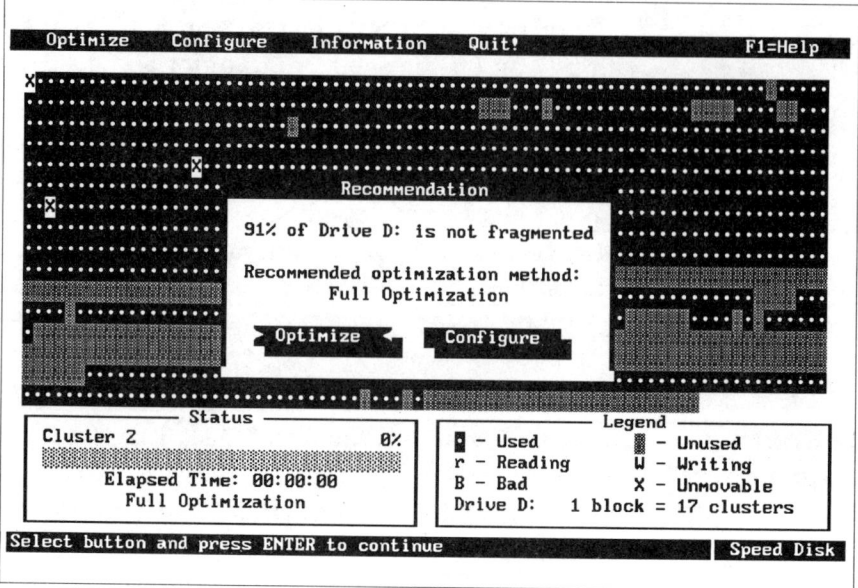

Figure 9.4 *Norton Utilities' SpeedDisk* visually shows how fragmented the hard disk is.

a "quickie" compress, where SpeedDisk will simply unfragment the individual files but leave gaps where future files might be placed, causing future fragmentation.

There is an inexpensive but time-consuming way to reorganize your hard disk. First, back up your entire hard disk, reformat it, and then restore all your files from the backup. (Procedures for backing up your hard disk are provided in Chapter 10, "Backing Up Your Hard Work") As the files are restored, they are saved to your hard disk one right after the other. This has the side benefit of assuring that you have at least one reasonably current backup of your hard disk available. The procedure will require an hour or two of your time.

Creating Smaller Partitions

Breaking up your one physical hard disk into several "logical" partitions is another disk-saver. You can take your one hard disk and break it up into drives C, D, E, and so on. (see Figure 9.5). By breaking the one hard disk into several drives, your computer can find information quicker. Also, the smaller partition may create a smaller cluster size of less than 2048 bytes. The advantage of this is that there may be less wasted space created than when you save a small file in an

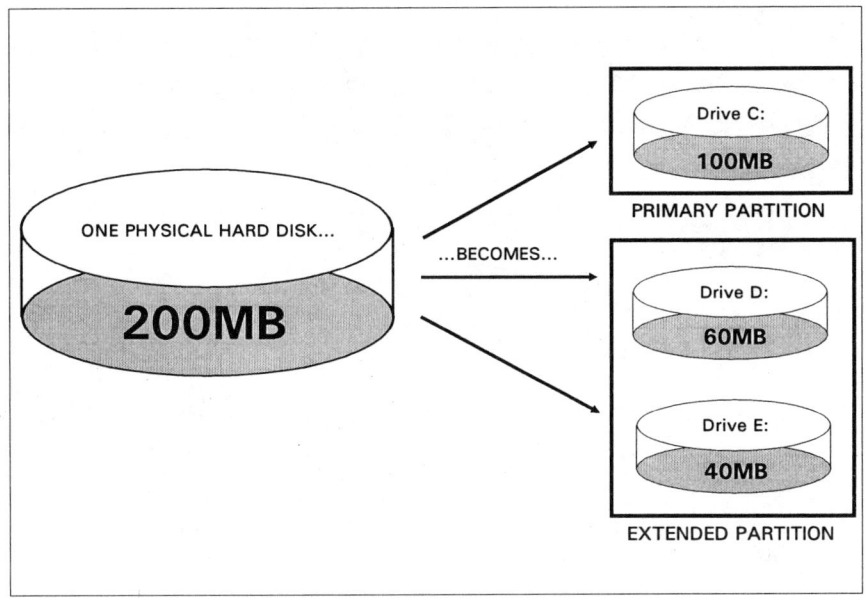

Figure 9.5 One physical hard disk can be broken into smaller, speedier "logical" drives.

unnecessarily large cluster.

To break your one hard disk into several partitions, back up your hard disk and then use the DOS utility FDISK. (When you use FDISK, the information on your hard disk is forever lost.) With FDISK, you create a primary DOS partition (drive C:) and then an extended DOS partition. From the extended DOS partition, you create several logical drives, such as D:, E:, and F:. After exiting FDISK, you format each partition and restore the backed-up files to the disk.

Going through the repartitioning process is not quick and easy. You must back up the hard disk, change the partition sizes, format each drive and restore the files. The process can easily take one to two hours. For detailed steps on repartitioning your hard disk, see the latter steps in the procedure for installing a new hard disk, given later in this chapter.

Changing the Interleave

The data transfer rate is determined by the hard disk controller. If you can increase the data transfer rate, you can save and retrieve information to and from your hard disk much faster. Outside of getting a new controller and/or hard disk, you can increase this data transfer

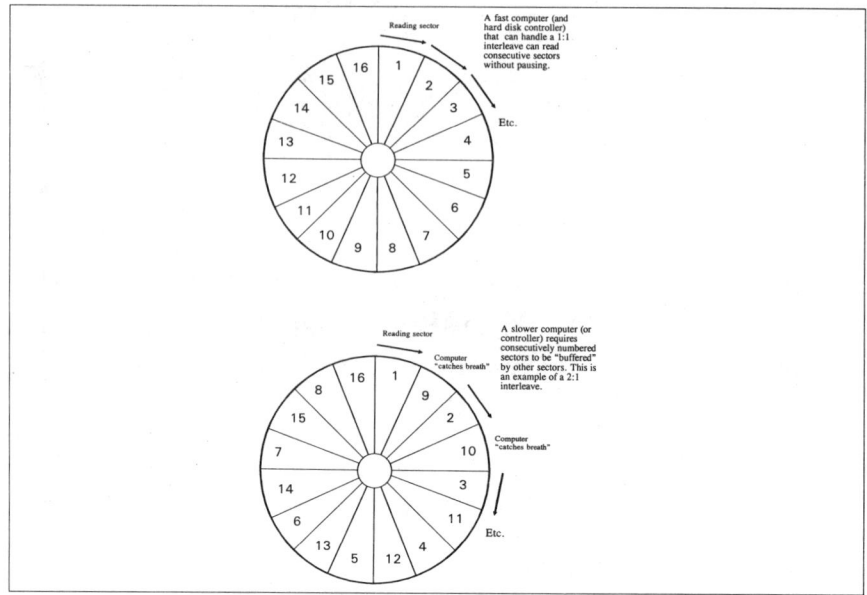

Figure 9.6 Compare these two drives with a 1:1 interleave and a 2:1 interleave. Without the buffer of other sectors, the 1:1 drive is faster at reading files.

rate by finding your disk's best *interleave factor*. (See Figure 9.6.)

The interleave factor is the layout of the sectors on your hard disk. When you request information from your hard disk, usually one sector is read followed by those after it. For example, retrieving a letter for your word processor may mean reading sector 2 followed by sectors 3 and 4. Your hard disk is spinning so fast — 60 times a second — that having the sectors placed in numerical order next to each other causes some to be missed, requiring the disk to spin around again for the next sector to be found. These extra rotations waste time.

The best interleave factor places sectors where they can be read in one rotation. Sometimes, this requires other sectors to be placed between consecutive sectors. For example, sector 1 may be followed by sector 9, and then sector 2. Sector 9 acts as a buffer so the hard disk can finish "digesting" sector 1 before reading sector 2. The ideal interleave is one in which the sectors are placed in numerical order, requiring no others in the way. The interleave factor is measured in a ratio. A hard disk that can read information from consecutive sectors has an interleave of 1:1. A hard disk that can only read every third sector in a single rotation has an interleave of 3:1. The interleave on the first IBM PC/XT had an interleave of 6:1.

Surprisingly, many hard disks are set with the wrong interleave. Their controllers can usually handle a smaller interleave, increasing the speed and reliability of your hard disk. Unfortunately, the interleave can only be changed on ST506 hard disks. These utilities do not work with IDE, SCSI, or ESDI drives. For example, I cannot use Norton Utilities' Calibrate to fine-tune the interleave on my IDE drive, but I still use it to test for possible defects. On SCSI and ESDI drives, you probably already have a 1:1 interleave since these are high-performance drives.

Some popular utilities for diagnosing and then changing your interleave include SpinRite from Gibson Research, DOSutils from Ontrack Computer Systems, OPTune from Gazelle, and Calibrate, the utility that comes with Symantec's Norton Utilities. Such utilities, usually costing under $100, first test your disk and then perform a low-level (physical) format on it. Fortunately, this formatting does not erase the information on your hard disk. A nondestructive format is used, preserving your work.

Changing the interleave is usually a one-time operation, although you should use these utilities to give your hard disk a quarterly "check-up." On an old 10-MHz AT computer, I used *Calibrate*. The 30MB hard disk was running with a 3:1 interleave. The software recommended a 2:1. The entire process took about one hour. After that, the hard disk was one-third faster. On XT-type computers, the process may take several hours.

Before using these utilities, back up your hard disk. (See Chapter 10, "Backing Up Your Hard Work" for tips on backing up your hard disk.) A power outage during the reformatting or an incompatibility with your hard disk could jeopardize all your work.

Adding a New Controller

Utilities that change the interleave are limited by the capacity of the controller. You could also replace the disk controller with one that supports a smaller interleave, such as 1:1. Some models include the Western Digital WD1003 and WD1006 as well as the Seagate ST22M/22R.

Most 1:1 hard disk controllers include built-in memory to speed up your hard disk. By continuously copying the most-wanted parts of your hard disk into this memory, your hard disk can give the processor what it wants much more quickly. These buffers tend to be between 8K and 64K. Often, these caches must be turned off to use a disk maintenance utility.

A disk caching controller provides the ultimate in hard disk controllers. These high-performance controllers are the hardware equivalent to software disk caching. Unlike typical controllers, these disk caching controllers provide more memory, usually the SIMM-type, and its own on-board computer to manage the cache. This hardware approach to disk caching, however, is expensive — between $400 and $1500 — and doesn't always offer a noticeable speed improvement over software disk caching. One advantage is that a caching controller uses its own memory, taking none from your computer.

The Full Disk Dilemma

A second complaint about hard disks is that they soon become full. Hours can be spent deleting old or unwanted files. The problem isn't getting better either; today's software takes up more megabytes of space than ever before. The operating system itself takes up megabytes; DOS 5.0 requires about 2MB. If you use Microsoft Windows, invest in as much hard disk as you can afford. The table below shows how much room the most popular programs consume:

Program	Disk space (MB)
Adobe Type Manager (30 fonts)	6
After Dark	2
Ami Pro 3.0	10
Borland C++ w/Application Frameworks	55
CorelDraw	12
Crosstalk for Windows	2
dBASE IV	5
Excel 4.0	8
Freelance Graphics for Windows	11
MS-DOS 5.0	2
Norton Desktop for Windows	9
The Norton Utilities	2

continued

Program	Disk space (MB)
(continued)	
Polaris PackRat	4
PC Tools	7
Publisher's Paintbrush	4
Ventura Publisher for Windows	12
Visual Basic	4
Windows 3.1	12

To discover your hard disk space:

How full is your hard disk? This is easy to find out using the DOS utility CHKDSK (Check Disk).

1. Turn on your computer.
2. From the DOS prompt (C:\ or A:\), type:

```
CHKDSK c: [Enter]
```

where c: is the drive whose size you want to check.

Your computer will then display various information about your disk drive space and memory. It may look like this:

```
105906176    bytes total disk space
4468736      bytes in 11 hidden files
174080 bytes in 66 directories
98244608     bytes in 2199 user files
2969600      bytes available on disk
2048         bytes in each allocation unit
51712        total allocation units on disk
1450         available allocation units on disk
655360 total bytes memory
585680 bytes free
```

3. Calculate the drive's capacity.

The first line shows the total disk space, in bytes. To find out how many megabytes large your hard disk is, divide this number by 1,048,576.

4. Calculate your free space.

   The last line in the first section shows how many bytes are available on disk. To find out how many megabytes you have remaining, divide this number by 1,048,576.

5. Calculate the percentage of free space.

   Divide the number in step 4 by the number in step 3. This is the percentage of disk space you have free.

6. Repeat this step for each drive letter you have, such as drive D:, E:, and so on.

IMPORTANT: Record these amounts of disk space in Appendix A: "PC Bio."

Making More Room

You have several options in dealing with a hard disk that is bursting at the seams. Several DOS files can be removed because they are unneeded. For example, the files 4201.CPI, 4208.CPI, and 5202.CPI are unneeded unless you own an IBM Proprinter or Quietwriter. Likewise, you may not use the DOS BACKUP and RESTORE utilities for your backup software; several superior backup programs are available to you. Here are some files to rid yourself of and why:

File name	Size (in bytes)	Why get rid of it
4201.CPI	6,404	Only needed by IBM Proprinters 4201 and 4202.
4208.CPI	720	Only needed by IBM Proprinters 4207 and 4208.
5202.CPI	395	Only needed by IBM Quietwriter.
APPEND.EXE	10,774	Dangerous utility.
APPNOTES.TXT	9,701	Lists programs and expansion cards incompatible with DOS 5.0.

File name	Size (in bytes)	Why get rid of it
BACKUP.EXE	36,092	Crude backup software best replaced by a commercial backup program.
COMP.EXE	14,282	Cruder version of FC.EXE. Use FC.EXE instead.
COUNTRY.SYS	17,069	Required for computers that need the date, time and currency in a non-U.S. format.
DELOLDOS.EXE	17,644	Not needed after you are satisfied with DOS 5.0. Run this program, which deletes the old version of DOS, and then delete it.
DISPLAY.SYS	15,792	Only needed for non-English languages.
DOSSHELL.VID	9,462	Only needed if you use the DOS 4.0 or 5.0 DOSSHELL.
DOSSHELL.INI	20,465	Same as above.
DOSSHELL.EXE	235,484	Same as above.
DOSSHELL.COM	4,632	Same as above.
DOSSHELL.GRB	4,421	Same as above.
DOSSHELL.HLP	161,763	Same as above.
DOSSWAP.EXE	18,756	Same as above.
DRIVER.SYS	5,409	Only needed for certain external and nonstandard disk drives.
EDLIN.EXE	12,642	A text editor that is bested by EDIT.COM.
EGA.SYS	4,885	Only needed for EGA monitors with the DOSSHELL.
EGA.CPI	58,873	Only needed with MODE command to display national characters.

File name	Size (in bytes)	Why get rid of it
EXE2BIN.EXE	8,424	Useful for programmers.
FASTOPEN.EXE	12,050	Sometimes causes more trouble than it's worth.
GORILLA.BAS	29,434	If you dislike games, delete it.
GRAFTABL.COM	11,205	Only needed for CGA monitors.
GRAPHICS.PRO	21,232	Only needed for IBM Proprinter.
JOIN.EXE	17,870	Sometimes causes more trouble than it's worth.
KEYB.COM	14,986	Only needed for non-English languages.
KEYBOARD.SYS	34,697	Only needed for non-English languages.
LABEL.EXE	9,390	Only needed to change volume name (no great loss).
LCD.CPI	10,753	Only needed for IBM Convertible.
MONEY.BAS	46,225	Crude personal finance program written in BASIC.
MSHERC.COM	6,934	Only needed for Hercules display adapter.
NIBBLES.BAS	24,103	If you dislike games, delete it.
NLSFUNC.EXE	7,052	Only needed for non-English languages.
PRINT.EXE	15,656	A second way to print text files.
PRINTER.SYS	18,804	Only needed for IBM Quietwriters and Proprinters to print non-English characters.
RECOVER.EXE	9,146	Creates more problems than it solves.
REMLIN.BAS	12,314	Needed only to convert other BASIC programs to QBASIC format.
RESTORE.EXE	38,294	See comment for BACKUP.EXE.

File name	Size (in bytes)	Why get rid of it
SETVER.EXE	12,007	Only needed to trick a handful of applications to work with DOS 5.0.
SMARTDRV.SYS	8,335	If you have SMARTDRV.EXE from Windows 3.1 or another disk-caching program, use it.
TOTAL SPACE SAVED	**1,034,576** (about 1MB)	

In Microsoft Windows 3.1, selecting the "Windows Setup" icon lets you remove some parts of Windows you may never need. By selecting "Add/Remove Windows Components" from the Options pulldown menu, you can remove those parts you don't need. For example, you can get rid of the Clock utility (CLOCK.EXE) or the several wallpapers (.BMP files) you don't like for your background. If you find you later need any files, you can easily reinstall them using this same utility. Between my DOS and WINDOWS directories, I've been able to trim over 3MB of files!

In your other directories, you can also find some space-wasting files. Look for read-me files, such as READ.ME or README.TXT. Such files contain last-minute documentation. You may want to print out this information and then delete the files. Also look for files that end with the extension .BAK. These are normally backup files. When you install new software, several printer and video drivers are copied to your hard disk. You can eliminate the ones you don't need. For example, WordPerfect has a printer driver called IBMPROPR.PRS for owners of IBM Proprinters. Another file, VIKING.VRS, runs the Viking brand of monitors. If you don't need these, remove them.

An alternative to ferreting out unwanted files is simply to use the DOS BACKUP utility or your backup software to archive files you presently don't need. Of course, you can also use the trusty COPY or XCOPY commands to offload some files to diskettes.

Compressing Files

You can compress groups of files so they require less space on the hard disk. One alternative is to use a compression program to archive a group of files until you need them. For example, using either

LHARC or PKZip, you can reduce files to a fraction of their size, up to 75 percent. When you need any of these compressed files, you use a companion utility to "unzip" or "unshrink" the ones you want.

However, compressing some files may be inconvenient, especially if you need frequent access to them. An alternative is to use PKLite from PKWare Inc. (the same company that makes PKZip). PKLite increases disk space by compressing only executable program files, that is, files with the extensions .EXE or .COM. PKLite reduces the size of these programs by an average of 40 percent. Compressing your executable files may not always work, particularly those that use overlays (.OVL companion files). However, PKLite warns you before attempting to compress a program that might present problems. Also, PKLite works only on DOS, not Windows, executable files. Despite these drawbacks, the program is a safe and convenient way to squeeze more onto your hard disk.

To use PKLite, select the executable files to be compressed. Fortunately, you can use wild cards, such as *.EXE, to compress several files in each directory. No memory is required to use PKLite. In fact, your programs may load faster since the smaller programs take less time to load. Once PKLite compresses your program files, it is done. As you install new software, you may want to run this utility again. PKLite sells for $47.

A more radical alternative is to use a data compression program such as Stacker or SuperStor. These products increase the capacity of your hard disk by about 100 percent or more, depending on the type of files your hard disk contains. How? As mentioned earlier, there is some waste, or slack, on your hard disk. Compression software keeps the content and trims the trash. As you request information from your hard disk, the information is decompressed on the fly with little or no wait. Once viewed as risky, data compression is now becoming a part of some operating systems. DR DOS 6.0 from Digital Research Inc. includes a variation of SuperStor. To increase the performance of this data compression, some manufacturers include an optional expansion card that uses a thinking coprocessor to speed the process.

These compression programs rely on device drivers or memory-resident programs to intercept your computer's commands to the hard disk. Besides requiring memory, these programs have one other shortcoming. Some disk utilities, such as disk defragmenters, will not work on compressed drives. Fortunately, the manufacturers include their own. Also, Windows does not like to work on a compressed drive. For example, the SmartDrive disk-caching software included with the program does not work with SuperStor-compressed drives. You also should not use a compressed drive for your Windows permanent swap file. On faster 80386 and 80486 computers, there is little performance lag when a compression program is used. For slower computers, compression can add a noticeable lag, possibly requiring the optional coprocessor card. Before using a compression program, have two fresh backups of your hard disk. You'd hate to compress yourself into oblivion.

Selecting a Larger Hard Disk

The obvious solution for ample storage is to buy another or larger hard disk. Yet, a hard disk can be a considerable investment — about 15 to 25 percent of your entire computer's price. Some computer owners have no hard disk at all, while others want to add a larger or second hard disk. How large a hard disk do you need and which interface should you select? The first IBM PC/XT had a 10MB hard disk. Today, 10- and 20-megabyte hard disks are nonexistent, except on the smallest laptop computers.

For most computer owners, the right hard disk size is about 100MB. That gives you enough storage for 30MB worth of applications (for example, a half dozen *Windows* programs, each requiring 4MB to 6MB), plus another 30MB for your work files, and another 30MB for the future. If you are involved with graphics, desktop publishing, programming, or computer-aided design (CAD), you will want to double your requirement to 200MB. Fortunately, the price per megabyte of storage costs less than ever. In 1987, one megabyte of hard disk cost $25.50. Today, that price is about $3 and still falling. In other words, a 200MB drive will cost you about $600.

An extremely large hard disk can pose problems. DOS 5.0 recognizes only up to 1024 cylinders in a single hard disk. You can get special utilities, such as *SpeedStor* from Storage Dimensions or *DiskManager* from Ontrack Computer Systems, to tame such large hard disks. However, these utilities may cause problems in some software programs.

Besides size, get the fastest drive you can. A fast computer should be matched with a fast hard disk. If you have an 80486-based computer, get a hard disk with an access speed in the low teens (under

15 milliseconds). Although a slower computer might not need such a fast drive, it can still benefit from one, especially for tasks that constantly need the hard disk, such as a database. You also need to select an interface: MFM, RLL, IDE, ESDI or SCSI. MFM interfaces are best for older computers, although the RLL interface can give you higher data transfer rates. Typically, the IDE interface will work best for most computers, although the SCSI interface is handy if you also have or intend to buy a CD-ROM drive or other SCSI devices.

Some hard disks or their controllers include a built-in memory cache. (This cache is different than the buffer provided with many hard disks.) This caching memory allows a subset of the hard disk to be read into it, providing your computer with faster access to the information than if it were to read the information from the much slower hard disk. Combining an internal disk cache with an external one, perhaps a software disk caching utility, is unnecessary and undesirable. Multiple caches can actually slow down your computer. Consider the chart below:

System	Interface
PC or PC/XT (8088- or 8086-compatible)	MFM, RLL or 8-bit IDE
80286 (AT) or 80386SX or DX (16 MHz)	MFM, RLL, SCSI, IDE with 1:1 interleave controller
80386SX or DX (25 or 33 MHz) or 80486	IDE, ESDI or SCSI
High-performance 80386 or 80486	ESDI or SCSI with a caching controller

Other speed-boosting technologies will be appearing in hard disks. One company is investigating a hard disk with two separate sets of read/write heads. This allows one set of heads to read information from one sector while the other set looks for the next one.

Installing a New Drive

Whether you are adding, replacing, or swapping a hard disk, the process is identical. When you order, you are offered either a bare drive or one with a kit. The more expensive kit includes the controller card, cables, installation hardware, and an instruction manual.

To install the drive:

1. If replacing your current hard disk with a new one, make two backups of your hard disk.

   Make at least two fresh backups (and test one) before replacing your hard disk. (See Chapter 10, "Backing Up Your Hard Work" for tips on backing up your hard disk.)

2. Turn off your computer and remove its case.

   For details on opening your computer, see the procedure in Chapter 3, "Cracking Open the Case."

3. Remove the current controller, if necessary.

   If you know you can use your current controller with the new hard disk, leave it in. Otherwise, remove it and use the disk controller card that came with the new hard disk. Floppy diskette drives in your computer, can be attached to the new controller. Most controllers can run up to two floppy diskette drives and two hard disk drives. Remove the floppy diskette flat ribbon cable from the current controller card. Next, remove the controller card.

4. Install the new disk controller card.

   You need to install the new disk controller card to run the hard disk. It's best to install this expansion card into the expansion slot where the previous controller resided or the slot nearest the power supply and drive bays. (The drive bays are areas in your computer where you install hard disks and disk drives.) If an expansion card already occupies this first position, remove it and place it in another slot.

   Remove the screw holding the rear metal bracket over the expansion slot. Next, remove the controller card from its antistatic bag. Insert the card straight down into the connectors on the motherboard. Push firmly, but not so much as to greatly bend the motherboard. It may break. Use the single screw to hold the controller card in place.

5. Install the hard disk (See Figure 9.7).

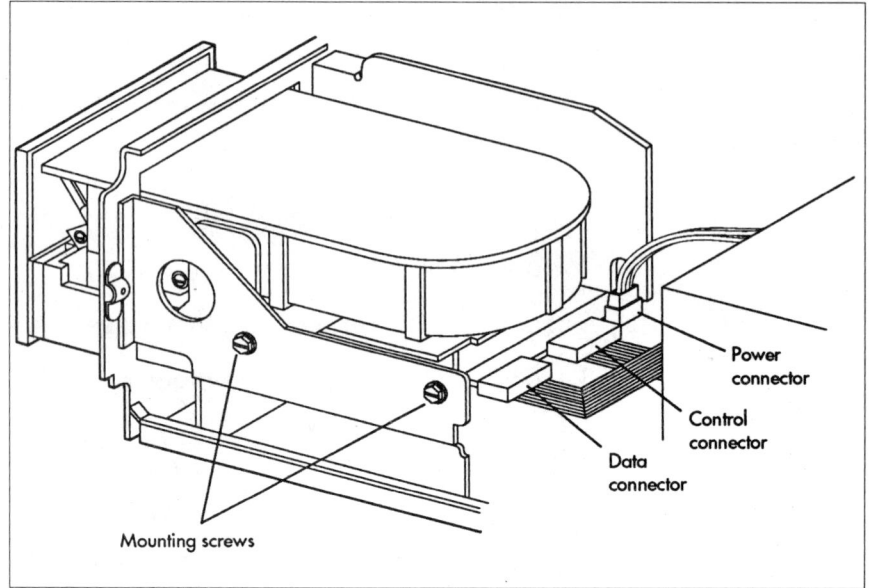

Figure 9.7 The hard disk is held in place by mounting screws and connected to your computer by data and power cables.

The hard disk slides into a drive bay, or cage, in your computer. Drives come in two sizes: half-height and full-height. Be sure the bay is tall enough for your new drive. You usually have to remove a plastic panel that covers the drive bay opening. Use the screws that came with your hard disk kit to mount the drive in place; typically, four screws are used to hold the drive in place. In some computers, plastic drive rails are used to mount the hard disk.

6. Connect the data cables to the hard disk.

Flat ribbon cables must be connected to the hard disk so it can "talk" to the controller card. This data cable carries the information from your hard disk to the controller and then to the rest of the computer. Some hard disks come with two cables: one 34-pin and one 20-pin. Others simply come with only a 20-pin cable. Consult your documentation for which ones you have.

Ribbon cables have a red or black stripe along one edge, identifying pin 1 of the cable. On the controller card, you also have a pin 1. This pin is probably marked "1" or "0." It is very important for pin 1 on the cable to be connected to the pin 1 on the controller card. Place the cable so the stripe aligns with pin 1 and press it into place. If you have a second cable, repeat this step.

Next, connect the ribbon cable(s) to the edge connectors on the hard disk. Most drives have connectors that prevent you from incorrectly attaching the cable. If not, again use the color stripe to line up the cable connector with pin 1 of the hard disk. Some hard disk cables have a connector in the middle of the cable. This is only used when two hard disks are installed in your computer. If you have only one hard disk, ignore this middle connector and use the end one (see Figure 9.8).

7. Connect the power cable to the hard disk.

You now need to connect a power cable to your hard disk. Look for a spare power cable coming from the power supply. This is a four-wire connector with a white plastic plug. Plug it into the four-pin power connector at the rear of the hard disk. This connector is shaped so the cable goes in only one way.

8. Set the jumpers, if needed.

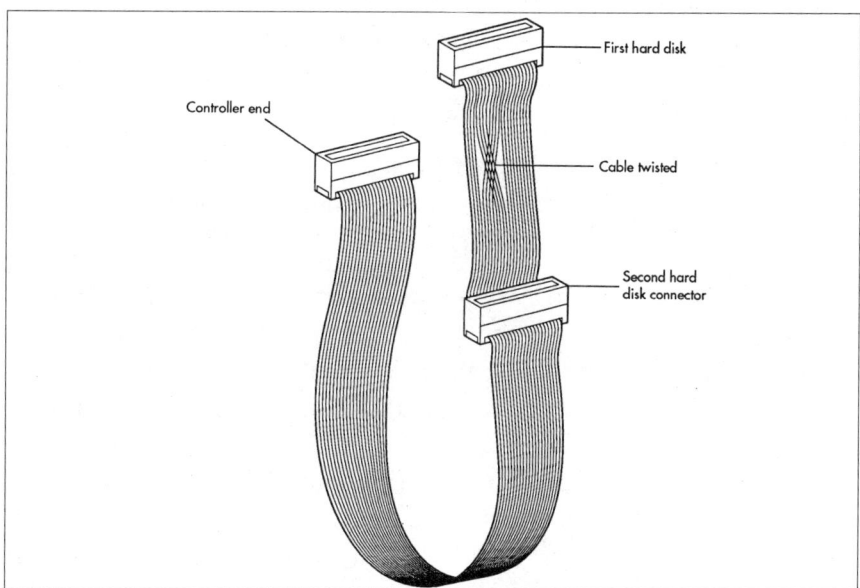

Figure 9.8 Use the end connector for a single hard disk. The middle one is for a second drive.

Most hard disks have a jumper that tells the controller whether it's the first or second drive. Refer to the drive's installation manual, and set the jumper in the first-drive position. If you don't have this information, assume it is set correctly. If the drive doesn't work, this jumper might have to be changed.

9. Attach the data cables to each floppy diskette drive.

   If the hard disk controller also can run floppy diskette drives, connect the data cable from each floppy disk drive to the controller. Consult your controller card manual for where to connect the diskette drive to the controller.

10. Attach the computer's power cord, monitor, and keyboard and turn on your PC.

    Do not put your computer's case on yet.

11. Tell your computer what type of drive you have.

    You now must tell your PC what type of drive you've just installed. Typically, you must run the computer's setup program. To get to the setup program, either press a key or two or run a software program that came with your PC. For example, you may have to press the Delete key or F1 as your PC warms up. Consult your owner's manual.

    Once in the setup program, you must change the drive type to match that of your new hard disk. The setup program already has a list of possible drives from which you can choose. Save the settings and exit.

    If the drive type is not listed, you have to tell the setup program about the drive by entering the number of cylinders, heads, sectors, and other information. You can get this from your hard disk owner's manual or from the hard disk's case where this information is stamped. If you can't identify the drive type, contact your dealer or the drive manufacturer. If you cannot enter the drive information, you may have to purchase a new BIOS (Basic Input/Output System) chip for your computer. A newer BIOS would list more drive types and provide other features to warrant the extra $50 to $100. Otherwise, you can purchase add-on ROM (read-only memory) chips that will augment your BIOS with additional drive types. Most computers have room for an extra pair of ROMs. One such ROM sold by Ontrack Computer Systems is called the SuperPROM. There are also software solutions when your drive isn't supported by your BIOS. The disk utilities such as SpeedStor or Ontrack Disk Manager can "pretend" your hard disk is not a hard disk, requiring a device driver (a small software program) to be loaded for your hard disk to be recognized. I don't recommend the use of device drivers since they require a portion of your computer's memory. I consider an up-to-date BIOS chip the best overall solution, since the new BIOS will support other features, such as high-density drives, VGA color monitors, and more.

12. Partition, or size, your hard disk.

You need to create a primary DOS partition on your new hard disk. Because there are different DOS versions, this procedure may be different. Typically, you place the original DOS diskette (or a copy of it) in the A: drive and restart your PC. At the DOS prompt, type:

```
FDISK [Enter]
```

From the menus, you need to select "Create DOS Partition" and then "Create Primary DOS Partition." Select the size for the partition (see Figure 9.9). This partition becomes drive C:.

Typically, DOS versions up to 3.3 (except for some manufacturer's versions) allow a maximum primary DOS partition of 32MB. DOS 4.0 and greater let you select as large a partition as you want. Be selective about the size of your partition. The larger the partition, the slower your hard disk will be. You can leave the remainder of your hard disk for an extended DOS partition, which will let you add more drives than drive C:. (Extended partitions are described next.)

13. Create additional logical drives (see Figure 9.10).

Forming two partitions makes organizing and backing up your work easier. After you create an extended DOS partition, you can create drives D, E, F, and more. Since these are part of the same one physical hard disk, they are called logical drives. From the

```
┌──────────────────────────────────────────────────────────────────────┐
│                                                                        │
│                        Create Primary DOS Partition                    │
│                                                                        │
│        Current fixed disk drive: 1                                     │
│                                                                        │
│                                                                        │
│                                                                        │
│                                                                        │
│                                                                        │
│        Total disk space is  202 Mbytes (1 Mbyte = 1048576 bytes)       │
│        Maximum space available for partition is  202 Mbytes (100%)     │
│                                                                        │
│        Enter partition size in Mbytes or percent of disk space (%) to  │
│        create a Primary DOS Partition................................: [ 20:  │
│                                                                        │
│        No partitions defined                                           │
│                                                                        │
│                                                                        │
│        Press Esc to return to FDISK Options                            │
│                                                                        │
│                                                                        │
└──────────────────────────────────────────────────────────────────────┘
```

Figure 9.9 With FDISK, select the size of your DOS partition. With DOS 5.0, you can enter percentages or the actual size in megabytes (MB).

main menu of FDISK, select "Create DOS Partition." Next, select "Create Extended DOS Partition." Accept the default to turn the rest of your hard disk into an extended partition. After creating the extended partition, you can create as many logical drives as you'd like.

14. Create an active partition.

Before leaving FDISK, be sure drive C: is the active partition. If it is not selected, you will not be able to start your computer from drive C:, even if you formatted it properly.

15. Format each drive.

Before you can use partitions, you must format each with the DOS FORMAT command found on your original DOS diskette. During formatting, each sector has a unique address written into it. Without an address, your computer cannot find the information it wants to retrieve for you. From the DOS prompt (A:\), type:

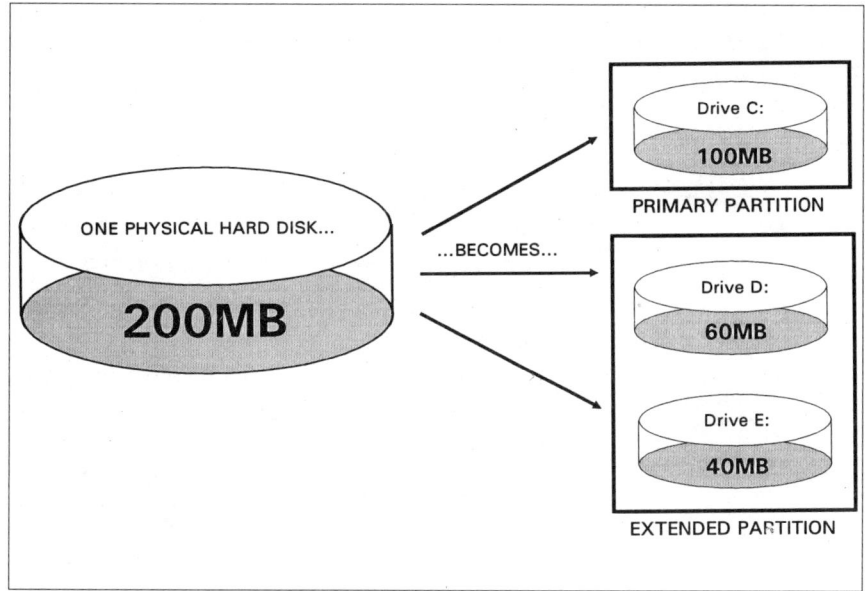

Figure 9.10 You can create several partitions, or logical drives, from one hard disk. This speeds up your hard disk by limiting its search.

```
FORMAT  C:  /S  [Enter]
```

Ignore the warning message and start formatting by entering "Y" and press the Enter key. The /S switch is crucial. It copies parts of the operating system to drive C: so you can start your computer from the new hard disk. For the other drives (D:, E:, and so on), type:

```
FORMAT  x:  [Enter]
```

where *x* is the letter of each logical drive you created from the extended partition.

16. Replace your computer's case and return your PC to working order.

17. Install your software.

    Install your various software onto the new hard disk. If you want to restore your hard disk using backup software, you first must install the backup software onto the new hard disk and configure it. Then use one of the backup sets of diskettes to restore your hard disk.

Adding a Second Drive

Adding a second hard disk is very similar to adding a single hard disk. When you want to add a second drive, your choices depend on the interface you already have.

If you have an ST506 controller, you can generally add a second ST506 drive of any capacity supported by your PC. Check your owner's manual or computer setup program to see what drive types are allowed. The only restriction is that both drives must use the same data coding scheme, MFM or RLL. However, you may have trouble finding an ST506 drive since they are becoming obsolete.

You can add a second ESDI drive with virtually any capacity, but the speed of the ESDI controller must match or exceed the transfer speed of the new drive. In other words, if you have a 10-MHz ESDI controller, you will want a 10-MHz drive. A controller can handle a slower drive but not a faster one. If you want to add a faster drive than your controller can handle, you will have to purchase a faster controller to match it.

Adding a second IDE drive may cause some compatibility problems. Because the original IDE specification was not well defined, some manufacturers' older drives will not work with those from other manufacturers. The ANSI AT standard was probably finalized after your first IDE drive was made. The best way to avoid compatibility problems is to purchase a drive made by the manufacturer of your first. Otherwise, insist the vendor let you return the new drive — without a restocking fee — if it is incompatible. Your second IDE drive doesn't have to match the capacity of your first.

Adding a second (or third) SCSI drive might pose some problems. Theoretically, you should be able to attach up to seven SCSI drives to your one SCSI controller. This "daisy-chaining" is simply not that easy. Like IDE, the SCSI standard has evolved over the years. Many early drives had several features that were optional, and different vendors have chosen to implement different options. Drives from two different vendors may not work together. Mixing devices — CD-ROM drives, printers, and so forth — is even chancier. To avoid problems, stick with the same manufacturer and make sure you have a liberal return policy.

In general, you can also mix interfaces when you add a second drive. For example, you can add a new SCSI drive to a system that already has an ST506 drive. However, you might need to change the address of one controller or both to avoid any kind of conflict.

Second Drive Pitfalls

Here are some caveats for adding a second hard disk. First, be sure your power supply can handle two hard disks. A second hard disk can demand another 25 to 40 watts from your power supply, causing it to work harder, creating unwanted heat and possible malfunctions. Refer to Appendix A: "PC Bio" to see at what capacity your power supply is operating. If you didn't complete this appendix, read Chapter 5, "Power: Keep Your Juices Flowing," to calculate the demand on your computer's power supply.

When connecting the data cables to your hard disks, use the middle connector of the flat ribbon cable for the second hard disk. On each drive, there is a terminating resistor that is needed on only the last hard disk. This terminating resistor is a plug-in DIP (dual in-line pin) chip. Your drive manual should indicate where this is located. This terminator must be either removed or disabled from the second drive (the one attached to the cable's middle connector). Some drive manufacturers might have a jumper or series of switches to turn off the resistor. The first drive attached to the end of the data cable should have a terminating resistor in place. Otherwise, twice the current is sent to the controller card, slowly ruining it.

> *Note:* IDE hard disks do not have terminating resistors.

You also need to set the *drive select jumper*. This jumper tells each drive what channel from the controller card to respond to. This jumper needs to be set on each drive. With two drives, the lowest-letter drive (usually C:) must be set to channel 1 (labeled DS0 or DS1) while the other is set to channel 2 (labeled DS1 or DS2) . Most computers use a controller cable that has an actual twist in it; several wires actually cross between the middle and end drive connectors. In this case, both drives should have their drive select jumpers set to the D: position.

One last piece of advice about second drives: Do not use

```
FORMAT C:  \S
```

for the new drive. This will destroy the information on your first hard disk. Simply use

```
FORMAT x:  [Enter]
```

where *x* is the letter of each drive you created on the new drive. Also, when using FDISK, you do not have to create an active partition on the second drive because your computer does not start from that drive but from the primary partition of the first drive.

Protecting Your Hard Disk

Like any mechanical equipment, a hard disk is going to fail someday. Unfortunately, you cannot predict the failure of your disk. While there is no foolproof way to gauge how long hard disks will last, manufacturers rate their products using a *mean time between failure (MTBF)* measurement. The MTBF is the best estimate of how long your hard disk will run before it breaks, or "crashes."

The good news is that your hard disk will probably become obsolete long before it fails. For example, some drives have an MTBF of 50,000 hours — or almost six years. Your drive most likely will not fail during its one or two-year warranty period. Still, your best protection is to buy a drive with a lengthy warranty and money-back guarantee. If your drive lives through its warranty, it probably will last several years beyond that.

Back Up!

Backing up your hard disk to floppy diskettes or a tape drive is your first step toward protecting yourself from catastrophe. The whole point of backing up is to be able to retrieve your data if your hard disk suddenly fails. Your first criteria for backup software is accuracy. The second is ease of use; if your backup software is too complex, you won't use it as frequently as you should. In Chapter 10, "Backing Up Your Hard Work," we provide tips for backing up your hard disk and criteria for picking a backup program.

Use a program that lets you select files easily from an on-screen directory tree. Good on-line help and documentation are also musts. The ability to choose among multiple skill levels keeps novices from issuing dangerous commands and eases the learning curve. If you typically back up files from the same directories, you'll want to do so automatically. Most important are scripts (or macros) that let you save the settings for a particular backup task so you don't have to reenter file specifications during every session. Macros let you replay command sequences — for example, to automatically back up your personal network disk after backing up your hard disk, or to automatically compare the backup with the original.

An effective backup strategy demands flexible options. You should be able to choose between full, incremental, and differential backups. A full backup copies every file you select. An incremental backup copies only the files that have changed since the last backup. A differential backup copies all files that have changed since the last full backup. You can combine full backups with either incremental or differential backups to save time and cut down on disks.

Most people do a time-consuming full backup once a week or month, appending incremental backups to it every day or week. Some people who update only a small set of files over and over prefer differential backups over incremental backups because they can back up less often and use fewer disks. The drawbacks: If you do a differential backup every day, it will take longer, and if you do one every week, you won't be able to go back and target a particular version of a file to restore. If you work with a wide variety of files, or if restoring specific file versions is crucial, incrementals make a lot more sense.

What gets backed up, must get backed down — and in its original condition. With luck, you'll never have to use your restore options, but chances are you will. Besides file selection features, look for special restore options that can save you time in getting your system back on line. For example, you should be able to restore only a particular version of a file and overwrite files that already exist on the hard disk. The ability to restore selected data to new locations is helpful if you need to restore data to a hard disk that has a different subdirectory structure.

Head Crash

The phrase "head crash" raises the eyebrows of most computer professionals. It is the most awesome disaster that can happen to your PC.

The hard disk's heads normally ride a cushion of air over the platters. If one of these heads ever touch a platter's surface, it can scour and destroy the disk. This is called a *head crash*; the head actually crashes into the drive's platters. The thin magnetic coating that allows you to record information to the disk becomes marred and the heads may become overheated and ruined. Even worse, the particles that are scraped off can contaminate other parts of the disk, possibly causing other heads to crash.

A head crash can be caused by several factors. For example, the hard disk may have some manufacturing defects. More likely, the hard disk may have received a jolt while it was being used. Hard disk drives are sensitive to vibrations and shocks. Because the heads fly so close to the surface, it doesn't take much to cause them to crash.

You can worry less about a head crash when your computer is turned off. Many hard disks automatically park their heads to a safe position on the disk when the power is turned off. The hard disks in older computers sometimes require you to type a command such as PARK to do the same thing. When a computer is turned off and the hard disk's heads are parked, it can be moved, but never dropped. Likewise, the hard disk can be removed and handled safely.

A Safe Environment

Your hard disk can live longer in the right environment. Believe it or not, leaving your computer on for long periods of time is best for your hard disk. Whenever your computer is turned on, the hard disk goes through enormous stress. It has to go from 0 to 3600 revolutions per minute in a few seconds. Also, your hard disk has to handle a 400+ watt surge every time it is started. I recommend you turn your computer on once a day and off once a day, and no more. Likewise, a power surge, sag, or outage can damage your hard disk. Using a surge protector is barely adequate. A better choice is a line conditioner or a more expensive backup power supply.

Hard disks are sealed and have an air filter, but the filters are not perfect. When a dust or smoke particle sits on a platter, the head crashes right into it at about 56 mph (if the particle is on the outer track). This crashing is inevitable; a dust particle is about 10 times taller than the gap between the head and the disk surface. Try to keep your work area clear of smoke and dust.

Keeping your hard disk at a near-constant temperature also extends its life. For example, the internal platters may expand or contract with the temperature. For example, some hard disks use inexpensive stepper motors that are sensitive to temperature changes. In a few minutes, your hard disk may go from room temperature to over 100 degrees. Saving information at one temperature may make it difficult to find when it is retrieved at a different temperature. When you first start your PC, do not use it immediately. Give it about 15 minutes to warm up. During that time, get ready for your work, grab a cup of coffee or read the paper. This will help extend the reliability of data saved to your computer.

Owners of laptop computers often take their computers from a hot or frozen car into an office only to have them die upon starting. Usually, the change in temperature and humidity causes condensation, leading to water droplets on the platters. Always give your computer time to adjust to the humidity and temperature of its surroundings before turning it on.

For more information on creating a good computing environment, refer to Chapter 2, "Environment: Clearing the Air" and Chapter 5, "Power: Keep Your Juices Flowing."

Verifying the Data

DOS allows you to "verify" a file has been safely saved to your hard or floppy disk drive. After writing the file, DOS checks that the file matches what was written seconds before. This command doesn't guarantee no physical error, only that the file wasn't saved to a bad sector. Still, it provides an extra assurance that crucial files are copied.

You can turn the DOS VERIFY feature on in your AUTOEXEC.BAT startup file so that it is always on. Otherwise, you can use the VERIFY feature only when you need it.

To have VERIFY on every time you start your computer, add this line to your AUTOEXEC.BAT file:

```
VERIFY ON
```

Otherwise, you can turn VERIFY on during your session by typing the above command from the DOS prompt. To turn VERIFY off, type:

```
VERIFY OFF [Enter]
```

You can also add the /V switch to the COPY or XCOPY commands to verify the copying of crucial files. When writing this book and feeling too tired to use my backup software, I would simply type:

```
XCOPY D:\BOOK\*.CHP A: /V [Enter]
```

This command copied all my chapters (.CHP) to a diskette in drive A: and verified the files were copied successfully.

Preventing Unwanted Formats

An accidental formatting of your hard disk could lose all your data. One way to prevent someone else from using the DOS FORMAT command on your hard disk is to rename it so it's more difficult to find. In the example below, the FORMAT.COM file is renamed to TAMROF (FORMAT spelled backwards). From the DOS prompt, you can type:

```
REN C:\DOS\FORMAT.COM C:\DOS\TAMROF.COM [Enter]
```

To protect yourself from using the FORMAT command, change the name as shown above but also create the following batch file that lets you format only drives A and B, your possible floppy diskette drives. To create a batch file, you must type the following in a simple text editor and save it as a plain ASCII file called FORMAT.BAT.

```
echo off (@echo off if you have DOS 3.3 or
higher)

if a== %1a goto formata

if %1 == A: goto formata

if %1 == a: goto formata
if %1 == B: goto formatb
if %1 == b: goto formatb
if %1 == C: goto formatc
if %1 == c: goto formatc
echo Your FORMAT command doesn't make sense.
goto end
:formata
tamrof a:
goto end
:formatb
tamrof b:
goto end
:formatc
echo ^G (this is Ctrl-G)
echo You are attempting to format your hard
disk!
echo This will destroy all information on it.
:end
```

Once created, you can use the FORMAT command by typing the phrase FORMAT and then the letter of the drive you want to format, like this:

```
FORMAT A:  [Enter]
```

The FORMAT.BAT file runs, using TAMROF.COM (the renamed FORMAT.COM file), and checks that you are formatting only drive A or B. If you try to format drive C:, you get a warning message.

If your hard disk is accidentally formatted, you may be able to rescue it. DOS 5.0 includes an UNFORMAT utility. UNFORMAT.COM can recover data from an accidentally formatted disk. If you used the DOS 5.0 Safe Format or Quick Format, the files are still on the formatted disk but simply removed from the File Allocation Table. This file information is placed instead on your disk in a hidden file. The Safe Format is the default method DOS uses to format already formatted diskettes. The Quick Format is the same as the Safe Format except it doesn't check for bad sectors on the disk.

To unformat a hard or floppy disk:

1. After discovering your accidental formatting, be sure you have UNFORMAT.COM available.

   If you formatted your hard disk, you will need to insert your original DOS diskette with the UNFORMAT utility on it. If you want to unformat a diskette in drive A:, the UNFORMAT.COM file is already in your DOS directory.

2. Start the UNFORMAT process.

   From the DOS prompt, type:

   ```
   c:\dos\UNFORMAT d:  [Enter]
   ```

   where *c:\dos* is the drive and path to your UNFORMAT.COM file and *d:* is the letter of the drive you want to unformat. If you have a path already defined to your DOS directory, you do not need to type *c:\dos*.

3. Answer "Y" (yes) that you want to update the system area on the formatted drive.

UNFORMAT restores your file information and recovers your disk. If unformatting a hard disk, you may have to restart your computer.

Resurrecting Deleted Files

DOS is pretty lazy when it erases/deletes a file. Rather than clearing the data from your disk, it simply replaces the first letter of the filename with an E5 hex marker to show the file's been erased. Last, the FAT is cleared of references to that file so the space can be used by other files. Since DOS doesn't erase the data, several unerase programs, including DOS 5.0's own Undelete, can restore files you've accidentally deleted. Of course, this unerasing is only successful if the clusters occupied by the erased file haven't yet been claimed by another file. This is why it is so important to unerase a file as soon as possible. In some cases, you may be able to retrieve only part of the file. However, retrieving 90 percent of a file is preferred to losing it all.

To use the UNDELETE command:

1. After accidentally deleting a file, type:

   ```
   UNDELETE  c:\path\file  [Enter]
   ```

   where c:\path\file is the drive, directory, and filename of the file you accidentally deleted. Deleted files are listed. In place of file, you can use wild cards, like *.LET to display deleted files ending with the letters .LET.

2. For each file displayed, answer "Y" to those you want to undelete.

3. For each file, provide the first letter of the name.

   If a file with the same name already exists, provide a different first letter.

Mirror, Mirror

Both the UNFORMAT and UNDELETE commands are greatly helped by using the DOS 5.0 MIRROR program. MIRROR.COM creates a delete tracking file that records the same information kept in the File

Allocation Table (FAT). Even if a disk is formatted with the unconditional (destructive) switch (/U), UNFORMAT can use the MIRROR information to restore the files.

When you load MIRROR, it creates either two or three files on a disk. MIRORSAV.FIL is a hidden file while MIRROR.FIL is a file that is read-only — you cannot delete it. If you use the optional /T switch with MIRROR, another file called PCTRACKR.DEL is created. This file is updated every time a file is deleted. This deletion tracking file is stored on your hard disk, often requiring no more than 2 percent of any disk. The larger the disk, the smaller percentage of the disk is required.

A small amount of your computer's memory is used when the /T switch is used, less than 7K. This memory used by the memory-resident portion of MIRROR is well worth it if you want to undelete almost any file.

To use MIRROR, add the following to the last line in your AUTOEXEC.BAT startup file:

```
c:\dos\MIRROR d: e:
```

where c:\dos is the drive and path to your directory of DOS files and d: and e: are the drives you want to protect. You do not need c:\dos if you already have a path pointing to your DOS directory. If you want the extra ability to track deleted files, instead use:

```
c:\dos\MIRROR d: e: /Td /Te
```

where /Td and /Te load the deletion-tracking portion of MIRROR for the drive letters you provide. To limit the size of the PCTRACKR.DEL file, you can use /Td-xxx, where xxx is the maximum number of deleted files you want tracked. If you are using DOS 5.0 and have upper memory available, instead use the line:

```
LOADHIGH c:\dos\MIRROR d: e: /Td /Te
```

Sometimes, you may want to disable MIRROR temporarily if you are about to delete or create many files you are certain you won't want to undelete. By disabling MIRROR, you can keep the PCTRACKR.DEL file from filling with this unwanted file information.

To Disable MIRROR

1. From the DOS prompt, type:

```
MIRROR /U [Enter]
```

If successfully turned off, MIRROR responds with "Delete Tracking removed from memory." If other memory-resident programs were loaded after MIRROR, you may be unable to remove MIRROR until the others are removed. For this reason, you may want to make the line that loads MIRROR the last one in your AUTOEXEC.BAT file to ensure it is the last memory-resident program loaded.

To Lower Levels

When you format your hard disk, you are only doing the logical formatting. The physical formatting was done at the factory. This physical formatting is called a *low-level format*. During a low-level format, the disk is tested for physical flaws and the sectors are mapped. Any flaws or bad sectors are marked as unusable. It is a natural process, since it is very difficult to make a perfect hard disk.

There are four basic reasons for you to low-level format your hard disk:

1. You've purchased either a new controller or new drive and want to ensure the two are matched to each other.

2. You want to refresh the sector addresses on your disk. Sector addresses are magnetic images on the disk. With age, these signals become faint, possibly creating errors such as "Sector not found." Some types of hard disks — especially those that use the older stepper motors — can benefit from a periodic low-level format without changing the interleave. An annual low-level formatting not only ensures the sectors on the disk are aligned with the heads but also identifies surface defects on the disk.

3. You want to change the interleave factor to speed up your hard disk. This was described earlier.

4. You suspect a faulty format.

Some hard disks come with low-level formatting utilities. Some drives come with a low-level formatting program right on the hard disk controller. You often have to use the DOS DEBUG program to run these programs. Consult your manual or dealer for information on accessing your built-in low-level formatting program. If your hard disk didn't come with a formatting utility, consider utilities such as DOSUtils, Norton Utilities or SpinRite. Remember, IDE drives cannot be low-level formatted. They are supposedly so perfect and self-adjusting that they do not need to be low-level formatted again.

Before you low-level format, restart your PC without any memory-resident programs, like disk caching software. Since a formatting program relies on the timing of your computer, such programs can jumble the results. Also, be sure you have two fresh backups of your hard disk (and test one). A low-level format usually clears the data from your hard disk, although some of the utilities mentioned above do not.

Hard Disk Troubles

The longer a disk is used, the more things can go wrong: Flaws can occur in the platters' magnetic coating; the read/write heads can drift away from their original position; the File Allocation Table can develop errors; and since DOS is designed to use the next available sector whenever it writes data, files can become fragmented across the disk, slowing disk reads and causing unnecessary wear and tear.

Your disk may give you a few clues of impending failure. For example, if you start getting an increasing number of disk errors such as "Sector not found," you can be sure that something is deteriorating in your disk. Conversely, a hard disk can fail quite suddenly. You switch on your computer and instead of a C:\> prompt, you see an ominous error message or nothing at all.

Some hard disk failures are easy to repair. For example, the battery that remembers your computer's setup may have died. This setup information tells your computer what kind of hard disk is installed. Many of these setup batteries are simple watch or AA batteries. Another easy-to-fix problem is that the hard disk controller or cables are loose. Check to see that the controller is seated in its socket and that all the cables between the controller and your disk are fully plugged in at both ends.

Beyond these simple solutions, you'll need to replace your hard disk or have a professional data recovery service retrieve the data from the ailing hard disk. Companies such as Ontrack Data Recovery charge several hundred dollars to repair a hard disk or recover the lost data. Although the costs of these services can surpass the price of the hard disk, the dollar value of your hours of work is often much greater. Such services should be used only when you need to retrieve vital information that you failed to back up.

Viruses

One of the biggest and possibly exaggerated threats to your computer is the *computer virus*. A computer virus is a small software program (usually less than 5K) that spreads from one computer to another. The virus either provides annoying messages or sometimes does actual damage to your data.

In 1986, there were about six known viruses. Today, there are more than 3,000 and growing. There are underground software packages, such as the Virus Creation Laboratory, that allow even computer novices to build dozens of viruses in a few hours. What motivates virus programmers? Typically, a sense of power, infamy, or just sheer boredom.

There are two general categories of viruses: *file* and *boot sector*. A file virus attacks files. They usually invade your program files, those ending with extensions of .COM or .EXE. They also invade overlay files (.OVL), device drivers (.SYS), and batch files (.BAT). All of these file types are called *executable files*, because they can be executed, or run. File viruses load themselves into memory whenever an infected file is run. They then spread to other uninfected program files as those files are run.

A boot sector virus spreads from PC to PC by placing itself on the boot sector of floppy diskettes and hard drives. The virus spreads to a hard disk if an infected diskette is in drive A: when your computer is turned on.

The widespread Stoned Virus is a boot sector virus. In 1992, the Michelangelo boot sector virus received great attention since it was scheduled to wipe out infected hard disks on March 6, the great artist's birthday. Contrary to popular opinion, you will not get infected by a virus by simply calling an online information service such as PRODIGY or an electronic bulletin board system (BBS). Most of these services use virus scanners before allowing an uploaded software program to be downloaded by its members.

How do you avoid viruses? Here are a handful of tips, although not all-inclusive:

- **Apply write-protect tabs to all program diskettes before installing new software or as soon as possible after installation.** Write-protecting these disks can prevent viruses from spreading to the original program files and therefore to other computers.

- **Do not install software if you don't know where it's been.** Watch out for demonstration and diagnostic floppy disks. These are often common carriers of viruses. Unfortunately, even new, shrink-wrapped software is not safe. The Michelangelo virus, for example, found its way onto thousands of new software packages.

- **Make your executable files read-only.** File viruses can be contained if you keep your executable files from being changed. Using DOS's ATTRIB command, you can make your files read-only, so they cannot be altered. From the top, or root, directory, use the following commands:

```
ATTRIB +R *.EXE /S [Enter]
ATTRIB +R *.COM /S [Enter]
ATTRIB +R *.SYS /S [Enter]
```

The /S switch applies the read-only attribute to files not only in the root directory but all directories underneath it. Repeat these commands for your other drives, like drive D:, E:, etc.

- **Limit sharing diskettes with others.** Boot sector viruses commonly spread this way. If an infected diskette is left in the drive A: and you turn on your computer, the virus will spread to the hard disk.

- **Back up your hard disk frequently.** For information on backing up your hard disk, see Chapter 10: "Backing Up Your Hard Work." Although your backup might be infected as well, you can at least restore your hard disk and then use an antivirus software package to remove the virus.

- **Avoid untested BBS files**. If you use a modem to dial electronic bulletin board systems, do not download new files that haven't been scanned for viruses yet by the system operator (sysop).

- **Stay away from pirated software.** Using copies of software you didn't buy is not only illegal and immoral but another avenue for receiving a virus. In this case, you get what you pay for.

- **Use a highly rated antivirus software package.** Antivirus software, such as Ontrack's *Dr. Solomon's Anti-Virus Toolkit* or Central Point's *Anti-Virus*, help prevent infection, as well as detect and eradicate computer viruses. Several antivirus software packages are available, but many are not equipped to detect certain viruses. For example, some viruses, called *polymorphic viruses*, try to avoid detection by changing the "fingerprints" these products use to track them down. *Stealth viruses* avoid detection by telling the antivirus software that the infected file is okay. Antivirus software is like wearing a seatbelt. You can certainly reduce the chances of an accident by driving carefully. But wearing a seatbelt is often reassuring.

How do you know if you have a virus? When a virus flares up, the symptoms are different. For example, the Jerusalem virus displays a blank box. The Cascade virus sends your monitor's letters crashing to the bottom of the screen.

Other symptoms include the following:

- Your PC suddenly slows to a crawl or programs take longer to load.

- The size of a file increases because the virus is attached to it.

- The time and date stamps of files mysteriously change although you haven't worked on them recently.

- Your drives work when they shouldn't, for instance, your floppy drive light turns on when you're not using it.

- Your available memory is reduced.

- Free space is suddenly decreased.

- Your programs are disappearing.

- Your computer restarts itself.

If you think you are the victim of a virus, immediately turn off your computer and purchase an antivirus software package. The package will provide you with the steps to take to remove the suspected infection. Typically, you will have to start your computer from a write-protected floppy disk and use the antivirus software to scan and repair your hard disk. You then must remove any infections from your floppy diskettes and backups.

Disk Utilities   Commercial disk utilities can help locate and even minimize the effect of some hard disk problems. Products such as Disk Technician Gold, SpinRite, Mace Performance, Norton Utilities, and PC Tools solve a variety of problems. These utilities are not "magic bullets" that solve your hard disk's physical problems. For example, they can prevent defective sectors from being used in the future, but such problems often indicate you could use a new hard disk.

   These utilities can help in at least three areas: surface testing, interleave setting, and low-level formatting.

**Surface
Testing**   The ability to find and lock out flaws in the disk's magnetic coating is the single most important feature a disk utility can offer. You'd hate to save perfectly good information on an imperfect sector. The best surface tests are both read/write (meaning they write to every sector of the disk and then read back the data to make sure it's correct) and nondestructive (meaning they save the data before starting the test and restore it afterward). Read-only tests are faster, and marginally safer, but they may not catch as many failing sectors. Testing should flag lost clusters, check and compare File Allocation Tables, and let you lock out bad sectors so they won't be used again. Testing should be accompanied by the ability to move data from a failing sector to a good one. Finally, it should verify that the hard disk controller is working correctly.

**Low-Level
Formatting**   When you receive your hard disk, two operations must be done for it to work. First, it must receive a low-level format. (This is done at the factory.) The low-level format process establishes tracks and sectors on the blank magnetic surfaces. Next, a high-level DOS format establishes a complex filing system that includes logical partitions (letter disks, like D:), subdirectories, and one or more File Allocation Tables (FATs). (You usually do the DOS format or have it done for you by the company that sold you your computer.)

   If the low-level format on your hard disk is rarely rewritten, it can fade in normal use. Also, wear and tear on disk hardware may cause the heads to drift away from the original tracks, causing data errors. (IDE, SCSI, and ESDI drives cannot be low-level formatted, because their controllers do not support it. Don't worry, though; these drives' sophisticated electronics adjust to the drifting of the heads.) The ability to rewrite this low-level format, thereby strengthening magnetic data and compensating for changes in the positions of the heads — all without losing any data — is almost as important as surface testing.

Also desirable, though not essential, is the ability to do a destructive low-level format. This is handy for brand-new hard disks as well as for XT-type computers, on which BIOS peculiarities make nondestructive low-level formatting needlessly tough on the hardware.

Interleave

The low-level format also establishes what's known as the interleave. The interleave is the order of the sector numbers around the hard disk's tracks. Sectors aren't always in sequential order. If they are, it's known as a 1:1 interleave.

A 1:1 interleave is a good idea on faster computers with faster hard disks but not for slower computers and disks. Why? By the time the microprocessor receives Sector 1 and requests Sector 2, Sector 2 has already spun past the read/write head. The controller then has to wait for Sector 2 to whiz by again. To reduce this idle time, some disks use interleaves that aren't sequential. For example, an interleave of 2:1 or 3:1 is often used, putting one or two other sectors, respectively, between consecutive sectors to compensate for the slower computer and disk. The wrong interleave will have a dire impact on how fast your disk reads and writes data. The best disk utilities test the interleave, tell you if it's optimal, and let you change it during the low-level format process.

In day-to-day use, hard disk utilities can indeed lessen chances of disaster. I primarily use *Norton Utilities*. In my AUTOEXEC.BAT startup file, I added the line:

```
NDD /Q
```

This is the Norton Disk Doctor with the "quick" switch on. NDD then gives my hard disk a quick "check-up" each time I start my computer. Although my hard disk is new, Norton Disk Doctor has discovered and corrected two FATs when they were out of synch. With hard disk utilities, you can preserve the health and well-being of your computer and resolve many of the problems affecting it.

Squeaky Drives

Some hard disks may squeal or squeak. How do you fix that? First, be sure the disk is lying flat or on its side. A slightly off-balanced drive will whine. Second, check that the drive is fully installed. Some drives are only supported on one side; if so, use a piece of cardboard to dampen the vibration. The third cause of noise is the *static wiper*, or *spindle ground strap*. The static wiper is a metal arm that is located over the center of the drive. Over time, the wiper becomes worn, causing it to rub unevenly against a nearby ball bearing. One solution is to use a fine emery cloth to shine the static wiper. You can dampen the vibration by attaching foam tape or rubber to it. Otherwise, place a drop of silicone putty on top of the wiper but not between it and the bearing. This extra mass may be enough to dampen the squeak. You can also lubricate the bearing using a Teflon-based lubricant. Do not use a silicone-based lubricant, such as WD40. The lubricant attracts contaminants.

(Not) Using CHKDSK

DOS includes a utility called CHKDSK (Check Disk) that crudely diagnoses and "fixes" damaged files. CHKDSK alerts you to errors in the FAT. If errors exist, CHKDSK can also fix them.

Unfortunately, the cure may be worse than the disease. CHKDSK usually "amputates" the corrupted files, causing a loss of data. The lost chains — files that have not been recorded in the FAT — can be saved in the root directory of your hard disk in the format FILE*nnnn*.CHK, where *nnnn* is the sequential number of the file. However, these files are often gobbledygook. Still, this utility is handy for the "garbage" files that are created if your computer is suddenly restarted or turned off while saving a file. For example, if your computer's power is shut off during *Microsoft Windows*, some temporary files may be created and need to be removed. Remember, CHKDSK only fixes logical errors, that is, errors to the file structure. If your hard disk has any physical defects, CHKDSK cannot help.

To use CHKDSK:

1. From your DOS prompt, type:

```
CHKDSK /F [Enter]
```

CHKDSK can only recover files if you have used the /F switch. The report on your screen shows information about your hard disk. If any of the files are damaged, you will see a message, like this:

```
10 lost allocation units found in 3 chains.
Convert lost chains to files?
```

2. Answer "Y" to convert the lost chains.

DOS saves the damaged files to the root, or top, directory, such as C:\ or A:\. These files are saved with the name FILE*nnnn*.CHK, where *nnnn* is the number of the file. The first file is FILE0000.CHK and so on.

3. Analyze the recovered files.

You can see if the recovered files might have some value. (They rarely do.) From the DOS prompt, type:

```
TYPE FILE0000.CHK [Enter]
```

The file is displayed to the screen. From this, you should be able to determine if the files have any value.

4. If desired, delete the recovered files.

If the files don't have any value, type:

```
DEL FILE*.CHK [Enter]
```

The recovered files are removed.

When a Hard Disk Isn't Right

The hard disk is not the best solution for everyone. Several mass storage options offer features attractive to some, including

- Hard cards
- Removable storage
- Rewritable optical
- Super floppy drives
- Portable drives

A hard card allows you to add a hard disk when there is otherwise no room in your computer's case for one. A hard card is a circuit card with a built-in hard disk designed to be inserted into the expansion slot of your PC. Since most slim-line computer cases have only three drive bays but ample expansion slots, a hard card is one way to add more storage. Hard cards often cost more than most regular hard disks, but installation is relatively easy. With the controller built into the card, they offer true plug-and-play installation. One popular manufacturer of hard cards is Quantum Corp. and its HardCards product line.

Removable storage is another storage option. You can save almost 100MB on a single cartridge and remove it at the end of the day for security reasons or to transport it elsewhere. Also, these cartridges make perfect backup devices. Unlike tape drives, removable storage devices let you copy the contents of your hard disk and instantly use the copy without wrestling with a restore process. The most popular removable storage is the Bernoulli Box from Iomega Corp. Another manufacturer is SyQuest. Removable storage is not slow; speed currently rivals that of most hard disks — under 20 ms. The drives can

Figure 9.11 A portable hard disk, such as the Sysgen MobileDisk, can connect directly to your computer's printer port. *(Photo courtesy of Sysgen Inc.)*

be expensive as well as the cartridges. Expect to pay more than $100 for a 90MB cartridge.

Rewritable optical drives are another alternative to data storage. Costing about $3000, rewritable optical drives offer 650MB of storage per cartridge. The cartridges cost about $200 per disk. For big storage needs, an optical drive is a good investment. A variation of the rewritable optical drive is the super floppy, or Floptical, drive. A super floppy drive provides 20MB of storage on an inexpensive ($25) 3.5-inch removable disk. At the same time, these drives double as a drive for 720K and 1.44MB diskettes. In some ways, a Floptical drive is like a poor man's Bernoulli Box. It isn't as fast, but you can back up assorted hard disks and directories affordably and easily.

If you want a hard disk that is on the go, consider a portable drive (see Figure 9.11). These handheld drives either attach to a SCSI expansion card or directly to your computer's parallel printer port (while allowing you to still print). When attached through the parallel port, these drives are not blazingly fast, but they provide ample speed for most work. A portable drive that attaches to your parallel port is ideal for moving large amounts of data between two or more computers.

QIC Is Quick

Another mass storage option is the tape drive. Unlike the previous storage options, tape drives are designed for backing up your hard disk. Instead of copying a 100MB hard disk to almost 85 diskettes, a tape drive can store the entire drive on one cartridge.

A tape backup system consists of a special tape recorder, cartridge tapes to hold your data and software to copy the files from your hard disk to the tapes. When necessary, this software must be able to restore these files to your hard disk. The most common type of tape drive is the DC2000, named after the type of cartridge tapes used. They are the least expensive, about $250 to $500, and can back up most hard disks. The tapes, about the size of a cigarette pack, can hold up to 250MB of data. (See Figure 9.12). If you require more storage, you can simply use more tapes.

These tape drives support the QIC (Quarter-Inch Committee) standards, which define the tape-drive controller cards, cartridge physical size, and the commands that control the drives. Theoretically, these tapes can be written in one manufacturer's tape drive and read

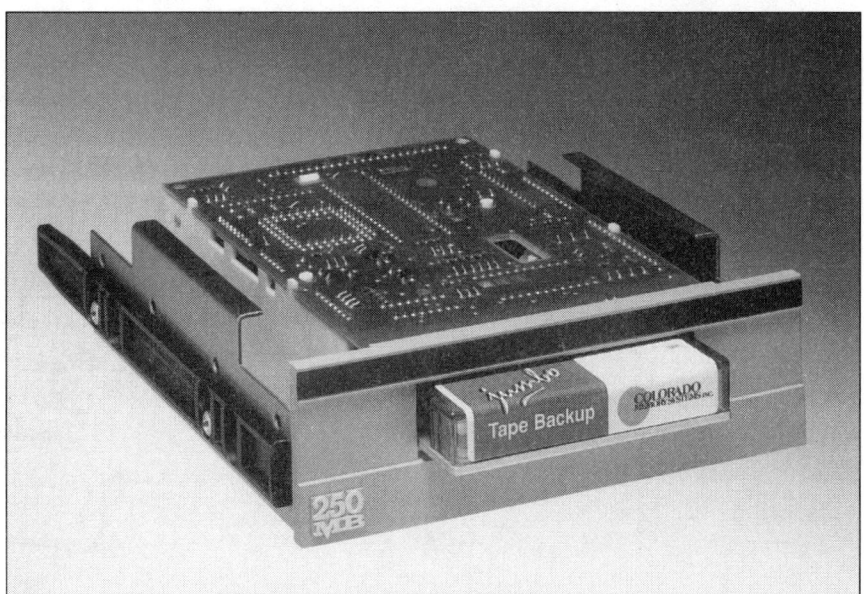

Figure 9.12. A tape drive can be either internal or external. This internal drive can hold 250MB of information. (Photo courtesy of Colorado Memory Systems Inc.)

back in a drive from another manufacturer.

To store more information on a tape, special techniques are used to compress the data. This compression may be provided either by the software used to back up your hard disk or by special expansion cards that control the drives. Software-based compression will slow down your backup, but may be worth it if you can get your entire hard disk on one tape instead of two, especially when the tapes cost more than $25 each. Of course, if your data is already compressed by a utility such as PKZip, further compression is unlikely.

The least expensive tape drives connect directly to the floppy disk controller card. If you have one floppy diskette drive, the tape drive uses the connection for the second one. If you have two floppy drives, a special Y-adapter kit usually can share the control lines between the tape and diskette drives. Unfortunately, using the floppy controller limits data transfer rates to about 500K per minute. This may seem reasonably fast, but backing up a 100MB hard disk may require up to two hours. If you want the data verified, this may take even longer. On the flip side, if you use your backup software's ability to run unattended or overnight, this slower process is of little concern.

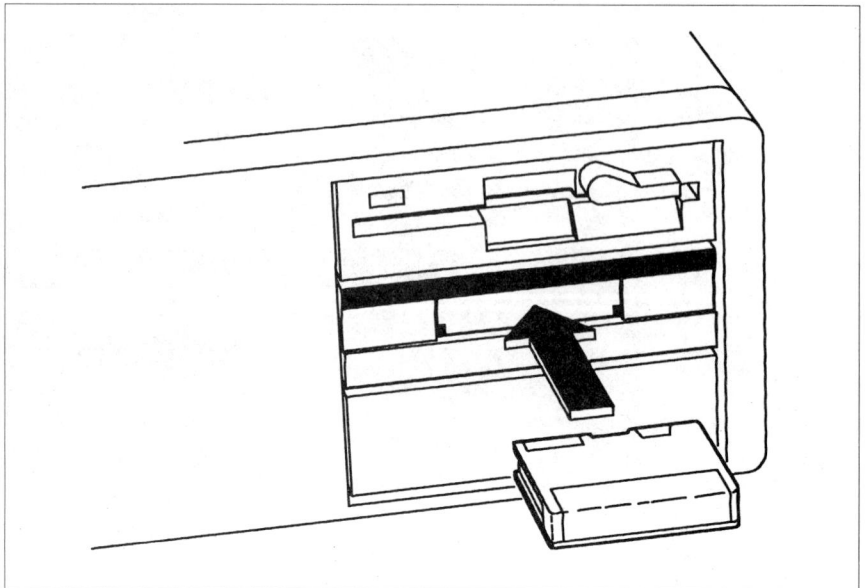

Figure 9.13 Once installed, the tape drive typically is first used to format tape cartidges before they can be used. *(Photo courtesy of Colorado Memory Systems Inc.)*

You can purchase an optional tape drive controller card. This expansion card lets you back up data as much as four times faster than the floppy controller. On my computer, I can back up and verify 212MB of data in less than 50 minutes. These interface cards require a single expansion slot and add $100 to $250 to the cost of a tape drive.

Besides selecting how you want to connect the tape drive to your PC you also must select where it should be mounted: internally or externally. An internal drive will be installed like any other half-height floppy drive. An external drive has its own case and usually its own power supply. One advantage of an external drive is that you can buy a second interface card and use the tape drive with another computer. You also would want an external tape drive if you have no drive bays left in which to mount an internal one. An internal drive has one advantage: It's less expensive, costing about $60 less than an external version.

Tape drives include a simple software utility for formatting the tapes and backing up your hard disk. Commercial software such as Norton Backup or Central Point Backup are much easier to use and are full-featured.

IMPORTANT: Before ordering such tape backup software, make sure it supports not only your tape drive but how it is connected. Some backup software does not support tape drives that use separate tape controller cards.

External tape drives are easiest to install. You simply put the controller card into an empty slot in your computer, close the case, and hook up the tape drive to the card's external connector. Installing an internal tape drive is slightly more difficult. You must mount the tape drive into one of the drive bays and attach the controller and power cables to the drive. Some pitfalls await you, however. For example, you may not have enough power supply connectors to run the tape drive, requiring you to get a Y-adapter to split the power with your hard disk or other powered device. Also, the controller cable for the tape drive differs between XT- and AT-type computers. If you get the wrong cable, none of your drives will work.

After you install a tape drive, you have to format each tape, unless they came preformatted (which costs extra). Formatting a single tape requires 40 minutes to one hour. After making a backup of your hard disk, test it out by restoring some of the files. For tips on selecting backup software and creating a backup strategy, consult Chapter 10, "Backing Up Your Hard Work."

Having enough storage is certainly a boon. You shouldn't have to worry about where to store your work. Your productivity should be limited only by your creativity and energy, not by the speed of your hard disk or the size of your tape drive.

10 Backing Up Your Hard Work

Regularly backing up your hard disk is your PC's insurance policy. You need it only when you're in trouble. Yet backups are useful for many purposes. Most important, they can be used to restore your data if your hard disk were to suddenly fail, or "crash." A crash can be caused by mechanical failure, an electrical jolt, fire, water, or even dust and smoke particles. Also, parts of your hard disk may fail. Portions of the disk can lose their magnetic signals, resulting in corrupt or lost data. Some hard disks contain hundreds if not thousands of hours of work. Protecting this work is crucial. A properly backed up hard disk can be restored within minutes.

Yet a failing hard disk is becoming rarer. Modern manufacturing techniques have created hard disks that probably will last longer than your computer, sometimes up to an average of 150,000 hours. Backups are useful for restoring individual files or directories you might accidentally delete. They are also useful for accessing older versions of a file. The backup can contain earlier versions of important files that you may want to retrieve.

Backups are also useful for unburdening your hard disk of rarely used programs and old data. By archiving megabytes of information, your hard disk can focus on present work and not last year's budget or old correspondence. Plus, you'll have more room for today's space-hungry programs. Archiving the information is safer than deleting files you may — gulp — need some day.

Backups are useful for transferring files from one computer to another. Whether moving the contents of your entire hard disk or just a few files, backup software provides an easy way to transfer files. You don't have to worry about how many files will fit on one diskette or what to do with very large files.

The value of a backup is often misunderstood. Your hard disk is equal to thousands of hours of your sweat and labor. The value is not only in your data — the files you created, the letters you wrote, the addresses in your databases. Backups also save you the trouble of reinstalling programs and configuring them to your liking. For example, I have tens of hours involved in customizing my installation of *Windows*. I have painstakingly removed unwanted files and tweaked my colors to my personal preferences. If that work was lost, I could certainly reinstall Windows from the original program disks, but that customization would be lost. For these reasons, I recommend people back up their programs as well as their data files.

The Backup Process

Backing up your computer involves copying files from your computer to another medium — a floppy diskette or, if you own a tape drive, a tape cartridge. Once done, the backup medium cannot be read directly by your computer; the files are often saved in a proprietary format to conserve space and prevent errors.

> *Note:* For information on tape drives, see Chapter 9, "Storage: It's a Hard Life." If you want to back up more than 30MB of data, I recommend a tape drive. Large floppy-disk backups can be tedious. At best, 30MB of data may require 10 diskettes; at worst, almost 90.

Keeping Track of It All

The backup process relies on the system of attributes. Each file on your computer has hidden marks to describe its status, as shown in the following table.

Letter	Meaning
A	Archive - needs to be backed up.
S	System - important file required for the operating system.
H	Hidden - this file is hidden from view.
R	Read-only - this file cannot be deleted or saved to.

The archive attribute, or flag, is DOS's way of determining if a file needs to be backed up. How do you find the attributes of a file?

To find the attribute of a file:

1. From the DOS prompt (C: or A:), type:

   ```
   ATTRIB *.* [Enter]
   ```

   A list of files is displayed. In the left-hand column of the screen, you will see the attributes of the files. If an "A" appears, it means the file has not been backed up. Backup software uses the archive attribute to determine what files get backed up.

Five Backup Options

There are five types of backup options:

1. Full
2. Full copy
3. Incremental
4. Incremental copy
5. Differential

The *full backup* backs up all files you select, whether the archive attribute is on or off. Usually, the entire hard disk is backed up, although you can perform a full backup of individual directories. Once the files are safely backed up, the archive attributes of all files are turned off. Every backup plan includes making at least one full backup of the entire hard disk.

The full copy backup backs up all selected files but does not turn off their archive attributes. Why? You may want to copy all the files and place them on another computer, such as a laptop. When you simply want to duplicate your files, leave the archive attributes un-

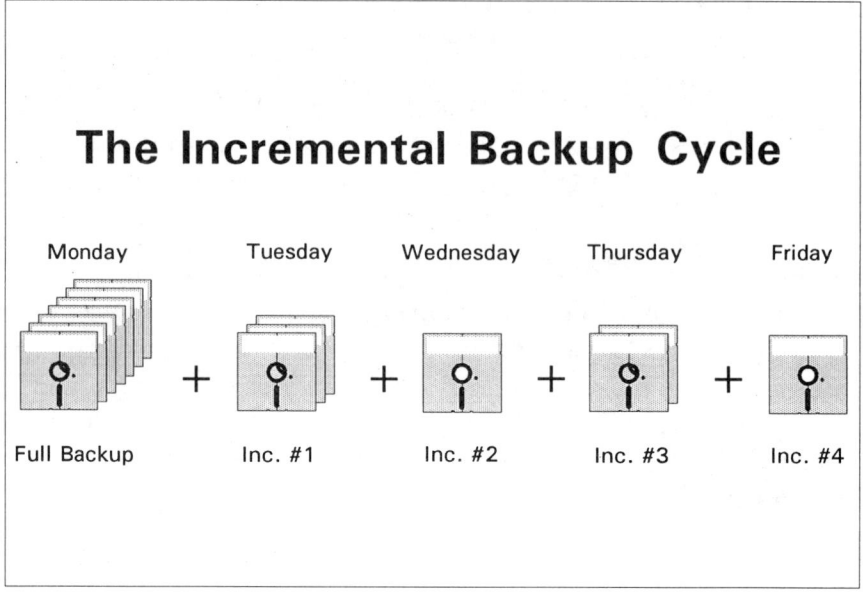

Figure 10.1 In an incremental backup, the files backed up vary from one partial backup to another.

changed to avoid muddying future backups.

The incremental backup backs up only those files that have the archive attribute turned on. In other words, it copies only the files that have changed or been added since the last full backup. Just like its name, the incremental backup stores the changes to your data in increments. The files being incrementally backed up are usually appended to the tail end of the full backup medium (see Figure 10.1).

Like the incremental backup, the incremental copy option backs up only the files that have changed since the full backup. However, the archive attributes are not turned off. The incremental copy option is often used to provide a duplicate of changed files for storage elsewhere or to update another computer.

An incremental backup is used after a full backup. With an incremental option, you must have the full backup set plus ALL the sets of incremental backups to restore your hard disk to the way it was up to the last incremental backup.

The differential backup is also a partial backup but acts differently than the incremental option. The differential backup stores the files that have changed since the last full backup (see Figure 10.2). However, the archive attribute is not changed. If a differential backup is

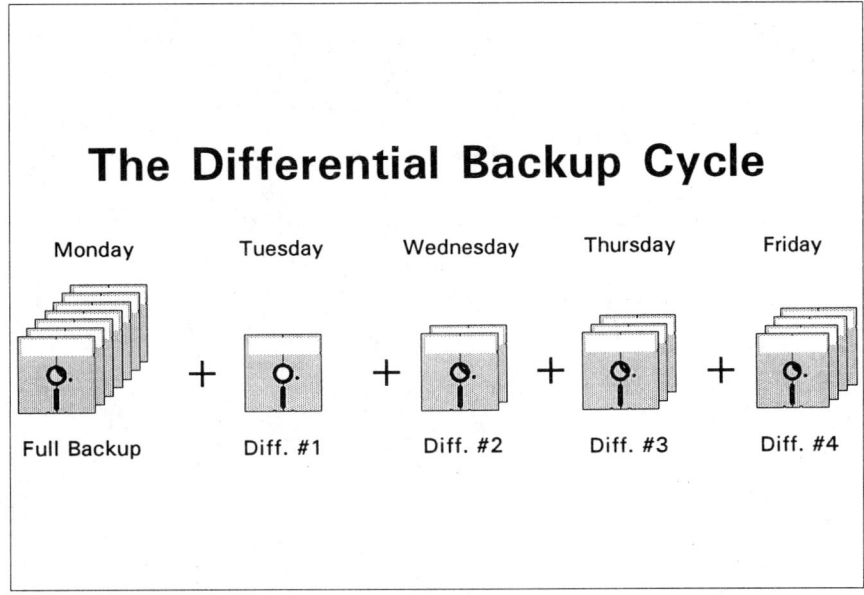

Figure 10.2 In a differential backup, the files backed up grow larger with each partial backup.

performed later, the same files are backed up plus any additional files that have been changed since then. In other words, the differential backup records all the changed files since the last full backup. With the differential option, the backup gets bigger and takes longer. The advantage is that the hard disk can be restored by having the full backup set and the single differential backup set.

Different Strokes for Different Folks

The different backup option you choose should reflect your personal style and the importance of your work. For example, you may want access to older versions of your files, or you may want to use as few disks as possible.

The Backup Cycle

Since every backup routine includes at least one full backup as its foundation, you need to determine the time between full backups. This is called the backup cycle. Two popular backup cycles are one week and one month. During this interval, you do partial backups, storing files that are new or have changed since the last full backup.

The backup cycle you select is determined by how many and to what extent your files change. If you do not use your PC much and the files do not change much or are not that important, you could opt for a longer backup cycle. If your work is very important and difficult to reproduce, or you use your PC quite often, then select a shorter backup cycle.

Besides the full backup cycle, you also need to select how often you will do the partial backup. For example, your backup cycle may be one month and you may want to do a partial backup every week. If your files change often during that week or are very important, you may want to do a partial backup twice a week. You know your computer habits best, but consider these three points:

1. If your number of backup media (diskettes or data cartridges) is limited, you need to estimate how many days they will last.

2. If your number of backup media is unlimited, you have more flexibility in selecting a backup cycle.

3. If you decide to save your backup off-site for the ultimate in safety, keep your backup cycle fairly short, say one week.

One general rule of thumb is that the number of days between your partial backups should never encompass more work than you can afford to lose.

The 3M Data Storage Products Division recommends the "Grand-father, Father, Son" principle to backups. Covering 12 weeks, this concept allows you to restore your computer's hard disk to the way it was three months ago.

Simply put, this principle requires a weekly full backup of your computer for three consecutive weeks. Label each backup set "Week 1," "Week 2" and "Week 3." Throughout the week, you do partial backups to store new or changed files. On the fourth week, do another full backup but label it "Month 1." Repeat this for the second month, but label the fourth week's backup set of the month "Month 2." Repeat this for the third month and create "Month 3."

No matter how often you back up, label your backup media clearly. One way to avoid mix-ups is to use a different colored label or floppy disk for each day of the week. Monday backups on red, Tuesday on blue, and so on. Monthly backups could be kept on black labels or disks. If you back up weekly, you can also follow a color scheme. For example, use a different color disk for each week of the month and a black disk for the end-of-the-month backup.

Don't Be Im-Partial

Besides selecting the length of your backup cycle, you also need to pick which kind of partial backup you will use between full backups: incremental or differential.

Incremental: Full Protection

The incremental backup is ideal if you either work with different files or require older versions of the same files.

If you frequently create several new files, like new correspondence, the incremental backup is ideal. With this option, each partial backup is both fast and efficient because it is recording only the files that are changed or new since the previous incremental backup. If you need access to prior versions of the same file, the incremental backup lets you choose the file from any of the prior incremental backups.

If you ever need to use your backups, you must restore the full backup and then ALL incremental backups since then. If using diskettes as your backup medium, you may find yourself running out, since each incremental backup requires its own diskette.

Differential: Simple and Plain

If you generally work with the same files each day, the differential backup is well suited for your partial backup. Also, the differential backup is ideal if you do not need to keep old versions of your files. With the differential backup, you use only two sets of backup media: the full backup set and the single differential backup set.

With the differential backup, the single partial backup records the changed or new files since the last full backup. For this reason, the differential backup grows larger and larger. Yet, if you tend to use the same files, the length of the backup may grow slowly. When you find the wait time and number of diskettes too burdensome, you can do a full backup and start over.

If you ever need to use your backup, you need to restore only these two sets: full backup and differential backup. This saves time and backup media (that is, fewer diskettes).

Off-Site and Safe

The best backup plan can be thwarted by fire, flood, theft, and other calamities. To assure you the best data protection, you should always keep a backup set off-site, such as in a safety deposit box, a neighbor's house, or at work. When making partial backups, keep the diskettes across the room away from your computer; thieves often steal the diskettes that are conveniently nearby.

How do you maintain a backup copy off-site if you might need it at your computer? You simply maintain two backup sets and rotate between them each backup cycle. For example, if your backup cycle is one week, place the first week's backup set and off-site. Then start the second week's backup set. The third week, you can either start a third backup set or reuse the first week's. In a worst-case scenario, the only work that would be lost if your on-site backup set were destroyed would be those few days since you stored the last backup off-site. Some programs have full copy and incremental copy backup options so you can duplicate the current backup cycle's work and store it off-site.

Free Backup Software with DOS

DOS versions 2.0 and greater come with free backup utilities: BACKUP and RESTORE. BACKUP stores a copy of your files onto one or more diskettes, and RESTORE recalls the files you want from the diskettes. However, these two commands are slow and cumbersome. They cannot detect errors that might occur during the backup process. Also, they do not compress data, so backing up takes longer and requires more floppies. Yet, they do work.

> *Note:* Avoid, if possible, the BACKUP/RESTORE in DOS 3.3. DOS 3.3's RESTORE couldn't read DOS 3.2 backups because directory names for version 3.2 used the forward slash (/) to separate the path names, while DOS 3.3 and later versions use the more usual backslash (\).

To use the DOS BACKUP:

1. Gather enough diskettes to back up your selected directories.

! **WARNING:** If you have a low-density 5.25-inch diskette drive (360K), do not use high-density, 1.2MB diskettes. The BACKUP program does not work correctly with these diskettes.

If you are backing up your entire hard disk, you will need several diskettes. How many? Here's a simple test. From your computer's hard disk, type:

```
CHKDSK [Enter]
```

> *Note:* If CHKDSK reports any corrupted files, do not back up yet. You may be able to use a disk utility to save the corrupted files or at least restore them from a previous backup set.

The first line of the Check Disk command shows how large your hard disk is in bytes. Record this number. Next, put a formatted floppy diskette in your disk drive and type:

```
CHKDSK A: [Enter]
```

Record the first line of how many bytes your diskette holds. Then, divide the size of your hard disk by the size of your floppy diskette. For example, imagine I had a 20MB hard disk and wanted to use BACKUP to back up all files to a 3.5-inch, 1.44MB diskette:

> *20,971,520 (20MB hard disk) ÷ 1,457,664*
> *(1.44MB disk) = 14.39, or 15 diskettes*

Gather 15 diskettes plus two extra ones (just to be safe). These diskettes do not need to be formatted and can even have old files on them. BACKUP will erase the old files, but it will not remove any subdirectories on the diskettes.

2. Place the first diskette in your diskette drive.

This diskette does not have to be formatted, since BACKUP can do this for you.

3. Select the files you want to back up.

    To back up your entire C: hard disk, type:

    ```
    BACKUP C:\ A: /S /M /F:size /
    L:drive:\path\logfile [Enter]
    ```

    To back up a directory and its subdirectories, type:

    ```
    BACKUP c:\path A: /S /M /F:size
    L:drive:\path\logfile [Enter]
    ```

    where *c:\path* is the drive and path to the directory you wish to back up.

What do these switches mean? See the following table.

Switch	Meaning
/S	Back up the files in the current directory and those in the subdirectories beneath it.
/M	Back up only files that have changed or are new since the last backup and then turn off the archive attribute to show the original files were backed up. If you want to do a full backup, then do not use this switch. Instead, use it later to copy only those files that have changed since the last full backup.
/F:size	(DOS versions 4.0 and higher only) formats the backup diskettes to a particular size, where *size* is: 360 — 360K double-sided, double-density 5.25-inch disk 720 — 720K double-sided, double-density 3.5-inch disk 1200 — 1.2MB double-sided high-density 5.25-inch disk 1440 — 1.44MB double-sided, high-density, 3.5-inch disk 2880 — 2.88MB, double-sided, ultra-density 3.5-inch disk (If you have already formatted some diskettes, you do not need to use the /F:size switch.)

Switch	Meaning
/L:*drive:* *path* *logfile*	Create a file of all files backed up. This file then can be used to track what files have been backed up and to where. Once this file is created, copy it to a diskette for proper storage. You can set the location and name of the file, such as /L:C:\\ DOS\\MYBACKUP.TXT. If no log filename is given, the default name becomes BACKUP.LOG.

4. Insert another diskette, if needed.

   Use as many diskettes as needed. Label each one so you can easily find files you may want to restore later. The BACKUP log file lists which disk has what files on it.

5. When done, verify the backup.

   You can verify the backup worked by checking for the presence of two files made by BACKUP. To check the backup, type:

   ```
   DIR A: [Enter]
   ```

   Each disk should contain the files BACKUP.*XXX* and CONTROL.*XXX*, where *XXX* is the number of the disk.

Appending Your Backup

You can add files to your current backup disks without deleting any files from the disks.

To add files to a current backup set:

Type:
BACKUP C:\ A: /A /M [Enter]
The /A switch tells BACKUP to add files to the backup disk, while the /M switch adds only newer files that don't already exist on the backup disk.

Restoring Files

The RESTORE command brings backed-up files to life.

To restore your files:

1. Insert the first disk of your backup into your diskette drive.

2. From the DOS prompt, type:

```
RESTORE  A:  C:\*.*  /P  /S  [Enter]
```

> *Note:* The C:*.* can be changed to restore only a certain directory or type of file, such as C:\DOS*.COM.

The two switches are:

/P Asks you to approve restoring files that are read-only or that have changed since the last backup.

/S Restores all subdirectories underneath the directory.

3. Insert other backup disks, if required, until done.

XCOPY: Simple and Effective Backup

XCOPY, available with DOS 3.2 and greater, allows a simple backup of a limited number of files. XCOPY is like the COPY command but has some backup-like powers and advantages:

- XCOPY is faster than COPY.

- XCOPY can copy files in subdirectories, preserving the structure of your hard disk.

- XCOPY can turn off the archive bit to track what files have been backed up.

- Unlike BACKUP, it can verify that the files were copied correctly.

- The backed-up files easily can be copied off the diskette, since they are in DOS format and not in any backup utility's proprietary format.

XCOPY cannot split large files over several diskettes, but it can be used to back up all your files to more than one diskette. If the largest file you want to back up fits on one diskette then indeed use XCOPY.

To use XCOPY to back up your hard disk:

1. Format some diskettes upon which to store your backed-up files.

    If you are backing up your hard disk, you will need to format several diskettes. Use the CHKDSK method described in the previous section to determine the number of diskettes. Unlike the diskettes used with the BACKUP command, these must be formatted.

2. Select the directory you want to back up.

    To back up your entire hard disk, go to your computer's root directory. If you want to back up a selected directory, move to that directory. If you are backing up your entire hard disk, type:

    ```
    CD\ [Enter]
    ```

3. Start backing up your hard disk.

    From the DOS prompt, type:

    ```
    XCOPY A: /V /S /E /M [Enter]
    ```

    The switches used are defined in the following table.

Switch	Meaning
/V	Verify that the files that are copied were copied correctly.
/S	Tells XCOPY to copy not only the files in the current directory but also the files in the subdirectories beneath the current directory. If you want to copy files in the current directory only, leave this switch out.
/E	Copy any subdirectories even if they are empty.
/M	Copy files that have the archive attribute on and turn off the attribute once the file is copied.

Two other switches may be useful for smaller backups:

Switch	Meaning
/D:date	Copy only those files modified on or after the date, where *date* is in the format MM/DD/YY, such as 04/01/93. (The format of *date* depends on the country for which your computer is configured.)
/P	Prompts you to confirm for each file if you want it copied.

The most important switch is the /M. It says: "Copy only the files that have not been backed up. Once the file is copied, mark it as being backed up." If you want to back up ALL your files, whether or not they have been backed up onto other diskettes, do not use the /M switch. After this initial full backup, you can then use the /M switch to back up only those files that have changed since the last backup.

4. Insert a new diskette, if more than one is required.

    XCOPY will fill up each diskette. Insert a new, formatted diskette and issue the command again (or just press F3 and Enter). XCOPY won't try to recopy files that are already backed up — the /M switch will have turned off the archive attribute for these files. Label each diskette so you can find files easily.

5. Continue this process for the remaining diskettes until you are finished.

6. If you had files that were too large to fit on a single diskette, use the DOS BACKUP command described earlier.

    XCOPY can be used to make important backups of work during a crucial period where a partial backup might be overkill. For example, I used XCOPY with the /M switch to make daily backups of the chapters for this book. The work was important enough to back up daily but I didn't want to use my tape drive every day. A batch file called BACK.BAT helped me back up the changed or new chapters. Here's the batch file:

```
@ECHO OFF
XCOPY D:\BOOK\*.CHP A: /V /M
ECHO Keep Your PC Cookin' backed up.
```

The /M switch backed up only those chapters that had the archive attribute turned on. In other words, only the new or changed chapters were copied to diskette. Once backed up, these chapters had their archive attribute removed.

When you use diskettes for your backup medium with XCOPY and BACKUP, remember that the data may get corrupted. Temperature extremes, humidity, and background radiation can corrupt the data on any floppy over time. If you wish to keep your backed-up files around for more than one year, then yearly make fresh copies of all files to new diskettes. Use the DOS DISKCOPY command to make a mirror copy of the diskettes. Then, use the DOS DISKCOMP command to verify the files were correctly copied.

Investing in Backup Software

Using a backup software program is the best way to assure safe, reliable backups. They're easier to use and more reliable. Many provide an error detection feature that reduces the possibility of a file being unreadable. Some programs even operate tape drives, making backup an easy, no-brainer process. Such programs usually provide a tree-like display of directories for easy selection of files and directories to be backed up.

What do you look for in a backup utility? Consider these features:

• Data security

The whole purpose of a backup utility is to protect yourself when an important file gets accidentally deleted or when your hard disk sputters and dies. Your backups should be accurate and restorable, even if the disks are badly damaged. If your backup software has this error-correction feature, turn it on.

The program must verify the backup can be read. I highly recommend you turn this verify feature on; if your data is truly important, then act like it is. Also, the program should warn you when you are going to overwrite disks used in another backup, or as a newer file with an older one.

- Ease of use.

  Find a program that lets you easily select files. Most programs use an on-screen directory tree from which you select drives, directories, and files to back up. Some programs allow you to select simpler skill levels; in this case, confusing or potentially dangerous options are not displayed.

  Some programs include scripts or macros. These recorded preferences or keystrokes allow you to back up chosen files or directories in a few keystrokes.

- Backup options

  You should be able to choose from several backup options: full, incremental, and differential backups. You should be able to include or exclude certain files, either by their name, such as *.BAK, or before or after a certain date. You should be able to back up your data to another hard disk, a network drive, removable media (like a tape cartridge), or floppy diskettes. If you have multiple drives, you should be able to back up all of them in one operation. Many programs provide data compression, thereby requiring fewer diskettes. On faster computers, such as a 20-MHz 80286 and greater, the extra time required to compress the files is negligible.

  If looking for backup software for a tape drive, be sure the software works with your tape drive and any other peripherals. For example, I use a Colorado Memory Systems Jumbo 250 tape drive with its optional FC-10 expansion card. The FC-10 speeds up the backup process. At the time, *Norton Backup* from Symantec did not support the FC-10 expansion card, although it did support the Jumbo 250. To use *Norton Backup*, I would have to disconnect the FC-10 and instead connect the tape drive to my IDE hard disk/ floppy disk controller card.

- Restore options

  What gets backed up must get backed down. Look for special restore options such as restoring a particular version of a file and overwriting those that already exist on your hard disk. Being able to restore files to new locations is helpful if you need to restore data to a hard disk that has a different subdirectory structure.

Once you purchase your backup program, test it using real-world conditions: your PC. Perform a small backup on your PC as it normally runs, memory-resident programs and all. Next, restore the files to a different directory or drive. Then, run DOS's COMPARE command on the original and the restored set. If they match, rest easy. If you install new memory-resident software, retest your backup software. If you add a new expansion card or hard disk, test your program's hardware compatibility. Many advanced packages support high-speed DMA transfers that can be subtly affected by newly added equipment.

Backing Up Your Programs

You can give yourself some backup protection when you install new programs. Most software manufacturers recommend you use the DOS command DISKCOPY to make a mirror-image copy of the new program's diskettes and use the copies for installation. This duplication gives you a backup of your program diskettes should the original disks fail or be destroyed. It's best to keep the second set elsewhere in case a calamity strikes your office. Always keep a copy of your backup software on diskette. Its manufacturer may go out of business or current versions may not be compatible with yours. Keep one copy off-site, such as at a friend's house; keep the other nearby. If the contents of your hard disk were destroyed, you could use the backup software to restore it.

With proper backups, you can protect yourself and your labor. Develop a thorough backup system that works for you — and use it religiously.

11 Preventing Floppy Fatalities

What goes into your PC usually needs to come out. This axiom justifies the floppy disk drive. On a single disk, you can place several important files and lock them away, give them to a friend, or transport them to the office. Floppy diskettes also provide an adequate backup medium. Many hard disk drives can be backed up onto a handful of diskettes.

A floppy drive is similar to a hard disk drive. Both have read/write heads that record and play back information from the disk's surface. Unlike a hard disk, a floppy drive is much slower, spinning at either 300 or 360 revolutions per minute instead of 3600 RPM. Also, a floppy drive has only one platter, the disk itself, while a hard disk may have five or more platters. When a floppy diskette is formatted, DOS does both the physical and logical formatting, mapping the diskette into sectors and clusters so data can be stored and retrieved quickly. The advantage of a floppy disk is that it can be removed from the drive.

Contents of a Floppy

A floppy disk consists of a thin circle of somewhat flexible, coated polyester film that must spin freely within a protective plastic jacket. The thin circle of film is formed from a foundation material that is coated on both sides with iron oxide and then burnished to a mirror-smooth finish. The iron oxide coating is what allows the diskette to hold information. The drive's read/write heads magnetize the coating so that the iron oxide particles hold information long after the diskette is removed from the computer. When retrieving information from the diskette, the heads read and amplify the small magnetic field contained in the coating.

The diskette's jacket is very important because it contains a liner that keeps the disk clean. The jacket also protects the diskette from heat. One diskette manufacturer likens a diskette rotating in a disk drive to running through the Sahara desert while trying to remember over 300 pages of information. Heat can cause the jacket to warp. And if a disk warps, information can be lost. Almost all diskettes can handle disk drive heat up to 125 degrees Fahrenheit before warping. With the thicker jackets, a diskette can handle up to 140 degrees.

Unlike 3.5-inch diskettes, 5.25-inch diskettes are stored in a sleeve or envelope to prevent contamination of the diskette. Some diskette manufacturers use sleeves cut from cardboard to store their products. Unfortunately, debris on the edges or in the bottom of the sleeve can touch the diskette's surface and destroy its information. Some jackets are formed of Tyvek, a DuPont product. Tyvek is the same material used in "clean suits" worn by workers in high-tech manufacturing plants. Tyvek helps reduce static and is free of such contaminants. For these reasons, buying high-quality diskettes is important. Being penny wise can be byte foolish.

Floppy disk drives support either of two sizes of diskettes: 5.25-inch and 3.5-inch. Also, the drive may be either of two sizes: *full-height* or *half-height*. Full-height drives are 3.25 inches high, 5.75 inches wide, and 8 inches deep. Older drives are often full-height. Half-height drives measure 1.625 inches high and either 5.75 or 4 inches wide, and 4 or 8 inches deep. The removable diskettes for each size drive store varying amounts of information because of the different densities possible on the magnetic media, as shown below:

Size	Density	Capacity
5.25-inch	Single-sided, double-density	160K*
5.25-inch	Single-sided, double-density	180K*
5.25-inch	Double-sided, double-density	320K*
5.25-inch	Double-sided, double-density	360K
5.25-inch	Double-sided quad (or high) density	1200K (1.2MB)

Size	Density	Capacity
3.5-inch	Double-sided, double-density	720K
3.5-inch	Double-sided, quad (or high) density	1440K (1.44MB)
3.5-inch	Double-sided, ultra (or extra) density	2880K (2.88MB)

*These drive sizes are obsolete.

Note: To prevent confusion, double-density diskettes and drives will be called "low density." Quad-density diskettes and drives will be called "high density." The new 2.88MB drive will be called "extra density."

Like a hard disk, floppy disks are measured in *bytes*, the amount of space required to store a single character. A kilobyte (K) is 1024 bytes. A megabyte (MB) is 1024K (about a million bytes).

How do you tell which size floppy diskettes you have? First measure them. The 5.25-inch diskettes are 5.25 inches on each side, while the 3.5-inch diskettes measure 3.5 inches square. More obviously, the 3.5-inch diskettes sport a hard plastic case, while the 5.25-inch diskettes don't.

Next, how do you tell a low-density diskette from a high-density diskette? The diskette box label or the diskette label may indicate double (low) or high density. Otherwise, you can tell at a glance what capacity diskette you have. The magnetic material used in a low-density 5.25-inch diskette is a chocolate brown color and has a hub on the inner circle. On a high-density 5.25-inch diskette, this material is a darker charcoal color. On a 3.5-inch diskette, you cannot tell so easily except by looking at its plastic shell. A low-density 3.5-inch diskette has one square hole and has "DS, DD," or "2S/2D" imprinted on its sliding metal shutter (see Figure 11.1). A high-density diskette has two square holes and "DS, HD" imprinted on the metal shutter. However, a small sliding switch may be covering one of the holes.

When you look at a 5.25-inch diskette, you notice several things. First, it has a hole in the center that is used to center the disk in the drive. Below this hole is an elliptical cut in the jacket, exposing the magnetic medium underneath. Do not touch this area! The oils from your finger can ruin data. On the right side of the diskette is a write-

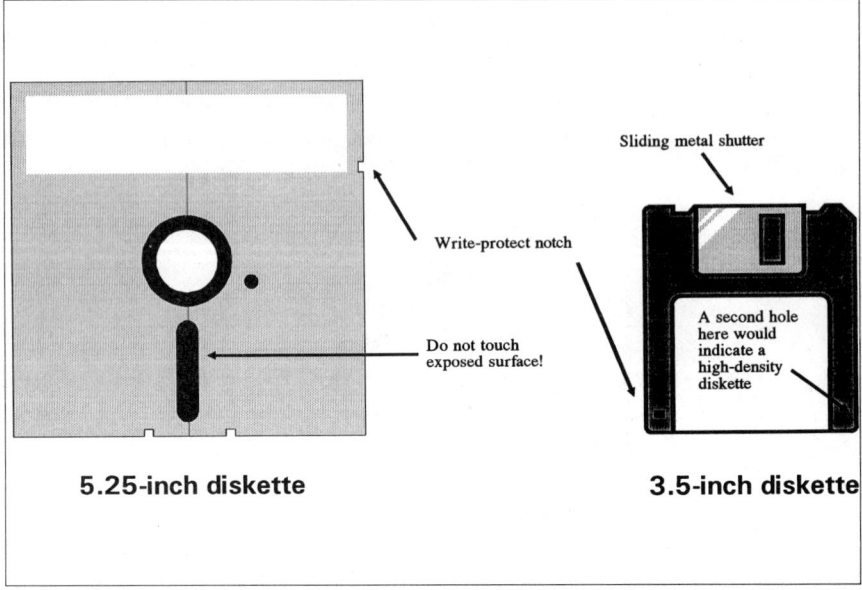

Figure 11.1 The various components of both sizes of floppy diskettes.

enable notch. When left uncovered, this notch allows information to be saved to the diskette. Adhesive tabs called *write-protect tabs* are usually included with a box of diskettes to cover this notch. When this notch is covered, you cannot delete or change information on the diskette. These are called *write-protected disks*. You can, however, copy the files from the diskette. The write-protect tab is handy when you have important work you want to protect.

When you look at a 3.5-inch diskette, the construction is more sophisticated (see Figure 11.1). Instead of a gaping hole in the center, this type of diskette has a metal hub.

Along one side of the diskette, a spring-loaded sliding metallic shutter protects the magnetic medium from being touched. On the right side, a sliding write-protect switch is used to write-protect the disk. Unlike the 5.25-inch disks, you do not have to attach an adhesive tab to the disk; you only have to move the switch.

When this sliding switch covers the hole, you can save information to the disk. When you can see through the disk, you cannot.

It's that simple.

Formatting Your Floppies

Before you can use a floppy disk to store your information, you must prepare it with the DOS FORMAT command. In general, you must format a disk at a capacity less than or equal to the capacity of the drive. For example, you can read a 360K diskette in a 1220K (1.2MB) drive. However, you cannot read a 1.2MB disk in a 360K drive.

To format a diskette:

1. Place the diskette into your disk drive.

   Place the diskette into the drive with the label up. For 5.25-inch diskettes, insert the diskette with the elliptical exposed area going in first and its indented notch on the left-hand side. Do not touch any exposed areas of the disk! For 3.5-inch diskettes, insert the diskette with the sliding metal shutter first. An arrow imprinted on the plastic shell shows the direction for inserting the diskette.

2. Begin formatting the diskette.

   From the DOS prompt (C:\), type:

   ```
   FORMAT a: [Enter]
   ```

   where *a:* is the drive letter of the diskette you wish to format. The drive begins to format the diskette.

   If you have DOS 4.0 or above, you can format a diskette to a lower (but not higher) capacity with the /F switch. Just type:

   ```
   FORMAT a: /F:size [Enter]
   ```

   where *size* is

   - 360 (360K)
   - 720 (720K)
   - 1200 (1.2MB)
   - 1440 (1.44MB)
   - 2880 (2.88MB)

   You can also use the FORMAT command to make a system, or boot, disk. Every computer owner should have a floppy "boot disk." This is a kind of emergency disk if your computer suddenly does not start from its hard disk. It may go through the motions of warming up, but somehow it simply doesn't bring you to a DOS prompt (C:\). For example, if you make a deadly change to the startup file CONFIG.SYS, your PC may not work. It won't be broken, but it won't let you work on it. Having a boot disk lets you bypass the CONFIG.SYS file and start your computer from the floppy drive. You can then get to your CONFIG.SYS and correct your error. To make a bootable diskette, place a blank diskette in drive A:, your first and possibly only floppy disk drive. (Boot diskettes usually do not work from drive B:.) From the DOS prompt, type:

```
FORMAT A: /S [Enter]
```

The /S adds system information to the diskette so it can start your computer when needed.

3. When done with the formatting, you will be asked to enter a name for the diskette.

    You can enter a volume name of up to 11 characters for this diskette or simply press the Enter key for no name. You can add a name later using the DOS LABEL command.

4. Answer "Y" (yes) or "N" (no) to format other diskettes.

    If you have other diskettes to format, enter "Y."

Whoops!

If you own DOS 5.0, you also can unformat a diskette. Why would you want to do this? Imagine you accidentally reformatted a diskette on which you had some important information. On recognizing your mistake, you can type:

```
UNFORMAT a: [Enter]
```

where *a:* is the letter of the floppy drive. UNFORMAT restores the disk to its condition at the time of the format. UNFORMAT does not work if you use the FORMAT command with the /U switch. The /U stands for "unconditional," which definitely formats your diskette and wipes the data from it. If you are using the DOS MIRROR utility, described in Chapter 9, "Storage: It's a Hard Life," you may be able to restore the diskette to its condition when you last used MIRROR.

Besides unformatting, you can also restore files you accidentally deleted from a diskette using DOS 5.0's UNDELETE command.

To undelete a file:

1. After accidentally deleting a file, type:

   ```
   UNDELETE  c:\path\file [Enter]
   ```

   where *c:\path\file* is the drive, directory, and filename of the file you accidentally deleted. Deleted files are listed.

2. For each filename displayed, answer "Y" to those you want to undelete.

3. For each filename, provide the first letter of the name.

   If a file with the same name already exists, provide a different first letter.

Besides DOS, other utilities can rescue your diskette, including Norton Utilities and PC Tools. For example, Norton Utilities includes a utility to revive the magnetic signals on a diskette. With age, a diskette can lose these signals.

The Trouble with 5.25-Inch Diskettes

There is one pitfall in sharing 360K disks between computers with 360K drives and those with 1.2MB drives—the 1.2MB disks are unreadable on the 360K drive, causing an "Abort, Retry, Ignore" error message.

Unlike 3.5-inch diskettes, these low- and high-density 5.25-inch diskettes have different numbers of tracks. The low-density 5.25-inch diskette has 40 tracks per side; the high-density version has 80. The 1.2MB drive, even operating in low-density mode, cannot overwrite the magnetic signals left in the wider track created by the 360K drive. The result is error messages when the 360K drive tries to read the same diskette. The solution is for the 1.2MB drive to format brand-new or bulk-erased low-density diskettes at 360K. To do this, type:

```
FORMAT a: /4 [Enter]
```

where *a:* is the letter of your 1.2MB drive. This command is supported in most versions of DOS. These 360K diskettes, with the narrower tracks, can then be used to swap data between the two different drives. Conversely, you should not and sometimes cannot format 1.2MB diskettes to 360K. The high-density disk is insensitive to the formatting signal, resulting in the FORMAT error: "Invalid media or Track 0 bad - disk unusable." As a general rule, format a diskette to its designated format capacity. A double-sided, double-density diskette should be formatted at 360K. A double-sided, high-density diskette should be formatted at 1.2MB. And so on.

Assign of the Times

If you have both 5.25- and 3.5-inch disk drives, you sometimes need to switch the drive letters. For example, some software programs install only from drive A:. If the installation diskette fits only in your drive B:, you cannot install the software. This command is also handy if you find yourself working on a computer where the disk drives are in an order opposite to yours. The DOS ASSIGN command temporarily allows you to switch drive letters. From the DOS prompt, simply type:

```
ASSIGN A=B [Enter]
```

This causes drive B: to think it is drive A:, although it also works as drive B:. A general rule of thumb is to think "Assign what letter (A) to (=) which drive (B)?" To make this change permanent, insert this command in your AUTOEXEC.BAT startup file. To clear the swap, simply type:

```
ASSIGN [Enter]
```

Adding a Floppy Disk Drive

To support another floppy drive, you need three components:

1. Drive controller card
2. The correct DOS version
3. Proper BIOS or BIOS extensions

It's in the Cards

To add a floppy drive, you must connect it to some type of drive controller card. Almost every PC has at least one floppy disk controller. XT-type computers normally can connect to two internal drives and, optionally, to two external drives. Most AT-type computers support two floppy drives and two hard disks. To run a certain type of floppy drive, you need a matching controller.

Your version of DOS must also support your new floppy drive. If your version of DOS doesn't support the drive's capacity, you won't be able to format and use it. Of course, having the most current version of DOS is best, but DOS version 3.3 supports all disk formats except the new 2.88MB size. (Only DOS 5.0 supports the 2.88MB disk drive.) If you have DOS 3.2, for example, you cannot add a 3.5-inch high-density (1.44MB) disk drive.

You also need a small program called the BIOS (Basic Input/Output System) to support your disk drive. The BIOS is placed on ROM (read-only memory) computer chips on the motherboard. Many older computers have a BIOS that does not support newer drives. For example, a BIOS dated before 11/15/85 does not support the 3.5-inch 1.44MB drive. If your BIOS doesn't support your type of floppy drive, you may still be able to use it. Sometimes, DOS may have a "workaround" solution (described later) or the drive controller may have some BIOS chips of its own to support the drive. When BIOS chips are on the controller, they are called BIOS extensions because they are an extension of the BIOS found on the motherboard.

Selecting a Floppy Drive

Because of intense competition, most floppy drives are of about the same quality, costing under $70. If you have a low-density (360K) 5.25-inch drive, you may want to either replace it with a 1.2MB high-density drive or purchase a 3.5-inch drive to supplement it. Conversely, you may have a low-density (720K) 3.5-inch drive and want to replace it with a 1.44MB drive.

Adding a high-density floppy drive to an older XT-type PC can be tricky. First, you need a special controller and cable. Since these computers have only 8-bit expansion slots, that is, one edge connector into which to place the card, you must order an 8-bit floppy controller or a 16-bit controller that can be set for 8-bit use. In the latter case, you can transplant the controller to your future AT-type computer. You also need the correct DOS version and possibly a new BIOS. All of these extra requirements increase the cost of this improvement. Unless your work absolutely demands it, add a low-density drive, such as a 720K 3.5-inch drive. If you still decide to order a floppy controller, ask if it will accommodate your specific floppy drive and computer. Be sure the vendor lets you return the controller—without a restocking fee — if it is incompatible.

If you own an AT-type PC (80286 and higher), you can get virtually any disk drive you choose. If you want to add a 1.44MB drive, you must install DOS version 3.3 or higher. At worst, you may need to buy a new BIOS.

When ordering, you simply need to tell the salesperson which size and capacity drive you want (see the following table).

Size	Capacity
3.5-inch	720K
3.5-inch	1.44MB
5.25-inch	360K
5.25-inch	1.2MB

If you are uncertain which drive to order, I recommend you buy a 3.5-inch drive. The diskettes are smaller (they fit in a shirt pocket or Daytimer), sturdier (I've thrown them across the room), hold more information, and—unlike 5.25-inch diskettes—do not require a separate sleeve in which to store the diskette. Also, the sliding shutter of 3.5-inch diskettes reduces contamination from dust and crumbs. If you own or plan to own a laptop computer, the 3.5-inch disk drive is a must if you want to share diskette-based information between your two computers.

In some cases, you may not have to choose which size to get. A new trend is the "combination drive," which provides both a 5.25- and 3.5-inch drive in a half-height space. These two-in-one drives, such as the TEAC FD505/02, simplify installation because one connector serves both drives. A jumper on this drive determines which one of the two is the A: boot drive. One advantage is that you can use your other floppy drive connector for a tape drive. Another is that the combo drive leaves you an extra drive bay in which to place a tape or CD-ROM drive.

Besides size and capacity, you also need to select either a half-height or full-height drive. The rarer full-height drives are 3.25 inches high, 5.75 inches wide, and 8 inches deep. Older drives are often full-height. Half-height drives measure 1.625 inches high, either 5.75 or 4 inches wide, and 4 or 8 inches deep. Open your PC to check whether the drive bay can support a shorter or taller drive. Most important, look for adequate holes for screws to hold each drive in place.

Installing a Floppy Drive

Once you receive your new drive, you can now install it. The installation procedure differs if you are installing a special controller into your computer to use an otherwise unsupported drive, perhaps putting a high-density drive into an XT-type PC.

To add a high-density drive to an XT-type PC:

Adding a 1.2MB or 1.44MB floppy drive to your XT-type PC can be tricky. Some people falsely believe that a new motherboard BIOS chip is needed to support one of these high-density drives. Rather, you need a special floppy drive controller. These controllers contain their own special ROM BIOS extension to support high-density drives. Still, you might need a new motherboard BIOS to be compatible with the controller.

1. Ensure you are using a DOS version that supports your new drive.

   To use a 1.44MB floppy drive, you need to have DOS version 3.3 or higher. To use a 1.2MB floppy drive, you need DOS 3.0 or higher. I recommend you use DOS 5.0. From the DOS prompt, type:

   ```
   VER [Enter]
   ```

   The version number your computer is using is displayed on the screen. If your version is older than the versions mentioned above, you should first install the new operating system.

2. Turn off your computer and remove its case.

   For details on opening your computer, see the procedure in Chapter 3, "Cracking Open the Case."

3. Select an expansion slot for your new floppy controller card.

   Select an expansion slot that is close to the drive bays where the disk drives are located. Remove the screw and bracket covering the slot.

4. Remove the controller card from its antistatic bag.

   Before touching the card, briefly touch a metal object, like your computer's case, to drain yourself of static electricity. Next, remove the card from its packaging, holding it by its edges or metal bracket.

5. Attach the cable to the controller card.

The way that most computers talk to floppy drives is through a flat, gray ribbon cable. Often, a twist is found in part of the cable. Analyze the cable that came with your controller and floppy drive. There probably are three to five connectors on the cable. The one by itself is the one that plugs into the floppy controller. This cable has either a red or black stripe along one edge, identifying pin 1 (or 0) of the cable. On the controller card, you also have a pin 1. This pin is probably marked "1." It is very important for pin 1 on the cable to be connected to the pin 1 on the controller card. Place the cable so the stripe aligns with pin 1 and press it into place. If incorrectly attached, your drives won't work.

6. Set any jumpers or switches on the controller card, if needed.

You may have to set some jumpers or switches on the card for it to work with your particular PC. Refer to the controller's instructions.

7. Install the controller card into the expansion slot (see Figure 11.2).

Next, reinstall the screw to hold the card in place.

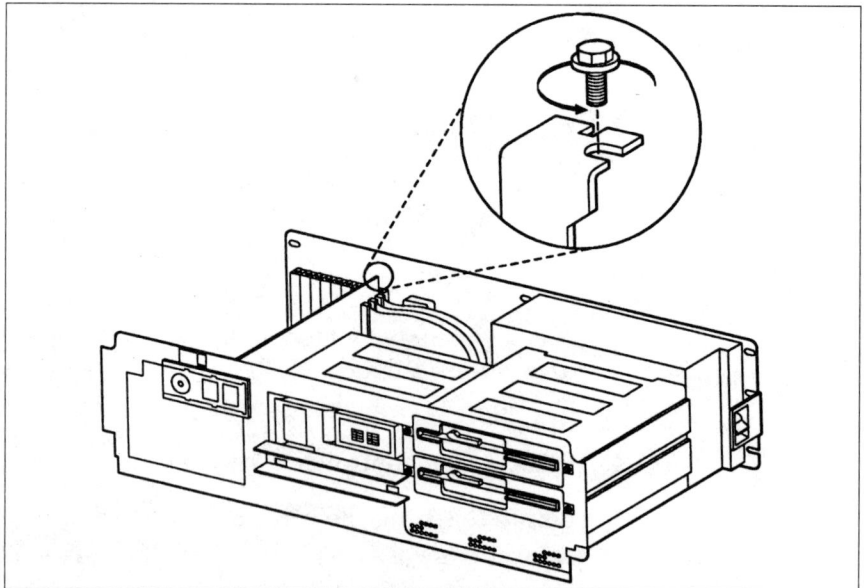

Figure 11.2 A single screw holds the controller card in place.

Grabbing the card by the edges, press it firmly into the slot.

8. Set the drive select jumper on each floppy drive, if needed.

   Occasionally, you may have to set a drive select jumper to tell a floppy drive which drive it is. These positions may be either DS0 through DS3 or DS1 through DS4. If there is a twist in the controller cable, you can skip this step. Most drives come with this jumper set in the second position, which is correct for most computers. If you are using a cable with no twist, you have to change this setting on one of the drives. If your cable supports only one drive, set the drive to the first drive-selecting position. Besides the drive select jumper, you may have to set a jumper or switch to tell the floppy drive whether you are using an XT- or AT-type computer. Consult your manual for details.

9. Set the terminating resistor, if needed.

   On 5.25-inch drives only, a terminating resistor is needed on the last floppy drive. This terminating resistor is a plug-in DIP (dual in-line pin) chip. Your drive manual should indicate where this is located. This terminator must be either removed or disabled from the second drive (the one attached to the cable's middle connector). Some drive manufacturers use a jumper or series of switches to turn off the resistor. The first drive attached to the end of the data cable should have a terminating resistor in place. Otherwise, twice the current is sent to the controller card, slowly ruining it.

10. Install the new floppy drive (see Figure 11.3).

    Unless you are swapping one drive for another, you first have to remove a cover plate over the drive bay where the drive will be placed. Next, slide the new drive into the empty bay. If adding a 3.5-inch drive, you may have to place it in an adapter to fit into a 5.25-inch drive bay. Make sure the floppy drive is facing the right way. Check that the electronic circuitry of the drive is facing down. After the drive is in place, use the mounting hardware—usually four screws—to hold the drive in place. In some PCs, plastic drive rails are used to mount floppy drives. If your drive didn't come with the proper mounting hardware, you can get a universal installation kit from most computer vendors.

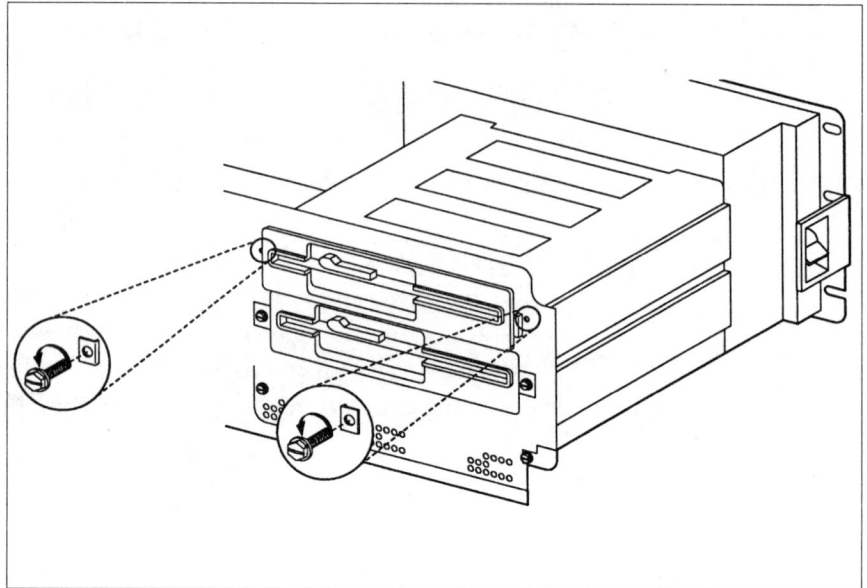

Figure 11.3 Typically two to four screws hold your floppy drive in place.

Tighten the screws only after the drive is flush with the other drives in your computer or with the front bezel.

11. Attach the controller cable to each floppy drive.

Flat ribbon cables must be connected to each floppy drive so it can "talk" to the controller card. This data cable carries the information from the floppy drive to the controller and then to the rest of the computer. The controller cable may have two pairs of connectors. Each pair supports either a header connector or an edge connector. The pair nearest the end of the cable is for drive A:, the drive desired as the first drive. The other pair of connectors is attached to drive B:, the second drive.

Note: If you are installing a new or replacement second drive and want it to be drive A:, you may want to rearrange the drives in the bays so that this drive is on top. Otherwise, the order of the installed drives doesn't matter.

In some cases, you may have only one connector per drive. If the connector doesn't fit the drive, your drive kit probably came with an adapter. If not, you can either get another cable to accommodate the old connector or go down to a Radio Shack store and get an insulation-displacement 34-conductor header connector. These can be attached with a pair of pliers.

Again, one edge of this cable has a colored stripe. This stripe needs to be plugged onto the connector at the back of the floppy drive with the colored stripe nearest pin 1 (or 0). If you are plugging in a 3.5-inch drive with a header connector, look at the PC board at the back of the drive. The connector pins will be labeled 1 through 34 (or 0 through 33). The stripe on the cable needs to be plugged in near to the pin 1 (or 0) designation. Most cables fit only one way.

12. Connect the power cable to each floppy drive.

    You now need to connect a power cable to each drive. If you have only one drive, look for a spare power cable coming from the power supply. This is a four-wire connector with a white plastic plug. Plug it into the four-pin power connector at the rear of the floppy drive. This connector is shaped so the cable fits only one way.

    If you don't have a spare power connector for your new drive, you can order a Y-cable for about $5 from most mail-order companies.

13. With the cover off, turn on your PC and test the drive.

    Your PC should automatically recognize it. As your computer warms up, the new floppy drive's indicator may light briefly. This is a good sign. Insert a diskette and format it.

    If the disk comes out formatted to 360K instead of the higher density, your BIOS probably doesn't support your drive. Go to the section, "Troubleshooting the Installation."

14. If your drive works properly, return your computer to normal operation.

To add a drive to an AT-type PC: Unlike an XT-type PC, you do not need to buy a new controller card for your AT-type computer; the disk controller that came with your computer will control both low- and high-density floppy drives. In fact, your computer probably came with a 1.2MB 5.25-inch drive. Only in rare cases will you need to get a newer BIOS. Sometimes, an older BIOS does not support the 720K or 1.44MB drive.

> **Note**: If you want to install a 2.88MB drive, you will need a new hard disk/floppy disk controller to support its 1-MHz data rate.

1. Be sure you are using a DOS version that supports your new drive.

   To use a 1.44MB floppy drive, you need to have DOS version 3.3 or higher. To use a 1.2MB floppy drive, you need DOS 3.0 or higher. I recommend you use DOS 5.0. From the DOS prompt, type:

   ```
   VER [Enter]
   ```

   The version number your PC is using is displayed on the screen. If your version is older than the versions mentioned above, you should first install the new operating system.

2. Turn off your PC and remove its case.

   For details on opening your computer, see the procedure in Chapter 3, "Cracking Open the Case."

3. If replacing an existing drive, remove it.

   Usually, four screws hold the drive in place. Remove these and then disconnect both the data and power cables connected to this drive.

4. Set the drive select jumper on each floppy drive, if needed.

   Occasionally, you may have to set a drive select jumper to tell each floppy drive which drive it is. These positions may be either DS0 through DS3 or DS1 through DS4. If there is a twist in the controller cable, you can skip this step. Most drives come with this jumper set in the second position, which is correct for most computers. If you are using a cable with no twist, you have to change this setting on one of the drives. If the cable supports only one drive, then set the drive to the first drive-selecting position.

5. Set the terminating resistor, if needed.

    On 5.25-inch drives only, a terminating resistor is needed on the last floppy drive. This terminating resistor is a plug-in DIP (dual in-line pin) chip. Your drive manual should indicate where this is located. This terminator must be either removed or disabled from the second drive (the one attached to the cable's middle connector). Some drive manufacturers use a jumper or series of switches to turn off the resistor. The first drive attached to the end of the data cable should have a terminating resistor in place. Otherwise, twice the current is sent to the controller card, slowly ruining it.

6. Install the floppy drive.

    Unless you are swapping one drive for another, you first have to remove a cover plate over the drive bay where the drive will be placed. Next, slide the new drive into the empty bay. If adding a 3.5-inch drive, you may have to place it into an adapter to fit in a 5.25-inch drive bay. Make sure the floppy drive is facing the right way. Check that the electronic circuitry of the drive is facing down. After the drive is in place, use the mounting hardware—usually four screws—to hold the drive in place. In some computers, plastic drive rails are used to mount floppy drives. If your drive didn't come with the proper mounting hardware, you can get a universal installation kit from most computer vendors. Tighten the screws only after the drive is flush with the other drives in your computer or with the front bezel.

7. Attach the controller cable to the new floppy drive.

    Flat ribbon cables must be connected to each floppy drive so it can "talk" to the controller card. This data cable carries the information from the floppy drive to the controller and then to the rest of the computer. The controller cable may have two pairs of connectors. Each pair supports either a header connector or an edge connector. The pair nearest the end of the cable is for drive

A:, the drive desired for your first drive. The other pair of connectors is attached to drive B:, your second drive.

Note: If you are installing a new or replacement second drive and want this drive to be drive A:, you may want to rearrange the drives in the bays so that this drive is on top. Otherwise, the order of the installed drives doesn't matter.

In some cases, you may only have one connector per drive. If the connector doesn't fit the drive, the drive kit probably came with an adapter. If not, you can either get another cable to accommodate the old connector or go down to a Radio Shack store and get an insulation-displacement 34-conductor header connector. These can be attached with a pair of pliers.

Again, one edge of this cable has a colored stripe. This stripe needs to be plugged onto the connector at the back of the floppy drive with the colored stripe nearest pin 1 (or 0). If you are plugging in a 3.5-inch drive with a header connector, look at the PC board at the back of the drive. The connector pins will be labeled 1 through 34 (or 0 through 33). The stripe on the cable needs to be plugged in near to the pin 1 (or 0) designation. Most cables fit only one way.

8. Connect the power cable to the drive.

    You now need to connect a power cable to the drive. If you have only one drive, look for a spare power cable coming from the power supply. This is a four-wire connector with a white plastic plug. Plug it into the four-pin power connector at the rear of the drive. This connector is shaped so the cable fits only one way.

9. With the cover off, turn on your PC and tell it about the new drive.

    As your PC warms up, the new floppy drive's indicator may light briefly. This is a good sign. You now must tell your computer what type of drive you've just installed. Usually on warming up, your PC will recognize that something has changed and will display an error message. From there, you can access your computer's setup program and make the changes. On older computers, this setup program is on a diskette. On newer computers, it's built into the BIOS. To get to your setup program, you either press a key or two or run a software program that came with your PC. For example, you may have to press the Delete key or F1 as your computer warms up. Consult your owner's manual. Sometimes, your PC will guess the change and simply have you approve the changes to the setup program.

If you are installing a 3.5-inch 720K or 1.44MB drive and it is not listed in your BIOS, select 360K. You then have to use the tips in "Troubleshooting the Installation" below.

10. Test the drive.

Once you have installed the drive, insert a diskette and format it. If the disk comes out formatted to 360K or 720K instead of the higher density, your BIOS probably doesn't support the drive. Go to the following section, "Troubleshooting the Installation."

11. If the drive works properly, return your PC to normal operation.

Trouble-shooting the Installation

After installation, a new floppy drive, the drive may work strangely or not at all. If you have checked that the power cables are secure and the controller cables are not put on backwards, you then must do a bit more work. The solution may be a combination of three factors:

1. Use the DOS DRIVPARM command to your CONFIG.SYS startup file.

2. Load DRIVER.SYS in CONFIG.SYS.

3. Buy a newer BIOS

These solutions allow you to teach your PC to handle the renegade drive. One caveat: DRIVPARM and DRIVER.SYS do not allow you to add 1.44MB or 2.88MB drives to computers whose BIOS does not support these drives.

**Adding
DRIVPARM**

For example, after installing a 720K drive into an XT-type computer, some people can use 720K diskettes but can format them only to 360K, half their capacity. This symptom indicates your PC is treating the drive as a low-density 5.25-inch, not 3.5-inch, drive. If your BIOS does not support a 720K drive and you own DOS 3.3 or greater, you can support it by adding a DRIVPARM command to the CONFIG.SYS startup file. The line to be added to CONFIG.SYS is

```
DRIVPARM=/D:x /F:y /I
```

where x is the number of the drive (A:=0 and B:=1) and y is the drive type (1.2MB=1, 720K=2, 1.44MB=7, 2.88MB=9). The /I switch tells DOS that this drive is not supported by your BIOS. If you have an older AT-type computer, add the switch /C, like this:

```
DRIVPARM /D:1 /F:2 /I /C
```

In this example, a 720K drive was installed as drive B: and the 720K drive is not supported by your BIOS. The /C switch provides *change-line support* so the disk drive can detect whether its drive door is open. This switch improves the performance of DOS by letting it know when one floppy disk has been replaced by another.

**Adding
DRIVER.SYS**

If the DRIVPARM command doesn't work or your DOS version doesn't support DRIVPARM, you have an alternative: DRIVER.SYS. This file provides built-in support for the 3.5-inch 720K drive without you having to buy a new BIOS.

Like DRIVPARM, you must add a line to your CONFIG.SYS file:

```
DEVICE=c:\dos\DRIVER.SYS D:x /F:y
```

where *c:\dos* is the drive and directory where your DRIVER.SYS file is located, x is the number of the drive (A:=0 and B:=1), and y is the drive type (1.2MB=1, 720K=2, 1.44MB=7, 2.88MB=9).

One difference between DRIVPARM and DRIVER.SYS is that DRIVPARM lets you give the drive any drive letter you want while DRIVER.SYS assigns the next available drive letter to the new drive. For example, imagine you just installed a 720K drive in addition to your drive A: (your floppy drive) and drive C: (your hard disk). When you use DRIVER.SYS, this new second drive becomes both drive B: and drive D:. You need to use the drive as drive D: when you want to format 720K disks. Otherwise, you can use it as drive B: for nonformatting purposes. If you format disks from drive B:, they will be formatted to 360K, not the full 720K.

Buy a New BIOS

If neither DRIVPARM or DRIVER.SYS works, you'll need either a special device driver (a small software program) or a newer BIOS that supports that particular drive. (I recommend the latter.) The drive controller could also be the problem. Check that any DIP switches and jumpers on the controller or the drive itself are configured for use with your computer. If you want your new floppy drive to be drive A:, your BIOS must list it. If not, you must install the new drive as drive B:. Purchasing a new BIOS is covered in Chapter 7, "CPUs: Boning Up on Brainpower."

Protecting Diskettes

Protecting your diskettes is vital. The diskettes are cheap, but your work isn't. For example, a paper clip can cripple a floppy disk. A paper clip from a magnetized dispenser becomes magnetized itself. Attach it and a note to a floppy diskette and your data could be lost forever. This is just one threat to your floppy diskettes. Another is power problems, such as a power surge or sag or even a complete outage. When a diskette file is opened, the computer copies the DCB (Data Control Block) from the disk into its memory. The DCB contains such information as filename, length, last records, and more.

As you work with a file, you may add or delete records, but the computer will not write the new DCB information on the diskette until you close the file. When the power is interrupted, the data is scrambled because the computer has information from the DCB that was not updated. Hence, a damaged file. Your loss depends on the software. Some software packages update the DCB information after each screen so that you would lose only the information on the last screen.

Your floppies are also threatened by contaminants. Coffee, eraser crumbs, and even smoke can prevent the read/write head of the disk drive from reading your data. In some cases, it can damage the disk drive. Small particles of dust, food, liquid, and lint can be major obstacles in the path of the heads. A smoke particle is more than twice as large as the gap between the read/write head and the diskette. The oil of your fingers can ruin a diskette, so don't touch its recording surface. The oil will attract dust and debris.

Any foreign matter on the diskette may cause the heads to be lifted from its surface and pass over data to be read. Even worse, the head may rise over this obstruction and drop on the other side. The falling head overshoots its normal flying position and "crashes" into the disk surface, removing the oxide coating and ruining not only the disk but the head as well.

There are several commonsense ways to keep your floppies from getting sloppy. For example, when not in use, diskettes should be kept in their protective envelopes and also in clean storage containers. For 5.25-inch diskettes, keep them upright so they don't warp.

The invisible and often overlooked enemy is magnetism. Because data is stored magnetically, diskettes should not be stored near anything that emits a magnetic field. The major magnetic culprits are monitors, electric typewriters, radios, vacuum cleaners, or any electrical device that has a motor or transformer. Even fluorescent lamps with transformers in their bases and magnetic text stands emit a magnetic field strong enough to erase data. Keep your data away from these and other magnetic hazards. How near is too near? Keep your diskettes at least six to 12 inches away from these devices.

One myth is that airport X-ray machines damage hard and floppy disks. Not so. X-rays are merely a type of light. What may damage your disks is the handheld and walk-through metal detectors, since these use magnetism, not light.

Yet, airport metal detectors should be gentle enough for diskettes. A power of 25 gauss, a measurement unit of magnetism, can affect a 360K diskette. For higher-density diskettes, even more magnetism is required. Metal detectors in the United States use no more than one gauss.

Heat is another enemy of the floppy. Most diskettes can handle temperatures of 50 to 125 degrees Fahrenheit. However, a diskette exposed to the sun is in danger. To avoid data distortion or loss, allow the diskette that has just arrived from somewhere else to shape itself to your conditions for 24 hours. Pretend it has jet lag.

Ballpoint pens and pencils also have inflicted damage on 5.25-inch diskettes. Labels should be written with a felt-tip pen to avoid making indentations on the diskette beneath its jacket. A paper clip can also cause a crease in your diskette. Also, never bend your diskettes. When you insert a floppy disk, be careful to not bend the jacket. Don't force it into the drive, but align and insert it carefully.

Washing Diskettes

If your diskettes ever get beverages spilled on them, don't panic. You can clean the diskette and salvage the information. First, carefully slit an edge of the floppy's outer cover. Next, remove the circular disk inside without touching its surface. Instead, grab the disk by its edges or inner hub. While holding the disk by the central hub, rinse it carefully in a sink of warm water.

Once rinsed, set the disk on a clean, soft cloth and wipe it with a damp, soft cloth. While it dries on a fresh dry cloth, find a blank 5.25-inch floppy that you can sacrifice. Slit it open and remove the disk, but keep the plastic cover. Carefully insert the now dry disk into the new jacket and tape the slit end. With this patchwork disk, insert it into the drive and make a backup of it as soon as possible.

Tip Top Shape

While the floppy drive's read/write heads are riding on the diskette's surface, they can accumulate the dirt and dust that were on the diskette. Also, the floppy drive is more prone to collect dust because this is one inlet for air to be pulled into your computer by its power supply fan. You can clean these heads with either a simple cotton swab or with a commercial floppy disk head-cleaning kit. A cleaning kit, costing less than $20, consists of a paperlike disk made of an absorbent material. Once cleaning solution is put on the disk, you insert it into the drive like a normal disk. As the drive attempts to read the disk, the heads are cleaned. Surprisingly, cotton swabs dabbed in isopropyl alcohol are much better than commercial kits because they are much gentler on heads. Also, you can be more thorough in cleaning the heads than these kits. Still, commercial head-cleaner kits are easier to use, especially if you can avoid opening up your PC to reach the drive heads.

I recommend cleaning the read/write heads every six months. If you work in a smoky or dusty area, clean the heads every three months. Cleaning them will not wear them out prematurely. If you clean the heads on your drives too often with head-cleaning kits, you will indeed wear down the heads. Using a cotton swab and alcohol, you can clean as compulsively as you'd like. You won't shorten the life of the heads.

Moving Your PC

If you are moving your PC a short distance, less than 50 miles, you do not need to put an old disk into each floppy drive to prevent head damage from vibration. The damage is done only if the two heads smack into each other. Yet, these heads are mechanically isolated and placed between a quarter-inch and a half-inch apart.

On the other hand, if you are transporting the computer a long distance, the constant vibration could deform some parts. To prevent this kind of damage, acquire one of the special cardboard inserts used by drive manufacturers and then close the head down onto the cardboard. Using a disk as an insert is bad for the heads because it provides little or no cushioning. Also, the constant contact between disk and head could either make the disk stick to the head or magnetize the heads.

By caring for your diskettes and having the correct sizes of floppy drives available, you can open up a range of possibilities. You can install software that comes only on high-density diskettes, and you can back up your hard disk to diskettes that you can safely store away. If your floppy diskette gets mangled, magnetized, or messed up, it can be replaced. Unfortunately, your work on it can't.

PART III

Desserts

12 Clear Vision

If the eyes are the windows to the soul, then your monitor is the window to your PC. Your monitor provides the link between you and your PC. You could get rid of your printer, disk drives, and expansion cards, but you couldn't sacrifice the monitor. Without a monitor, you would be operating blind. You couldn't see the results of your calculations or the typing errors on the screen.

The first microcomputers were small boxes without displays. Instead, you waited for the final output from a printer. When a monitor was added, the computer became more attractive to a wider audience. This trend continues today with graphical user interfaces like Microsoft Windows.

Like Cable TV?

A monitor is very similar to a cable television set. Instead of getting HBO or CNN, the cable attached to your computer lets you see your computer at work. A monitor may use any of several display technologies. By far, the most popular is the cathode ray tube (CRT) technology, the same technology used in television sets. CRTs consist of a vacuum tube enclosed in glass. One end of the tube contains an electron gun. The other end contains a screen with a phosphorous coating.

When heated, the electron gun emits a stream of high-speed electrons that are attracted to the other end of the tube. On the way, a

307

focus control and deflection coil steer the beam to a specific point on the phosphorous screen. When struck by the beam, the phosphor glows. This is the light that you see when watching TV or your word processor.

This electron beam moves very quickly. It sweeps the screen from left to right in lines that move from top to bottom in a pattern called a raster. During its sweep, the beam strikes the phosphor wherever an image should appear on the screen. It also varies in intensity to produce different levels of brightness. Since the glow fades almost immediately, the electron beam must continue to sweep the screen to maintain an image, a practice called redrawing or refreshing the screen. Most displays have a refresh rate (also called a vertical scan rate) of about 70 Hertz (Hz), meaning that the screen is refreshed 70 times a second. Low refresh rates cause the screen to flicker and contribute to eyestrain. The higher the refresh rate, the better.

Monochrome versus Color

Monochrome monitors produce images of one color. The most popular is amber, followed by white and green. The color of the monitor is determined by the color of the phosphors on the CRT screen. Some monochrome monitors with white phosphors can support many shades of gray.

Monochrome monitors cost less than color models. For example, NEC offers the MultiSync GS2A that supports up to 64 shades of gray. This 14-inch monitor can be purchased for as little as $99. A monochrome monitor is ideal for character-based applications: word processing, spreadsheet analysis, database management, and computer programming. However, such monitors may not work as well with Windows software as the more expensive color monitors. Large monochrome monitors designed for specialized applications, like desktop publishing and CAD/CAM, however, cost hundreds of dollars more than color monitors.

Color monitors use more sophisticated technology than monochrome monitors, which accounts for their higher prices. While a monochrome picture tube contains one electron gun, a color tube contains three guns arranged in a triangular shape referred to as a delta configuration. Instead of amber, white, or green phosphors, the monitor screen contains phosphor triads, which consist of one red, one green, and one blue phosphor arranged in the same pattern as the

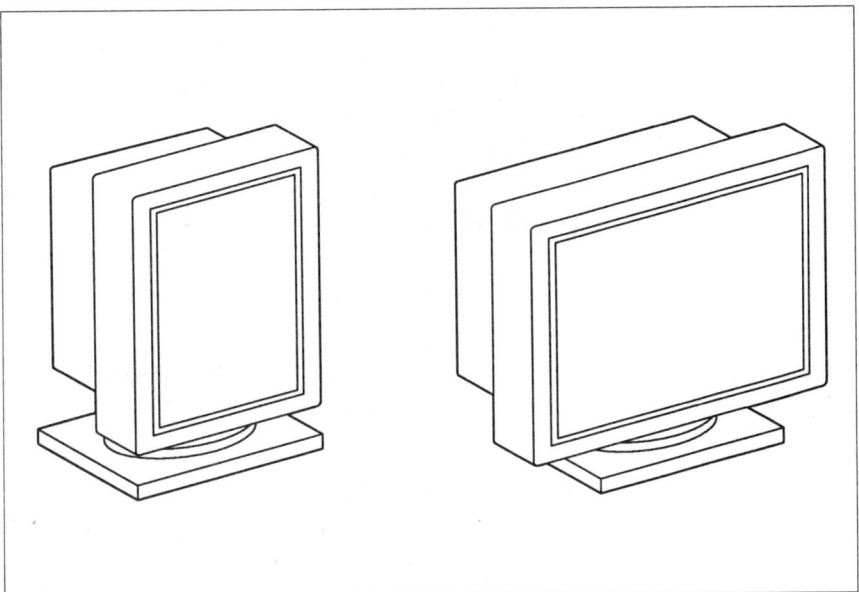

Figure 12.1 A portrait (tall) and a landscape (wide) monitor.

electron guns. These three primary colors can be mixed to produce other colors. Although color monitors cost more than monochrome monitors, they are more versatile, allowing you to take advantage of color software, perhaps for presentations.

The Right Size

Monitors come in different sizes, from an inexpensive 12-inch monochrome monitor to a 21-inch color monitor. The larger the monitor, the more you will pay. The larger monitors are handy for uses like desktop publishing. With a larger monitor, you can see an entire 8.5 x 11-inch page in a 100 percent view. In other words, what you see on the screen virtually matches the page to be printed. This is called *what-you-see-is-what-you-get (WYSIWYG)*. By seeing the whole page at its actual size, you can save yourself from printing several drafts before you get it right.

Also, these monitors come in both *portrait* and *landscape* shapes (see Figure 12.1). The screen on a portrait, or full-page, monitor is higher than it is wide, enabling you to view an entire page of a document. They differ from standard monitors because they stretch image height to about 66 lines, enabling you to see the equivalent of a full printed page on one screen. A landscape, or dual-page, monitor is suitable for viewing two pages, side by side, at once. Although most general purpose monitors are landscape, monitors with this orientation are larger and wider. Landscape models usually cost more than portrait models. When considering a portrait monitor, you should double-check that it supports your software. Some monitors require special video drivers, small software programs, to work with a software package.

Understanding Resolution

Resolution is the amount of detail the monitor can render. This quantity is expressed in the number of horizontal and vertical picture elements, or *pixels*, contained in the screen. The greater the number of pixels, the more detailed the images are. The resolution required depends on the application. Character-based applications, like word processing, require little resolution, while graphics-intensive applications, like desktop publishing or Windows software require a great deal.

The term *pixel* refers to the smallest unit that the monitor uses to produce an image. In a monochrome monitor, the picture element is a screen phosphor, but in a color monitor, the picture element is a phosphor triad. This difference raises another consideration called *dot pitch*, which applies only to color monitors. Dot pitch is the distance, measured in millimeters (mm), between phosphor triads. Screens with a smaller dot pitch contain less distance between the phosphor triads. As a result, the picture elements lie closer together, producing a sharper picture. Conversely, screens with a larger dot pitch tend to produce less clear images. Most monitors have a dot pitch between 0.25 and 0.52 mm. To avoid grainy images, look for a dot pitch of 0.28 mm or smaller for 12- and 14-inch monitors, or 0.31 mm or smaller for 16-inch and larger monitors. Watch out for the monitors with 0.41 mm or greater dot pitches. On fine text and graphics, the lack of clarity is appalling.

Some monitors support *interlaced* resolution. In *noninterlaced* (conventional) mode, the electron beam sweeps the screen in lines from top to bottom, one line after the other, completing the screen in one pass. In interlaced mode, the electron beam also sweeps the screen from top to bottom but in two passes, sweeping the odd lines first and the even lines second. Each pass takes half the time of a full pass in noninterlaced mode. Therefore, both modes refresh the entire screen in the same amount of time. This technique redraws the screen faster and provides more stable images. You should be familiar with interlacing; television transmissions broadcasted in the United States are interlaced.

The drawback is that interlacing depends on the ability of the eye to average two nearly identical lines separated by a gap into one solid line. While television pictures have nearly identical lines, computer graphics do not. Since unmatched lines produce flickering and shimmering images, interlacing is reserved for only high-resolution monitors.

The Birth of Video Standards	Like any computer device, a monitor requires a source of input. The signals that run your monitor come from a video circuit inside your computer. A few systems, like the IBM PS/2 computers, contain this circuitry on the motherboard, your computer's main circuit board. Most systems, though, use a separate circuit board that fits into an expansion slot. Expansion cards that produce video signals are called *video cards*, *video adapters*, or *graphics cards*.

Most video cards follow one of several industry standards. The first IBM PC had a monochrome display that used the *Monochrome Display Adapter (MDA)*. (Actually, the MDA card doubled as a video and printer card.) The MDA video card could display text in a resolution of only 720 horizontal by 350 vertical pixels (720 x 350). A company named Hercules released its own video card called the Hercules Graphics Card, or HGC. This card displayed sharper text and could handle graphics, like bar charts.

The first color video card was the *Color Graphics Adapter (CGA)* from IBM. This card had a lower text resolution than the MDA, typically 320 x 200 pixels, and could display only four colors from a palette of 16. One drawback of a CGA video card is that it produces *flicker* and *snow*. Flicker is the annoying tendency of the text to flash as you move the image up or down. Snow is the flurry of bright dots that can appear anywhere on the screen. The *Enhanced Graphics Adapter (EGA)*, also from IBM, increased resolution to 640 x 350 pixels. Also, you could show 16 colors at one time from a palette of 64. The IBM *Professional Graphics Adapter (PGA)*, introduced in 1984, was a more powerful version of EGA, but, PGA never caught on.

In 1987, the IBM Personal Systems/2 (PS/2) computers were introduced, sporting the video standard known as *Virtual Graphics Array*, or *VGA*. (Some people mistakenly call VGA "video graphics adapter.") The current standard, VGA adapters produce a maximum resolution of 640 x 480 pixels, able to display up to 256 colors from a palette of 256,000. That's a lot of crayons. The *Multi Color Graphics Array (MCGA)* is a cut-down version of VGA for some PS/2 models. Today, you can buy a Hercules video card for as little as $20, while a VGA card costs as little as $50.

Too many video standards to comprehend? Industry leaders agree. Some companies are pushing for standardization in the microcomputer industry. In 1988, nine vendors of graphics products (ATI Technologies, Genoa Systems, Orchid Technology, Renaissance GRX, STB Systems, Techmar, Headland Technology [formerly Video Seven], Western Digital Imaging/Paradise Systems, and NEC) formed the Video Electronics Standards Association, or VESA. Led by NEC Home Electronics, VESA intends to establish standardized timing parameters for the *super-VGA (SVGA)* video standard, which provides a maximum resolution of 800 x 600 pixels and the same colors as VGA. There are also video cards that do 1024 x 768 pixels — XGA (Extended Graphics Array) and 8514/A, for instance.

Most microcomputer monitors support at least one video standard, allowing them to operate with video cards and software compatible with that standard. For example, a monitor that supports VGA may operate with VGA video cards and VGA software. A monitor that supports many different video standards is called a *multiple frequency monitor*. One example is the NEC MultiSync 4D, which supports all popular video standards. Different vendors call their multiple frequency monitors by different names, including *multisync, multifrequency, multiscan, auto synchronous,* and *auto tracking*.

Picking the Right Combination

After years of a CGA or monochrome monitor, you may want to move up to a new video card and monitor. Improving the resolution of your PC involves three parts: a high-resolution video card, matching monitor, and often, software.

Standardizing on a Video Standard

Which video standard do you select? The standard so far is VGA, with super VGA (SVGA) becoming more prevalent. (Many video cards support both.) Start by looking at the software you currently use or would like to run. Many games, for example, require VGA. Avoid EGA video cards, since they are limited to 16 colors and are only 62 percent as sharp as a VGA card. Also, VGA and super-VGA cards let you run CGA and EGA software on your VGA monitor.

SVGA is very popular for many reasons. If you want to use multimedia (the melding of sound, sharp graphics, and information from a CD-ROM disk), you want to purchase an SVGA video card. This is the minimum requirement mandated by multimedia standards. SVGA is also convenient for Microsoft Windows, allowing you to get more icons and groups on the screen without having to scroll up or down to make your selections. SVGA is also better for your eyes, since it has higher refresh rate than VGA — about 72 Hz. When the screen is refreshed more often, your eyes will not feel as fatigued.

Some SVGA cards also support a resolution of 1024 x 768 pixels, but such a high resolution requires a 16-inch or larger monitor to comfortably read the text. Also, such high resolution slows down your monitor, since the video card must draw all those pixels. On typical 14-inch monitors, this resolution crams too much detail into too small an area.

Often, you can select how much memory you want on your video card — 256K, 512K, or 1MB. Finding 256K on a VGA card is rare; most cards come with at least 512K. The 512K or 1MB of memory does not speed up your video card. Rather, it allows your monitor to display more colors and/or higher resolutions. For 256 colors drawn from a palette of 256,000, you'll need at least 512K of video memory. At 1024 x 768 pixels, you need at least 1MB. If you currently don't need this ability, bypass the extra memory. The next generation of video cards will probably provide other features you may need or want.

Another difference between video cards is the type of expansion slot they fit: 8-bit or 16-bit. The 8-bit video card has only one edge connector that fits into your expansion slot. The 16-bit card has two edge connectors that slide into the slot. With the two connectors, the 16-bit cards are faster than 8-bit ones, but only if your computer supports them. If you have an older XT computer (which accepts only 8-bit cards), you'll have to shop carefully. Most, but not all, 16-bit video cards can work in these 8-bit computers. They usually have switches that allow them to pretend they are 8-bit cards. To ensure your video card supports your older computer, ask before you buy and insist on a money-back guarantee if it does not.

If you are shopping for a video card to provide super VGA or sharper resolutions, you will need special software drivers for each of your software programs to take advantage of this resolution. Otherwise, your video card will act as a typical VGA card. For example, if you use the desktop publishing program *Ventura Publisher Gold* (GEM version), you will need a software driver for your SVGA video card to display more of the page on the screen. When shopping for a higher-resolution video card, be sure it has drivers that support the software packages you own. Otherwise, your software will operate in the typical VGA mode. Don't expect many drivers to be available. Drivers are usually provided for only a handful of the following programs: AutoCAD, Autoshade, CADKEY, Framework, GEM Desktop, Lotus 1-2-3, Microsoft Windows, Microsoft Word, P-CAD, Symphony, Ventura Publisher, VersaCAD, WordPerfect, WordStar, OS/2 Presentation Manager, and Quattro Pro.

Windows Shopping

Some video cards offer exceptional speed. How? They include a "thinking" video chip that frees your computer from having to draw the screen's images. Such video cards are called *video accelerators*. These special video cards are also called *Windows accelerator cards* because they can speed up all Microsoft Windows software (see Figure 11.2). Since Windows software is so graphic, your screen may be slowly redrawn every time you resize a program group or move an icon. In some ways, these special video cards should be called Auto*CAD* accelerators. When used with the popular computer-aided design (CAD) program, these video cards can really shine, improving video speed tenfold. However, more people own Windows than own AutoCAD.

A video accelerator card replaces the video card in your PC. In DOS mode, it functions as a normal VGA or SVGA card. Almost all your present software applications run flawlessly and perhaps a little faster than they currently do. When you enter Windows or another supported application, you'll truly see some speed.

An accelerator card is built around a video coprocessor, a special

Figure 12.2 A *Windows* video accelerator card, such as the Diamond Stealth VRAM, relieves your computer from managing graphical screens. *(Photo courtesy of Diamond Computer Systems Inc.)*

computer chip mounted on the video card. This coprocessor may come from S3, Western Digital, Texas Instruments, or Weitek. The coprocessor performs many video duties with little or no help from your computer's processor. With an accelerator card installed, your PC can concentrate on what it does best — handling data and responding to your needs. In other words, the accelerator card's video coprocessor relieves your computer from handling the pixels, lines and other visual data. That reclaimed power is focused on other tasks. Not only does the video coprocessor handle the work faster, but it also can address more memory at one time — through linear addressing — than conventional video cards.

To free your PC from these video duties, a video accelerator card requires a software driver that, once installed, tells Windows to let the video card handle the visual work. How much work is saved? Your computer can spend up to 40 percent of its time drawing your screen. In my own real-world experiences, my computer has been accelerated about 10 to 20 percent.

There are several video accelerator cards on the market, based on several different video coprocessor chips. Almost all will run Windows at resolutions up to 1024 by 768 pixels in both interlaced and noninterlaced modes with either 16 or 256 colors. You will, of course, need a monitor that can match that performance. Some models have a built-in mouse port and mouse. If you buy one of these, make sure it will accept a Microsoft-compatible or Logitech-compatible mouse so that you can replace the mouse in the future without having to replace the entire accelerator card. (Mice do die and need to be replaced.)

If you want 256 colors at high resolutions, make sure the board has 1MB of video RAM (VRAM) installed. If 16 colors are adequate, 512K is enough. Some boards include the Sierra high-color RAMDAC chip that will allow 32,768 colors in 800 x 600 mode. Dual-ported VRAM provides faster performance when using 256 or more colors at one time. Most of these video cards have drivers for Windows and for DOS applications like AutoCAD, GEM, Generic CADD, Lotus 1-2-3, Ventura Publisher, and WordPerfect. Make sure your video accelerator card supports the applications you plan to use.

Picking a Monitor

The trick is to pick a monitor that works with your selected video card. You can save money by purchasing a single-standard (fixed-frequency) monitor and a matching video card. For example, you can order a VGA monitor and a VGA video card. For greatest flexibility, get a multiscanning monitor that accommodates a range of standards, including those standards not yet formalized.

With these monitors, you must match the range of horizontal and vertical frequencies the monitor accepts with those generated by your video card. The wider the range of signals, the more expensive but versatile the monitor. Your video card's vertical and horizontal frequencies must fall within the ranges supported by your monitor. The vertical frequency (or refresh/frame rate) determines how stable your image will be. The higher, the better. Typical vertical frequencies range from 50 to 90 Hz. The horizontal frequency (or line rate) ranges between 31.5 and 59 kHz.

To keep the horizontal frequency low, some video cards use interlacing signals, alternately displaying half of the lines of the total image. With some monitors, interlacing can produce a pronounced flicker. For this reason, your monitor should synchronize to twice the vertical frequency of the video card. For example, the IBM XGA video standard uses a frame rate of 43.5 Hz. To match those signals, a monitor must accept a vertical frequency of 87 Hz and a horizontal frequency of 35.5 kHz.

When shopping for a VGA monitor, make sure the monitor supports a horizontal frequency of at least 31.5 kHz, the minimum a VGA card needs to paint a 640 x 480 screen. The VESA super-VGA (800 x 600) standard requires a 72-Hz vertical frequency and a horizontal frequency of at least 48 kHz. The sharper 1024 x 768 image requires a vertical frequency of 60 Hz and a horizontal frequency of 58 kHz. If the vertical frequency is upped to 72 Hz, the horizontal frequency must be 58 kHz. If flicker-prone interlacing is used, a 1024 x 768 video card needs a monitor with a a 43.5 Hz vertical frequency and a 35.5 kHz horizontal frequency.

If you don't know whether your prospective monitor supports your video card, get the salesperson's assurance that the monitor will work. Also, you should verify that the monitor plugs into your video card. Older monitors may use a 9-pin connector instead of the VGA-standard 15-pin. Also, the cord from the monitor to the video card should be included with the monitor.

Consider the size of your desk before you think about monitors 16 inches or larger. A 16-inch monitor is typically at least a foot and a half deep, and a 20-inch monitor will take up two square feet. (Typical 14-inch monitors are 16 to 18 inches deep.)

Picture-tube quality is another consideration. Many monitors are curved because it's easier to send an electron beam across them. Flat-screen monitors, which are a bit more expensive, look better to most people. As a general rule, the less curvature a monitor has, the less glare it will reflect. You also should check the dot pitch of the monitor — the lower the number, the better. You can save money by picking a smaller monitor with a higher dot pitch. The trade-off in clarity is often tolerable. Selecting a monitor with a 0.31-mm dot pitch over one with a 0.28-mm dot pitch may save you up to $75.

Get a monitor with horizontal and vertical positioning and image controls that can be easily reached. Look for more than basic contrast and brightness controls; some monitors let you adjust the width and height of your screen images. A tilt-swivel stand should be included with your monitor, allowing you to move the monitor to the angle best for your use. If ordering by mail, watch out for excessive shipping costs. Better yet, try to find a vendor that includes prepaid shipping for such a large purchase. When your new monitor finally arrives, check for external damage to the box.

Tire-Kicking a Monitor

A monitor is such an important part of your computer that knowing its technical specifications doesn't go far enough. Knowing the monitor has a 0.28-mm dot pitch doesn't necessarily tell you that it is ideal for you. It's best to "kick the tires" of your new monitor at a showroom or, with a liberal return policy, in the privacy of your office.

To test your monitor:

- Load a black-on-white word processor or graphics program, like Microsoft Windows' Paintbrush. Stare at one side of the monitor and take in the screen without focusing on it. Then chomp your teeth while looking directly at the screen. Does the screen flicker or pulsate? If it does, you'll find that even a couple of hours of work at this monitor will tire your eyes and give you a headache.

- Draw a circle with the graphics program. If the result is an oval, not a circle, this monitor won't serve you well with graphics or design software.

- Type some words in 8- or 10-point type (one point = 1/72 inch). If the letters are fuzzy or if the black characters are fringed with color, select another monitor.

- Are the brightness, contrast, power, and other controls at the front of the monitor? Controls at the front are more easily accessible than those on the back or side.

- Turn the brightness up and down while examining the corner of the screen's image. If the image blooms or swells, it's likely to lose focus at high brightness levels.

- Load *Windows* to check for uniform focus. Are the corner icons as sharp as the rest of the screen? Are the lines in the title bar curved or wavy? Monitors are usually sharply focused at the center, but seriously blurred corners indicate a poor design. Bowed lines may be the result of a poor graphics card, so don't dismiss a monitor without double-checking with another card.

- Is the screen prone to glare? A showroom's subdued lighting can make glare hard to detect, so instead look for excessively curved screens that catch light from many directions. A less curved or flat-screen monitor will reduce glare.

Upgrade Over Time

Buying a new monitor and video card can be costly, especially since these are the most expensive parts in your PC. Improving your monitor over time may be your best move. By spreading the costs over several months, you can stay within your budget.

The first step is to buy a new video card. A VGA video card can cost as little as $50. Most video cards can bridge two or more video standards. In other words, they can work with your monochrome or CGA monitor until you can afford a new monitor to match it. If you adopt this strategy, be sure you choose the a video card that supports both the video standard used by your old monitor and the standard that will be supported by your new one. Fewer cards are supporting the older video standards.

An alternative is to purchase a VGA or SVGA video card and a monochrome VGA monitor. A monochrome VGA monitor works well with your VGA card. You'll enjoy sharp graphics and text now, rather than enduring the low resolution of your current monitor. One drawback is that instead of colors, you will see 64 shades of gray. A monochrome VGA monitor, such as the NEC MultiSync GS2A, can be purchased for less than $100, saving you $150 to $250 over a VGA color monitor. When you can afford the color monitor, you can hand down the monochrome VGA monitor to another in your company or family, sell it, or keep it for a backup.

Installing the Video Card

Installing a new video card can spring some traps. If, for some reason, the new video card doesn't work correctly, you won't be able to see anything on the screen, so you won't know why the card is misbehaving. And if you have any software that depends on the video card you are removing, it may not run correctly on the new card. Usually, you install the video card into your computer, tell your computer of the change, and change your software, if necessary, to support the new video standard and resolution.

To install a video card:

1. Disable or remove any software that relies on your current video card.

   Your computer's startup files may rely on your video card. When you replace your card with another, the software may be surprised by the different video card. For example, if you automatically have Windows start each time you turn on your computer, you must disable this line from your AUTOEXEC.BAT file to keep it from launching. Otherwise, the new video card may be put into service before the Windows Setup program has been run to recognize the new card. I once replaced a Trident SVGA card with a Diamond Stealth VRAM Windows accelerator card. I ran the Setup utility to return Windows to a plain VGA configuration.

   Some people may need to disable their EGA- or VGA-enhancing software. For example, some people use UltraVision from Personics. Also, memory managers — like QEMM-386, 386Max, or DOS 5.0's EMM386.EXE and HIMEM.SYS duo — may need to be disabled so they don't place any data in video RAM. Once these software changes are complete, reboot your computer .

2. Turn off your PC and remove its case.

   For details on opening your PC, see the procedure in Chapter 3, "Cracking Open the Case."

3. Remove or disable the current video card.

   If your computer has a video card built into its motherboard rather than on an expansion card, you must disable the card. Most computers with a built-in video card allow you to turn off this internal circuitry by either changing a jumper or a DIP (dual in-line pin) switch. In most cases, an on–off switch labeled "VGA" must be turned off. Check your owner's manual for directions.

   If you are replacing an existing video card, you must find and remove it from its slot. To avoid static electricity, first briefly touch a piece of metal, like, your computer's cover. Next, remove the screw holding this expansion card in place and lift the card straight up. Grab the card by its metal bracket or edges, not by its components.

4. Configure your new video card.

Before inserting the new video card, you may need to configure it using the card's switches or jumpers. In most cases, the factory default settings should work fine. For example, some cards allow you to disable the software interrupt used to avoid conflicts with a network card. Others require you to set the scan rate of the card so it is compatible with your monitor. The documentation should tell you the purpose of each and suggest the situations in which a setting is useful. Even if you decide to use the default or factory settings, look at the board carefully to make sure it is set to the defaults.

5. On some computers, select the type of video card being installed.

If you own an XT-type computer, you must set a DIP switch or jumper to tell it you are installing a certain type of video card. To install a color video card, you have to turn switches 5 and 6 of SW1 to the ON position. On some older AT-type computers, you may have to change a jumper on the motherboard. For example, if you are upgrading from a monochrome to color monitor, you may have to change a jumper. Check your PC's owner's manual.

6. Install the new video card.

Hopefully, the new video card will fit in the expansion slot from which you removed your original video card. If your video card was built into your computer's motherboard, select an empty expansion slot and remove its slot cover. If you have an AT-type computer and want to install a 16-bit video card, you should install the video card into a 16-bit slot to take full advantage of your computer's speed. If you removed your original video card from an 8-bit slot in your AT, select a different slot that accepts the new 16-bit video card.

Insert the video card into the expansion slot. Firmly press the gold-fingered edge connector of the card into the expansion slot until it snaps into place. Use the screw removed from the slot to fix the card in place.

7. Plug in your computer, monitor, and keyboard.

Before assembling the rest of your computer, you should test the new video card. Plug in your computer and monitor. Connect the keyboard to your computer. Don't forget to plug in the monitor cable from the monitor to the new video card.

8. Turn on your PC and test the video card.

Turn on first your monitor and then your computer. When you turn on your computer, the new video card's copyright notice should appear on the screen almost immediately. If so, you know it is working correctly.

If you have an AT-type computer, you must now tell it what type of monitor you have. If you didn't change between monochrome and color, you may not have to change anything. If you did change from monochrome to color, your computer probably sensed a different video card and reported an error. Typically, you must run your computer's setup program. To get to the setup program, you either press a key or two or run a software program that came with your PC. For example, you may have to press the Delete key or F1 as your PC warms up. Consult your owner's manual. Once in the setup program, you must change the primary display to match that of the video card. Your setup program already has a list of possible displays, such as "Monochrome," "VGA/PGA/EGA," or others. Save your settings and exit.

If you notice anything wrong as your PC warms up, turn it off immediately, remove the card, and study it to see if you have set a switch incorrectly. If you specify the wrong kind of monitor in your computer's setup program, you may get an error message. Check your settings and try again. If the monitor still doesn't come to life, you may need a new ROM BIOS (read-only memory basic input/output system) chip for your computer. Older computers may have a ROM BIOS that doesn't support VGA. For more information on the BIOS, refer to Chapter 7, "CPUs: Boning Up on Brainpower."

9. Replace your computer's case and return your PC to working order.

10. Set up your software to work with the new video card.

When you get to the DOS prompt, install the new card's software. Some cards include a DOS-based program to tune the monitor and the video card.

If you went from a monochrome to a color video card, tell your software about it. For example, you now can pick a color palette for your word processor or spreadsheet. If you added a super-VGA (or higher-resolution) card, you must use special software drivers to take advantage of its 800 x 600 resolution. Otherwise, the SVGA card mimics the typical VGA standard. These drivers are included with your video card on a diskette or two. Assorted utilities — which you may never need — are also included.

Some software programs have built-in support for a higher-resolution video card. For example, Microsoft Windows has drivers for most video cards, although your video card may have a newer, more powerful version. Once the software driver is installed for its intended program, your video card will exhibit top performance. For example, you may be able to see more on your screen. Characters on the screen will be easier to read because more pixels are being used to form the letters, and graphical images will be smoother and more representative of how they will look when printed. If you use *Windows*, you'll need to run the *Windows* Setup program from DOS to install the new video card's drivers. Because the new video card may have a different resolution than your previous card, you may need to use the monitor's horizontal and vertical controls to center the image on your screen.

Other Video Software

You can also get software utilities that enhance your VGA video card. For example, the characters displayed on your monitor, or screen fonts, do not take full advantage of this higher resolution. One way around this is to use a software utility that provides a replacement font for those that are now used.

One popular product is UltraVision from Personics. This program, selling for less than $100, gives you an assortment of fonts you can substitute for the VGA and EGA default characters. It also lets you change screen colors and number of rows and columns of text. With

UltraVision, you can shift to sharper text, and have your computer use this quality of text for all of your DOS applications. Unfortunately, the program won't improve on super-VGA fonts.

Eyestrain: A Glaring Problem

After a few hours of work at your computer, your eyes may ache and become tired. Most likely, the glare from your computer's monitor is the culprit. Glare is light that is bounced off your screen directly into your eyes. Because most monitors are slightly curved, they channel the light from the sides at you. Although a glare problem may not be obvious, it eventually takes its toll on your eyes. Your work can be slowed and accuracy impaired.

You can easily tell if you have a glare problem. First turn off your monitor. If parts of your screen have an especially bright spot, such as a window reflection or other light source, you may have a problem. Glare can easily be reduced. The best solution is to buy a monitor with a flat screen and either etched or coated glass designed to reduce glare. If you cannot afford a new monitor, here are some affordable ways to reduce glare.

First, change the light that is bounced off your screen. Point your screen away from any bright light sources like windows and lamps. Also, avoid facing a window directly. Looking at a monitor with a bright window in front of you is especially straining. To avoid looking out a window is tricky, since you also want to avoid having a window behind you, which casts reflections on your monitor. It's best to have windows to the left or right of your screen. Also rearrange the other lights in your room. Window blinds can control outside light. Meanwhile, try to reduce the amount of surrounding light without relying on a single reading lamp. A single lamp causes uneven lighting, which also causes eye fatigue. Your goal is to have indirect, uniform lighting.

You can change the position of your monitor. Tilt your screen down slightly, about 10 to 15 degrees below eye level. While an upward-tilting screen is ideal to look at for bifocal and contact-lens wearers, it reflects more light than one perpendicular to your desk. Also, you should sit more than 18 inches from your monitor. When setting the monitor's brightness, start out at a low level to avoid headaches and eye fatigue. How low? Load a program that has a light background and set the brightness accordingly. You'll not only avoid eye problems but also lengthen the life of your monitor.

You can use software to change your screen. It is best to have dark characters on a light screen, rather than the more prevalent light characters on a dark background. Microsoft Windows and other programs enable you to change your colors. For black text on a white background at the DOS prompt, use ANSI.SYS's color mapping. Enter the following line to your CONFIG.SYS startup file:

```
DEVICE=C:\DOS\ANSI.SYS
```

Next, restart your computer. Then, insert the following line in AUTOEXEC.BAT:

```
PROMPT $e[7m$p$g
```

After restarting your PC, you should have black text on a white background.

A filter of tinted glass or plastic can improve your monitor's contrast by darkening the screen uniformly. These are called *glare filters* or *antiglare screens*; they are available for as little as $50. Because of the filter, you may need to increase the monitor's contrast and brightness — in that order — so the screen seems as bright as usual. You can get an inexpensive black mesh screen, but it may cause more problems than it solves. These screens reduce glare by absorbing any light that isn't traveling perpendicular to the screen. Unfortunately, mesh screens absorb light that comes in at sharp angles from the side, producing glare. Also, the coarser meshes may interfere with the screen's images.

Safe Haven

Like anything electronic, your monitor won't last forever. Here are some tips to extend its life.

First, keep all the ventilation holes and slots free and clear. Never place paper or anything else on top of the monitor. Poorly ventilated monitors become hot, which eventually deteriorates the insulation of the components and circuits. Excessive heat can also alter the properties of some components, possibly causing outright failure. If you notice dirt accumulating on the openings, use a toothbrush or vacuum cleaner to clear them.

Leave your monitor on as much as possible: It's better not to turn your monitor on and off more than once or twice a day. There are several reasons for leaving your monitor on. Each time you turn your monitor on or off, the surge of electricity may stress some components. Also, the temperature swing between on and off may prematurely age some components. In some cases, poor-quality electrical connections may fail or become intermittent. Some people recommend leaving a monitor on permanently, using a software "screen saver" to turn off the screen after a specified idle time. The cost of electricity for operating a typical monitor is about 16 cents per day. Another important reason to leave your monitor on is that most screens require up to an hour to stabilize. During this period, image centering, black level, focus, and screen brightness can vary greatly, affecting the screen's readability and your comfort.

If you leave a color monitor on continuously, make sure that you degauss it periodically to stave off a loss in color purity. If you have a degaussing button, be sure to press it at least once a week. Otherwise, turn your monitor off for at least half an hour from time to time. When you start up the monitor again, it will degauss itself automatically. Degaussing eliminates built-up magnetic fields that alter the correct scan of the electron beams. This affects the purity of the screen colors, focus, and convergence. My NEC MultiSync 4FG monitor has a degaussing button that should be pressed no more than every 20 minutes.

Fading Star

The brightness of your screen fades with time. A few years down the road, you may be squinting to see the dim images. Your monitor fades for two reasons: Both the cathode that generates the light beams and the phosphor coating that the beams illuminate become less efficient over time.

Buy a monitor that is brighter than you really need. This extra reserve will compensate for the slow dimming as well as for bright, sunny days. Also, the extra brightness may be needed if you put an anti-glare screen on your monitor. To check the brightness of a monitor, use it with a program that has a bright background with areas of contrast. Increase both the screen brightness and contrast controls while watching how sharply defined text or objects become.

Beware the ELF

Several medical studies indicate that your monitor may be hurting you. Your monitor generates electromagnetic emissions; these electromagnetic emissions may cause health problems — miscarriages, birth defects, and cancer. The risk may be low, but if you spend a third of your day (or more) in front of a computer monitor, that risk is multiplied.

The concern is that VLF (very low-frequency) and ELF (extremely low-frequency) emissions somehow affect your body. These two emissions come in two forms: electric and magnetic. Some research indicates that ELF magnetic emissions are more threatening than VLF emissions, because they interact with the natural electric activity of body cells. Monitors aren't the only culprits; significant ELF emissions come from electric blankets and power lines. ELF and VLF are not considered radiation; they are actually radio frequencies below that of broadcasting.

These two frequencies are covered by the new Swedish monitor-emission standard called SWEDAC, named after the Swedish regulatory agency. In many European countries, government agencies and businesses buy only low-emission monitors. How well a monitor reduces emissions varies because the emissions guideline that the industry follows — the so-called SWEDAC standard — became stricter in 1991. Whether or not real dangers exist, low-emission monitors are here to stay.

A low-emission monitor costs about $20 to $100 more than similar, regular-emission monitors. When shopping for a low-emission monitor, don't just ask for a low-emission monitor. Find out if the monitor limits specific types of emission, particularly ELF magnetic fields; or ask if the monitor complies fully with the new 1991 Swedish standard.

If you decide not to buy a low-emission monitor, you can take other steps to protect yourself. The most important is to stay at arm's length (around 28 inches) from the front of your monitor. After a couple of feet, ELF magnetic emission levels usually drop down to those of a typical office with fluorescent lights. Also, monitor emissions are weakest from the front of a monitor, so keep at least three feet from the sides and backs of nearby monitors and five feet from any copier — a strong source of ELF.

However, electromagnetic emissions should not be your only concern. You should also be concerned about screen glare, monitor flicker, computer noise, and unbroken stretches of keyboard work. In fact, some anti-glare screens not only reduce eyestrain but also cut ELF and VLF electric — but not magnetic — fields. You can prevent health problems by taking regular breaks to ease eye and hand strain. Also, use a chair that encourages good posture and a comfortable typing position. Make sure your workspace has good lighting, and use a flicker-free monitor with adequate screen resolution.

Cleaning the Monitor

Screen cleaning is the easiest way to maintain your monitor. If you often point your fingers at the screen, a smudge will remind you to do the chore. Even if the screen isn't smudged, perform regular cleaning. When you clean the monitor, use a soft, lint-free cloth and a nonalcohol glass cleaner. Always spray fluid on the cloth and not on the screen; excess fluid on the screen could stain the casing or seep inside the monitor to damage its electronics.

By arming yourself with the three elements of a good video system — a video card, a monitor, and software — you'll have more pixels to play with, giving you more detail and less fatigue. Proper and regular maintenance and cleaning of your monitor will provide these benefits much longer. In this case, seeing is believing.

13 Multimedia: Sound and More

Interested in adding high-quality sound to your PC? How about animation, or even full-motion video? You can do it on an extremely wide range of levels, ranging from the simple to the sophisticated and expensive. These exciting new capabilities all fall under the hottest new buzzword in the PC world: multimedia.

Multimedia embraces a gamut of technologies, including the ability to merge sound, still images, animation, and video on a PC at the same time. Most multimedia software is designed for education, entertainment or reference. Multimedia applications range from talking encyclopedias and arcade-style games, to databases of stored video clips and complex multimedia development tools.

You may want to get a CD-ROM disk drive to simply enjoy some multimedia applications. Or you may want to create your own multimedia, which on a basic level, can be accomplished fairly easily. For example, with a voice-annotation tool and Windows' Object Linking and Embedding (OLE), you can embed different forms of media, such as audio or animation, into your documents and files. An Excel user can add voice notes to a spreadsheet before sending it to a co-worker.

If you want to view or create higher-level multimedia, involving animation or video, you'll need additional software and hardware, including a PC with a fast processor and plenty of RAM, a video card, heavy-duty storage, and video-based system software such as Apple's QuickTime for Windows or Microsoft's Video for Windows.

This chapter concentrates on some simple improvements that will bring your PC into the multimedia world. It also points the way toward additional enhancements that will allow you to play and create advanced applications involving video.

Sounds Great

You can take advantage of multimedia on its most basic level by enhancing the sound capability of your PC. Then you'll be able to enjoy the growing number of sound-savy products supported by Microsoft Windows 3.1. For this type of sound, you'll need a sound card.

Sound cards fall into two groups: 8-bit and 16-bit. Eight-bit sound cards do not provide as rich a sound as the 16-bit models. (If you have an XT-type computer, however, an 8-bit sound card is your only choice. Sixteen-bit sound cards are used in AT-type computers.) Although 16-bit cards sound better, the extra cost may not be worth the improvement, especially if the card is just used for games.

Adding a sound card is not that expensive. For example, a $100 8-bit Thunderboard sound card from MediaVision and a couple of speakers give you much better sound than your computer's built-in speaker. Most sound cards typically support either of two audio standards: Sound Blaster or Ad Lib. The Thunderboard card supports both.

The Ad Lib Gold, Sound Blaster Pro and ProAudio Spectrum-16 are second-generation 16-bit sound cards, usually costing about $200 (see Figure 13.1). All vastly improve the average computer by providing professional-quality sound. They do this through sampling: the cards use an analog-to-digital converter (ADC) to turn sound waves into a digital format. A digital-to-analog converter (DAC) replays the digital file. This CD-quality audio is the yardstick against which sound cards are compared.

Some sound cards provide other options, such as a SCSI (Small Computer Systems Interface) port for connecting other devices through the same card. For example, a CD-ROM drive — required for multimedia — can be attached through this port. (The Sound Blaster Pro uses its own interface for connecting a CD-ROM drive.) Other features include a game port for attaching a joystick, text-to-speech conversion software and a MIDI interface to attach an electronic synthesizer.

Figure 13.1 A sound card gives you great sound not only in games but in Microsoft Windows 3.1.

You can sometimes add a sound card by simply plugging a small device into your PC's parallel printer port. MediaVision, for example, offers the AudioPort. It gives laptop and desktop computers sound capabilities without opening the case. For under $150, the AudioPort includes a built-in speaker for playback, a microphone jack for sound input and a speaker jack for external speakers. It runs on batteries and is compatible with both Ad Lib and Sound Blaster software. The Audio-port comes with voice-annotation software from Lotus Development Corp. that lets you leave voice notes in supported Windows software.

Windows Sound Cards

You can get sound cards designed especially for Microsoft Windows. Microsoft itself offers the Windows Sound System audio card. This hardware/software bundle lets you add verbal comments or instructions to a Windows file for others to act on. For example, you can add such a voice annotation to a spreadsheet file or database record.

The Sound System also lets you record voice commands for basic Windows menus. It even proofreads spreadsheet numbers by reading them back to you. For under $300, the Windows Sound System provides business audio you can afford.

Compaq is also getting into the game. The computer manufacturer has added built-in Windows sound capabilities to its Deskpro/i line of PCs. Developed along with Microsoft and Analog Devices Inc., Business Audio allows you to record voice files and add them to Windows applications via Object Linking and Embedding (OLE) technology. This built-in capability will make it all the more easier to add voice annotations.

Adding Speakers

Sound cards usually do not include speakers. You can use headphones or connect a cable from one of the card's audio ports to a stereo boom box, the amplifier in your stereo system or a self-amplified speaker. Sometimes, special speakers are needed to prevent your computer's electronic "noise" from being heard. Deluxe speakers include sub-woofers that increase the range of bass sounds the speakers can play. When considering a speaker, look for an easy-to-reach volume control and long cords. Many require batteries or include an AC adapter.

If you simply want better sound than your computer's speaker at the lowest possible price, consider the $39.95 Disney Sound Source. This device is about the size of an answering machine and includes its own speakers. It plugs into the parallel port while allowing you to still use your printer. Non-Disney programs will soon support the Sound Source since its code was licensed to Phoenix Technologies whose customers will, in turn, build this technology into internal sound products.

Improving Sound and Graphics

You can improve both sound *and* graphics with a single card. MediaVision offers the Thunder and Lightning card, which boasts 24-bit video and 8-bit sound. The card has 1MB of video memory that provides VGA, Super-VGA and 1024 x 768 resolutions. It also plays Sound Blaster- and Ad Lib-compatible sounds. The card sells for under $300.

Using Sound with Windows

Once the sound card is installed, you can go into Windows 3.1 and activate some of the sound options. The Control Panel contains drivers for MIDI devices and sound cards. A utility called Sound is also new to the Control Panel. With it, you can assign audio special effects to system events, such as replacing the error beep with a chime. In the Accessories group, a utility called the Sound Recorder plays, records and edits sound files. The Media Player controls audio devices, such as audio CD drives. And screen savers, such as After Dark, can add exotic sounds to your computer.

Recording With a Microphone

To records your own sounds, consider a microphone. For as little as $20, you can find a good one at Radio Shack. A digital sound card will capture sounds coming from a microphone and convert them into a digital format. These digitized sounds then can be converted back to audio. Microsoft calls this ability *waveform audio*. In other circles, it is called digital audio and sampled sound. (Saving these digital audio files may be difficult; CD-quality sound eats up about 10MB of hard disk per minute.)

Recording With MIDI

A sound card also lets you connect an external electronic synthesizer to your computer. This synthesizer uses a protocol called MIDI (Musical Instrument Digital Interface). MIDI was developed in the early 1980s to connect electronic music synthesizers and controllers, such as keyboards and electronic wind instruments. When a MIDI keyboard is connected to your MPC sound card, the computer can store the MIDI files, which can then be manipulated and mixed with other MIDI data. Finally, these MIDI files can be played back through your speakers. For example, you can play one instrument at a time on the synthesizer and combine them later into a multilayered compositions.

Going Further: The Multimedia PC

If you want to go beyond sound to really take advantage of all multimedia has to offer, you'll require an enhanced level of hardware capabilities. Don't expect an inexpensive journey. The Multimedia PC Council (MPC), a group of hardware and software manufacturers, defines a multimedia PC as a computer having at least the following:

- 80386SX computer.
- 4MB of memory.
- 30MB hard disk.
- Super-VGA (800 x 600) monitor and video card.
- 1.44MB 3.5-inch disk drive.
- CD-ROM drive.
- Digital sound card.
- A pair of speakers.
- Multimedia Windows (either Windows 3.0 with Multimedia Extensions for Windows or Windows 3.1).

Products with the MPC logo on them essentially promise that the product meets minimum MPC standards or works on MPC equipment. However, the MPC is reevaluating these standards, and some multimedia technology is still being developed. IBM, on the other hand, is creating its own standards with its Ultimedia products.

In other words, nothing is set in stone.

If your computer already meets the MPC requirements for processing capability, RAM, and display, you can convert it the rest of the way with a multimedia upgrade kit. These are sold for between $700 and $1200 and include a CD-ROM drive, sound card and Multimedia Windows. A multimedia upgrade kit simplifies installation and technical support, and often costs about as much as if you were to shop around and mix and match the various components. An example of a deluxe multimedia upgrade kit is the MediaVision CDPC. It offers great audio, a CD-ROM drive and two high-performance speakers. The CDPC is housed in a sleek box that sits atop your computer. It attaches to your PC through a cable inserted into a single expansion card, making it one of the easier-to-install upgrade kits.

CD-ROM: The Heart of Multimedia

The heart of a multimedia system is the CD-ROM (compact-disc read-only memory) drive (see Figure 13.2). A CD-ROM drive is like a hard disk in that it stores large quantitles of information. However, the storage capacity of a CD-ROM goes far beyond that of a hard disk: each CD-ROM disk can store over 600MB, which is equal to about 250,000 pages of text, or the capacity of more than 400 high-density diskettes!

There are some other differences between a hard disk and a CD-ROM. First, you cannot save information to a CD-ROM. Second, a CD-ROM drive is up to 20 times slower than a hard disk. However, you can remove and insert various CD-ROM disks, and you can even play your own audio CDs on these drives.

There are hundreds of CD-ROM disks you can play now without having to invest in a high-powered multimedia-ready PC. If you only want to use simple text databases on CD, you can settle for a slower drive that costs as little as $300. You can select either an internal or external model. An internal version costs about $100 less, although an external drive is portable. However, for multimedia, you want to select a CD-ROM drive with a data transfer rate of at least 150 kilobytes per second (kbps). You also want a built-in buffer of at least 32K and hopefully 64K to provide jitter-free moving video. For multimedia, look for access speeds of under 400ms. The lower this average random access time, the faster your drive.

Most CD-ROM drives are connected to your computer through an interface card placed into an expansion slot (although some external CD-ROM drives even can be attached to your printer port). This interface card either supports SCSI or a proprietary interface. A

Figure 13.2 A CD-ROM drive gives you access to the equivalent of 250,000 pages of text. *(Photo courtesy of Sony Corp.)*

multimedia sound card can usually double as the controller for your CD-ROM drive. Some sound cards support the SCSI (small computer systems interface) interface; others use a proprietary interface that locks you into one vendor's products.

Buying a CD-ROM Drive

When you order your CD-ROM drive, make sure an interface card is included. Also, buy the interface card with the fastest possible data transfer rate. The faster this card can accept information from the CD-ROM drive, the faster you can get your work done.

Look for a drive that has dust protection, usually a door that seals the motors and optical elements against contaminants, and a mechanism that cleans the lens automatically. Most CD-ROM drives play audio CDs and include a headphone jack and volume control. If you want to amplify this sound, look for RCA phono jacks you can connect to an amplifier or sound card.

CD-ROM Formats

Unfortunately, not all CD-ROM drives are the same, making multimedia shopping difficult. There are several incompatible CD-ROM formats, each with its own logo.

Here is a brief list of some CD-ROM formats:

- **CD-ROM XA (CD-ROM Extended Architecture).** This format is used by both the Sony Multimedia CD Player and IBM's Ultimedia products. It is becoming more popular for stand alone CD-ROM drives. It goes beyond the MPC specifications in combining audio and video data.

- **Ultimedia.** Another variation of the CD-ROM XA specification, Ultimedia is the standard for IBM's Multimedia Personal Systems.

- **MMCD (Multimedia CD-ROM).** Developed by Sony for its portable Multimedia Player, this CD-ROM format is based on CD-ROM XA. Most conventional CD-ROM disks won't work on this player. However, IBM Ultimedia PC owners don't have to worry, since their PCs support the XA format.

- **Kodak Photo CD.** A variation of the CD-ROM XA standard, this file format provides high-resolution photographic images you display on your TV. The CD-ROM can be appended to with new photographs, which can then be displayed, edited and printed by the user.

- **CD-I (Compact Disk Interactive).** This standard was developed by Philips for CD-ROMs that work on a standalone player. Without a computer, the player simply attaches to your TV. One popular CD-I title is Time-Life 35mm Photography, which teaches you better photographic techniques.

Portable CD-ROM

Multimedia is even going on the road. The Sony Multimedia CD-ROM Player is a handheld, portable device. Costing under $1000, it includes a keyboard and LCD screen, and also can be connected to a 256-color monitor. (See Figure 13.3)

The portable CD-ROM Player uses the CD-ROM XA technology and conforms to Sony's Multimedia CD Player (MMCD) standard. Because it can only play MMCD CD applications, Sony emphasizes its use as a platform for custom business applications. It is not compatible with most commercially available CD-ROM software. However, it does play audio CDs, which may be a boon when you're on the road.

Figure 13.3 Multimedia is even going on the road, with a two-pound portable Multimedia Player. *(Photo courtesy of Sony Corp.)*

Speeding Up Your CD-ROM Drive

You can speed up your CD-ROM drive with some simple changes. When adding a CD-ROM drive, you must load a DOS program called MSCDEX.EXE. This DOS extension allows your CD-ROM drive to be recognized like any other drive. Usually a line is added to your AUTOEXEC.BAT startup file to load this extension. For example, it might read:

```
LOADHIGH C:\PROAUDIO\MSCDEX.EXE /D:MVCD001 /M:10 /V
```

You can speed up your CD-ROM by increasing the memory set aside for the cache. This is done by the /M switch shown above. If there is no /M switch, the default value of 10 buffers is used. (Each buffer uses 2K of memory.) Increase the number to one that provides the best balance of speed and memory use. If you use DOS 5.0, these buffers can be used from upper memory blocks, or UMBs, preserving your conventional memory. You should also use a good disk caching program, such as Super PC-Kwik Disk Accelerator. This disk cache will speed up the information that is provided to your computer. Also, increase the size of this cache to as large as possible.

With multimedia and CD-ROM drives gaining broad appeal, the future is sounding and looking brighter. And volumes of information are available at our fingertips without our having to enter the library.

Bringing Your PC Alive With Video

Affordable video is the Achilles' heel of multimedia. The images are often jerky or less than full-screen. Why? Full-motion video — such as that you see on your television — requires 30 images or frames per second (fps). The storing and retrieving of these images requires managing huge files.

Consider this: a single, full-screen color image requires almost 2MB of disk space; a one-second moving video would require 45 MB! Also, any video transmission that you may want to capture for use on your PC must be converted from an analog NTSC (National Television Standard Committee) signal to a digital signal your computer can use. On top of that, the video signal must be moved inside your computer at 10 times the speed of the conventional bus structure.

To play or record video on your multimedia-ready PC, you'll need some extra hardware and software:

- Video system software, such as Apple's QuickTime for Windows, or Microsoft's Video for Windows.

- A compression/digitization video card that allows you to digitize and play large video files.

- An NTSC-to-VGA adapter that combines TV signals with computer video signals for output to a VCR.

System Software for Video

In order for your PC to process and play video, it requires a system software extension for managing video files. Both Apple and Microsoft have recently brought Windows video software to market.

In March 1992, Microsoft joined Intel to announce the Digital Video Media Control Interface (DV MCI), a set of protocols that lets Windows programs control digital video devices, such as CD-ROM drives, sound cards and various digitizing and video capture boards. Now Microsoft has released the MCI-compliant Video for Windows system extension, which is based on the Windows Audio Video Interleaved (AVI) file format. It includes tools for capturing, editing and playing back video, as well as a compression scheme. The $199 retail version of Video for Windows also includes a CD-ROM containing hundreds of sample video clips. This software basically standardizes video on the PC.

Not to be outdone in the war for the hearts and minds of PC multimedia enthusiasts, Apple has released it own video system extension for Windows, named QuickTime for Windows. It's based on QuickTime for the Macintosh, which came to market over a year ago. Unlike Video for Windows, QuickTime for Windows is not being sold as a retail product, but rather as a $295 "developer's kit" for those who want to add QuickTime playback capabilities to their applications. Because of Apple's head start in desktop video, a large number of QuickTime resources (such as video clips), have already been developed, meaning that "off-the-shelf" video products for QuickTime currently outnumber those available for Video for Windows. With QuickTime for Windows, you can embed a QuickTime movie in a Windows application. However, editing is not yet possible, and the Apple product does not currently support the MCI protocol.

Additional Video Hardware

If you want to go further than just viewing video applications that others have created; if you want to start creating your own multimedia, you'll need some video editing software, and perhaps even a multimedia authoring system. You'll also have to upgrade your PC with video capture and compression cards.

NTSC-to-VGA Adapters

NTSC-to-VGA adapters are plug-in cards that take NTSC signals (such as those from a VCR or camcorder) and overlay computer graphics (such as captions) and export them as a combined signal to a television monitor or VCR. A good example of this type of card is the 8-bit, 256-color Bravado from Truevision Inc., a $1,295 video-in-a-window card for IBM-compatible PCs running Microsoft Windows.

These cards provide an inexpensive way to make videotaped presentations that combine computer graphics, animation and captions with full-motion video. Most lack mature editing features for top-notch presentations. However, the SCSI-based version of the $4,995 Video Toaster from NewTek is an exception. The Video Toaster allows you to create special effects, such as digital wipes and chromakeys, that were previously only available with equipment costing $250,000 or more.

Compression Cards

Despite the growing affordability of full-motion video, the storage requirements for such images is overwhelming. However, compression/digitization video cards are providing breathing room for hard disks burdened by megabytes of images. They genarally provide better performance than the software-based compression built into QuickTime and Video for Windows.

These expansion cards use a variety of techniques to turn the analog NTSC signal into a digital signal that can be used by your VGA monitor. Once displayed, you can edit and store the image.

So far, two compression techniques are prevalent in these cards. The first is Intel's Digital Video Interactive (DVI) compression algorithm used in its $1,895 ActionMedia 750 Delivery expansion card. This card plays back full-motion video and true-color still photographs as well as high-quality audio. The companion $695 ActionMedia 750 Capture board lets you capture video from a VCR. Intel has an RTV (real-time video) version of DVI compression that compresses images by an impressive ratio of 150:1.

The second video compression method is JPEG (Joint Photographic Experts Group). By better preserving the original quality of the image, this method has a compression ratio of 20:1. With this technique, storing 16 minutes of video would require about 1 gigabyte (1,000 MB) of storage. The MediaStation board from VideoLogic also uses JPEG and lists for $2,995. An up-and-coming compression specification is MPEG (Motion Picture Experts Group).

Video Accelerator Cards

Since multimedia requires so much video horsepower, you may want to get an accelerator video card that uses a video coprocessor like the Diamond Stealth VRAM, the ATI Graphics Ultra, or the Orchid Fahrenheit 1280°. This video coprocessor speeds up your screen by personally handling the drawing of images. Future multimedia standards may require a video card that provide TV-quality video.

You may also want to get a 24-bit video card that can display up to 16.8 million colors. The ability to display this many colors allows realistic images on your PC. The SpeedSTAR 24 video card from Diamond Computer Systems provides 24-bit video for under $300.

The Revolution Continues

As the multimedia revolution continues, some of these technologies will emerge to become long-lasting standards, while others fall by the wayside. It's hard to predict which products and architecture will survive. Still, with just a modest investment, you can tap into the lower rungs of this brave new world for PCs. Adding sound or video to your applications can be fun and productive, while adding a CD-ROM drive will allow you to enjoy hundreds of useful and entertaining multimedia products.

14 Printer Panaceas

Finding the perfect printer is like finding the perfect president—impossible. Each printer has its strengths and weaknesses. One may be fast, while another offers typeset quality. One may do envelopes, another may excel at mailing labels. Instead of seeking perfection, you must find a printer that balances the most features for the best price. As with everything else in the computer industry, the prices of printers have fallen drastically. Laser printers, which once cost more than $5000, now can be purchased for under $600.

Printer Categories

There are generally two families of printers: *impact* and *nonimpact*. Impact printers involve striking the page and leaving an impression. These printers are ideal for inexpensive printing or printing that requires duplicate copies from carbon or carbonless forms. Without the impact, no duplicate can be made.

One of the first impact printers for the personal computer was the *daisywheel printer*. This printer used a rotating wheel with "petals" for each character. Once the wheel rotated to select the correct character, a small hammer struck the character against the ribbon, forming an image on the paper. Although of letter quality (the print quality of an electric typewriter), daisywheel printers were slow and noisy.

Another impact printer is the *dot matrix printer* (see Figure 14.1), which forms images out of dots. Several wire pins in the printer are

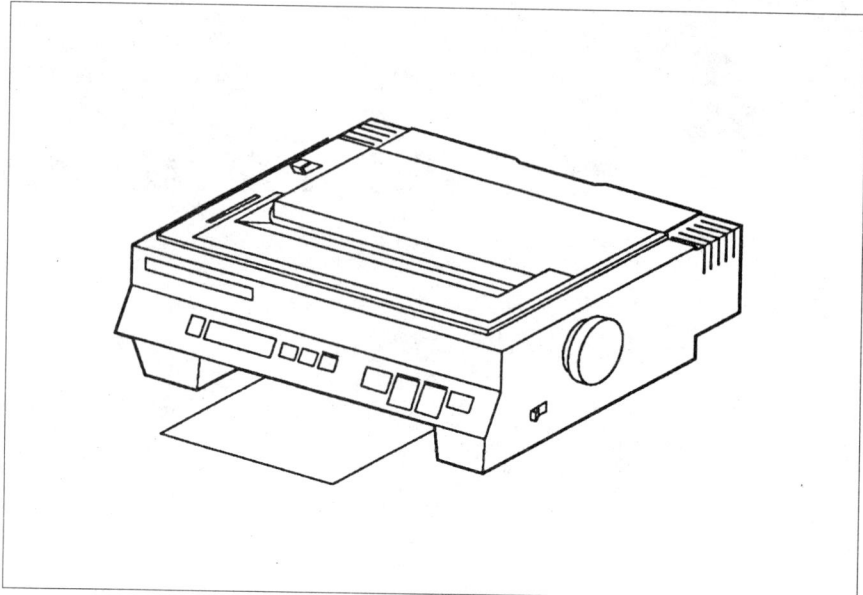

Figure 14.1 A typical dot matrix printer.

struck by small hammers to leave an impression. The more pins used, the better the image. There are basically two types of dot matrix printers: 9-pin and 24-pin. Nine-pin printers are used for inexpensive, fast printing. At best, these printers provide *near letter-quality (NLQ)* print. This quality is adequate, but not good enough for your important letters. The 24-pin dot matrix printers provide *letter-quality (LQ)* print. Although typically slower than 9-pin printers, 24-pin printers can be used for correspondence. They can also be scaled back to draft mode so you can print quickly using a handful of the 24 pins.

The speed of impact printers is usually measured in *characters per second*, or *cps*. The speed may be given for both draft and NLQ/LQ modes. For example, a Citizen GSX-140 Plus dot matrix printer has a draft speed of 220 cps and a letter-quality speed of 72 cps.

Nonimpact printers silently produce superior print quality without relying on striking. These printers are typically faster than impact printers, measuring speed not in characters per second but in pages per minute, or ppm. The most popular nonimpact printer is the *electrophotographic printer*. Doesn't sound familiar? The common name is the *laser printer*, although a laser is not always used (see Figure 14.2).

The laser printer requires a rotating drum to be charged with a high voltage. A negative copy of the image is painted onto the drum by

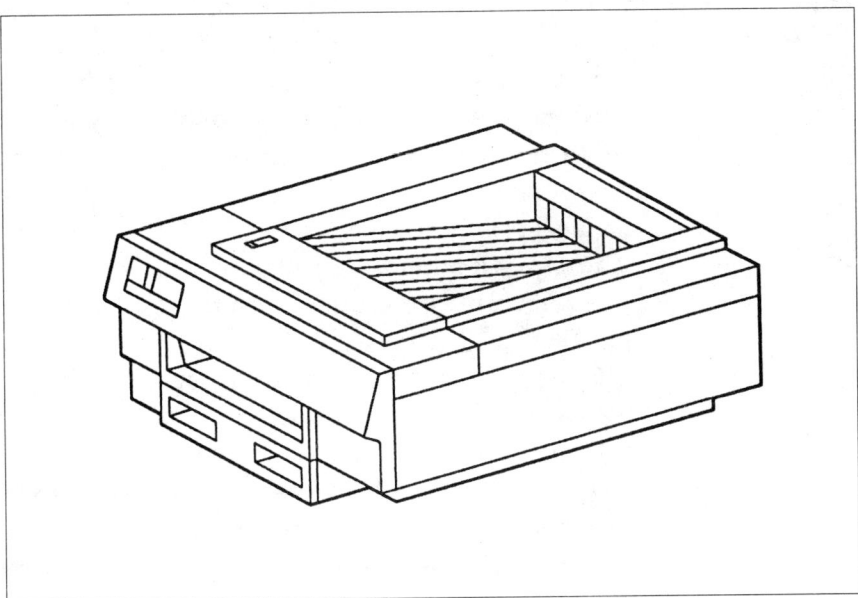

Figure 14.2 A typical laser printer.

a light source. Where the light falls onto the drum, the drum is discharged. A toner (ink) adheres to the charged portion of the drum. Next, the drum "melts" (fuses) the image onto the paper by pressure and heat. A variation of the electrophotographic printer uses several LEDs (light-emitting diodes) instead of a laser for its source. These are often called LED page printers and supposedly have fewer moving parts, reducing the chances of mechanical failure.

The most popular laser printers are the Hewlett-Packard LaserJets, which include the LaserJet II, LaserJet III, and LaserJet 4. Several laser printers imitate the LaserJet. Other LED laser printers are those from Okidata, like the OkiLaser 400.

Another nonimpact printer is the ink jet printer, such as the Hewlett-Packard DeskJet 500. Such printers spray a fine quick-drying ink onto the page from several small nozzles. Despite earlier problems with ink smudging and fading, the latest printers are inexpensive and quiet, but not fast. If you consider the falling prices of laser printers, the ink jet printer does not provide as good a value. One niche for the ink jet printer is as a portable printer for laptop computers. An ink jet printer like the Canon BJ-10e is the size of a notebook computer and sells for less than $300.

Label Printers

Some printers only do labels, saving you from having to print a single envelope or label from your conventional printer. For as little as $200, you can have a printer that easily prints a label or envelope when you need it. These printers usually connect to your computer's serial, or COM, port, rather than using your parallel printer port. (Usually, you have your primary printer connected to the parallel port.) Some popular label printers include the Avery Personal Label Printer, the CoStar AddressWriter, and the Seiko Smart Label Printer.

A label printer is ideal for printing one label at a time, and most can print up to 100 labels at once. They are not designed for large quantities and some cannot print on large shipping labels. Usually, you load a software utility before you use your word processor or other software. When you need a label, you switch to this memory-resident software to print the address that is on the screen. Not only can these printers do labels, but many print the Postnet bar codes used by the United States Post Office to encode ZIP codes, thereby speeding your mail delivery. The only drawback to label printers is their use of near-letter quality.

Fun Fonts

A laser printer deserves more than just monospace Courier typewriter type. The growth of desktop publishing and *Windows* software demand that your pages look better than ever. Fonts are the solution that add flavor to the printed page.

To understand fonts, you must know a few simple typographic terms. First, a *typeface* is a family of type. Specifically, it is the design of a set of characters. For example, Courier (used by many typewriters) is a typeface. So are Helvetica, Swiss, Dutch, and Times—a handful of many popular typefaces. The confusion often comes when describing a font. A *font* is a subset of a typeface. It is a set of characters of a particular style and size generated from a particualar typeface design. For example, 10-point Courier bold is a font. (A *point* is a typographic method of measurement; 72 points equal one inch.) Often, many people confuse fonts with type families. For example, a printer that includes 26 fonts sounds like a versatile printer, no? But those 26 fonts may actually only cover four typefaces, or families of type.

The fonts available to you start with your printer. Printers come with fonts built in; the total number varies with each printer. Built-in fonts are called *resident fonts*, because they reside in your printer.

The wealth of fonts and high-quality printing is spreading to more and more computer owners. By selecting and taking care of yours, you can fulfill the democratic idea of a printing press on everyone's desk. As someone once said: "Freedom of the press only applies to those who own one."

Page Description Languages

Most laser printers understand one of two page description languages that have become standard in the printer industry. A *page description language*, or *PDL*, is the computer language that describes how text and graphics should be placed on a page for display or printing. Because of their role, PDLs determine what fonts work with your printer. Therefore, selecting a printer with a certain PDL may limit what fonts you can use with it. It also affects the price of your printer, often by several hundred dollars.

The most prevalent page description language is the *Printer Control Language (PCL)*, developed by Hewlett-Packard for its LaserJet printers. However, *PostScript*, developed by Adobe Systems, has become the standard PDL for desktop publishing. Your font options depend on which of these two languages meet your output requirements.

PCL for the People

The mogul of laser printers is Hewlett-Packard. HP sells about $3 billion of laser printers a year. HP's line of LaserJet printers use PCL. The first LaserJet printers of the 1980s had few fonts. However, LaserJet printers allow you to add other fonts by plugging a *font cartridge* into a slot in the printer.

Font cartridges contain bitmapped fonts, a pattern of pixels, or dots, that make up a typeface's characters. A bitmapped font is set in stone; it is of a certain size, style (like italic or bold), and resolution and cannot be changed. These fonts can be accessed just like the printer's built-in fonts.

There are several manufacturers of font cartridges, for example Pacific Data Products and IQ Engineering. If your needs are limited and you don't anticipate moving into desktop publishing, cartridge fonts may be enough. Installation is a snap; just plug the cartridges into the printer and install the software driver for your application.

One disadvantage of cartridge fonts is that font size and variety are limited by your printer's built-in memory.

Soft fonts are also available. You load soft fonts from a diskette into your computer. These fonts are then downloaded to your printer when you're ready to use them. Some of the original soft font packages, like Bitstream's *Fontware,* required you to generate the fonts first and store them on your hard disk. Not only do these programs create printer fonts, but they also generate matching screen fonts for your application—a step toward the elusive goal of "what you see (on the screen) is what you get (off the printer)." This is called WYSIWYG (pronounced "wiz-ee-wig"). For example, I use Fontware with Ventura Publisher for GEM to create printer and screen fonts.

Using soft fonts does take a toll. First, these fonts are trickier to install than cartridges and must be downloaded from your hard disk to your printer each time you print, which can be time-consuming. Also, fonts eat away at precious hard disk space. Like cartridge fonts, soft fonts are bitmapped, immutable fonts; they are of a certain size and style. If you want others, you must create them. Creating soft fonts from the original outlines can require several minutes to several hours, depending on both the number and size of the fonts selected.

These problems created the rise of type managers, such as Adobe Type Manager (ATM). Type managers make working with fonts much easier while requiring less disk space. Type managers store only the font outlines. When you need a specific font, the type manager creates it on the fly. Under Windows, each font is available for every Windows application. The type manager also creates matching screen fonts for your display. You are then able to see on your screen what the printed output will look like.

Since PostScript printers use Adobe type and Adobe's ATM is available for LaserJets, LaserJet-compatibles, and dot matrix printers, you now can generate PostScript fonts on several different printers. In fact, all the new type managers send fonts to PostScript printers, LaserJets, and dot matrix printers.

PCL with a Twist

With the introduction of the LaserJet III, Hewlett-Packard broke away from its bitmapped past and introduced scalable fonts. The LaserJet III and LaserJet 4 have scalable outline fonts that can be printed in any size from 4 to 999 points. Two scalable fonts (and two fixed-pitch fonts) are built in. Scalable fonts are made possible by PCL Level 5, the newest release of HP's page description language. An advance in the LaserJet III is the addition of Resolution Enhancement Technology, or RET. This technology makes the printed page look sharper than the laser-standard 300 *dots per inch (dpi)* by "smudging" the toner on the page to fill in the jagged edges of type. The results are quite nice, making the LaserJet III produce text with almost 600-dpi clarity. The LaserJet 4 actually prints text at 600 dpi.

PostScript: The One to Beat

PostScript from Adobe Systems is the other major page description language. Unlike Hewlett-Packard, Adobe Systems does not sell laser printers. Rather, the company licenses PostScript to other manufacturers who then place PostScript into their printers. Adobe then collects royalties on each printer sold. These royalties cause PostScript printers to be more expensive than HP's laser printers.

PostScript is popular, especially with people who use desktop publishing. Most important, PostScript uses scalable outline fonts. An outline font allows one set of characters to store the information needed to generate all the sizes you would ever want from a given typeface. From a single outline, you can print characters at virtually any size. PostScript outline fonts are called PostScript Type 1 fonts. Because outline fonts create characters of different sizes as required, Type 1 fonts require little disk space. Also, PostScript allows drawing of complex graphics and manipulation of type. With PostScript, text is treated as a graphic element that can be scaled to any size, rotated to any orientation, stretched, skewed, reflected, shadowed, filled with any pattern, outlined, reversed out, or printed in any shade of gray.

PostScript is also printer-independent. The same language commands will cause different printers to work in different ways, but in the end they will all generate the same printed page—or nearly the same. PostScript allows the same language instructions to make two printers work at different quality levels. So the same commands that operate a 300-dpi laser printer will signal a high-resolution PostScript typesetting machine to create a page at 2500-dpi resolution. You simply print your document to a disk file instead of to paper. This disk is sent to a service bureau where the PostScript file is printed at a higher resolution. This capability is perhaps the single most important reason why PostScript is the favored desktop-publishing printer language. You can preview the same PostScript output file on an inexpensive laser printer, then later send it to a typesetter for camera-ready artwork.

One of the most attractive features of PostScript printers is that they have 35 Type 1 fonts already built in. Many users get along quite well without having to buy any additional fonts. But if you do outgrow the built-in fonts, the Adobe Type Library offers a wide selection of high-quality designs. Also, other type foundries, like Monotype and Linotype, provide thousands of Type 1 fonts for use with PostScript printers.

PostScript isn't for everyone, however. Compared to standard laser printers, PostScript printers, with their royalties, can be expensive. Support is another concern. Although software support is now commonplace among the major applications, there are still categories of products, such as the vast majority of accounting packages, that have yet to offer PostScript drivers. (You can, however, print non-PostScript files on a PostScript printer with utilities like Printer Control Panel from LaserTools.) To further complicate buying decisions, numerous "PostScript-compatible" printers have hit the market. These often are competitive in features and aggressively priced, but total compatibility with Adobe PostScript isn't a sure thing.

Another complaint about PostScript is that it is slow. Because PostScript is an interpreter, it is slow, requiring an interpreter for its codes, commands, and data. Some printers use speedy RISC (reduced instruction set computing) processors to overcome PostScript's nagging performance limitations. Despite PostScript's current edge in generating higher-quality output, the percentage of office workers who actually take their documents beyond 300 dpi is small.

TrueType

An up-and-coming standard is TrueType, developed jointly by Apple and Microsoft corporation TrueType is a font technology introduced with Windows 3.1 that lets you use scalable typefaces to produce an onscreen image that looks as it would on paper. Windows 3.0 alone couldn't do this; its screen and printer fonts were jagged, driving people to purchase Adobe Type Manager or Bitstream FaceLift. With TrueType, you can select any typeface outline you have on your computer and use it at practically any point size. It doesn't matter if the font isn't supported by your printer; TrueType sends the page as a picture, requiring no fonts from your printer. And adding other TrueType fonts is easy, costing as little as $25 for 20 TrueType typefaces.

Selecting a Printer

Selecting a printer involves answering four questions:

1. What quality does your printing require?
2. How fast do you need your printing?
3. How much printing do you intend to do?
4. Does your software support the printer?

A printer should never be selected on price alone. For example, the printing speed and memory capacity are important. Graphics, for example, take more time to print and demand more memory. Watch out for stripped-down printers. For some, you must pay extra for the 250-sheet paper tray. For a dot matrix printer, a cut-sheet feeder that feeds individual sheets is also optional. What good is fast printing if your printer requires you to feed it individual sheets? Similarly, why have crisp-looking text if you have only a couple of fonts available? Why bother to get a printer for desktop publishing if it doesn't have enough memory to print a page full of graphics?

Connect the Dots

Selecting a dot matrix printer is relatively easy. Compatibility with your software is rarely a problem, since most printers emulate either an Epson printer or IBM ProPrinter. The features from which to select include:

- **24- versus 9-pin.** A 24-pin printer provides letter quality text. If you want to save money and can tolerate lower print quality, select a 9-pin printer. This printer can print at near-letter quality; but if you demand letter quality, stay with the 24-pin printer.

- **Wide or narrow carriage.** A dot matrix printer may come in either of two sizes: *wide carriage* or *narrow carriage*. These sizes are also called *132 column* and *80 column*, respectively. The wide carriage can handle 11 x 17-inch ledger paper and wide invoices. If you can live with printing 8.5 x 11-inch paper, you can save yourself about

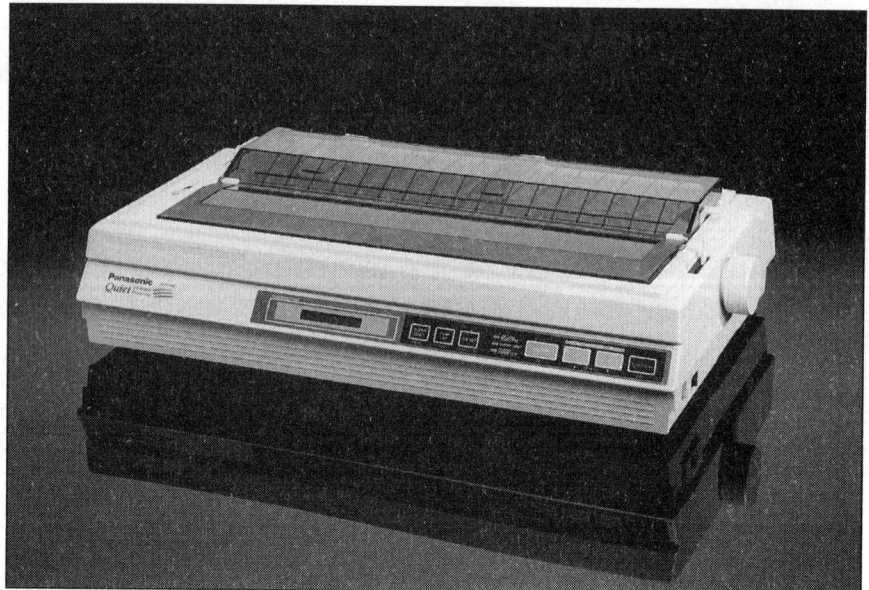

Figure 14.3 The Panasonic KX-P2624 printer allows you to have high-speed, impact printing that doesn't interrupt the quiet of the office. *(Photo courtesy of Panasonic Communications & Systems Co.)*

$100 by selecting a narrow-carriage printer over a wide-carriage model.

• **Print buffer.** Some printers include a small amount of memory, up to 64K. This memory is used to store your document in the printer until it is ready to print it. About 3K holds one page of text. The bigger this buffer, the sooner you can work on something else. If you print shorter documents (fewer than 10–20 pages), this memory can be a boon. Unless you use a print spooler, such as *Windows* Print Manager, you must wait for your printer to finish before you can continue your work.

• **Paper paths.** Besides the pin-fed tractor feed, you should have other paper options. For example, you may want to feed your printer individual letterhead or purchase the optional cut-sheet feeder so you can print single sheets without hand feeding them. If you are going to use both single sheets and continuous paper, look for a paper-parking feature, which pulls the continuous paper out of the way. If you work with labels, envelopes, and other heavy paper, you will want to print as straight through the printer as possible.

Look for printers with front-, rear-, or bottom-feed paths. If you use multi-part forms, be sure your printer can print on the last page of the ones with four or six parts.

- **Noise reduction.** Some printers provide a "quiet" mode that slightly reduces the noise of the printer. Other printers, such as the Panasonic 2624, are specifically designed to print as quietly as a laser printer.

- **Fonts.** Most dot matrix printers include six or seven bitmapped fonts. Some printers, such as the Epson ActionPrinter 3250, even include scalable fonts. For additional fonts, you may need to use soft fonts. An alternative is to use font cartridges, for which some printers have slots.

At the Speed of Light

Selecting a laser printer is more difficult, especially since the resolution for all is typically the same: 300 dpi. Use these criteria to find the best printer for your needs:

- **Speed**. Laser printers typically come in two speeds: 4 ppm and 8 ppm. If your printing needs are modest (fewer than 10-20 pages per day), you can save considerable dollars by buying a 4-ppm printer. An 8-ppm printer is designed for the busy home or small office.

- **Size.** As a rule, 4- to 6-ppm printers tend to be smaller, requiring less desk space. Their paper trays can often be flipped up and out of the way. Faster models are generally bulkier, requiring their own printer stand or a wing of your desk.

- **Processor.** One important point for you to consider is that the rated speed of a laser printer, such as 4 ppm, is the top speed at which the printer can print. The more complex the page design—one containing several typefaces, several font sizes, and/or graphics—the slower your printer. The speed of the printer's processor is often more important. For example, the HP LaserJet IIP Plus features a 16-MHz instead of the 10-MHz processor given the original IIP. The actual number of pages that can be printed is dramatically improved with the faster processor despite the same engine speed.

- **Emulation.** Almost every laser printer emulates the LaserJet II, which uses the PCL4 page-description language. Your software can then use its LaserJet driver for your new printer. You can also select a printer that uses PostScript, although these printers are more expensive because of the royalties paid to Adobe Systems. Likewise, not all software supports a PostScript printer. Some printers provide both emulations—for a price. If you use older software, check whether it will work with your printer's emulation.

- **Memory.** Most laser printers include at least 512K of memory. This memory is used to prepare a page for printing and is adequate for printing just simple text. If you intend to use software-based fonts with your printer or wish to print a full page of graphics, you may require 1MB of memory or more. Check how much memory your printer can accommodate if more is required. One plus is a laser printer that accepts industry-standard SIMM or DRAM type of memory, since this memory is less expensive than memory you must buy from the printer's manufacturer.

- **Fonts.** Most laser printers include 14 to 35 fonts. Some printers, such as the HP LaserJet 4, even include scalable fonts. You'll probably want some business typefaces, such as Helvetica and Times. For additional fonts, you may need to use soft fonts or font cartridges.

- **Paper capacity.** Some laser printers hold only 50 sheets of paper, requiring frequent reloading for large print jobs. An optional paper tray may cost $100 to $200 more. Others include trays that handle 200 letter-size sheets. Check that your laser printer can handle envelopes and transparencies.

Dot Matrix Maintenance

Dot matrix printers are the workhorses of most offices. They are used for drafting letters, reports, labels, and invoices. Keeping that horse from being sent to the glue factory requires some simple routine maintenance.

First, the printhead should move freely. Otherwise, the letter spacing in the text may be uneven. The track on which the printhead moves back and forth requires cleaning and lubrication. Wipe it periodically with a soft cloth and use a light oil such as sewing machine oil. Avoid WD-40, since it doesn't contain enough lubricant, and don't use heavy oil (such as 10W-30), since it creates a gummy mess after attracting paper dust.

Your ribbon is also a concern. A ribbon not only provides the ink for your character but also preserves the life of your printer. Ribbons are soaked in lubricant and ink to keep the pins of the printhead lubricated. Cheap or re-inked ribbons may not contain enough lubricant. For this reason, you want to use a manufacturer-recommended ribbon.

A build-up of ink may cause one or more of your printer's pins to stick. You will see a continuous white horizontal line through your type or graphics. Try cleaning the printhead with isopropyl alcohol on a cotton swab. If that doesn't work, remove the printhead and liberally spray the impact tips with a penetrating lubricant, like WD-40. Let it soak and then wipe it thoroughly. Another method is to soak a section of an old ribbon with WD-40 and run a few test prints with the saturated ribbon. If these tips don't loosen the clog, send your printer in for repair.

The best way to extend the printhead's life is to adjust the gap between the printhead and the platen (the surface behind your paper) according to the paper you are using. For example, you want a bigger gap between the printhead and the platen when you are using thick paper, like labels or thick multipart forms. Having the proper paper gap keeps the printhead from prematurely dying.

If you feed continuous paper through your printer, don't make your printer pull it up from the floor to your desktop. Paper is heavy, and the tractor mechanism in a printer isn't designed for heavy lifting. The strain may result in uneven line spacing. If you want to avoid buying a new printer stand, consider stacking your paper near the level of your printer.

Life for Your Laser Printer

Despite its reliable operation, your laser printer can use some tender, loving care to live a full life. The best advice is to clean your printer regularly. Many owners tend to ignore their laser printer until it sputters and dies. However, a few minutes each week can increase the life of your printer and improve its print quality.

Most printer manuals describe how to clean your printer. Typically, you need to clean the corona wires and fuser. The corona wire creates the electric charge that attracts the toner to the paper. If it gets dirty, it won't apply the proper charge to the paper. If this happens, you'll get light or even blank streaks on your page. The fuser is the part that melts the toner onto the page. If it is not kept clean, the toner may not stick. Again, streaking can result. You should clean these parts often with a soft cloth and cotton swabs. Solvents and cleaners can damage the printer. Avoid breaking any wires or else your printer will be disabled.

Your laser printer has a photosensitive drum that should not be exposed to light for long periods. This drum is usually covered by a shield. If you frequently open this shield and expose the drum to light, you'll ruin its effectiveness. Keep the drum in the printer as much as possible. If you have to remove it, keep the shield closed and put the drum in a dimly lit area.

Toner can also affect the life of your printer. Your printer's toner cartridge should always be kept level. Tilting it or storing it on one side will shift the toner to one side, causing a spill or uneven printing.

Every 3000 pages or so, your laser printer will run out of toner, requiring you to replace it. Sometimes, that toner cartridge still may have some life left. Remove the cartridge and gently shake it back and forth to loosen and evenly distribute any remaining toner. Reinsert the cartridge into your printer and check if the "Toner Empty" message is still displayed. If not, continue using the cartridge until it is empty. To extend the life of the toner, you can turn down the darkness, or print density, of the toner until you are ready to print the final version of your document. For example, I keep my LaserJet's toner dimmed to about 7 instead of the normal setting of 5.

To get solid black printing from your LaserJet printer, print four or five totally black pages first. This large amount of black printing will refresh the toner development system. Create a desktop publishing document that prints solid blacks (see your instruction manual). To get the best print quality on an important document, print four or more copies of this solid black document until the ink coverage is uniform. Then print your document.

To save money, some people use recycled, or remanufactured, cartridges. Toner cartridges can be recycled because there's a lot more to them than just toner. A typical toner cartridge also contains most of the other replaceable parts of your laser printer—the drum, the corona, and the excess toner bin. Each of these parts can last longer than 3000 copies. Consider taking your used toner cartridge to a company that recycles them and buying a recycled toner cartridge. You can save some money doing this, as well as feel good about contributing less to your local landfill.

Some recycled cartridges are not as good as others. Look at a test print of the recycled toner cartridge. If a sample isn't provided, ask for one before purchasing. The toner cartridge should arrive in a box to avoid exposure to light. Also, avoid a recycled cartridge with an unusually low price. Most recycled toner cartridges save you between 30 and 50 percent over a brand-new cartridge.

Proper Paper

Selecting the right paper for your laser printer is as important as selecting the printer. The ideal paper can greatly improve print quality. Use relatively smooth, uncoated paper, since textured papers may be pulled into the printer and print unevenly. Conversely, the shiny surface of coated papers may come off in the laser printer and cause damage.

Laser paper should be very opaque (light-blocking) with a brightness (light-reflection) of 85 percent or more to improve reading and better copies. A paper's weight is measured by the weight of a ream (500 sheets) of 17 x 22-inch sheets. A good laser paper should be just a little heavier than the 20-pound copier paper; 24-pound Finch Laser Opaque, Hammermill Laser Plus, Weyerhauser First Choice, or Nekoosa Ardor would be a good choice.

Never use transparencies or sheets of labels unless they are specifically made for use with a laser printer. Otherwise, they bake under the printer's extreme heat and melt. The result may be serious damage to either your laser printer or its $70 toner cartridge. When possible, consider using recycled paper designed for laser printers.

A Filter Change

Besides changing toner, you may also have to replace your printer's ozone filter. While ozone gas is good in the upper atmosphere where it blocks harmful ultraviolet rays, it is unhealthy here at ground level. Ozone can damage the lungs, skin, and eyes.

Many laser and LED-based printers use high voltages on their drums to create their images. Unfortunately, these voltages also generate harmful ozone. An ozone filter in these printers minimizes the amount of ozone released by trapping it before it leaves the air vents in your printer. These filters are made of activated charcoal and must be replaced regularly because of the toner, paper dust, and ozone that accumulates in them. For example, a typical laser printer should have its ozone filter replaced every 50,000 pages or two years.

Replace the filter more often if you work in a dry or dusty environment or work alongside your printer. These filters cost between $10 and $45. Sometimes, an ozone filter can be replaced only by the dealer. Consult your printer's owner manual.

Exploding Toner

If you ever spill toner inside your laser printer or on the floor, do not use a vacuum cleaner to pick it up. Most toner powder is so fine that it will pass through conventional vacuum filter bags and out the rear of the cleaner, only to end up all over the upholstery.

Also, if you mix air and toner under pressure in a hot place — conditions met in a vacuum cleaner — there's a possibility of explosion. That's why special toner vacuum cleaners are manufactured by companies such as 3M.

The best policy for avoiding problems is to be extremely careful when changing toner, and clean up spills by hand.

Turbocharging Your Laser

Even a laser printer can use a boost. With sophisticated desktop publishing or documents that use several fonts, printing a four-page newsletter may take up to an hour. Similarly, some laser printers balk at printing a full page of graphics, delivering only half a page because of low memory. Other printers could benefit from sharper resolutions than the typical 300 dots per inch.

The most basic enhancement to a laser printer is extra memory. Laser printers require extra memory to print extensive graphics and fonts that come from software, not the printer's own built-in, internal fonts. Most Hewlett-Packard laser printers come with either 512K or 1MB of memory. The IIP, for example, comes with 512K of memory and can be expanded to 4.5MB. For fonts that are downloaded to the printer or for complicated pages, more memory is required. Extra memory is often placed on a circuit board that is inserted into the laser printer.

Laser Utilities

Software utilities that add zip to your laser printer are popular. At first, these utilities made it easier to set up your laser printer—to change from one default font to another, for example. Although laser printers now are much friendlier, laser utilities are still prevalent. Almost 200 different printer utilities are available. They form three categories: printer feature access, print spooling, and PostScript emulation.

To control your printer, you can use a utility such as *LaserMenu* from MicroLogic Software. This program allows you to change the default combination of features available on your printer and insert macros in text files to provide underlining and font changes at selected points. The same features are available in *PrintMenu*, the utility from the same company for dot matrix printers.

Other utilities allow you to reduce the waiting time for your pages to come out of the printer. For example, *PrintCache* from LaserTools Corp. is a print spooler. A print spooler sits in your computer's memory, scoops up data as fast as your software sends it, and then stores the data until the printer is ready to receive it. Meanwhile, your computer becomes free faster for other work. A *Windows* version, *PrintCache for Windows,* is also available. With a print spooler, you may even be able to print full-page graphics on a laser printer with 512K. Some products have built-in graphics data compression. Even if you don't need data compression, you'll want a print spooler for its skill at compressing the time you spend waiting for your printer.

The speed improvements you get from a print spooler depend on your software and the work you do. The best results come with applications that print only in the foreground, locking up your computer from doing other work. For example, a Ventura Publisher file that normally ties up my computer for 71 seconds now lets me resume work in 9 seconds thanks to a print spooler.

PostScript on Disk

You no longer have to choose between the two industry-standard printer languages: Hewlett-Packard's PCL and Adobe's PostScript. Laser printers not armed with the PostScript language are often less expensive than their PostScript peers because no royalty fees are paid for the built-in PostScript. Sometimes, a penny-wise decision results in PostScript-envy. For example, if you prepare your work on a PostScript printer, you can then bring the final file to a service bureau where your pages can be printed at a very high resolution. A typesetter such as a Linotronic 300, for example, can print at a resolution of about 1250 dpi. In other words, you can use your 300-dpi PostScript printer as a proofing tool but have the final work printed at a high resolution for literal sharp-looking output. A service bureau often charges $6 to $10 per page for these typeset-quality pages.

Several software packages let your printer talk PostScript. These PostScript-emulation software packages often work only on LaserJet or LaserJet-compatible printers. Some emulation packages include: Color Age's Freedom of Press and Freedom of Press Light, LaserGo's GoScript and GoScript Plus and PM Ware's UltraScript.

Figure 14.4 The WinJet 300 is an expansion card that closes the door on slow Windows printing to you Hewlett-Packard LaserJet II or III printer. *(Photo courtesy of LaserMaster Corp.)*

With a PostScript emulator, you either print your PostScript files to a disk file and then use the software to print the files to your printer or you print directly from your software program. PostScript is also available through cartridges that plug into your laser printer. Pacific Data Products, a manufacturer of several font cartridges, offers PacificPage, a cartridge for LaserJet II and compatibles. Hewlett-Packard also has PostScript cartridges for its printers.

Replacing Your Printer's Brains

You can give your laser printer PostScript capability, speed up printing, or increase print resolution with the aid of add-in boards. These printer controllers go beyond soft fonts, plug-in laser cartridges, and extra memory. Enhancement boards that plug into your computer and take over the "brains" of your laser printer can vastly improve the quality of your laser's text and graphics.

For example, you can plug an advanced printer controller board into your computer, attach it via a supplied cable to the alternate I/O port on the back of the LaserJet (or most other printers based on the Canon SX or CX laser engine). You'll get at least twice the print quality of the LaserJet alone; and, in most cases, you'll also get scalable fonts and faster printing. The result is an affordable, high-resolution alternative to the nearby service bureau that charges $6 to $10 per page for PostScript printed output.

How can you get sharper text and graphics from a printer accustomed to printing 300 dpi? Several companies discovered that the Canon laser engine—which is found in Canon, Ricoh, Brother, and HP printers—is capable of running at resolutions in excess of the 300 x 300 dpi that's the standard for personal laser printers. Such controllers take over from the laser printer's built-in controller the job of controlling the laser beam that "paints" the image of a page onto the printer's drum.

LaserMaster Corp. has been known for its TurboRes technology, which it uses in several products. The company's proven Professional controller squeezes up to 800 dpi from a typical laser printer. The increased resolution and printing speed can be dizzying. Graphics print about 10 times faster. The increased resolution makes a dramatic difference in text quality and brings laser printers very close to the level of low-end typesetters. Two newer products, the WinJet 300 and WinJet 800, provide fast printing, especially when used with *Windows* software. These printers use part of your computer's horse-power to prepare each page for printing. One benefit is that your printing becomes faster when you purchase a faster, next-generation computer.

But even at 800 dpi, a high-resolution printer controller is less than half the 1250 dpi used by low-level typesetters. If you use your printer only to create proofs for pages to be printed by a service bureau, an add-on controller isn't worth the money. But if you want high-quality printing on your desktop, nothing else brings you so much improve-ment at so reasonable a cost.

15

Input Devices: Of Mice and Manicures

No matter how loud you yell at it, your PC won't do a thing. The information entered into your PC is called input. The way you enter this information is by an *input device*. Whether you type words from a keyboard or select a menu option with a mouse, you are telling your computer what to do. Several input devices are:

- Keyboard
- Mouse
- Trackball
- Digitizing tablet
- Pen
- Scanner
- Speech recognition
- Joystick

The Popular Keyboard

A keyboard is the most popular way to communicate with your computer. This part of your computer is often overlooked. Unfortunately, most computers come with an inexpensive keyboard, usually costing less than $30. A keyboard has four parts:

1. **Typing area**, such as letters and numbers.
2. **Numeric keypad**, where 10-key operators can nimbly add up numbers.

3. **Cursor and screen controls**, for paging up or down or moving the cursor one character or line at a time.

4. **Function keys** (F1 through F10 or F12) for calling special features in a software program ("Press F1 for Help," for example).

The first IBM PC had an 83-key keyboard. The 10 function keys (F1 through F10) were on the left-hand side of the keyboard. One criticism was that the often-used Enter key was too small. In 1985, the IBM PC/AT keyboard was introduced. This 84-key keyboard corrected many of the 83-key keyboard's problems. The Enter key was enlarged and LED (light-emitting diode) lights were added to indicate if the Caps Lock, Scroll Lock, or Num Lock keys were on.

Today, computers often come with a variation of the IBM's Enhanced 101-Key keyboard. Unlike the previous two keyboards, this one has the function keys across the keyboard's top. Where did the extra 17 keys come from? A separate numeric keypad was added apart from the cursor keys (the up/down, left/right arrow keys). This separate numeric keypad let people with 10-key skills use the numeric keypad and have access to the arrow keys. Two extra function keys, F11 and F12, were added. Such keyboards are simply called "enhanced" keyboards.

Keyboards plug into your computer using a five-pin connector called the DIN-5. (PS/2 computers use a six-pin connector but, with an adapter, can use the five-pin cables.) Newer keyboards can be used with older computers. Often, a switch on the belly of the keyboard lets you switch between XT (8088/8086) and AT (80286 and higher) modes. This switch does not always make your newer keyboard work with an older computer. Sometimes, the older computer cannot recognize the keyboard or does not allow some of the new added keys (such as F11 and F12) to work.

Newer keyboards have LED (light-emitting diode) lights to show whether the Caps Lock, Num Lock, and Scroll Lock keys are on. If you use such a keyboard with an XT-type computer, these lights remain dim since the these computers do not support them.

To determine if your PC supports a particular keyboard, check to see if the light above your Num Lock key turns on when you start the PC. The numeric pad should also work. One exception: Some computer setup programs intentionally allow you to disable the Num Lock key each time your computer starts. Small software programs loaded in your computer's AUTOEXEC.BAT startup file — like NUMOFF — do the same thing.

Replacing Your Keyboard

You may use your keyboard several hours each week. Since a keyboard can be such a constant companion, you may want to invest in one that fits your unique needs. Some even come with a built-in solar-powered calculator! What do you look for in a keyboard? There are three factors: keyboard layout, touch, and compatibility.

You should look for an enhanced keyboard; it's a strong design that has evolved over time. However, there are variations of this design. Some replacement keyboards let you swap a handful of individual keys to your liking. For example, you can swap the Caps Lock, Alt, and Ctrl keys or the asterisk and backslash (\) keys.

QWERTY versus Dvorak

The most popular keyboard layout is the QWERTY. A rarer but intriguing keyboard layout is the Dvorak keyboard. Designed by August Dvorak in 1936, the Dvorak keyboard increases typing speed, comfort, and accuracy by placing the most often used letters in the center, or home, row. According to tests, 90 percent of typing effort is reduced. The five vowel keys, AOEUI, are on the left-hand side. The five most frequently used consonants, DHTNS, are on the right-hand side. The Dvorak keyboard was approved by the American National Standards Institute (ANSI) in 1982. A Dvorak keyboard requires no changes to your computer. However, you do have to learn the new style of typing.

If you already know how to use the Dvorak keyboard and are using Microsoft Windows, it's quite simple to change your computer to use the Dvorak keyboard. First, open the Windows Control Panel. Then, double-click on the International option. Under the Keyboard layout, choose "US-Dvorak." Depending on which keyboard setup you had initially, you might have to insert one of the original Windows disks so that Windows can find the correct driver. Finally, click on OK to complete the command and close the dialog box. At this point, all your Windows applications will respond to the key placement used by the Dvorak keyboard.

If you want to sample the Dvorak keyboard with your DOS software before investing in one, you can use a memory-resident program that remaps the keyboard. Two such utilities are Prokey Plus from CE Software, which sells for $99, and Smartkey from No Brainer Software, which sells for $50. (Smartkey comes with a predefined macro that converts your existing keyboard to Dvorak.) These packages are more than just Dvorak-imitators; they are designed to run macros (a series of recorded keystrokes) from your keyboard.

The touch of a keyboard is crucial. Some people prefer keyboards that "click," telling them with each keystroke that the key was indeed pressed. This is called a *click-tactile* keyboard. Others prefer silent, or nontactile, keyboards. If you are a fast typist or work in an office environment, you may prefer a quiet keyboard over the staccato of pressed keys.

As mentioned earlier, compatibility should not be an issue. Some replacement keyboards, however, provide switches to make the keyboard compatible with some brands of computers and networks. For example, some keyboards slow down with some versions of Novell's NetWare. Others do not work with Tandy 1000 or AT&T 6300 computers.

Figure 15.1 The Northgate OmniUltra keyboard is an alternative to the generic keyboards included with most computers. The OmniKey/ Ultra features two sets of function keys, and the top 12 can be programmed as shifted keys. (*Photo courtesy of Northgate Computers, Inc.*)

When you type on a keyboard, you are actually pressing the keycaps, the plastic covers for each key. Underneath each keycap is a keyboard switch. When you press the keycap, the switch is completed and sends a signal to your computer that you pressed, for example, the "A" key. The type of switch underneath varies. It could be mechanical, conductive rubber dome, or membrane. Most newer keyboards use membrane switches underneath each key. These switches can last up to 50 million key presses. When ordering a keyboard, ask how many key presses the keyboard can handle in its lifetime. This is more important than the type of switch it uses.

One favorite keyboard of mine is the Northgate OmniKey/102. This keyboard, costing about $90, has function keys on both the left-hand side and the top. Key Tronic Corp. is another popular keyboard manufacturer. One manufacturer, Prometheus Pro, provides a keyboard that you can rearrange. The Switchboard lets you rearrange the typing area, the cursor pad, and the numeric keypad. For example, left-handed people like myself may want the numeric keypad on the left. An optional trackball is also available.

Cleaning behind the Keys

To maintain your keyboard, it's best to clean it periodically. The accumulated dust and dirt can make the key stick or sometimes not respond. Vacuum the keyboard weekly or use a can of compressed air. Before using compressed air, turn the keyboard upside down so the contaminants can fall out.

For more extensive cleaning, remove each keycap and remove any debris. To remove a keycap, use either a special chip-puller or keycap remover. You simply hook the left and right undersides of the keycap and lift up. Otherwise, you can take two inexpensive flat-blade screwdrivers and bend the last quarter inch of each blade into a right angle. Use both screwdrivers to pry up and lift the keycap from both sides.

After removing each keycap, spray some compressed air into the space under the cap to dislodge any contaminants, like dust, hair, and crumbs. Then replace the keycap and check the action of the key. Never remove caps of "big" keys, like the space bar.

If you ever spill a beverage into your keyboard, the damage can be fixed. As soon as possible, flush the keyboard with distilled, not tap, water. The distilled water won't leave any mineral residue. Next, disassemble part of the keyboard and wash the components with the distilled water. Remove the screws from the base of the keyboard. Once the base bottom is removed, do not remove any internal screws.

If the liquid has dried, let the keyboard soak in some of the water. Once the keyboard is clean, pour another gallon of distilled water over it and through the key switches. After the keyboard fully dries, try it. If the keyboard is not dry, it may short circuit and be ruined.

A Second Skin

If you work in an environment where there are several contamination threats, you can get a plastic skin for your keyboard. From cookie crumbs to grease, these second skins protect your keys. These plastic covers are see-through, allowing you to see the keys you are typing. Your protective cover must exactly match your keyboard layout. As mentioned earlier, there are various designs of keyboards. One such cover is SafeSkin from Merrit Computer Products. One complaint in using these products is that they slow down typing; the material between keys is not recessed enough to avoid accidentally depressing other keys. Newer designs provide a tighter fit.

Keyboard Accelerators

You can speed up your keyboard to make it more responsive. Simple programs called *keyboard accelerators* let you more quickly move your cursor to where you want it or repeat a certain character. Unfortunately, a keyboard accelerator doesn't speed up your typing. A keyboard accelerator lets you change the repeat rate and repeat delay of your keys. Such accelerators are often memory-resident utilities that must be loaded. Unfortunately, these utilities require memory that could be used elsewhere.

Some ROM BIOS (read-only memory basic input/output system) chips let you change the "typematic" rate of your keyboard. Some keyboards, such as the Northgate OmniKey/102, also let you accelerate your keyboard. A new BIOS chip or keyboard does not require any memory.

You can bypass all these options and accelerate your keyboard yourself. If you use DOS 4.0 or higher, you can use DOS's MODE command to make your keyboard more responsive. Simply add this line to your AUTOEXEC.BAT startup file:

```
MODE CON: RATE=32 DELAY=1
```

After restarting your PC, you should find your keyboard to be much faster. You can enter RATE values from 1 to 32; the default is around 20. The higher the number, the faster the keys will repeat. The values for the DELAY range from 1 to 4; the default is 2. The DELAY value denotes time in quarter-second increments. Unfortunately, this command will not work on older 83-key, XT-type keyboards.

Plugging Problems

The major keyboard difficulty arises from the cord being disconnected. It can become unplugged from either the back of the system unit or the rear of the keyboard. Another common problem is accidentally bumping the switch on the rear or bottom of the keyboard that switches it between XT and AT modes. If bumped to the wrong mode, the keyboard won't be recognized no matter how firmly plugged in it is. Otherwise, computer keyboards are so inexpensive yet difficult to fix that getting a new one may be the best cure for an ailing keyboard.

Mousing Around

The trend of the 90s is more visual software. Graphical user interfaces (GUIs) in Microsoft Windows, DESQview, and Geoworks rely on various elements. To make computing easier, the GUI (pronounced "gooey") uses icons, small pictures that represent programs or peripherals. For example, you might click on a picture of a document to start your word processor and open a certain document.

Pull-down menus are another GUI hallmark. Instead of typing commands, such as FORMAT, you select your choices from various menus. When working with a GUI (pronounced "gooey"), you use a pointing device like a mouse, trackball, or light pen.

The most popular pointing device is the *mouse*. Mice are small plastic objects about the size of your palm (see Figure 15-2). A mouse usually has two or three buttons used to select items. You move the mouse around your desk to move a corresponding pointer on the screen. This pointer usually is called a mouse cursor and is shaped like an arrow or a box. There are four basic mouse techniques: pointing, clicking, double-clicking, and dragging.

When you move your mouse, it points the corresponding mouse

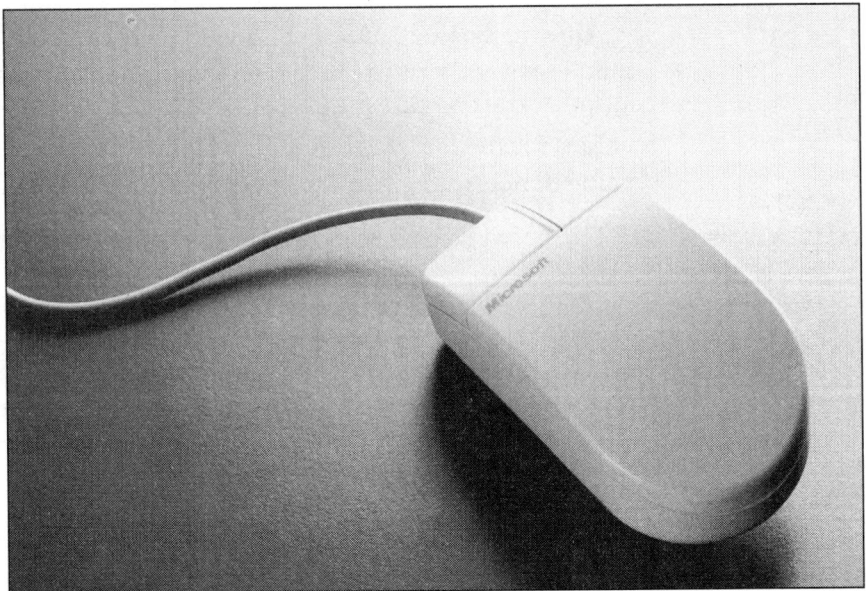

Figure 15.2 The Microsoft Mouse is one of the most popular models today. *(Photo courtesy of Microsoft Corp.)*

cursor at different parts of the screen. Once the pointer is where you want it, you click the mouse button to select an item. When you click, you press and quickly release the mouse button. Double-clicking means quickly pressing and releasing the button twice. Often, clicking is used to open an item and double-clicking is used to close it. Sometimes, you need to move objects around your screen, and that's where you use dragging. To drag an object, you hold down a mouse button and move the pointer while keeping the button held down. Dragging also lets you select a portion of the screen for resizing. Learning to use a mouse is all "thumbs" at first, but with time you will master it.

Selecting a Mouse

The most popular mouse is the Microsoft Mouse. Because of this, most mice are Microsoft-compatible. Your mouse usually has a "tail," a cord that connects to your computer. (There are also cordless mice that transmit their movements to a receiver in your computer.) There are two types of mouse connections: serial or bus. A serial mouse connects to one of your computer's serial, or COM, ports. These are 9-pin or 25-pin connectors on the back of your computer. Most PCs have at least one 9-pin port. Some, like the PS/2, have a dedicated mouse connector. To add a serial mouse, you just plug it into the serial or dedicated mouse port, if present.

Bus mice come with an expansion card you must insert into your PC. The mouse then plugs into this bus card. You must open your computer to add a bus mouse. Although a serial mouse is easy to install, the bus mouse preserves a serial port for other uses, such as an external modem.

Besides selecting a bus or serial mouse, you must also select which type. You have a choice between optical and mechanical. The mechanical mouse has a ball in its belly that rolls across your desk as you move the mouse. This rolling ball moves a pair of wheels or rods that measure horizontal and vertical movement. An optical mouse uses light to track where the mouse has moved. The light reflects off a special pad that has a grid pattern. As you move across the pad, the mouse uses these grid lines to determine how far it has moved.

Are there any advantages to one mouse over another? A mechanical mouse is more prone to collect dust and dirt off your desktop, but it can be easily cleaned. An optical mouse requires you to use its

Figure 15.3 The Logitech TrackMan Portable, which lets you have a mouse without using any desk space, is also ideal for laptop computer users on the go. (*Photo courtesy of Logitech Inc.*)

special pad, although many people use a mouse pad anyway to provide better traction for the mouse ball. Supposedly, an optical mouse provides more precision when used with high-end graphics software, like desktop publishing or computer-aided design (CAD).

There are various mouse designs. Some are designed for left-handed people; others are designed to look like a beetle or small rodent. Some mice even include other buttons—such as the Esc and function keys, for example. There are even mice that attach to the side of your laptop or desktop computer. Microsoft's Ballpoint Mouse and Logitech's TrackMan Portable Mouse clamp onto the side of your PC, forming an extension of the keyboard. Microsoft's product has four buttons, and it can be tilted in relation to the keyboard; Logitech's has three buttons, and it sits at a 45-degree angle to the keyboard. It will also work as a stand-alone device.

Once installed, a mouse must have special software to bring it to life. If you are only running Microsoft Windows 3.0 or 3.1, you have all you need. Windows automatically detects the mouse and resurrects it. The software to run your mouse is called a *mouse driver*, a small software program that tells DOS how to use your mouse. For a Microsoft Mouse, for example, two drivers are provided: MOUSE.SYS and MOUSE.COM. You only need only one. MOUSE.SYS is loaded from your CONFIG.SYS startup file. If you always need a mouse, you can load this driver in CONFIG.SYS. The MOUSE.COM driver is useful when you occasionally require a mouse. When needed, you can simply type from the DOS prompt:

```
MOUSE ON [Enter]
```

When you no longer require the mouse, type:

```
MOUSE OFF [Enter]
```

I often make batch files (.BAT) that will load the mouse driver and run the program that requires it. When done, this batch file removes the mouse driver from memory. For example, here is a batch file I use with Ventura Publisher:

```
@ECHO OFF
C:\MOUSE\MOUSE ON
C:
CD \VENTURA
```

```
DRVRMRGR VPPROF %1 /S=SDFVGAH5.VGA /M=03
C:\MOUSE\MOUSE OFF
CLS
```

Some mice have setup programs that allow you to change the sensitivity of the mouse—how fast it accelerates as you move it, or the pause between clicks before registering a double-click. With the Microsoft Mouse, this is called the Control Panel (not to be confused with the Windows Control Panel.)

For software that doesn't directly support a mouse, like older DOS programs, you can make mouse menus. Many mice come with software that let you add pull-down menus for virtually any program. Of course, some time is required to make the menus for each program.

Mouse Maintenance

The only maintenance you can do for a mouse is to keep it clean. With a mechanical mouse, watch for the mouse cursor skipping pixels or the ball sliding more than it is rolling. These symptoms indicate a dirt-riddled mouse. You can usually gain access to the mouse rollers and ball by simply removing a round cover in the bottom of the mouse. Typically this cover will either turn or slide off.

Once the cover is off, you can remove the ball, if one is used, and/or remove lint and dirt that is sticking to the rollers. Use a pointed nonmetal object such as a toothpick to remove the dirt. First pry off the larger chunks of dirt from each roller. Next, use a cotton swab lightly dipped in isopropyl alcohol to clean off the remaining dirt. You can use a can of compressed air to clear loosened dirt from the mouse's body. If your mouse gets dirty often, examine your work area. Do you leave food crumbs or spills on your desk area? Are papers nearby that your mouse runs over, collecting paper dust? Removing these hazards will help keep your mouse clean.

On the Fast Track

A trackball is like a mechanical mouse on its back (see Figure 15.4). Instead of you moving the ball in the mouse across the desk, a trackball is stationary, requiring you to use your palm to move the ball. Two or three buttons are placed in front of the ball. If you are short on desk space, a trackball is ideal since it doesn't need to be

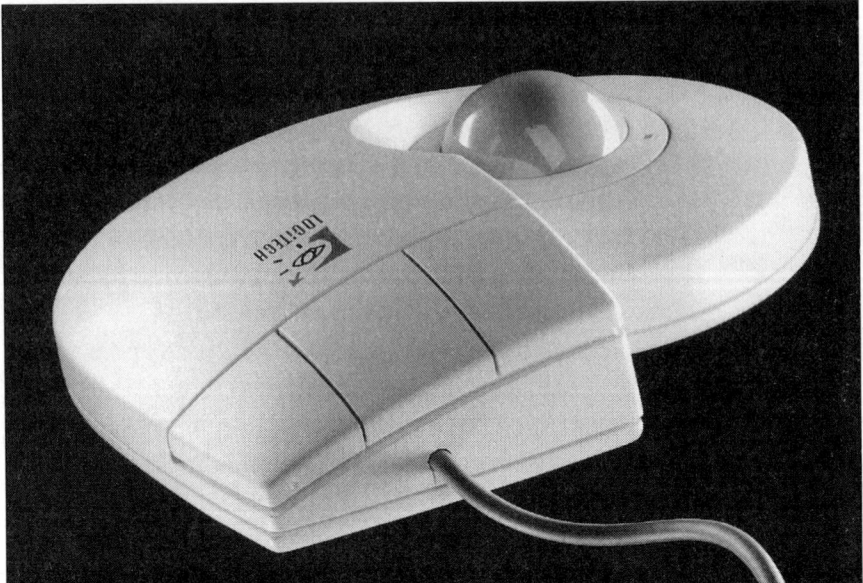

Figure 15.4 The Logitech TrackMan is an example of a trackball. *(Photo courtesy of Logitech Inc.)*

moved about as a mouse does. You also don't have to move your arm or wrist. Otherwise, a trackball works the same as a mouse, requiring a software driver to make it work. A trackball, like the Logitech TrackMan, costs about as much as a mouse, about $75.

Mightier than the Mouse?

The pen is the most common instrument we use for communicating. The pen can also be used in lieu of a mouse or trackball to communicate with your PC. The first pen-based tool was the digitizing tablet. A digitizing tablet resembles a sketch pad. You draw on the pad with a pen or a mouse-like cursor (sometimes called a puck). This pen is attached to the computer. For artists, the digitizing tablet is ideal, since it allows them to trace a drawing and save it to a file. There's a price for this convenience; a digitizing tablet can be expensive: between $400 and $3000.

A light pen is a variation of the digitizing tablet that eliminates the tablet. Instead, you point to the screen. The pen is attached to a phone-like cord. When not in use, it attaches to the side of your monitor. The tip of the pen is sensitive to light and reacts to changes in brightness on the screen. The pen tells your computer when it "sees" a portion of the screen light up. Unlike the mouse, the light pen is not widely supported—yet. FTG Data Systems, for example, includes a driver that emulates a mouse so that software that works with a mouse will work with the pen.

Scan Magic   A scanner can improve your desktop publishing and word processing work. A scanner is basically the inverse of a printer. Instead of turning data into paper, a scanner turns printed matter into data. You can scan text from magazines and books; if you can photograph it, you can scan it.

Scanners are based on the same technology as photocopying machines. Photosensitive cells in the scanner record the appearance of a page by reflecting light off the material and measuring the reflection of the light back to the cell. White portions of the page reflect the most light, black portions the least. The photosensitive cells measure the reflected image, and the scanner generates a series of bits that corresponds to the intensity of reflected portions of the image. This bit image is then saved to a file format by the software program bundled with the scanner. The same software program controls all the scanner's functions, sets the conversion format of the scanned material and the scanning resolution, and performs various editing functions.

There are two scanner types: *image* and *OCR (optical character recognition)*. Image and OCR scanners differ in how they handle the content of resulting images. Image scanners merely copy pictures from paper, ignoring the content and converting the complete image to digital form. Most image scanners save the file as a *TIFF (Tagged Image File Format)* file. This file can then be converted to other formats, such as the popular PC Paintbrush PCX format. Essentially, this type of scanner operates as electronic microfilm, copying originals into a more compact electronic storage form.

Image scanners are handy for saving photographs, signatures, and artwork to a computer file. For example, I once sent out 500 letters. Instead of signing every one, I scanned my signature and placed the resulting file as a graphics file on the letter. The clarity of the scanned image depends on the resolution of the scanner and its ability to capture gray tones. Most scanners offer a scanning resolution of 300 dots per inch (dpi) and up to 256 shades of gray.

OCR scanners, on the other hand, use elaborate pattern-recognition schemes to identify individual text characters and convert the characters into ASCII files that can be used by your word processor. Many OCR scanners, such as the Caere Typist Plus, can place the scanned text directly into your word processor at your cursor. In my work, for example, I can scan a company's press releases or product specifications into a story I am writing. Some scanners can do both image and OCR work.

OCR scanners face a difficult task. They must recognize characters from different typefaces in various sizes. Sometimes, not all the characters are read properly. In such case, the scanning software typically replaces the unreadable character with a special character, such as a tilde (~). These kinds of mistakes can then be found easily with a spelling check. OCR scanners give you the opportunity to scan text to computer files and then destroy or archive the paper documents, saving file space. I've found that once the sensitivity of the scanner is adjusted to the document being scanned, accuracy is very high. I've often scanned several pages with no errors.

Scanners typically come in two sizes: *flatbed* and *handheld*. Both

Figure 15.5 The Caere Typist Plus doubles as an image and OCR scanner. (*Photo courtesy of Caere Corp.*)

require a scanning expansion card to be placed inside your computer. The cords from both are then plugged into this card. The Caere Typist Plus, for example, is a four-inch-wide handheld scanner (see Figure 15-5). If text or images to be scanned are wider than four inches, you can move the scanner across the page to capture any width. Flatbed scanners require you to place the image on a flat, glass panel. The Hewlett-Packard ScanJet, for example, has a scanning mechanism that then travels down its length to scan the image. Some flatbed scanners come with an automatic document feeder that holds several sheets. The HP ScanJet has a feeder that holds up to 20 sheets of paper. The long-awaited paperless office has yet to occur, but scanners can help reduce the paper burden.

Let Your Voice Be Heard

Someday, you may be able to speak to your PC, a la HAL in *2001: A Space Odyssey*. Speech recognition technology lets you instruct your PC with simple voice commands. Most speech recognizers store sets of words you speak into a microphone. You are essentially training

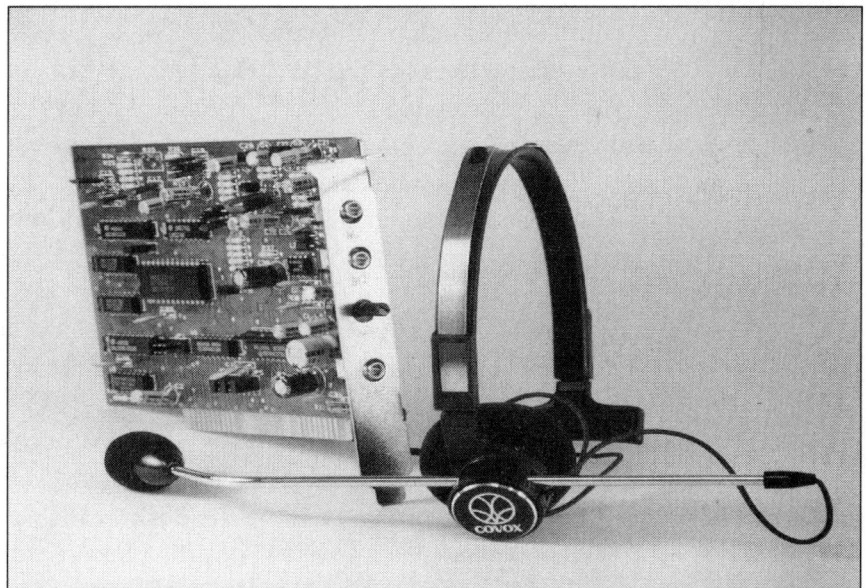

Figure 15.6 The Voice Master uses an expansion card and headset so you can give your computer voice commands rather than lift a single finger. Up to 1023 words can be stored in a single file.

the computer to recognize your voice by repeating sounds over and over. One popular product for the Apple Macintosh is the Voice Navigator II from Articulate Systems Inc.

Few voice-recognition products are available for IBM-compatible computers. One popular product is Voice Master from Covox, which sells for less than $250. The Voice Master software is memory-resident, requiring about 20K of memory. It includes a library of over 1000 voice commands from which you can create recorded keystrokes, or macros. After your voice commands are created, you talk to your computer through a microphone headset. The software sends your verbal commands to either an expansion card installed in your computer or an external device attached to a parallel port. Voice Master then runs your macro and performs your command. Although you must train Voice Master to work with your unique voice, you can create different configuration files to allow several people to use the software. Soon, voice-recognition software will be available for Microsoft Windows.

Pure Joy

Your PC is more than a business tool. Color screens and fast, inexpensive computers make the IBM PC ideal for gameplaying. Most computer games rely on a joystick instead of a keyboard. Flight simulation, combat, and car racing games are best enjoyed with a joystick.

Most joysticks have the same features. At least two firing buttons are included. Some joysticks provide dual buttons to accommodate left-handed gamesters. Selecting a joystick depends more on your individual hand size and shape. Some people prefer a joystick that is fast and loose; others favor one that is stiff. Some joysticks resemble a jet plane's flightstick. The Flight Yoke 2000 from Winner Products features dual grips so you can use both hands to control your game vehicle.

Many joysticks include suction cups used to stick them to your desk. However, you must have the desk available. An alternative is to get a smaller joystick that fits in the palm of your hand. Joysticks usually provide vertical and horizontal controls with which to calibrate the stick.

Many PCs come with a game port, a connector into which to plug your joystick. However, a game card is ideal to provide the best control in your game. This card is an expansion board that is plugged into your PC. Why a dedicated game card? Some faster computers get confused by the inexpensive game ports. During the heat of battle, for example, you may find your plane suddenly upside down or spiraling out of control. This is one sign that your game port is inadequate. A dedicated game card also includes software to set the correct speed and centering for your joystick. Most cards have dual ports to accommodate yours and someone else's joysticks. This way, you can enjoy a game with a friend.

By being well connected to your computer, you can work (and play) faster. A responsive keyboard, a clean mouse, and a nimble joystick make computing all the more enjoyable.

16 Bad Connections

We may wrestle with which computer, printer, or modem to buy, but most of us fail to think about the cables that join them. Often, computer problems stem from bad cables or their connections. A loose keyboard cable, for example, may cause your computer to warn: "No keyboard present."

Since cables are so small and inexpensive compared to your main purchase, they are easy to overlook. Often, we rely on the cables that either came with our PC or were chosen for us by the salesperson. Thanks to industry standards, you can get cables almost anywhere. For example, the parallel printer cable can be purchased anywhere and will work with your IBM-compatible computer and printer. In most cases, your hardest decision may be whether you want a 6- or a 10-foot cable.

Cable Construction

What makes up a cable? Several insulated conductors, or wires, travel from one cable end to the other, usually bundled within a protective plastic sheath. At each end, a wire is soldered to a pin within a connector attached to the end of the cable. The two cable connectors mate with connectors on two pieces of hardware (such as your computer and printer) so that each line in the cable has a source and a destination for the electrical signals it carries. Some lines carry data signals, some transmit hardware control signals, and others provide power or grounding. To prevent an electrical short, the lines in a cable are insulated from each other by a coat of polyvinyl chloride (PVC) plastic. To protect these wires from abuse, they are bundled inside a sheath of PVC.

For longer distances, you can buy special *low-capacitance* cables that use more expensive polyethylene insulation. Polyethylene lowers the capacitance between the lines in a cable, which lets high-frequency signals travel farther.

The End Justifies the Means

Every cable must come to an end. The wires in a cable must attach at each end within a connector. Most cable connectors are one of three types: a *D-shell* connector, which comes in various sizes and numbers of pins; a *Centronics* connector, which is the edge connector on a parallel printer; or a *DIN* connector, the tubular plug that attaches a keyboard to your computer.

These connectors use different numbers of pins to make it more difficult to plug the cable into the wrong connector. (What do you call someone who plugs an electrical cord into your RS-232 port? A *serial* killer!) Gender is also used to reduce error. While a serial port on your computer uses a male D-shell connector (with pins), parallel printer ports use a female D-shell connector (with sockets for pins). The cables that plug into them must be of the opposite gender. A good connector must also provide a strong mechanical connection between cable and peripheral. You don't want wires to separate from their pins after repeated plugging and unplugging, or if someone trips over a cable.

Ads sometimes use phrases like male-to-female, male-female, M/F, or M/M to indicate the gender of the two connectors on a cable. The first gender should refer to the end that plugs into the PC.

Built-In Shielding

Some cables provide built-in shielding from airborne electric fields. Shielding contains the electromagnetic fields generated within the cable that could cause trouble as *radio frequency interference (RFI)*. For example, a nearby radio may "squawk" each time you print a document to your laser printer. Shielding also protects the signals carried within the cable from outside *electromagnetic interference (EMI)*, which can come from many sources including fluorescent lights, nearby appliances, and laser printers. These outside "noises" may distract the signals traveling down the cable.

Braided copper shielding and foil are used for shielding. Either one is adequate for use in most offices, while the combination (double shielding) will stop most noise. For long distances, shielding is a must because it helps conducted signals stay cleaner longer. How much shielding do you need? Almost any shielded cable can prevent RFI emissions. If you work in a crowded residential area or commercial/residential building, you'll want to make sure you buy shielded printer and modem cables so that you don't ruin your neighbors' TV and radio reception.

To protect data within the cable from EMI depends on how far the cable will run, how electrically noisy the area that it must pass through is, and how sensitive to noise the connected printer or modem is.

Besides your cables, your computer or one of its peripherals may generate RFI. For this reason, the FCC requires that all computers be tested, approved, and granted an FCC Class A or Class B license. Computer products to be used in homes must have the more stringent Class B licenses.

To earn FCC certification, a manufacturer submits a sample of each product model for testing. After a machine passes a number of tests, it is approved and given an FCC number for each model. The manufacturer then creates a label and applies it to the back of each computer. Unfortunately, many manufacturers avoid the expensive tests, which cost up to $6000 per model. Some smaller companies would rather risk getting caught than dole out this amount of cash.

To discover how much RFI noise your computer or its peripherals creates, place a portable AM/FM radio next to it. Tune it in between channels on the AM band and see how far you have to walk away from the computer before the RFI noise disappears. You may find that you have to go out of the house before you lose the signal —not good.

To reduce RFI, you can simply move your computer to another location and plug it into another outlet. Instead of plugging your monitor into your computer's electrical outlet, let it have its own. The surest way to avoid the RFI dilemma is to buy only products that carry an FCC Class B label.

Going the Distance

Running cables down the hall may require more than just shielding. While shielding keeps outside noise from disrupting cable signals, it doesn't keep the lines within a cable from interfering with each other. Separating the lines into pairs and evenly twisting one line with the other reduces crosstalk between lines and increases the distance a cable can reliably carry signals.

Parallel printer cables are typically limited to about 10 feet. Serial cables can send data farther than printer cables, up to 200 feet with shielded cables. However, the higher the frequencies you send, perhaps transmitting 19,200 bits per second (BPS) between two computers, the shorter the distance. If you stick with slower transmission, you may be able to stretch a cable farther.

The ultimate long-distance cable, however, is low-capacitance cable. It uses single or double shielding to cut EMI, twisted-pair conductors to cut crosstalk, and low-capacitance polyethylene insulation on 24-gauge wire to make high-frequency signals go farther. A low-capacitance cable can increase distance by 50 to 100 percent. One thing you shouldn't do is link together several shorter cables to make one long one. Every additional connector reduces transmission.

You can double PC-to-printer distance with a $30 to $50 *line booster*, which strengthens cable signals when you connect two shorter cables together to make a longer one. *Electronic line extenders* provide even more travel; a small transmitter unit attaches to your PC's printer port and sends signals through inexpensive four-line telephone cable (RJ-11) to an equally small receiver attached to your printer's Centronics port. These units run $50 to $150 by mail order, depending on how far they transmit. Some work to several hundred feet, others to almost 10,000 feet.

For both monitor and keyboard, you can buy extender cables that provide enough slack, another 6 or 10 feet, to move your computer processing unit off your desk and onto the floor. The cables are often sold in sets of three: one for the keyboard, one for the video data cable, and one for the monitor power cable. Because keyboards consume a relatively high amount of current, the cord can't be too long. You shouldn't, for example, connect two keyboard extension cables to make a long cable.

A Safe Port

The most commonly used cables are the *parallel printer cable* and the *serial (RS-232) cable*. The parallel printer cable (or just printer cable) connects to the parallel port on the back of your computer and then to your printer. Your computer may have more than one parallel port. Each parallel port has a name: LPT1, LPT2, and LPT3. (LPT stands for line printer.) The connector to your computer is a male DB-25. In other words, the connector contains 25 individual protruding pins. These pins are arranged in two parallel rows of 12 and 13 pins. The other end has what's called a 36-pin Centronics connector.

One disadvantage of printer cables is that the signals that travel through any of the 25 wires may bleed over to the others, corrupting the printing that is occurring. This is called *crosstalk*. The longer the cable, the greater the chance of crosstalk. For this reason, most manufacturers recommend parallel cables be no longer than 10 feet. If you want to put your printer more than 10 feet away from your computer, you should buy a special double-shielded or low-capacitance printer cable. With a shielded cable, you can count on 50 feet, and a special low-capacitance cable stretches the distance to between 75 and 100 feet.

Serial: RS-232

Selecting a *serial* (or *RS-232*) cable is more difficult. The name RS-232 comes from the name of the standards developed by the Electrical Industries Association. Most computers use the serial port to attach modems or mice. Some printers can also use the serial port, although they require special cables. Like the parallel port, each serial port has a name: COM1, COM2, COM3, or COM4. Your computer most likely has at least two COM, or communications, ports.

Unlike the parallel printer port, there are two types of serial ports and therefore two types of serial cables (see Figure 16-1). The "traditional" RS-232 port has 25 pins in a D-shell connector, also called a DB-25 connector. The newer design has nine pins (DB-9). The two work the same; in fact, you can buy a serial cable adapter to convert a 25-pin cable to the 9-pin connector. In either case, the serial cable has a female connector. In other words, the connector shows holes instead of pins.

When you order a serial cable, you must know whether you'll be using it with a 9- or 25-pin port, and also whether that port is male

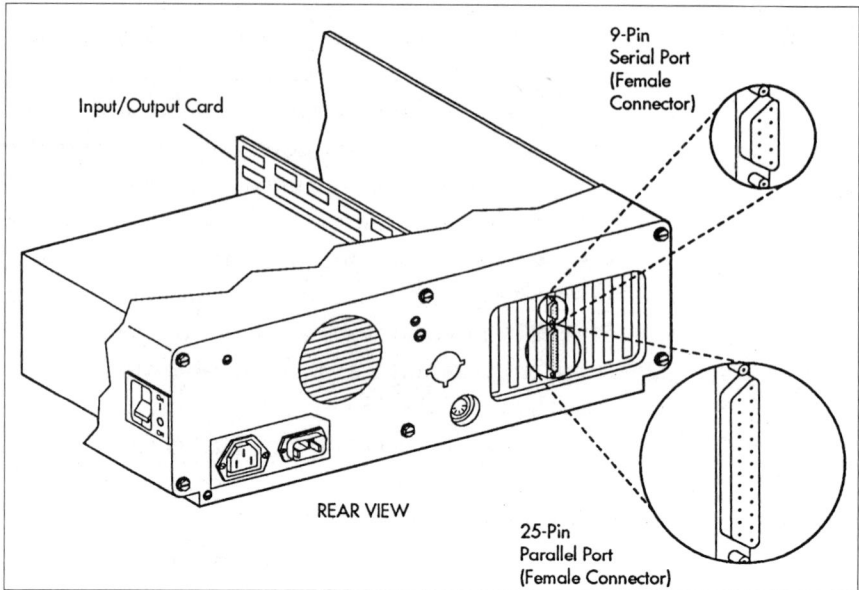

Input/Output Card

9-Pin
Serial Port
(Female
Connector)

REAR VIEW

25-Pin
Parallel Port
(Female Connector)

Figure 16.1 There are two serial ports, and your computer may support both types.

or female. Typically, the port connector is male, requiring a female DB-9 or DB-25 connector. A few older computers—some Tandy computers, for example—have female serial ports.

Although two serial cables may look the same, they may not be. Modem cables don't work for serial printers, for example. This is because there are two types of serial equipment: data terminal equipment (DTE) and data communications equipment (DCE). Computer and serial printers are configured as DTE, and modems are DCE. A different serial cable is required for each.

Convenient Cables

Some cables accommodate your computer arrangement. For example, you can buy a right-angle printer cable that lets your printer sit closer to the wall when space is tight. You can also get cable extenders to lengthen your keyboard and monitor cables, letting you move your system unit from a crowded desktop to the floor. Only vendors that specialize in cables are likely to carry these items.

You can also get specialty items to share printers or connect two computers together. I use an A-B DB25 switch box (this is not a brand name but a type) to switch between my two printers. To use this switch box, I had to purchase another printer cable and a special 25-pin male/male cable. This special cable connects to the middle of three ports on the back of the switch. The two printer cables then connect from the other two ports to their respective printers. Of course, you can also connect two computers to one printer. You can buy cables with Centronics connectors of either gender on both ends to hook up to such switch boxes.

I also use a null-modem adapter, which is a short plug that attaches to one end of a serial cable. This adapter fools my computer into thinking it is attached to another computer by a modem. With the null modem cable in place, I can transfer data between two computers at a blazing 19,200 bps (bits per second), about eight times faster than downloading a file from the typical electronic bulletin board system (BBS).

| **Seeing is Believing** | Monitor cables are somewhat brand-specific. There are two standard connectors at the computer end, a 15-pin D-shell connector for analog monitors (VGA, Super VGA, 8514/A, and XGA), and a 9-pin D-shell connector for older TTL monitor types (MDA, CGA, and EGA). The connector used at the monitor end varies with the brand, however. Most have 9-, 15-, or 25-pin connectors. |

You can find cables for popular brands like Sony and Mitsubishi by mail order for $4 to $10. Some mail-order cable vendors also sell adapters (9- to 15-pin and 15- to 25-pin) that can make an existing cable work with a different monitor. Then again, you may have to go to the monitor manufacturer to find what you're looking for. Some multiscanning monitors have two cables, one for analog and one for digital signals. Monitor cables carry high-frequency signals and should always be shielded.

| **Buying a Cable** | If you buy a computer peripheral (such as a printer or modem) by mail-order and a standard cable will suit your needs, you might as well buy the cable to go with it. Most mail-order companies charge a reasonable price and don't charge extra shipping and handling for |

the cable. If you're replacing a bad cable or buying several cables, consider shopping around for the best price. Obviously, mail-order companies provide better prices than most local stores. If you are ordering several cables, some vendors can customize the cables to your desired lengths.

Don't forget quality, however. Mail-order companies are unlikely to include an inferior cable with your modem or printer if it will endanger the new purchase. Cable vendors offer various qualities of cables. However, troubleshooting a faulty cable can cost more than you saved.

If you're buying several cables, first buy a sample and disassemble it for inspection. Clean, neat internal connections indicate reliability. An Underwriters Laboratories-listed cable has been tested already for mechanical pull strength and connector durability. A UL listing is a good indication of high-quality materials and construction. When cable shopping by phone, don't expect many answers to your detailed questions. At this point, you know more than they do. The most you can expect to find out is whether the cables are shielded and have a UL listing.

Vendors that supply special cables, bulk orders, or custom cables should answer your specific questions, because they often sell different grades of cable for different purposes. Cable specialists generally charge 25 to 50 cents per foot for single-shielded cable with a connector at each end. More generalized vendors will charge prices that come out to 50 cents to $1.50 per foot. Additional shielding and low-capacitance insulation add to the price.

When comparing prices, include shipping and handling costs. When you see prices for a 6-foot cable for less than $10, you can assume an additional cost of $4 to $12 for shipping and handling. A few vendors have minimum order amounts of $25 or $50.

In general, consider buying shielded cables to make a peripheral run more reliably and to prevent RFI problems. To get the correct cable, the most important thing you can know is what's going to be connected at each end. In some cases, it's enough to specify a parallel printer cable and the length you want. In other cases, you'll have to know the type or even brand of peripheral that's going to use the cable. You don't always have to think too hard about cables, but a little planning can prevent a lot of problems.

Cable Care   Improperly replugging any cable connector, or wedging the computer against a wall, can bend or break the fragile connector pins. When replugging a cable, grab it by its connector and push it straight onto the connector on your peripheral or computer. When unplugging, pull the connector straight off. Mouse and keyboard cables are the ones most prone to damage. With a mouse, for example, the weakest link is where the cable joins the mouse, because it is constantly being flexed. Frequently disconnecting a keyboard can diminish the friction used to hold its connector in place.

Sometimes, a computer may have several cables connected to it. For example, my computer has 12 cables streaming from it. Often, these cables become entangled, keeping me from moving the mouse or using my handheld scanner. One solution is to take garbage-bag twist ties to bundle cables together. You can also buy special-purpose flex tubing that acts as a conduit for various cables. You can use this flexible plastic tubing to make your own cable protector. Buy about 20 feet of flexible plastic tubing about 1.5 inches in diameter. Cut the tubing to the correct lengths for the groups of cables you're about to encase. Thread the cables through the tubes. If there are several cords to put through the tubing, or cords with large connectors, simply slit the tubing lengthwise to accommodate them.

By paying more attention to your cables, you can be sure your work gets to where it's going, whether to a printer or a modem. Buying the correct cables and taking care of them is one step toward a healthy computer.

A PC Bio

POWER SUPPLY

Power supply wattage (in watts)	☐ 135W ☐ 150W ☐ 200W ☐ 220W ☐ 250W ☐ 300W ☐ Other _____
Power supply capacity	_____ %
Power supply switch	☐ Paddle ☐ Rocker ☐ Push button
Remote switch	☐ Yes ☐ No

CASE

☐ Desktop ☐ Baby AT ☐ Slim-line desktop
☐ Tower ☐ Mini-Tower ☐ Other _____

DRIVES (Check those that apply.)

☐ Floppy: Drive A	☐ 5¼″ ☐ 3½″ ☐ Half-height ☐ Full-height
☐ Floppy: Drive B	☐ 5¼″ ☐ 3½″ ☐ Half-height ☐ Full-height
☐ Hard Drive 1	☐ 5¼″ ☐ 3½″ ☐ Half-height ☐ Full-height
☐ Hard Drive 2	☐ 5¼″ ☐ 3½″ ☐ Half-height ☐ Full-height
Drive C: Total disk space	Total bytes: _____ Total megabytes (÷ 1,048,576): _____

DRIVES (*Continued*)

Drive C: Available space	Total bytes: _____ Total megabytes (÷ 1,048,576): _____
Drive C: Free space	(Available space ÷ Total disk space) _____ %
Drive D: Total disk space	Total bytes: _____ Total megabytes (÷ 1,048,576): _____
Drive D: Available space	Total bytes: _____ Total megabytes (÷ 1,048,576): _____
Drive D: Free space	(Available space ÷ Total disk space) _____ %

EXPANSION SLOTS

Total: ____	# of 8-bit: ____ # of 16-bit ____
Used: ____	# of 8-bit: ____ # of 16-bit ____
Free: _____	# of 8-bit: ____ # of 16-bit ____
Full-length expansion cards	☐ Yes ☐ No

PROCESSOR

Type	☐ 8088 ☐ 8086 ☐ 286 ☐ 386DX ☐ 386SX ☐ 486DX ☐ 486SX ☐ Other ____
Speed (in megahertz)	☐ 4.77/5MHz ☐ 6MHz ☐ 8MHz ☐ 10MHz ☐ 12MHz ☐ 16MHz ☐ 20MHz ☐ 25MHz ☐ 33MHz ☐ 40MHz ☐ 50MHz ☐ Other _____
Months old from chart on page 40	_____

MEMORY

Memory banks	☐ 2 banks ☐ 4 banks ☐ Other ____
Vacant memory banks	☐ 1 bank ☐ 2 banks ☐ 3 banks ☐ Other ____
Memory chip design	☐ DIP ☐ SIMM ☐ SIP ☐ Combination ☐ Other _____

MEMORY *(Continued)*

Memory speed (in nanoseconds)	☐ 150ns ☐ 120ns ☐ 100ns ☐ 90ns ☐ 80ns ☐ 70ns ☐ 60ns ☐ 50ns ☐ Other ____
Total memory (in K)	☐ 512K ☐ 640K ☐ 1024K ☐ 2048K ☐ 4096K ☐ 8196K ☐ 16384K ☐ Other _____
Total megabytes (MB) if more than 1024K (total memory ÷ 1024 and rounded up to next whole number)	☐ 1MB ☐ 2MB ☐ 3MB ☐ 4MB ☐ 5MB ☐ 6MB ☐ 8MB ☐ 9MB ☐ 12MB ☐ 16MB ☐ Other _____
Free memory (in K)	_____ K before changes _____ K after changes
Percentage of free memory (Free memory ÷ 640K)	_____ % before changes _____ % after changes
Total EMS memory (in K)	_____ K before changes _____ K after changes
Free EMS memory (in K)	_____ K before changes _____ K after changes
Contiguous extended memory (in K)	_____ K before changes _____ K after changes
Available contiguous extended memory (in K)	_____ K before changes _____ K after changes
Available XMS memory (in K)	_____ K before changes _____ K after changes
MS-DOS resident in High Memory Area	☐ Yes ☐ No

OPERATING SYSTEM

Version	☐ 2.0 ☐ 2.1 ☐ 3.0 ☐ 3.1 ☐ 3.2 ☐ 3.3 ☐ 4.0 ☐ 4.01 ☐ 5.0 ☐ Other _____
Maker	☐ Microsoft MS-DOS ☐ IBM PC-DOS ☐ Digital Research DR-DOS ☐ Other _____

MOTHERBOARD

☐ XT ("baby AT") (8.5 x 13.5 inches or smaller)
☐ AT(12 by 13.5 inches or smaller)

B Resources

Ad Lib Inc.
220 Grande Allee E. Ste. #850
Quebec City QB CD G1R 2J1
800-463-2686
Ad Lib Gold 1000 ($300)
Ad Lib Gold 2000 ($400)

AddStor Inc.
1040 Marsh Rd.
Menlo Park CA 94025
800-732-3133
SuperStor ($100)

Adobe Systems Inc.
P.O. Box 7900 1585 Charleston Rd.
Mountain View CA 94039-7900
800-833-6687
Adobe Type Manager for Windows ($99)

American Megatrends Inc.
6145-f Northbelt Pkwy.
Norcross GA 30071
800-828-9264
AMI BIOS

Avery Dennison
818 Oak Park Rd.
Covina CA 91724-3624
800-462-8379
Personal Label Printer ($249)

Bitstream Inc.
215 First St.
Cambridge MA 02142-1270
800-522-3668
FaceLift for Windows ($99)
FaceLift for WordPerfect ($99)

Caere Corp.
100 Cooper Court
Los Gatos CA 95030
800-535-7226
Typist Plus Graphics ($695)

Canon U.S.A. Inc.
One Canon Plaza
Lake Success NY 11042
800-652-2666
BJ-10ex ($499)

CE Software Inc.
P.O. Box 65580 1801 Industrial Circle
West Des Moines IA 50265
800-523-7638
ProKey ($99)

Central Point Software Inc.
15220 N.W. Greenbrier Pkwy. Ste. 200
Beaverton OR 97006
800-445-4208
Central Point Anti-Virus ($129)
Central Point Backup ($129)
PC Tools ($179)

Colorado Memory Products
800 S. Taft Ave.
Loveland CO 80537
800-432-5858
FC-10 ($129)
Jumbo 120 DJ-10 ($250)
Jumbo 250 DJ-20 ($350)

ColorAge Inc.
900 Technology Park Dr.
Billerica MA 01821
800-437-3336
Freedom of Press ($495)
Freedom of Press Light ($98)

CoStar Corp.
22 Bridge St.
Greenwich CT 06830-5238
800-426-7827
AddressWriter ($595)

Covox Inc.
675 Conger St.
Eugene OR 97402
503-342-1271
Voice Master Key System II ($240)

Creative Labs Inc.
  (subsidiary of Creative Technology)
1901 Mccarthy Blvd.
Milpitas CA 95035
800-998-5227
SoundBlaster ($150)
SoundBlaster 16 ($349)
SoundBlaster PRO ($299)

DiagSoft Inc.
5615 Scotts Valley Dr. Suite 140
Scotts Valley CA 95066
800-342-4763
QAPlus ($160)

Diamond Computer Systems Inc.
532 Mercury Drive
Sunnyvale CA 94086
408-736-2000
Diamond Stealth VRAM ($445)

Digital Research Inc.
  (subsidiary of Novell Inc.)
70 Garden Court, Box Drive
Monterey CA 93942
800-274-4374
DR DOS 6.0 ($99)

Disk Technician Corp.
1940 Garnet Ave.
San Diego CA 92109
800-847-5000
Disk Technician Gold ($150)

Epson America Inc.
(subsidiary of Seiko Epson Corp.)
20770 Madrona Ave.
Torrance CA 90509-2842
800-922-8911
ActionPrinter 3250 ($299)

Fifth Generation Systems Inc.
10049 N. Reiger Rd.
Baton Rouge LA 70809-4562
800-873-4384
Mace Performance ($69)

Gazelle Systems Inc.
305 North 500 West
Provo UT 84601
800-786-3278
OPTune ($100)

Gibson Research Corp.
22991 Lacadena
Laguna Hills CA 92653
800-736-0637
SpinRite II ($89)

Hewlett-Packard Co.
3000 Hanover St.
Palo Alto CA 94304
800-752-0900
DeskJet 500 ($599)
HP LaserJet IIP Plus ($1249)
HP LaserJet III ($2395)
HP LaserJet 4 ($2199)
HP ScanJet IIP ($1095-$1295)

Hyperware
Rt. 1, Box 91
Pall Mall TN 38577
615-864-6868
HyperDisk ($49)

Intel Corp.
2200 Mission College Blvd.
Santa Clara CA 95054
800-538-3373
ActionMedia 750 Delivery Board
($1995-$2495)

Intel Corp. *(Personal Computer
Enhancement Operation)*
5200 N.E. Elam Young Pkwy.
Hillsboro OR 97124
800-538-3373
Intel Math Coprocessor
AboveBoard Plus I/O ($339)

International Business Machines
Old Orchard Rd.
Armonk NY 10504
800-426-3333
OS/2 2.0 ($195)

Iomega Corp.
1821 West 4000 South
Roy UT 84067
800-777-6004
Bernoulli Boxes ($699-$2749)

Kingston Technology Corp.
17600 Newhope St.
Fountain Valley CA 92708
800-835-2545
SX/Now!

LaserGo Inc.
9369 Carroll Park Dr. Ste. A
San Diego CA 92121
619-450-4600
GoScript ($149)
GoScript Plus ($299)

LaserMaster
6900 Shady Oak Road
Eden Prairie MN 55344
800-950-6868
WinJet 300 ($495)
WinJet 800 ($795)

LaserTools Corp.
1250 45th St. Ste. 100
Emeryville CA 94608-2907
800-767-8004
PrintCache ($149)
PrintCache for Windows ($149)

Logitech Inc.
6505 Kaiser Drive
Fremont CA 94555
800-231-7717
Logitech TrackMan ($139-$149)
Logitech TrackMan Portable ($169)

Media Vision Inc.
3185 Laurelview Ct.
Fremont CA 94538
800-348-7116
AudioPort ($199)
CDPC ($1295)
Pro AudioSpectrum Plus ($199)
Pro AudioSpectrum 16 ($299)
Thunder and Lightning ($349)
ThunderBOARD ($179)

Merrill & Bryan Enterprises Inc.
P.O. Box 900069
San Diego CA 92190
619-689-8611
Turbo EMS ($100)

Merritt Computer Products Inc.
5565 Red Bird Center Dr. #150
Dallas TX 75237
214-339-0753
SafeSkin

MicroLogic Software Inc.
1351 Ocean Ave.
Emeryville CA 94608
800-888-9078
LaserMenu ($100)
PrintMenu ($70)

MicroProse Software Inc.
180 Lakefront Dr.
Hunt Valley MD 21030
800-879-7529
F-117A Nighthawk Stealth Fighter ($80)

Microsoft Corp.
One Microsoft Way
Redmond WA 98052-6399
800-227-4679
Microsoft Ballpoint Mouse ($175)
Microsoft Mouse ($125)
Microsoft Windows ($150)
Windows Sound System ($289)
MS-DOS 5.0 ($100)

NEC Technologies Inc.
(subsidiary of NEC Corp.)
1414 Massachusetts Ave.
Boxborough MA   01719
800-632-4636
MultiSync 2A ($499)
MultiSync 4FG ($899)

NewTek Inc.
215 Southeast 8th St.
Topeka KS   66603
800-847-6111
Video Toaster ($4995)

No-Brainer Software Inc.
P.O. Box 1906
Big Bear Lake CA   92315
800-748-4499
SmartKey Advanced ($90)

Northgate Computers
P.O. Box 59080
Minneapolis MN   55459-0080
800-548-1993
OmniKey/102 ($129)
OmniKey/Ultra ($129)

Okidata Corp.
(division of Oki America Inc.)
532 Fellowship Rd.
Mt. Laurel NJ   08054
800-654-3282
OkiLaser 400 ($999)

Ontrack Computer Systems Inc.
6321 Bury Dr. Ste. 15-19
Eden Prairie MN   55346
800-752-1333
Disk Manager ($125)
DOSutils ($100)
Dr. Solomon's Anti-Virus Toolkit ($150)
SuperPROM ($100)

Pacific Data Products Inc.
(subsidiary of Digital Communications
Associates Inc.)
9125 Rehco Rd.
San Diego CA   92121
619-552-0880
PacificPage ($499)

Panasonic Communications
   & Systems Co.
2 Panasonic Way
Secaucus NJ   07094
800-742-8086
KX-P2624 ($650)

PC Power & Cooling Inc.
5995 Avenida Encinas
Carlsbad CA   92008
800-722-6555
TurboCool 300S power supply ($189)

PC-Kwik Corp.
15100 S.W. Koll Pkwy.
Beaverton OR   97006
800-274-5945
Super PC-Kwik Disk Accelerator ($80)

Personics Corp.
(subsidiary of Datawatch Corp.)
234 Ballardvale St.
Wilmington MA 01887
800-445-3311
Laptop Ultravision ($100)

PKWare Inc.
9025 N. Deerwood Dr.
Brown Deer WI 53223
414-354-8699
PKLite ($47)
PKZip ($47)

PM Ware Inc.
346 State Place
Escondido CA 92029
800-845-4843
UltraScript & UltraScript Plus ($195-$495)

Prometheus Products Inc.
9524 S.W. Tualatin Sherwood Rd.
Tualatin OR 97062
800-477-3473
Switchboard ($240)

Qualitas Inc.
7101 Wisconsin Ave. Ste. 1386
Bethesda MD 20814
800-827-0486
386MAX ($100)
Move 'Em (included with above)

Quantum Corp.
500 Mccarthy Blvd.
Milpitas CA 95035
800-624-5545
Hardcard EZ ($269-$749)

Quarterdeck Office Systems
150 Pico Blvd.
Santa Monica CA 90405
800-354-3222
DESQview ($130)
QEMM-386 ($100)
Manifest (included with above)

Quiet Technology Inc.
500 Executive Center, Ste. 3c
P.O. Box 18216
West Palm Beach FL 33416
800-745-3623
The Silencer ($70)

Seiko Instruments U.S.A. Inc.
1130 Ringwood Court
San Jose CA 95131
800-888-0817
Smart Label Printer Plus ($249)

SONY Corporation of America
655 River Oaks Pkwy.
San Jose CA 95134
800-352-7669
Multimedia CD-ROM Player
  (MMCD) ($995)

SOTA Technologies, Inc.
2200B Zanker Road
San Jose, CA 95131
800-933-7682
SOTA 386si ($200-$400)

Stac Electronics
5993 Avenida Encinas
Carlsbad CA 92008
800-522-7822
Stacker ($149)

Storage Dimensions Inc.
  (subsidiary of Maxtor Corp.)
1656 Mccarthy Blvd.
Milpitas CA 95035
408-954-0710
SpeedStor ($100-$150)

Symantec Corp.
10201 Torre Ave.
Cupertino CA 95014-2132
800-441-7234
Norton Backup ($129)
Norton Utilities ($179)

Sysgen Inc.
556 Gibraltar Dr.
Milpitas CA 95035
800-821-2151
Sysgen MobileDisk ($550-$1250)

TEAC America Inc.
7733 Telegraph Rd.
Montebello CA 90640
213-726-0303
TEAC FD-505 ($249)

Truevision Inc.
  (subsidiary of RasterOps Corp.)
7340 Shadeland Station
Indianapolis IN 46256-3925
800-344-8783
Bravado ($1295)

Weitek Corp.
1060 East Arques Ave.
Sunnyvale CA 94086
800-468-3167/408-738-8400
Abacus 3167
Abacus 4167

Western Digital Corp.
8105 Irvine Center Dr.
Irvine CA 92718
800-832-4778
WD1003 Controller
WD1006 Controller

Winner Products Inc.
821 S. Lemon Ave. Ste. A-9
Walnut CA 91789
714-595-2490
Flight Yoke 2000 ($90)

Index

403